D0508352

ANGEL CITY

Town Without Pity

AN ONI PRESS PUBLICATION

May 18

ANGEL CIT

Town Without Pity

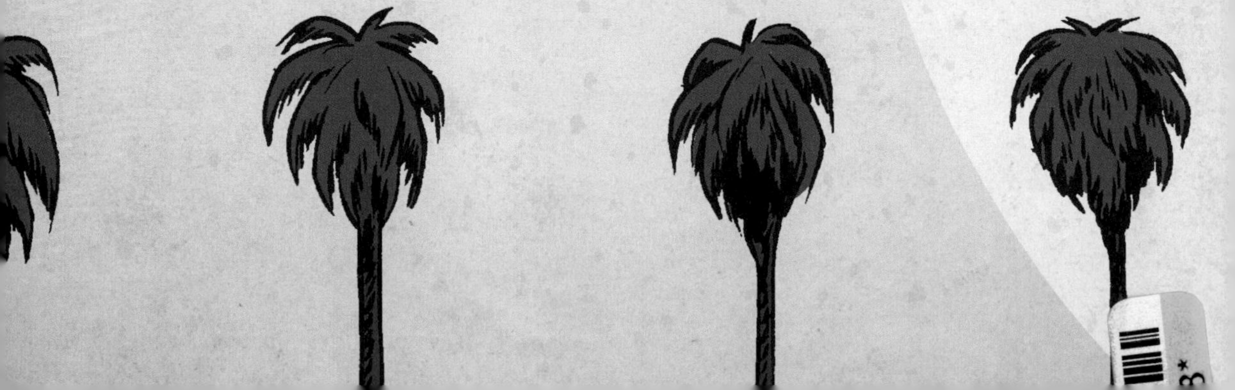

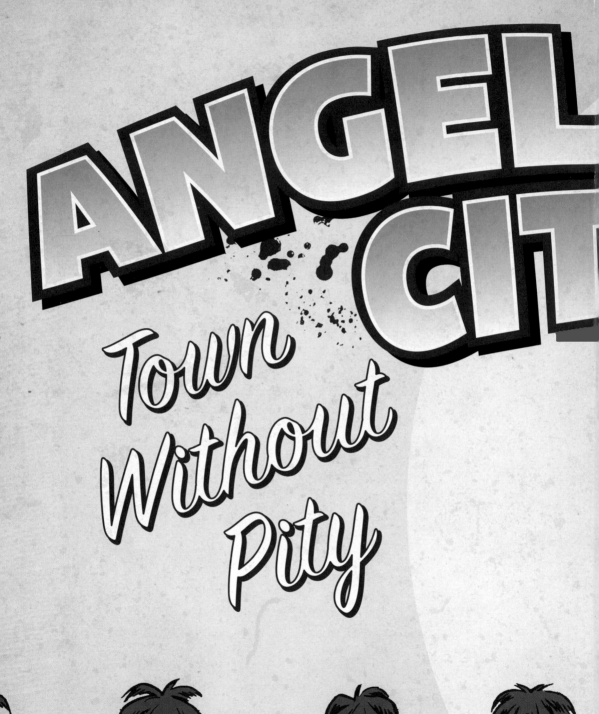

WRITTEN BY
Janet Harvey

ILLUSTRATED BY
Megan Levens

COLORED BY
Nick Filardi

LETTERED BY
Crank!

DESIGNED BY
Hilary Thompson

EDITED BY
Ari Yarwood

PUBLISHED BY ONI PRESS, INC.

Joe Nozemack, publisher

James Lucas Jones, editor in chief

David Dissanayake, sales manager

Rachel Reed, publicity coordinator

Troy Look, director of design & production

Hilary Thompson, graphic designer

Angie Dobson, digital prepress technician

Ari Yarwood, managing editor

Charlie Chu, senior editor

Robin Herrera, editor

Alissa Sallah, administrative assistant

Brad Rooks, director of logistics

Jung Lee, logistics associate

**ORIGINALLY PUBLISHED AS ISSUES 1-6
OF THE ONI PRESS COMIC SERIES *ANGEL CITY*.**

1319 SE MLK Jr. Blvd,
Suite 240
Portland, OR 97214

onipress.com
facebook.com/onipress
twitter.com/onipress
onipress.tumblr.com
instagram.com/onipress

@janetharvey
@sadmegangirls
@nickfil
@ccrank

First Edition: August 2017
ISBN 978-1-62010-426-2
eISBN 978-1-62010-427-9

1 3 5 7 9 10 8 6 4 2

Library of Congress Control Number: 2017932448

Printed in China.

For Dave,
without whom this book would not exist.
My Dearest Friend:
You are always with me.
You inspire me every day.
I love you forever.

— Janet Harvey —

For my parents, for never once
suggesting I get a "real job."

— Megan Levens —

For my fiancée Shannon,
and my sweet 12-year-old dog Deniro.

— Nick Filardi —

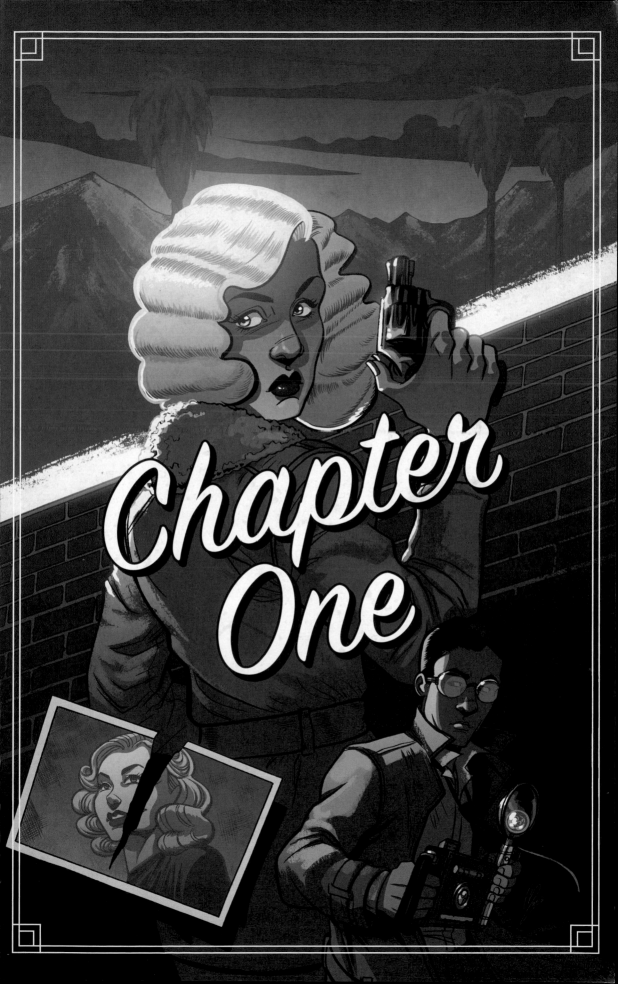

Chapter One

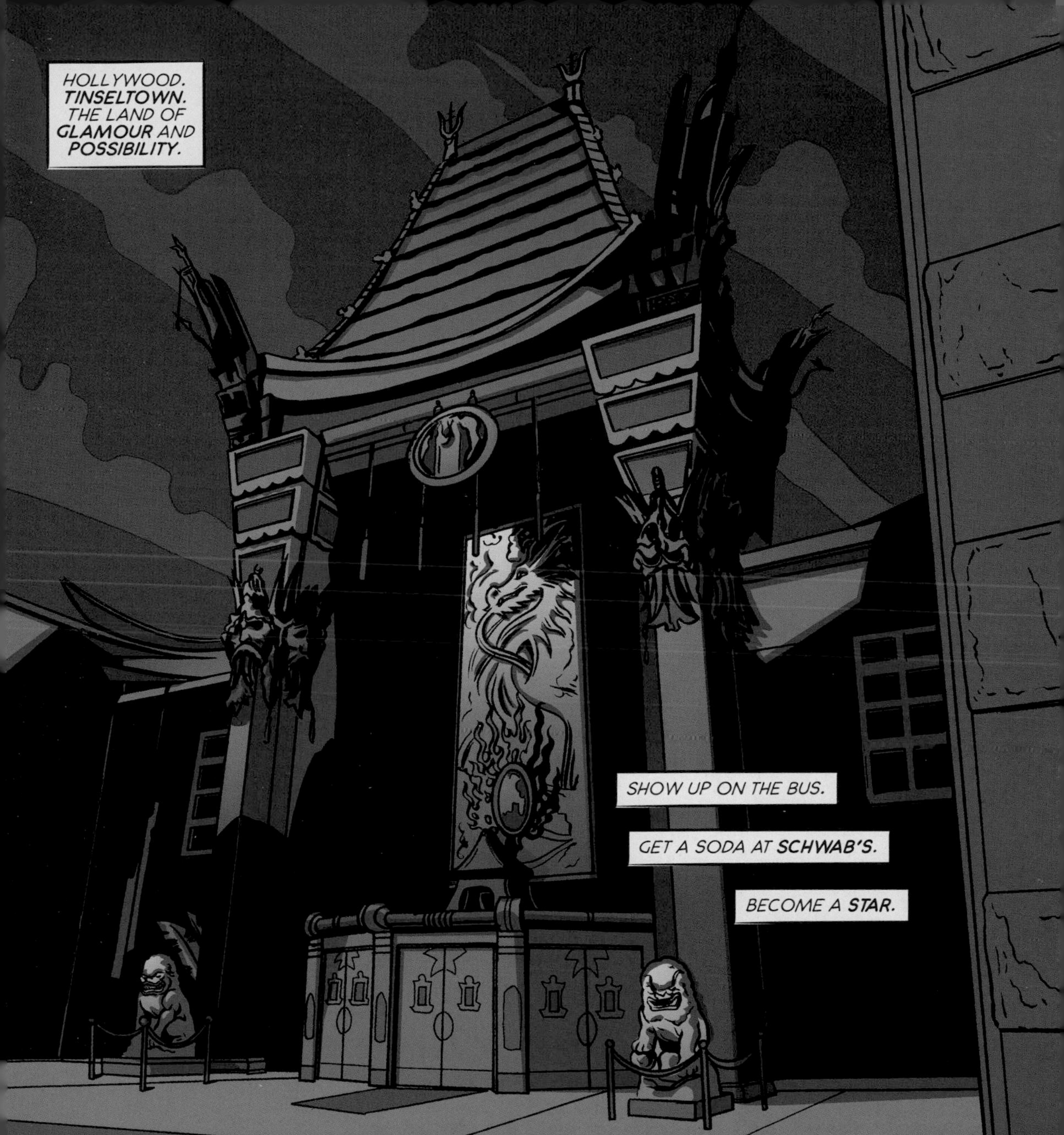
HOLLYWOOD. TINSELTOWN. THE LAND OF GLAMOUR AND POSSIBILITY.
SHOW UP ON THE BUS.
GET A SODA AT SCHWAB'S.
BECOME A STAR.

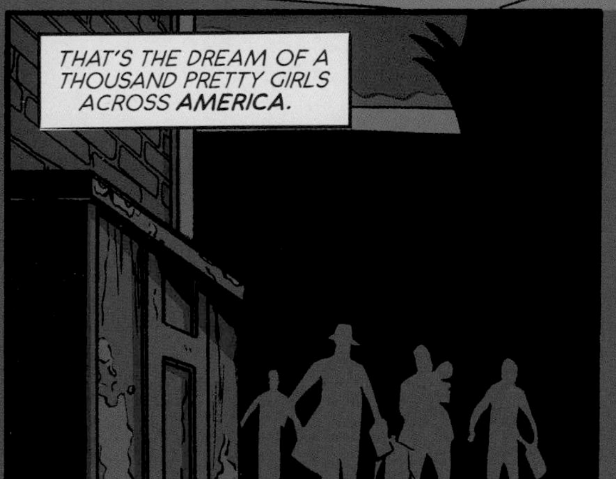
THAT'S THE DREAM OF A THOUSAND PRETTY GIRLS ACROSS AMERICA.

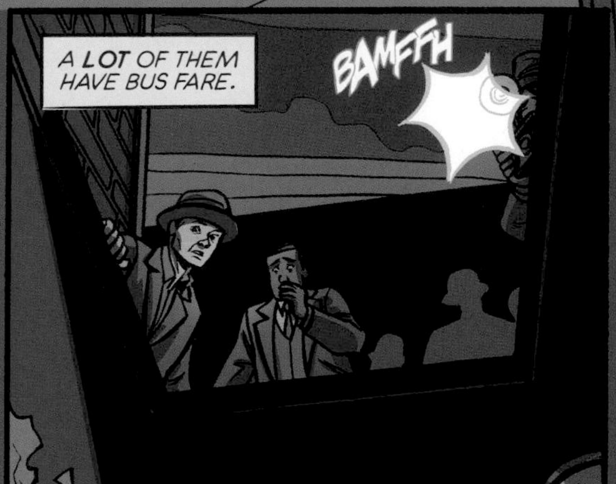
A LOT OF THEM HAVE BUS FARE.
BAMFFH

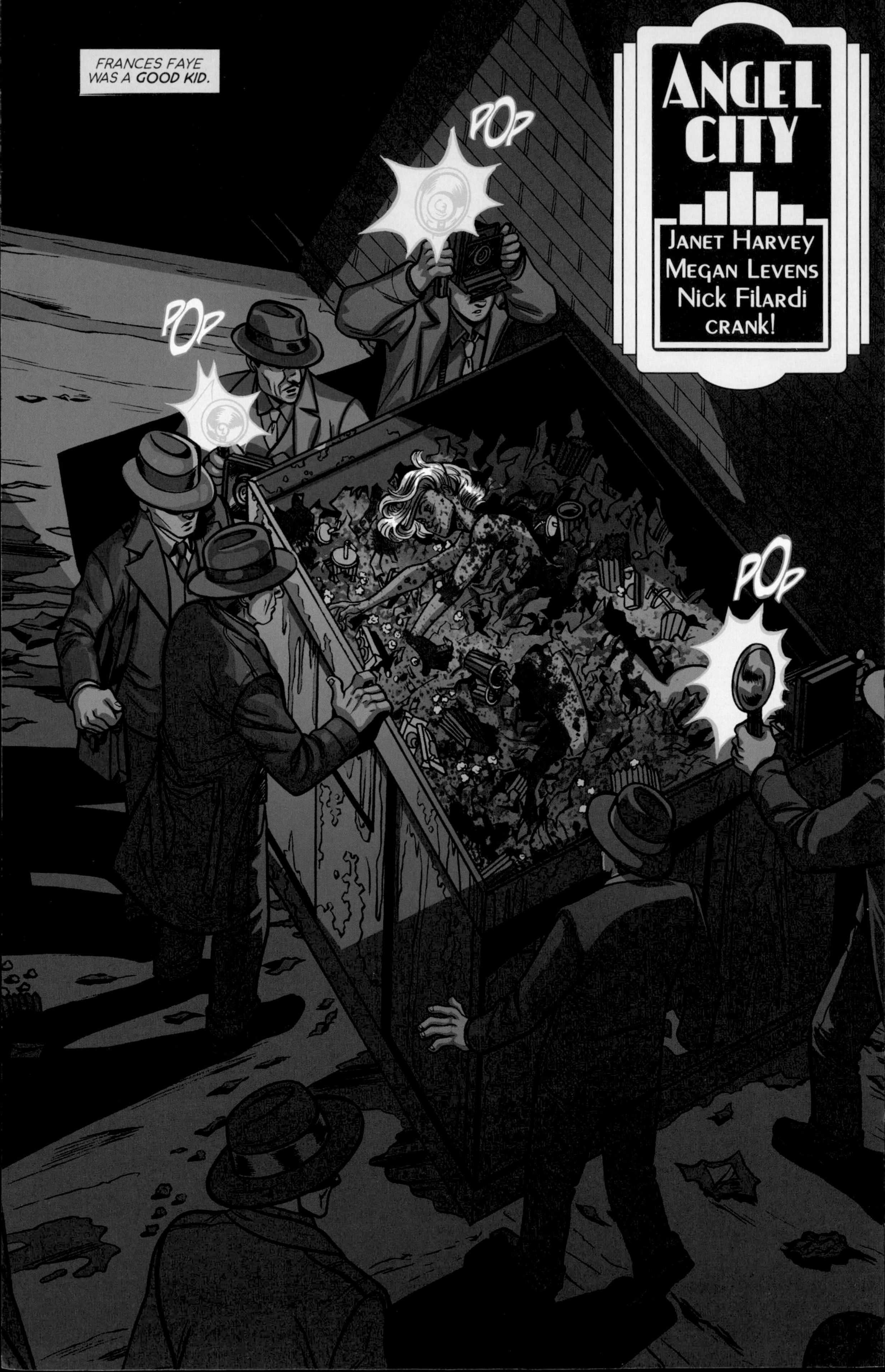
FRANCES FAYE
WAS A GOOD KID.
POP
POP
ANGEL CITY
JANET HARVEY
MEGAN LEVENS
Nick Filardi
CRANK!
POP

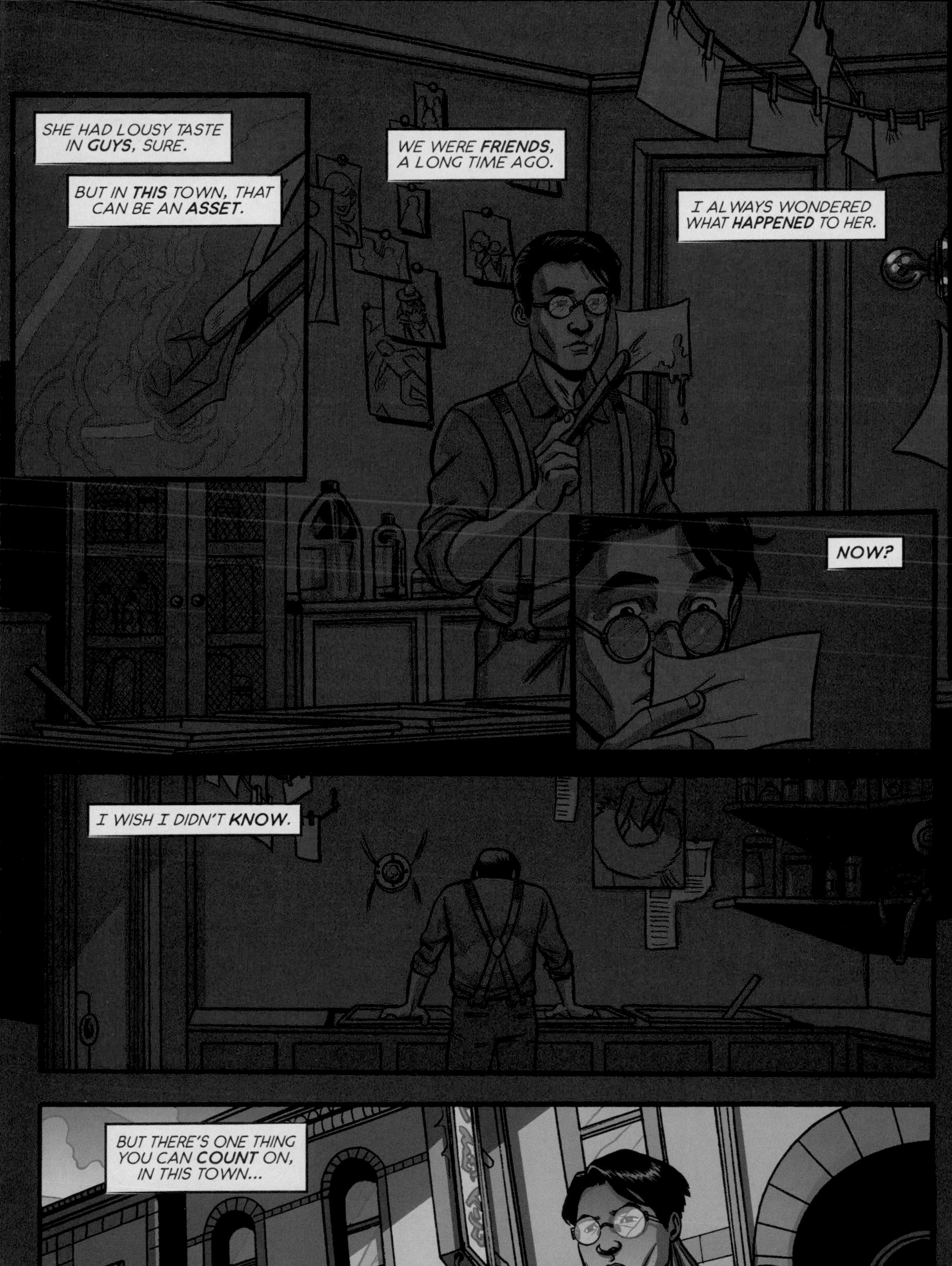
SHE HAD LOUSY TASTE IN GUYS, SURE.
BUT IN THIS TOWN, THAT CAN BE AN ASSET.
WE WERE FRIENDS, A LONG TIME AGO.
I ALWAYS WONDERED WHAT HAPPENED TO HER.
NOW?
I WISH I DIDN'T KNOW.
BUT THERE'S ONE THING YOU CAN COUNT ON, IN THIS TOWN...

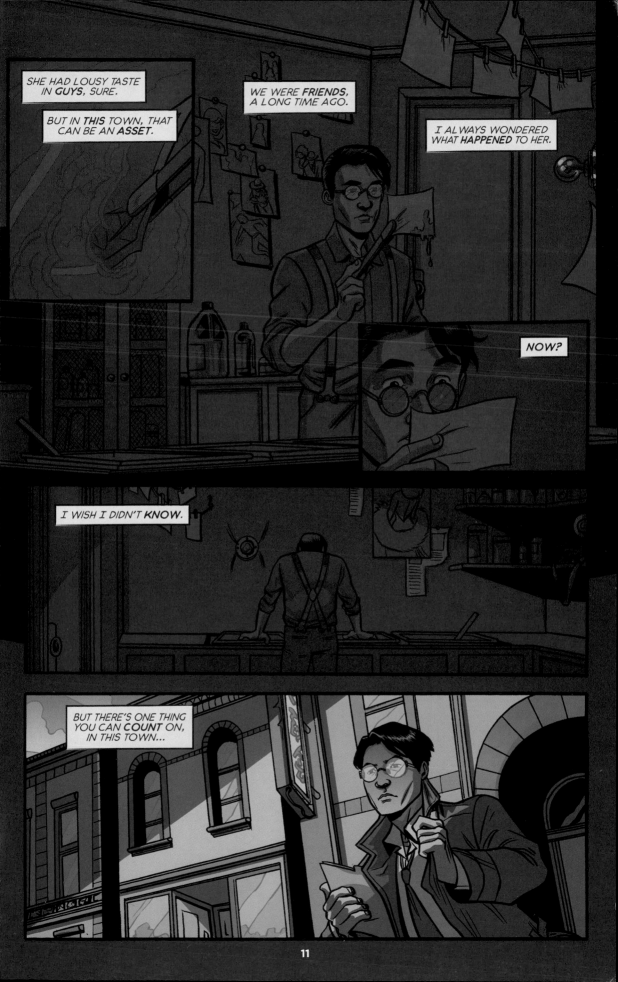

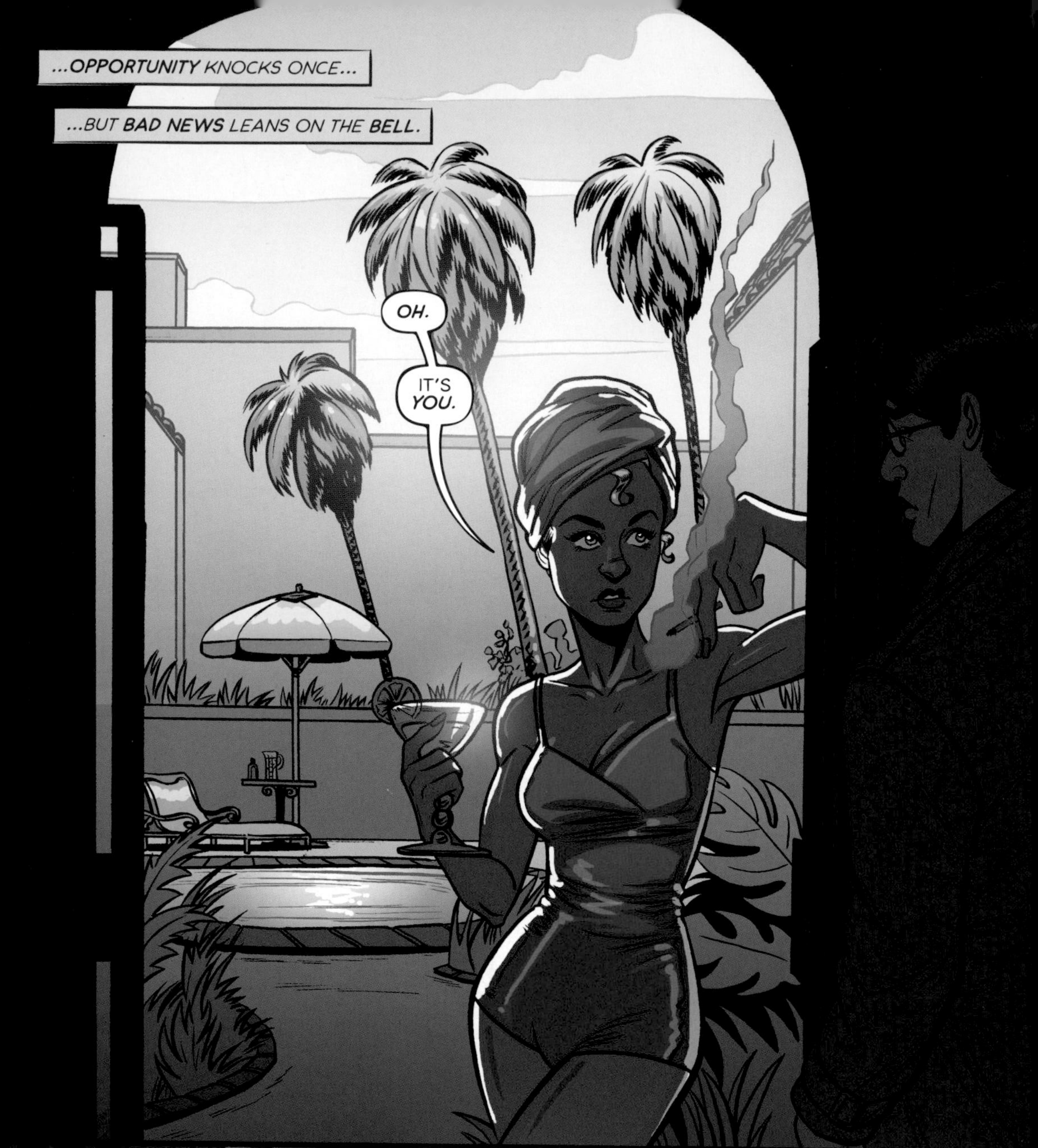
...*OPPORTUNITY* KNOCKS ONCE...
...BUT **BAD NEWS** LEANS ON THE **BELL**.
OH.
IT'S *YOU.*
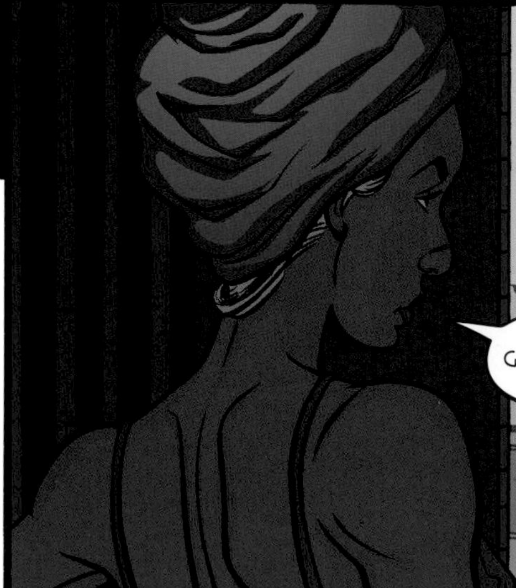
DON'T GET *CUTE*, JOE.
WHATEVER YOU *WANT*, MAKE IT QUICK.
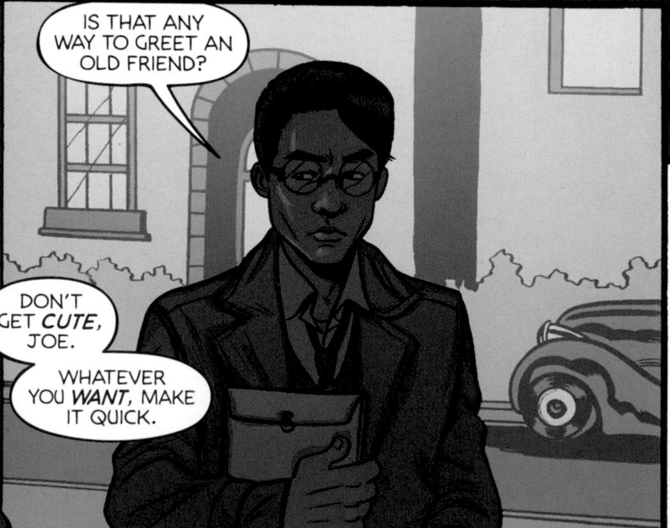
IS THAT ANY WAY TO GREET AN OLD FRIEND?

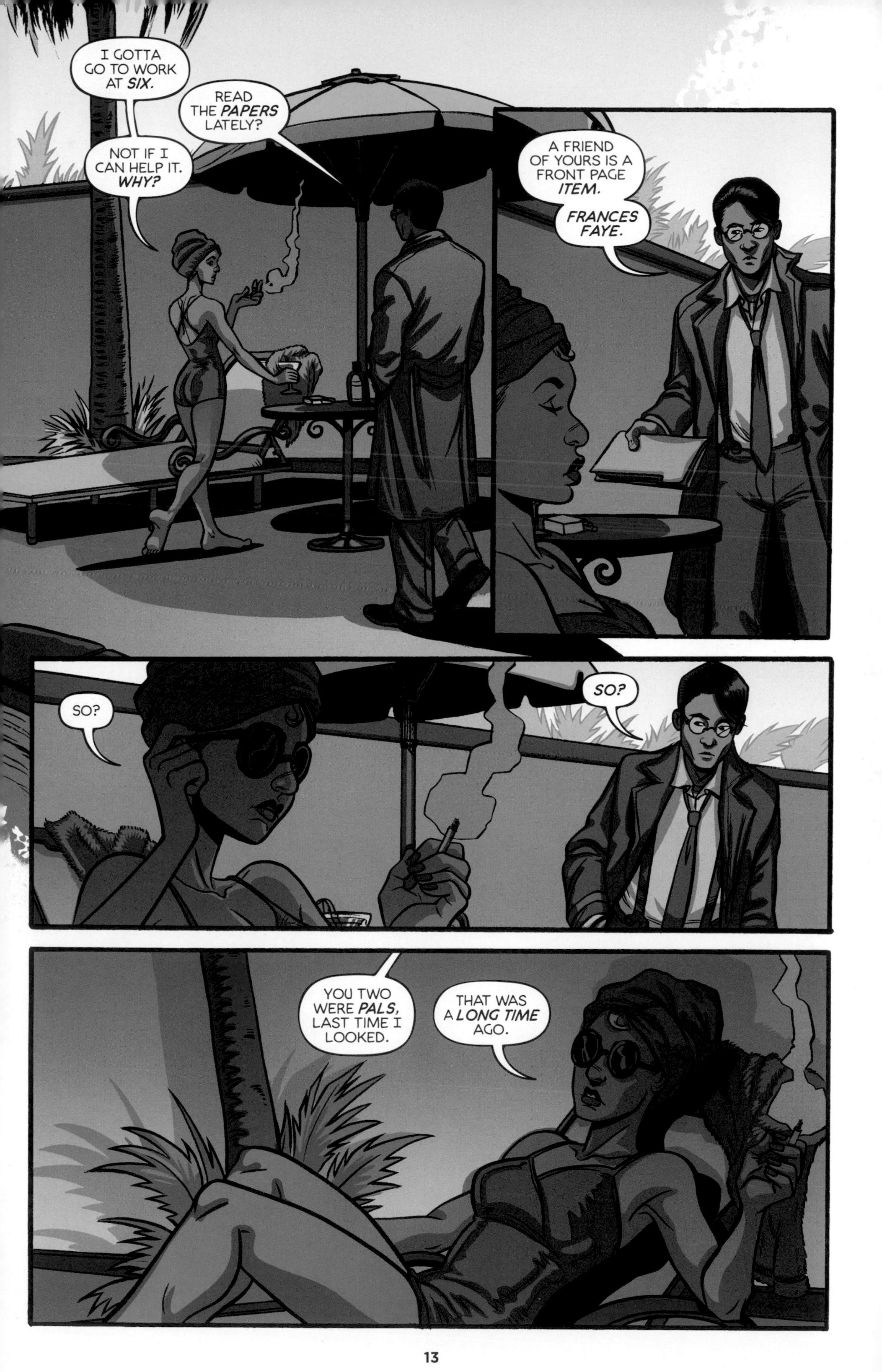
I GOTTA GO TO WORK AT *SIX.*
READ THE *PAPERS* LATELY?
NOT IF I CAN HELP IT. *WHY?*
A FRIEND OF YOURS IS A FRONT PAGE *ITEM.*
FRANCES FAYE.
SO?
SO?
YOU TWO WERE *PALS,* LAST TIME I LOOKED.
THAT WAS A *LONG TIME* AGO.

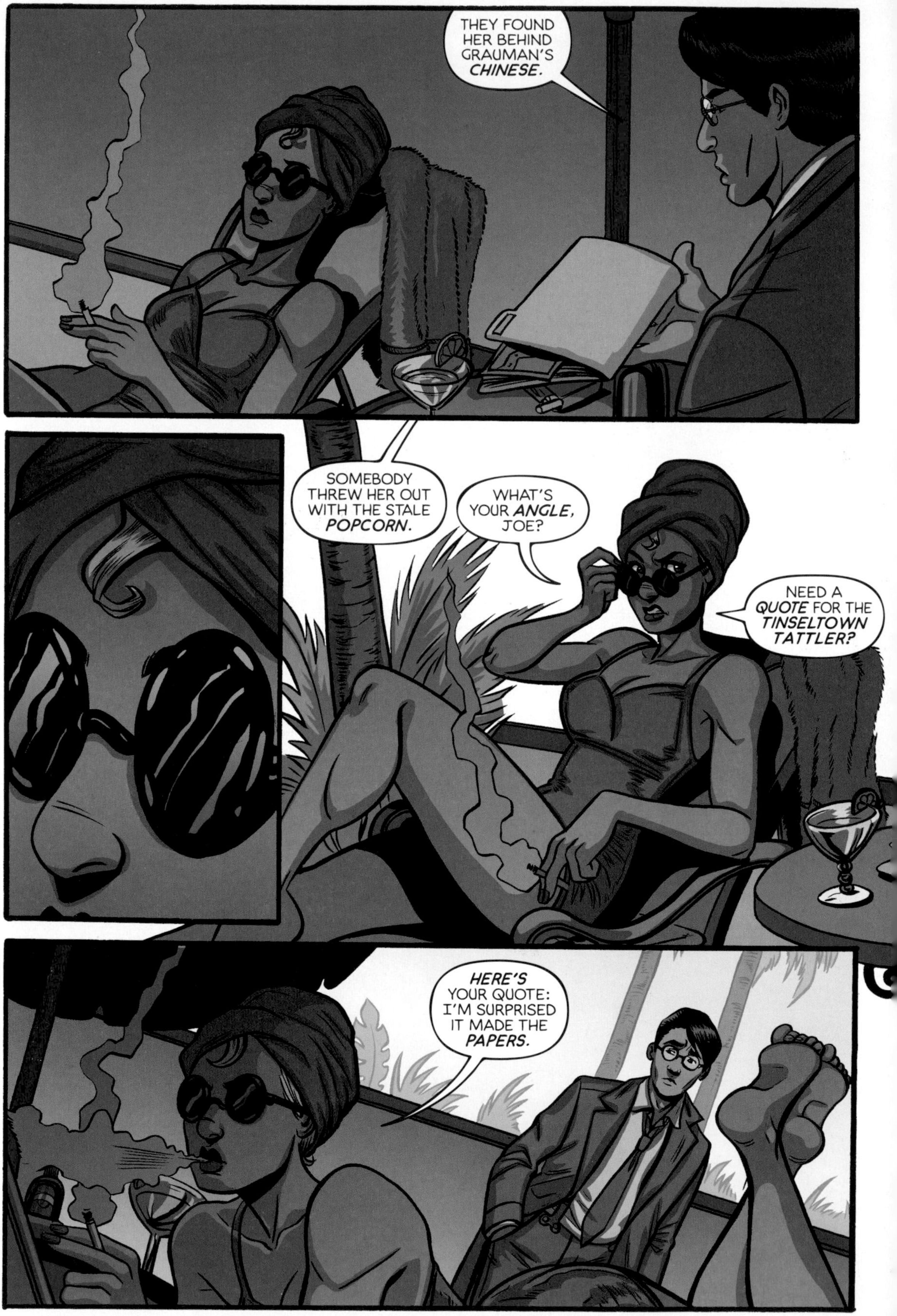
THEY FOUND HER BEHIND GRAUMAN'S *CHINESE*.
SOMEBODY THREW HER OUT WITH THE STALE *POPCORN*.
WHAT'S YOUR *ANGLE*, JOE?
NEED A *QUOTE* FOR THE *TINSELTOWN TATTLER?*
HERE'S YOUR QUOTE: I'M SURPRISED IT MADE THE *PAPERS*.

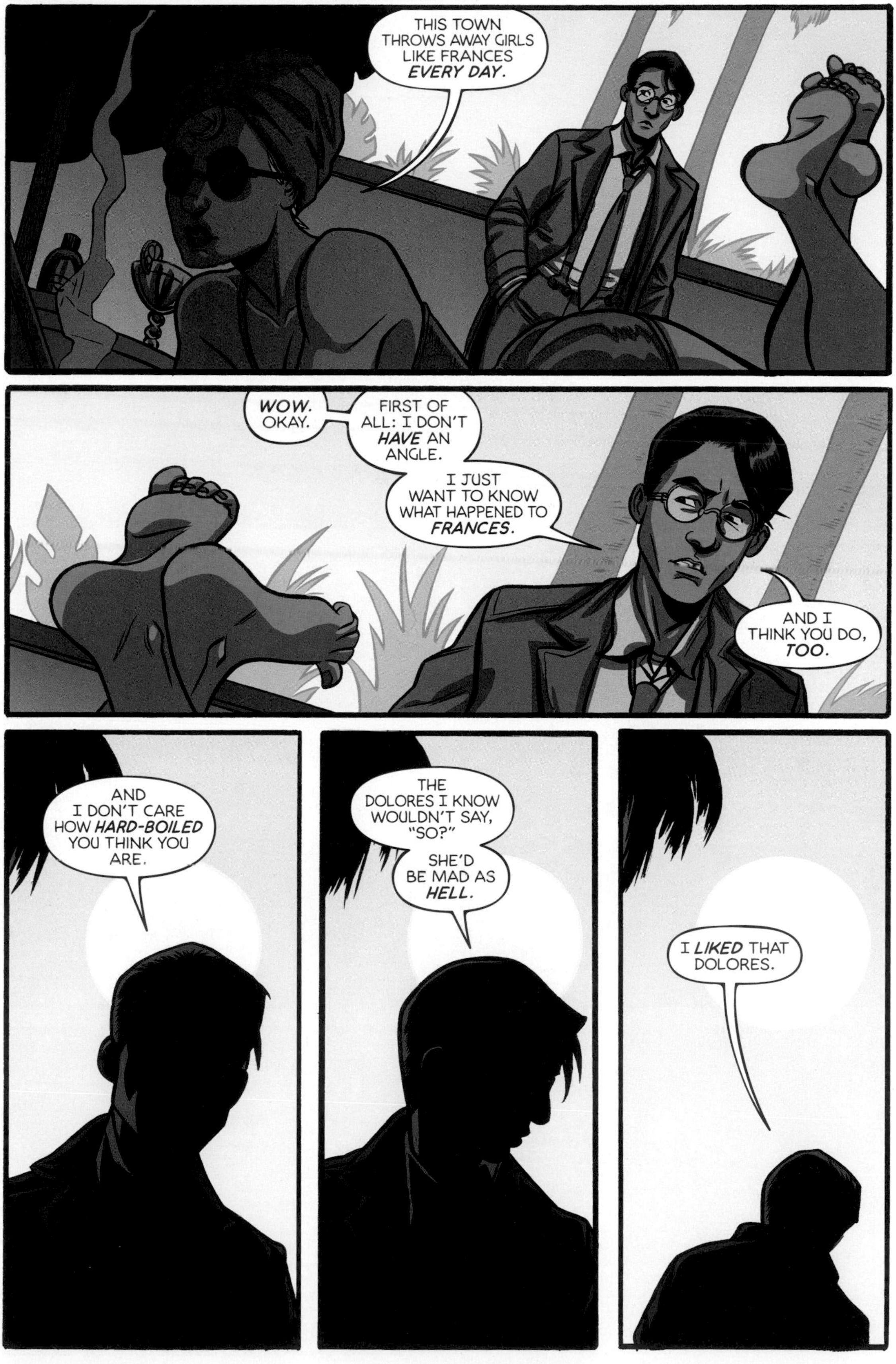
THIS TOWN THROWS AWAY GIRLS LIKE FRANCES *EVERY DAY*.
WOW. OKAY.
FIRST OF ALL: I DON'T *HAVE* AN ANGLE.
I JUST WANT TO KNOW WHAT HAPPENED TO *FRANCES*.
AND I THINK YOU DO, *TOO*.
AND I DON'T CARE HOW *HARD-BOILED* YOU THINK YOU ARE.
THE DOLORES I KNOW WOULDN'T SAY, "SO?"
SHE'D BE MAD AS *HELL*.
I *LIKED* THAT DOLORES.

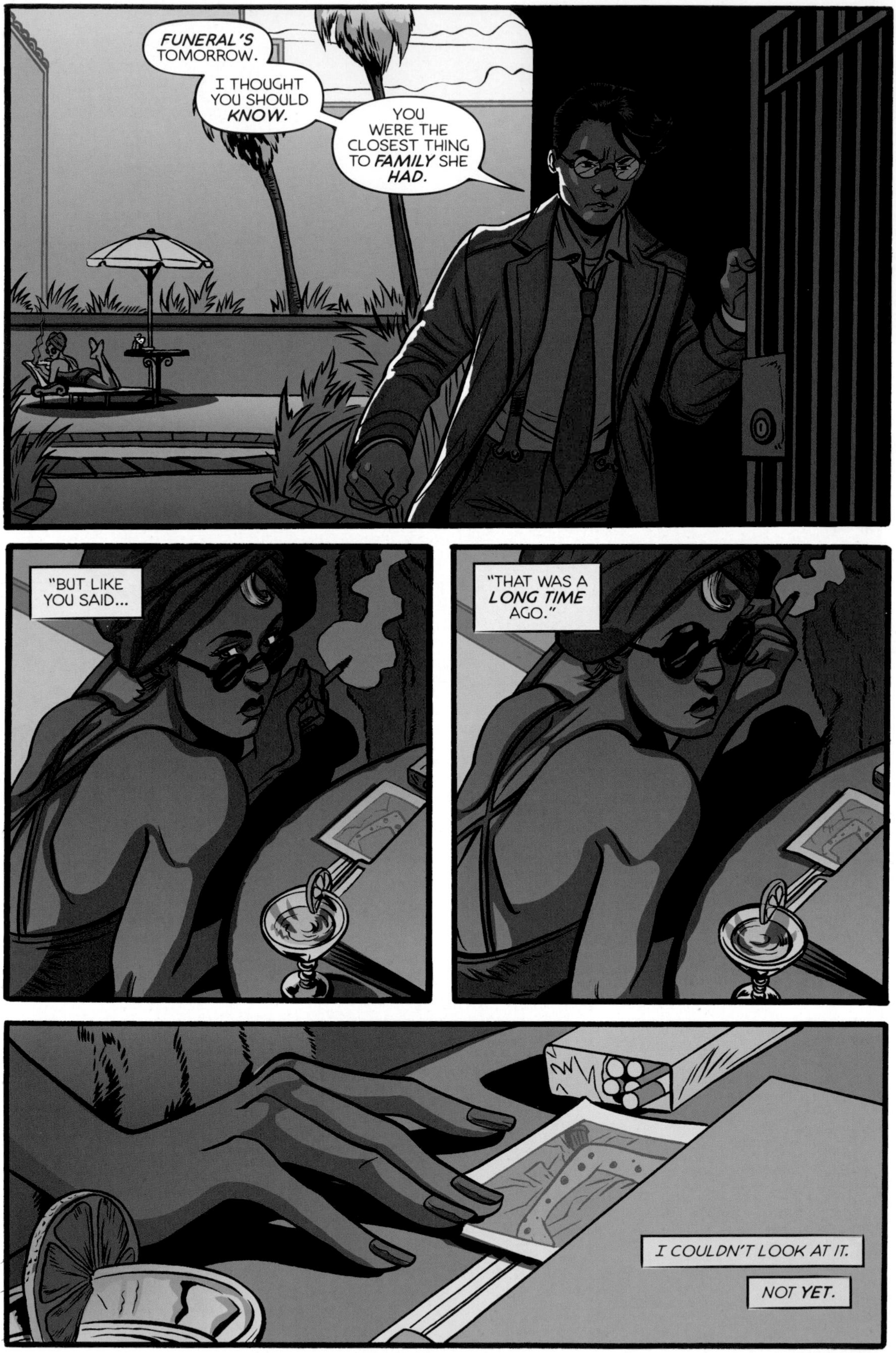
FUNERAL'S TOMORROW.
I THOUGHT YOU SHOULD KNOW.
YOU WERE THE CLOSEST THING TO FAMILY SHE HAD.
"BUT LIKE YOU SAID...
"THAT WAS A LONG TIME AGO."
I COULDN'T LOOK AT IT.
NOT YET.

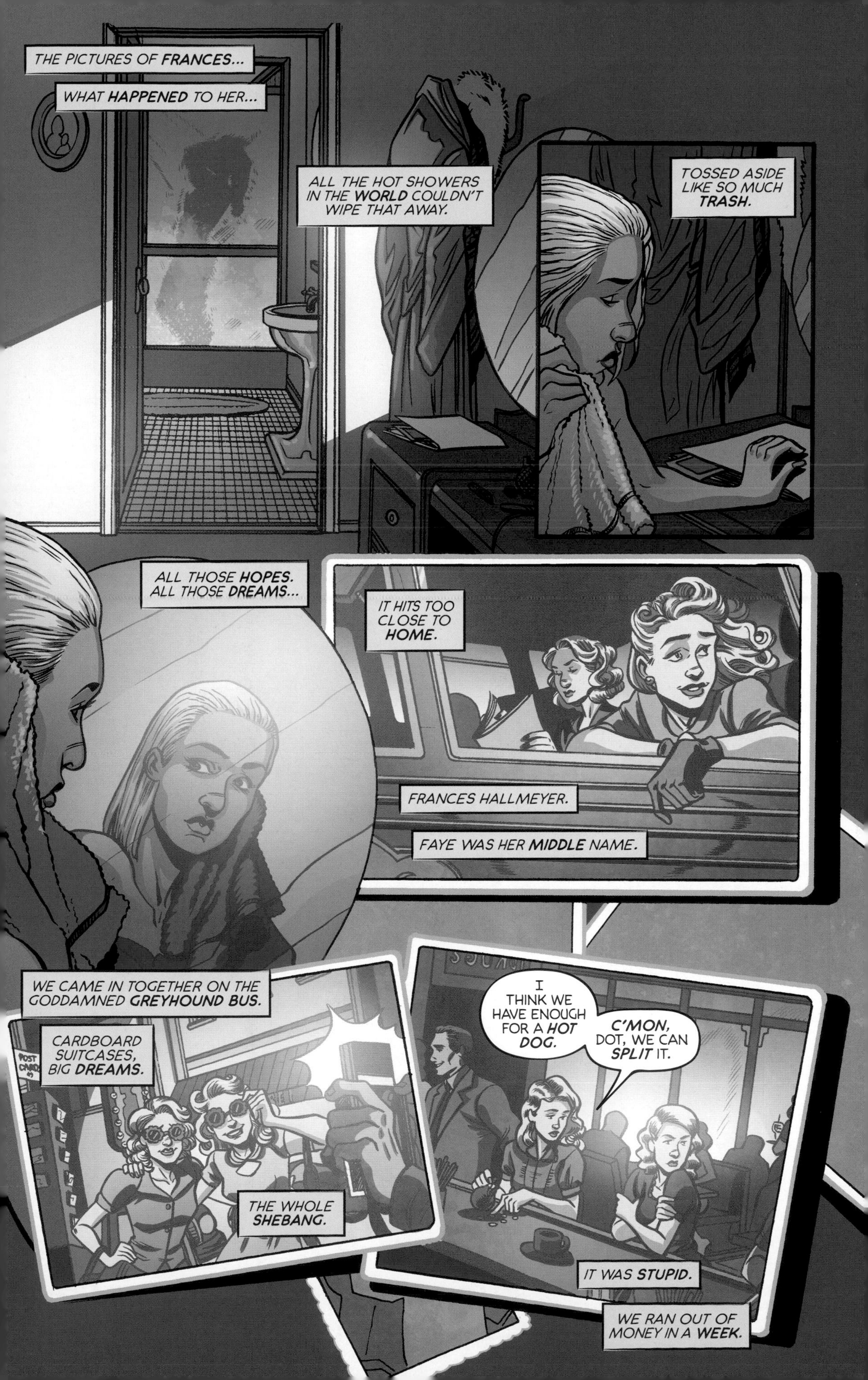
THE PICTURES OF FRANCES...
WHAT HAPPENED TO HER...
ALL THE HOT SHOWERS IN THE WORLD COULDN'T WIPE THAT AWAY.
TOSSED ASIDE LIKE SO MUCH TRASH.
ALL THOSE HOPES. ALL THOSE DREAMS...
IT HITS TOO CLOSE TO HOME.
FRANCES HALLMEYER.
FAYE WAS HER MIDDLE NAME.
WE CAME IN TOGETHER ON THE GODDAMNED GREYHOUND BUS.
CARDBOARD SUITCASES, BIG DREAMS.
THE WHOLE SHEBANG.
I THINK WE HAVE ENOUGH FOR A HOT DOG.
C'MON, DOT, WE CAN SPLIT IT.
IT WAS STUPID.
WE RAN OUT OF MONEY IN A WEEK.

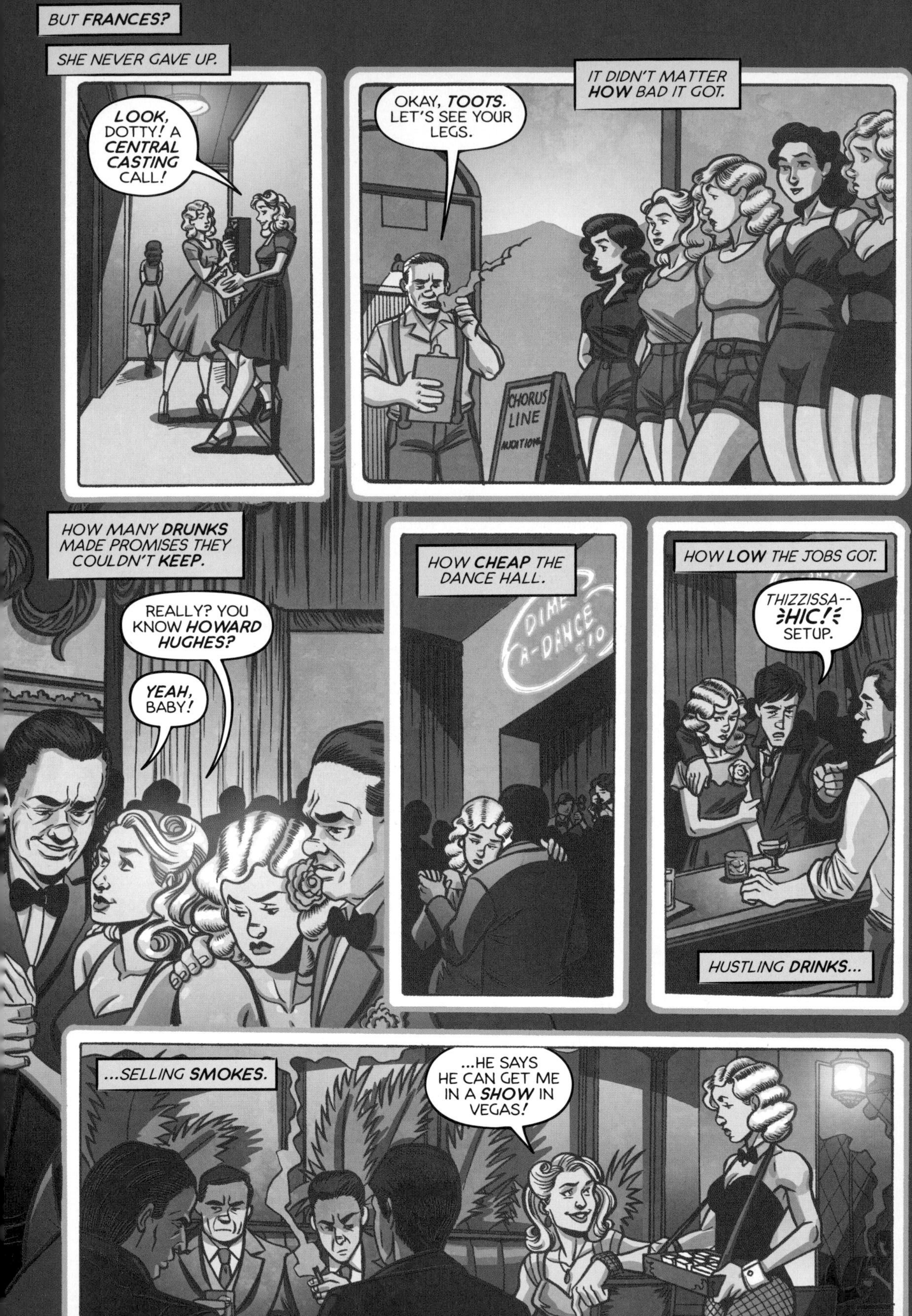
BUT FRANCES?
SHE NEVER GAVE UP.
LOOK, DOTTY! A CENTRAL CASTING CALL!
IT DIDN'T MATTER HOW BAD IT GOT.
OKAY, TOOTS. LET'S SEE YOUR LEGS.
CHORUS LINE AUDITIONS
HOW MANY DRUNKS MADE PROMISES THEY COULDN'T KEEP.
REALLY? YOU KNOW HOWARD HUGHES?
YEAH, BABY!
HOW CHEAP THE DANCE HALL.
DIME-A-DANCE
HOW LOW THE JOBS GOT.
THIZZISSA-- HIC! SETUP.
HUSTLING DRINKS...
...SELLING SMOKES.
...HE SAYS HE CAN GET ME IN A SHOW IN VEGAS!
FRANCES ALWAYS HAD HOPE.

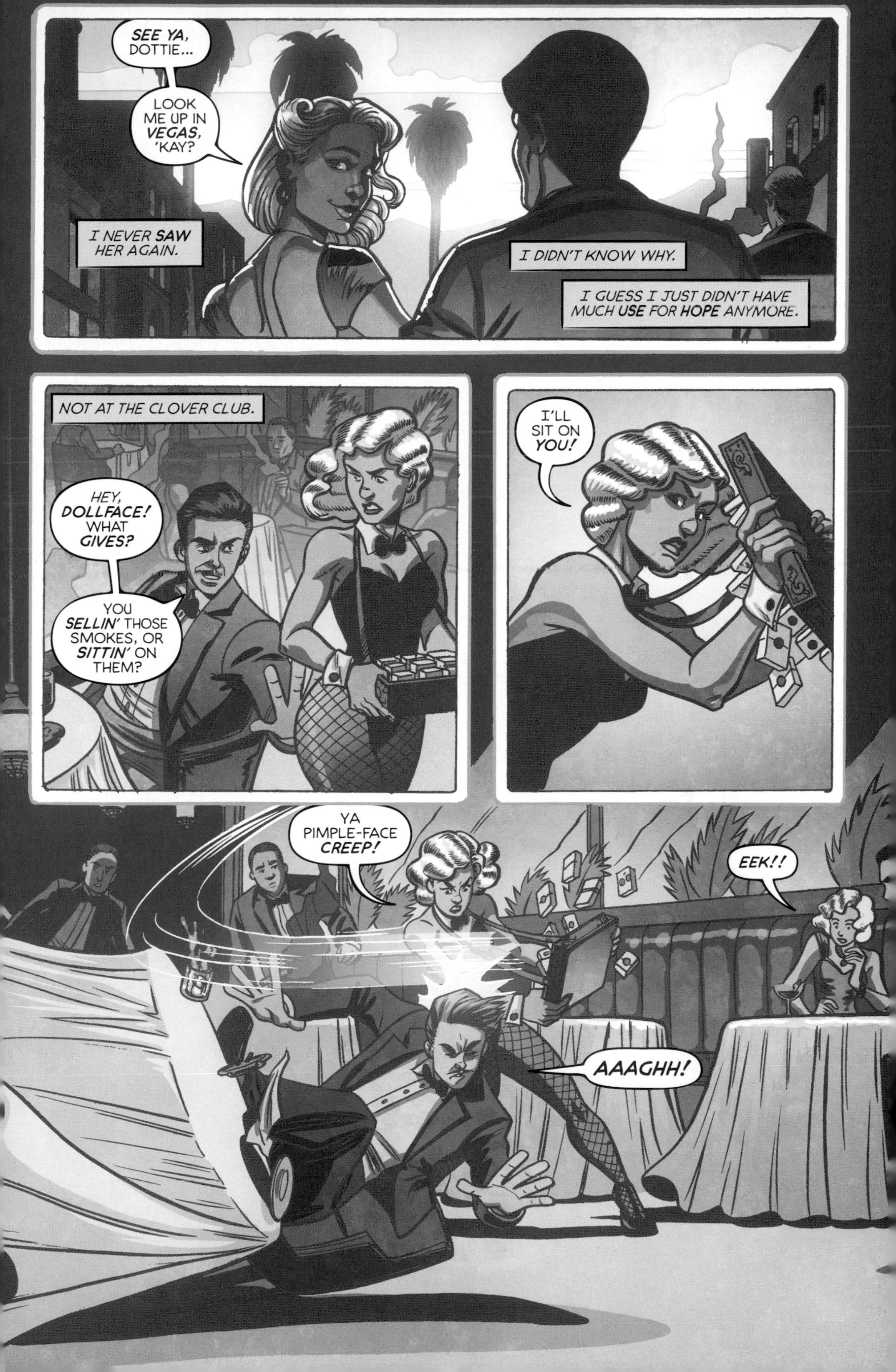
SEE YA, DOTTIE...
LOOK ME UP IN VEGAS, 'KAY?
I NEVER SAW HER AGAIN.
I DIDN'T KNOW WHY.
I GUESS I JUST DIDN'T HAVE MUCH USE FOR HOPE ANYMORE.
NOT AT THE CLOVER CLUB.
HEY, DOLLFACE! WHAT GIVES?
YOU SELLIN' THOSE SMOKES, OR SITTIN' ON THEM?
I'LL SIT ON YOU!
YA PIMPLE-FACE CREEP!
EEK!!
AAAGHH!

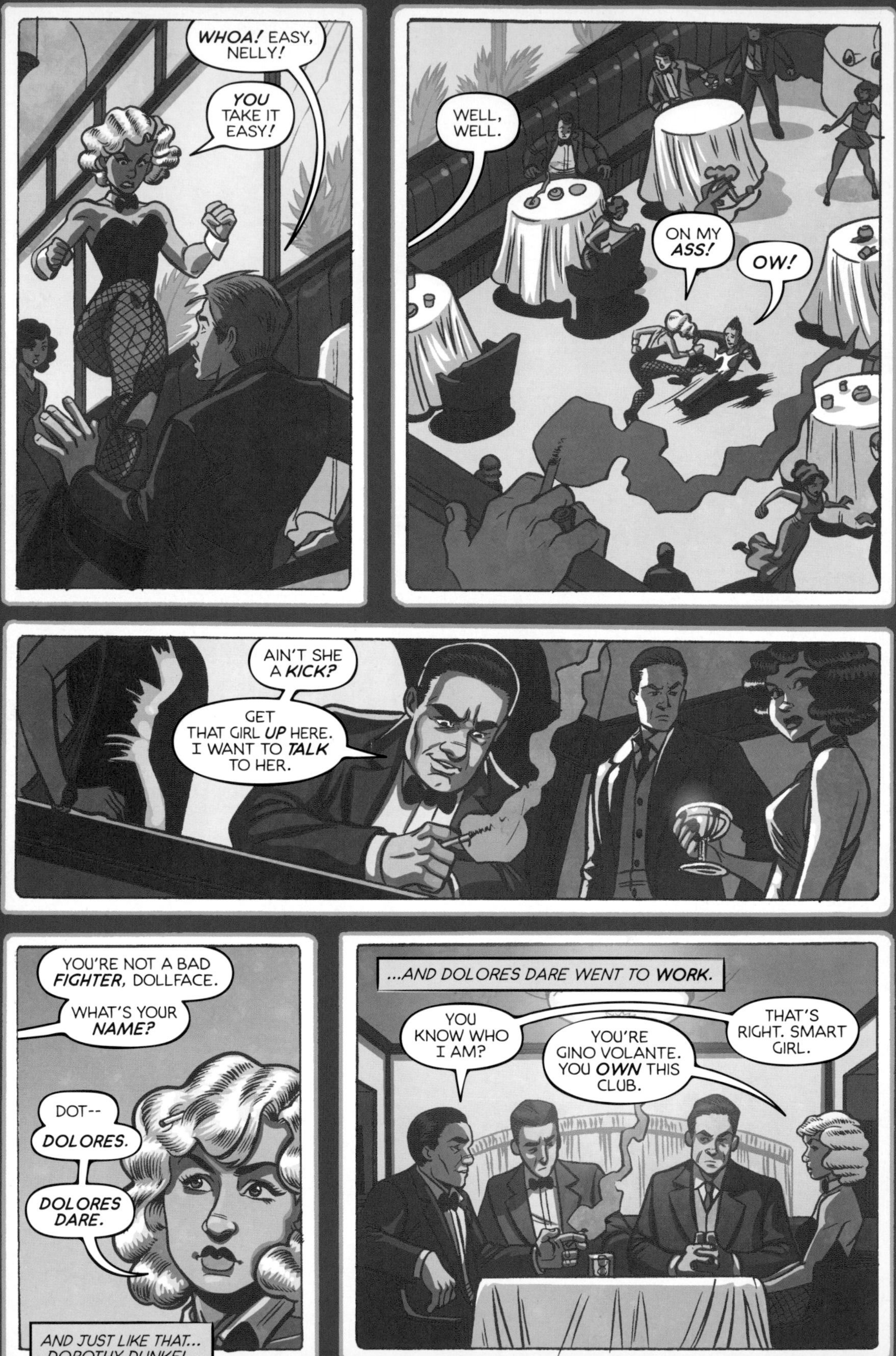
WHOA! EASY, NELLY!
YOU TAKE IT EASY!
WELL, WELL.
ON MY ASS!
OW!
AIN'T SHE A KICK?
GET THAT GIRL UP HERE. I WANT TO TALK TO HER.
YOU'RE NOT A BAD FIGHTER, DOLLFACE.
WHAT'S YOUR NAME?
DOT--
DOLORES.
DOLORES DARE.
AND JUST LIKE THAT... DOROTHY DUNKEL DISAPPEARED.
...AND DOLORES DARE WENT TO WORK.
YOU KNOW WHO I AM?
YOU'RE GINO VOLANTE. YOU OWN THIS CLUB.
THAT'S RIGHT. SMART GIRL.

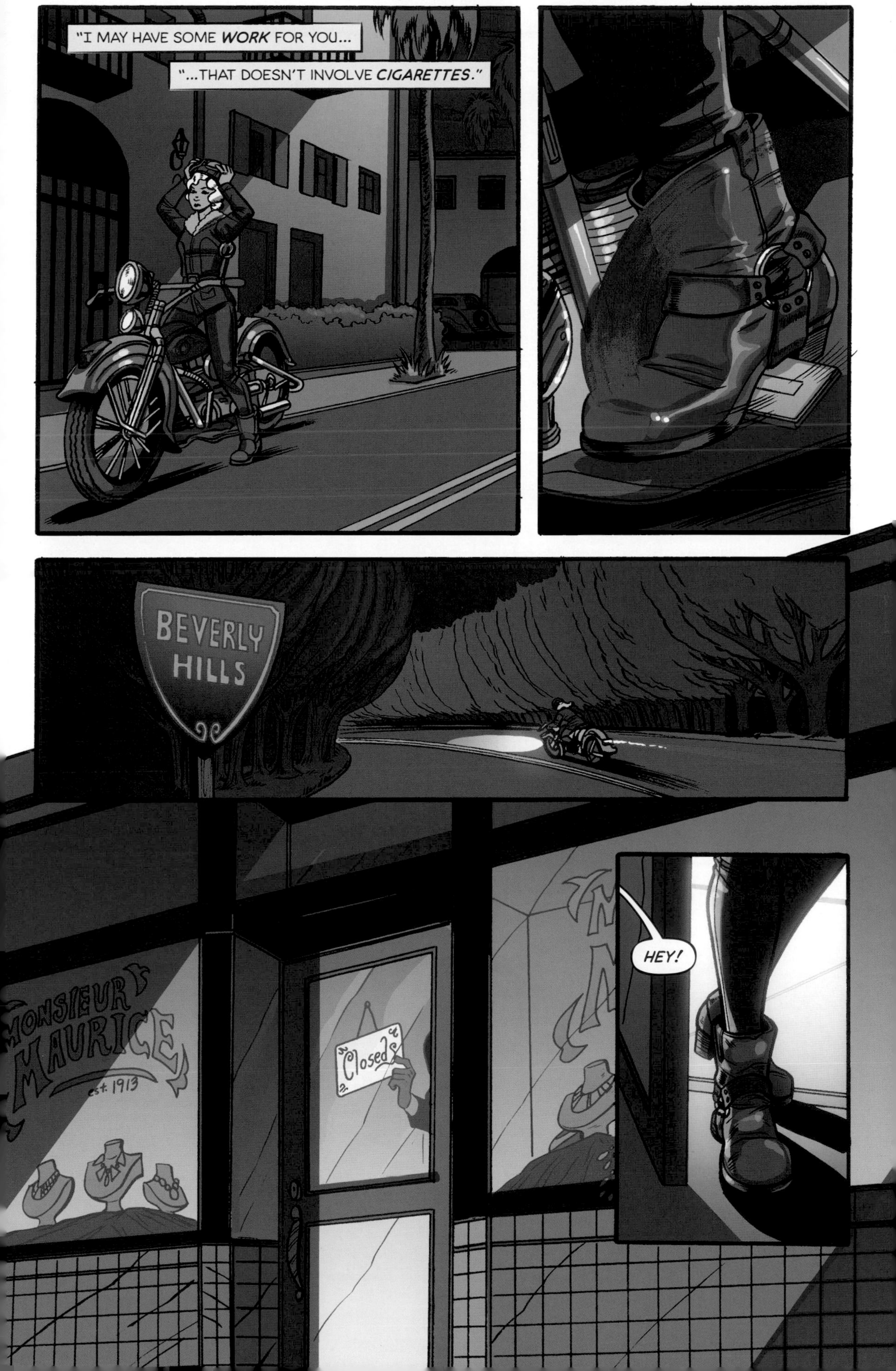
"I MAY HAVE SOME *WORK* FOR YOU...
"...THAT DOESN'T INVOLVE *CIGARETTES*."
BEVERLY HILLS
MONSIEUR MAURICE
est. 1913
Closed
HEY!

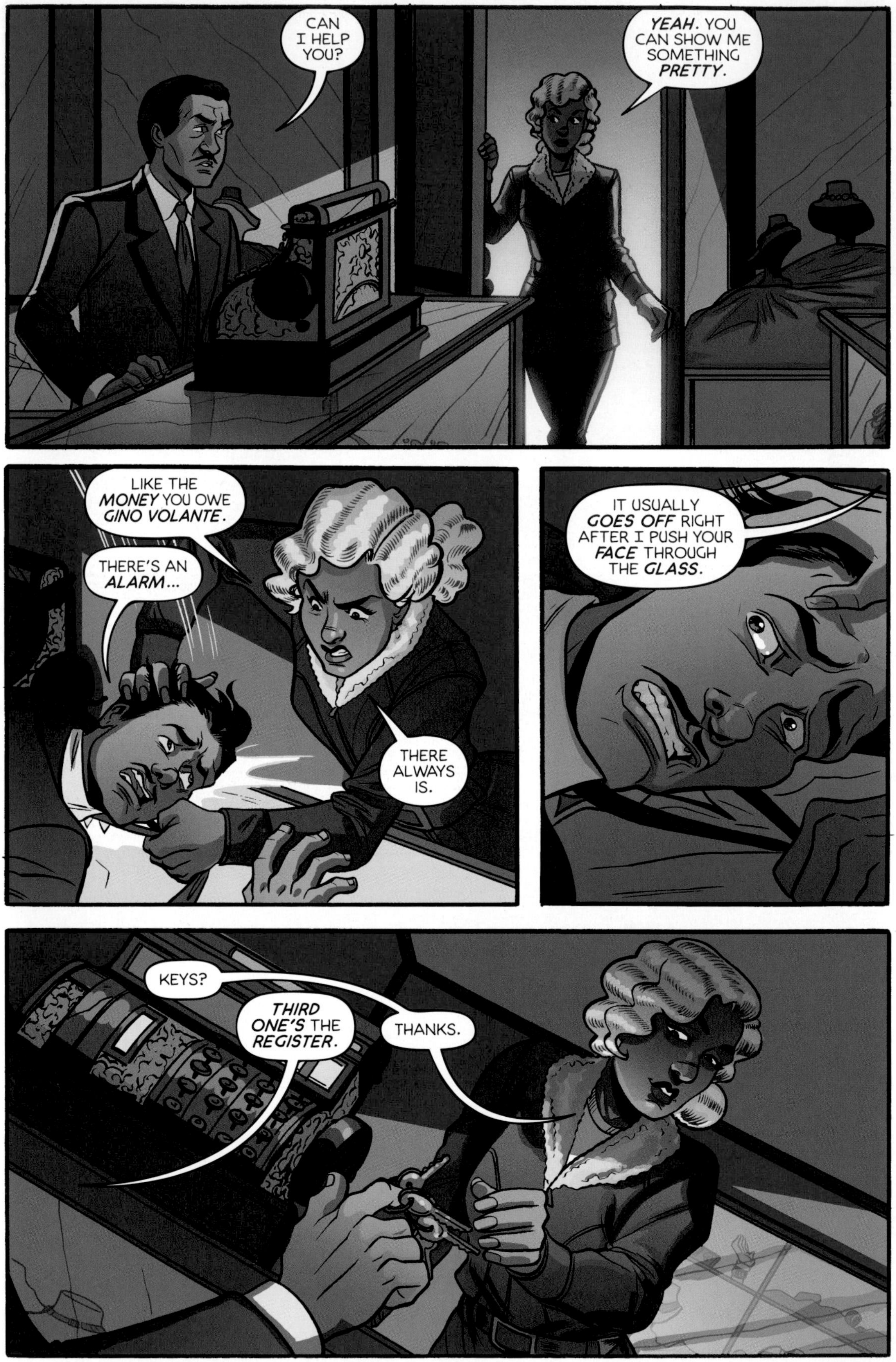
CAN I HELP YOU?
YEAH. YOU CAN SHOW ME SOMETHING PRETTY.
LIKE THE MONEY YOU OWE GINO VOLANTE.
THERE'S AN ALARM...
THERE ALWAYS IS.
IT USUALLY GOES OFF RIGHT AFTER I PUSH YOUR FACE THROUGH THE GLASS.
KEYS?
THIRD ONE'S THE REGISTER.
THANKS.

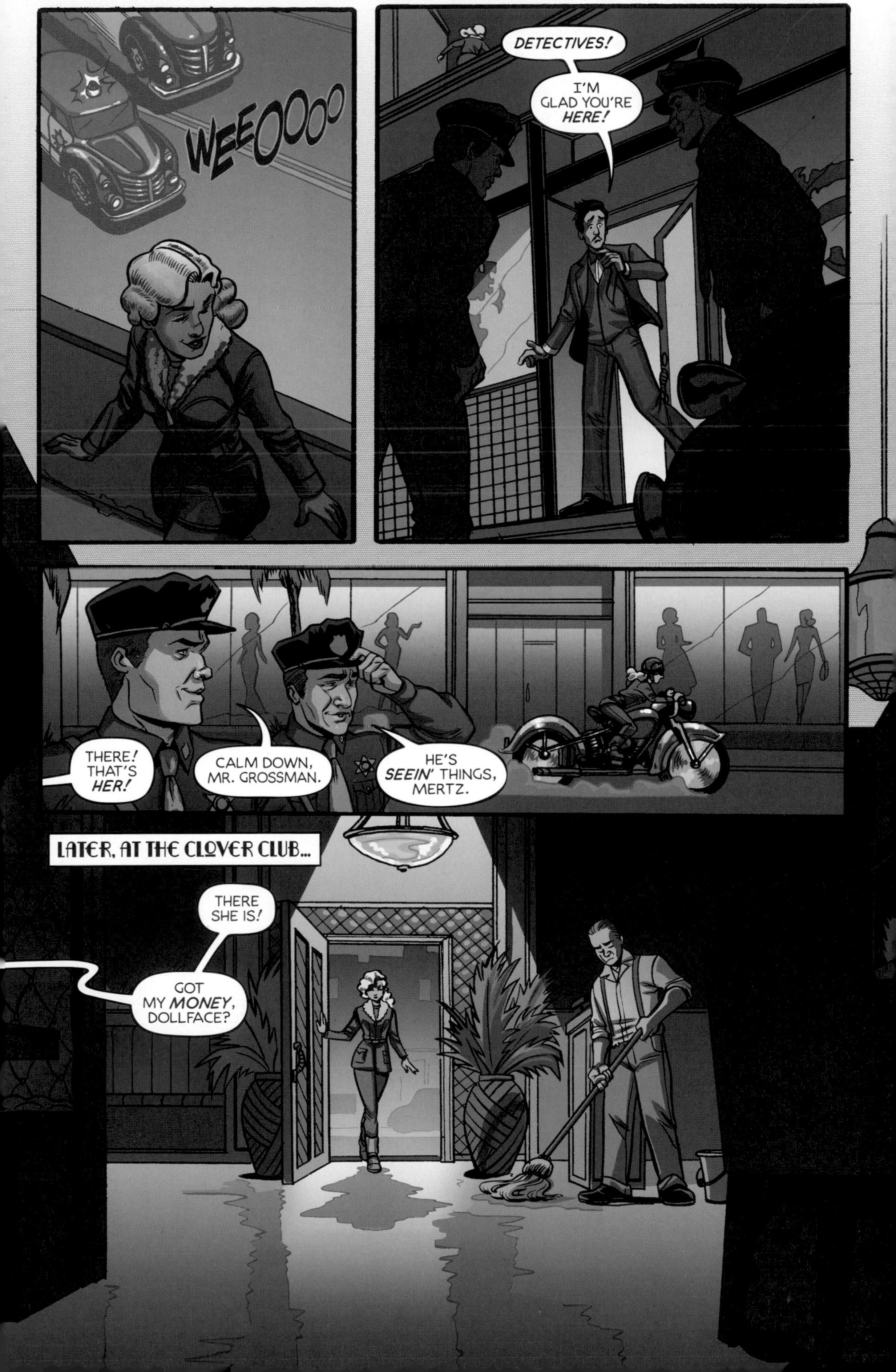
WEEOOOO
DETECTIVES!
I'M GLAD YOU'RE *HERE!*
THERE! THAT'S *HER!*
CALM DOWN, MR. GROSSMAN.
HE'S *SEEIN'* THINGS, MERTZ.
LATER, AT THE CLOVER CLUB...
THERE SHE IS!
GOT MY *MONEY*, DOLLFACE?

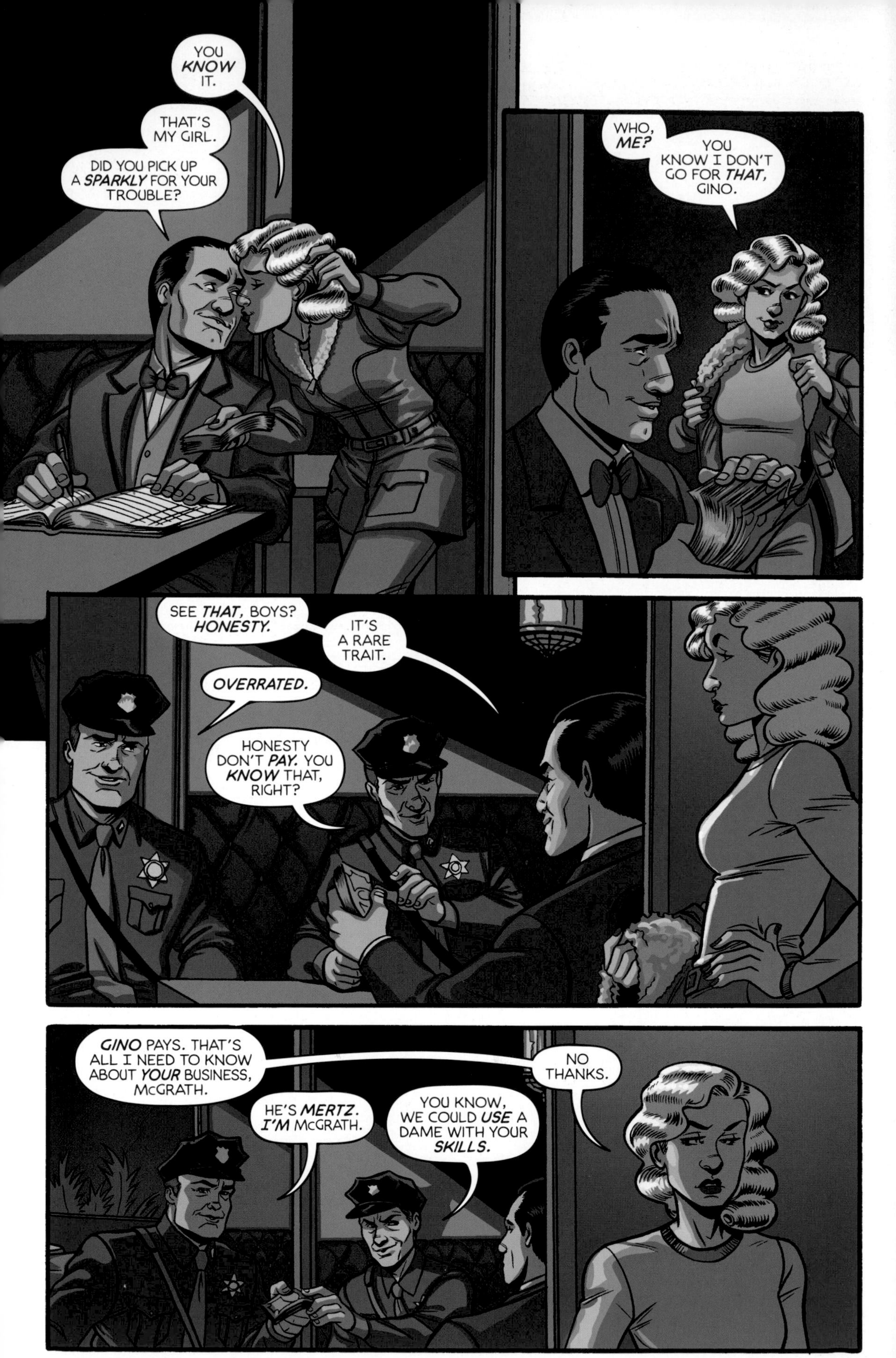
YOU *KNOW* IT.
THAT'S MY GIRL.
DID YOU PICK UP A *SPARKLY* FOR YOUR TROUBLE?
WHO, *ME?*
YOU KNOW I DON'T GO FOR *THAT,* GINO.
SEE *THAT,* BOYS? *HONESTY.*
IT'S A RARE TRAIT.
OVERRATED.
HONESTY DON'T *PAY.* YOU *KNOW* THAT, RIGHT?
GINO PAYS. THAT'S ALL I NEED TO KNOW ABOUT *YOUR* BUSINESS, McGRATH.
HE'S *MERTZ. I'M* McGRATH.
YOU KNOW, WE COULD *USE* A DAME WITH YOUR *SKILLS.*
NO THANKS.

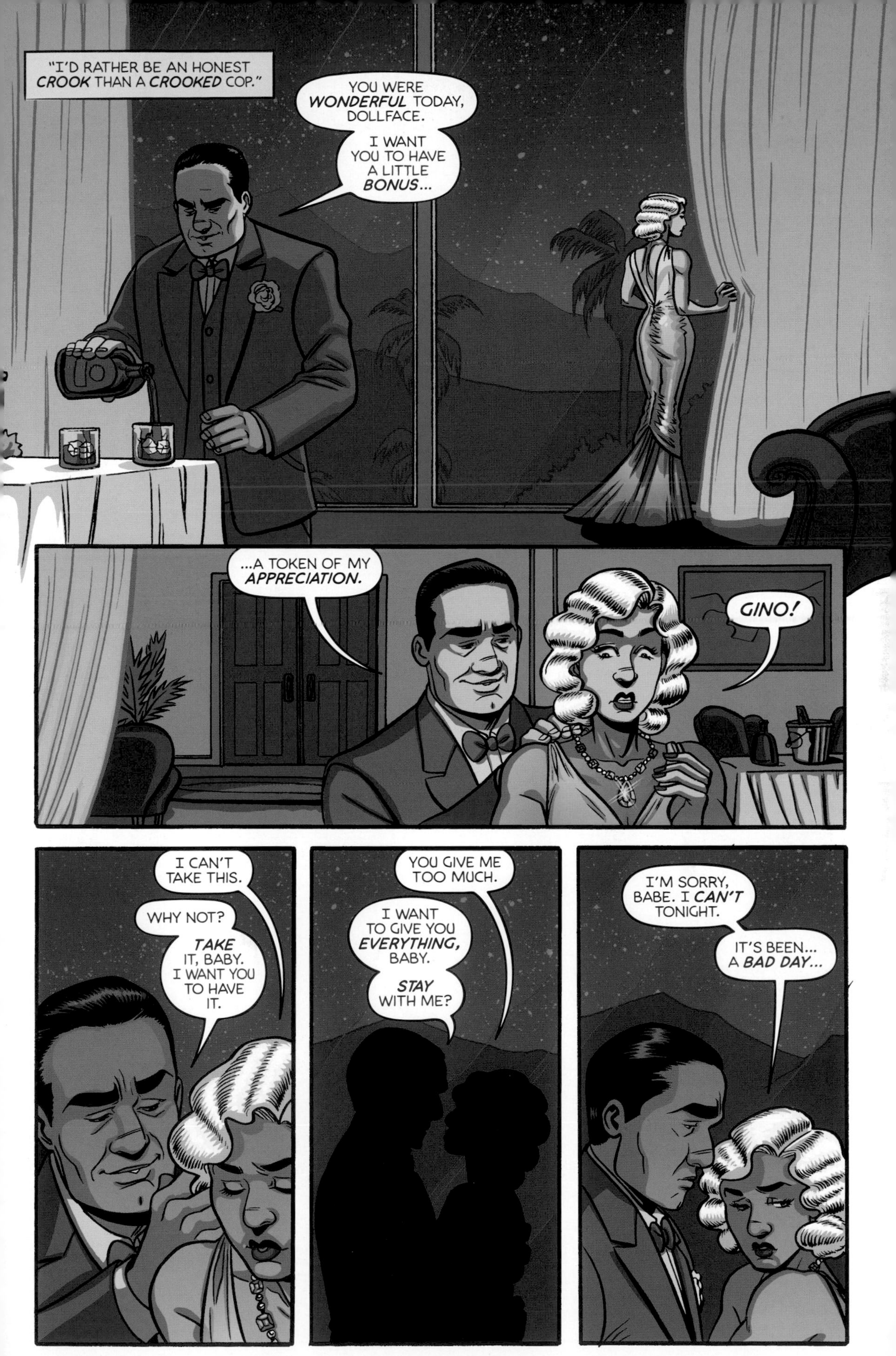
"I'D RATHER BE AN HONEST CROOK THAN A CROOKED COP."
YOU WERE WONDERFUL TODAY, DOLLFACE.
I WANT YOU TO HAVE A LITTLE BONUS...
...A TOKEN OF MY APPRECIATION.
GINO!
I CAN'T TAKE THIS.
WHY NOT?
TAKE IT, BABY. I WANT YOU TO HAVE IT.
YOU GIVE ME TOO MUCH.
I WANT TO GIVE YOU EVERYTHING, BABY.
STAY WITH ME?
I'M SORRY, BABE. I CAN'T TONIGHT.
IT'S BEEN... A BAD DAY...

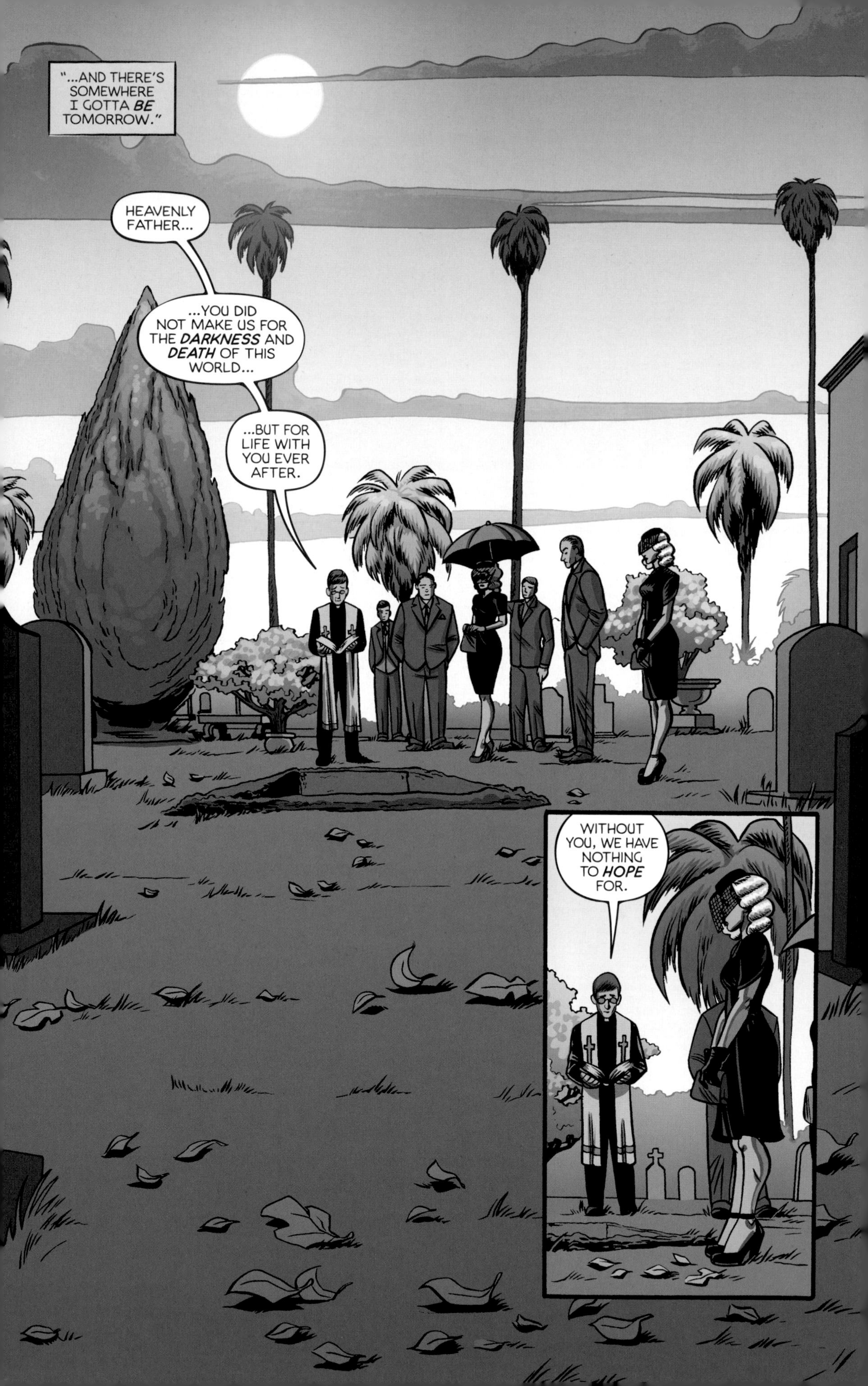
"...AND THERE'S SOMEWHERE I GOTTA *BE* TOMORROW."
HEAVENLY FATHER...
...YOU DID NOT MAKE US FOR THE *DARKNESS* AND *DEATH* OF THIS WORLD...
...BUT FOR LIFE WITH YOU EVER AFTER.
WITHOUT YOU, WE HAVE NOTHING TO *HOPE* FOR.

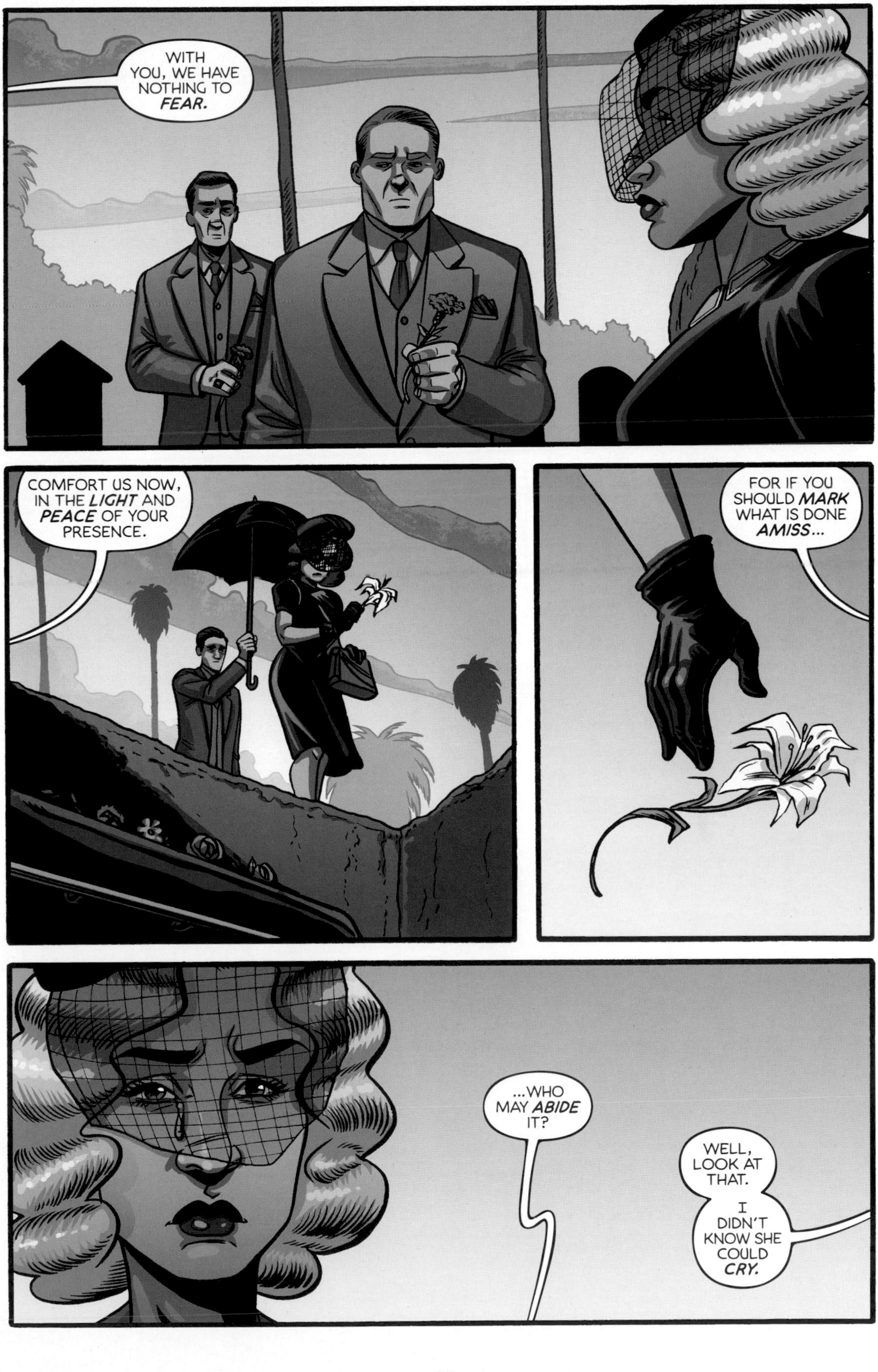
WITH YOU, WE HAVE NOTHING TO *FEAR.*
COMFORT US NOW, IN THE *LIGHT* AND *PEACE* OF YOUR PRESENCE.
FOR IF YOU SHOULD *MARK* WHAT IS DONE *AMISS...*
...WHO MAY *ABIDE* IT?
WELL, LOOK AT THAT.
I DIDN'T KNOW SHE COULD *CRY.*

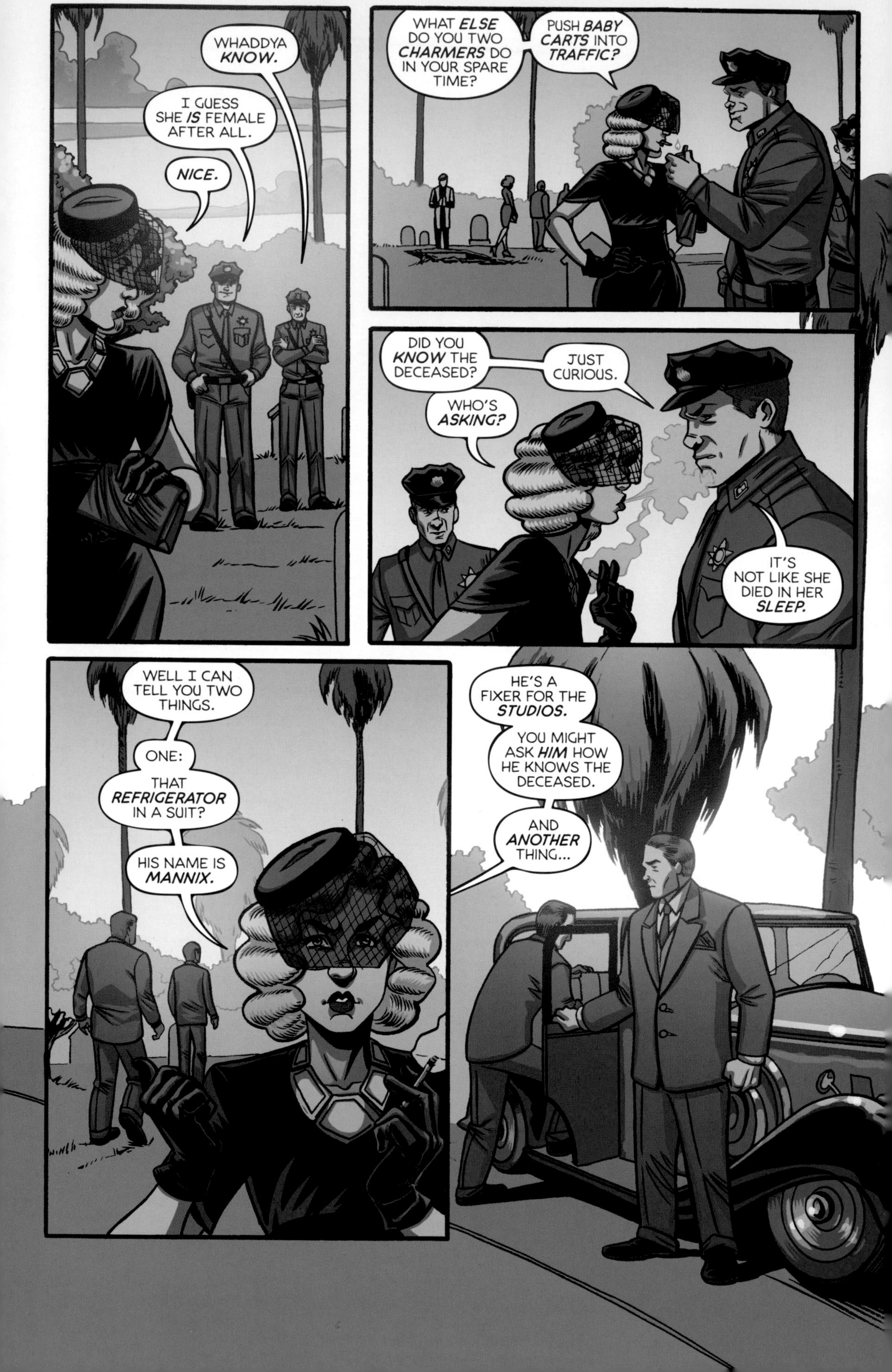

WHADDYA KNOW.
I GUESS SHE IS FEMALE AFTER ALL.
NICE.
WHAT ELSE DO YOU TWO CHARMERS DO IN YOUR SPARE TIME?
PUSH BABY CARTS INTO TRAFFIC?
DID YOU KNOW THE DECEASED?
WHO'S ASKING?
JUST CURIOUS.
IT'S NOT LIKE SHE DIED IN HER SLEEP.
WELL I CAN TELL YOU TWO THINGS.
ONE:
THAT REFRIGERATOR IN A SUIT?
HIS NAME IS MANNIX.
HE'S A FIXER FOR THE STUDIOS.
YOU MIGHT ASK HIM HOW HE KNOWS THE DECEASED.
AND ANOTHER THING...

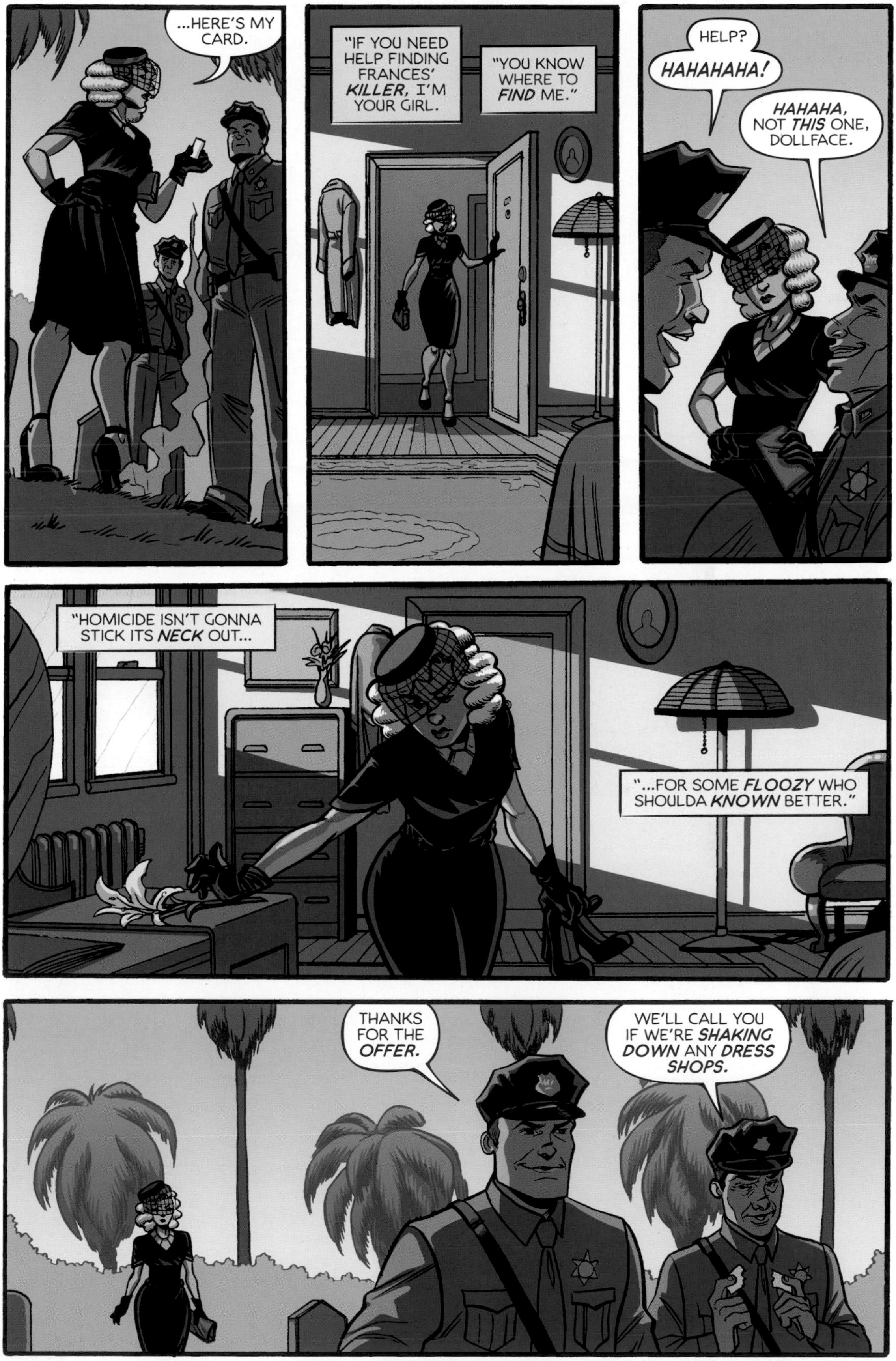
...HERE'S MY CARD.
"IF YOU NEED HELP FINDING FRANCES' KILLER, I'M YOUR GIRL.
"YOU KNOW WHERE TO FIND ME."
HELP?
HAHAHAHA!
HAHAHA, NOT THIS ONE, DOLLFACE.
"HOMICIDE ISN'T GONNA STICK ITS NECK OUT...
"...FOR SOME FLOOZY WHO SHOULDA KNOWN BETTER."
THANKS FOR THE OFFER.
WE'LL CALL YOU IF WE'RE SHAKING DOWN ANY DRESS SHOPS.

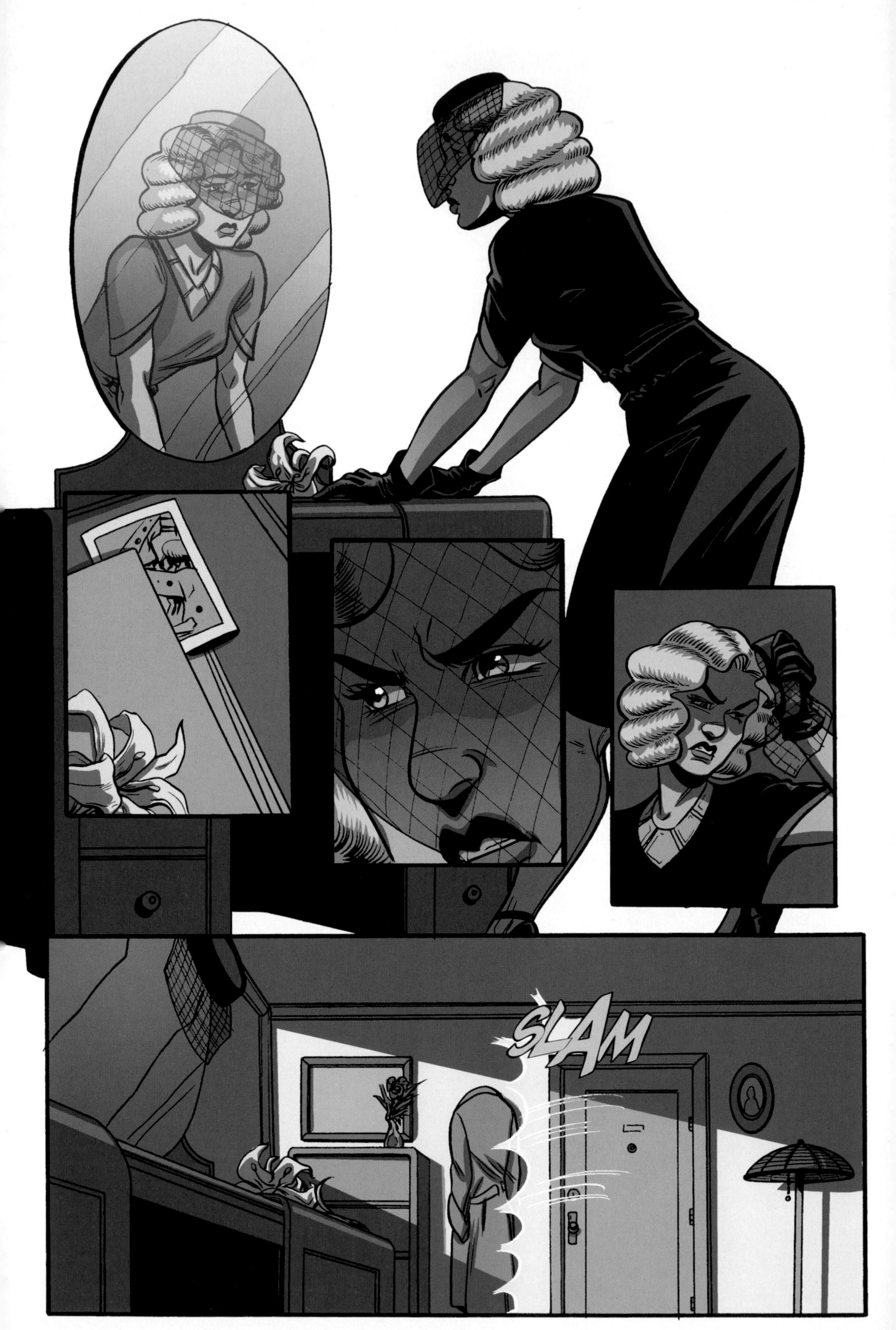
SLAM

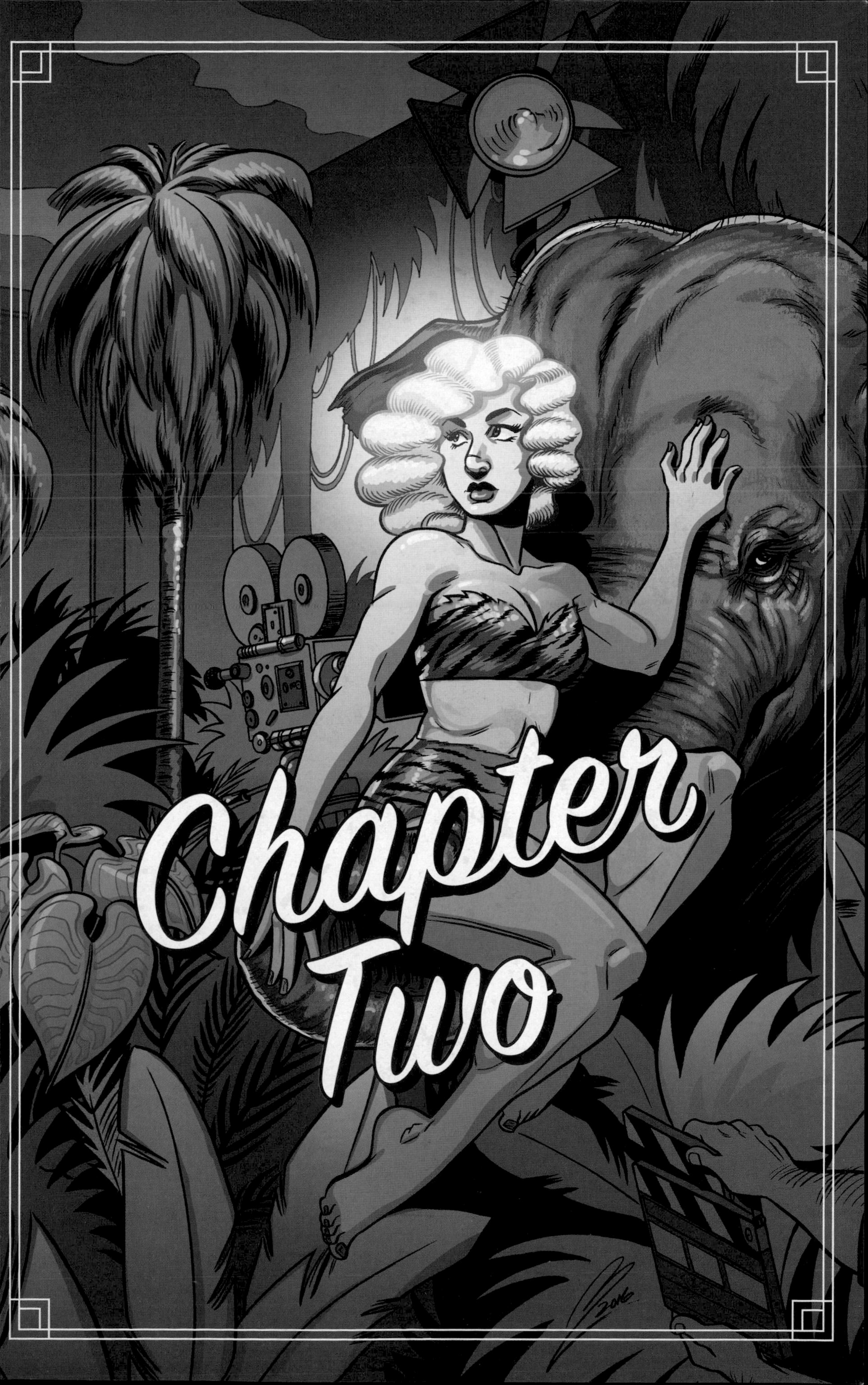
Chapter
Two

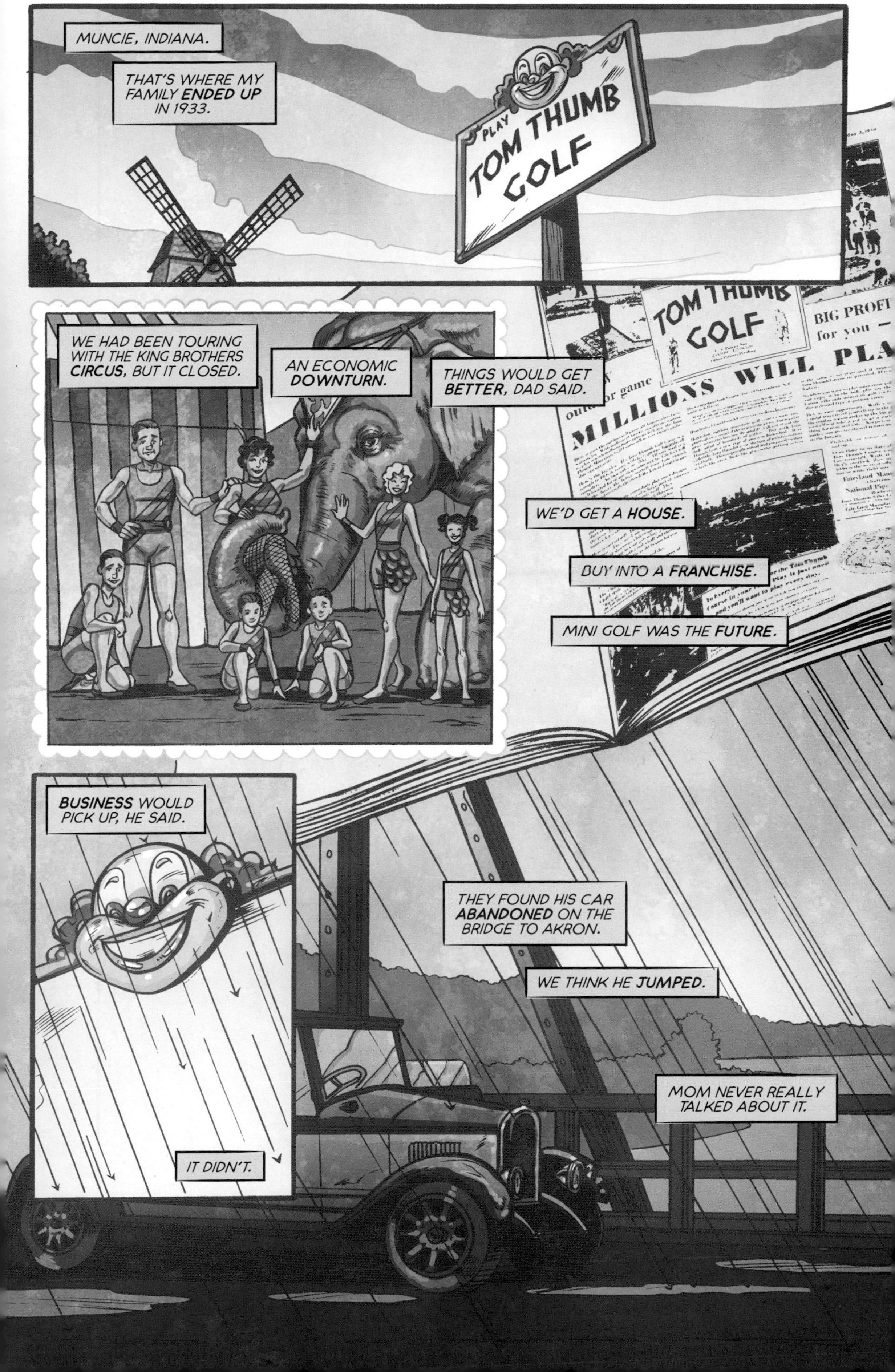
MUNCIE, INDIANA.
THAT'S WHERE MY FAMILY ENDED UP IN 1933.
PLAY TOM THUMB GOLF
WE HAD BEEN TOURING WITH THE KING BROTHERS CIRCUS, BUT IT CLOSED.
AN ECONOMIC DOWNTURN.
THINGS WOULD GET BETTER, DAD SAID.
TOM THUMB GOLF
BIG PROFI
for you —
MILLIONS WILL PLA
WE'D GET A HOUSE.
BUY INTO A FRANCHISE.
MINI GOLF WAS THE FUTURE.
BUSINESS WOULD PICK UP, HE SAID.
IT DIDN'T.
THEY FOUND HIS CAR ABANDONED ON THE BRIDGE TO AKRON.
WE THINK HE JUMPED.
MOM NEVER REALLY TALKED ABOUT IT.

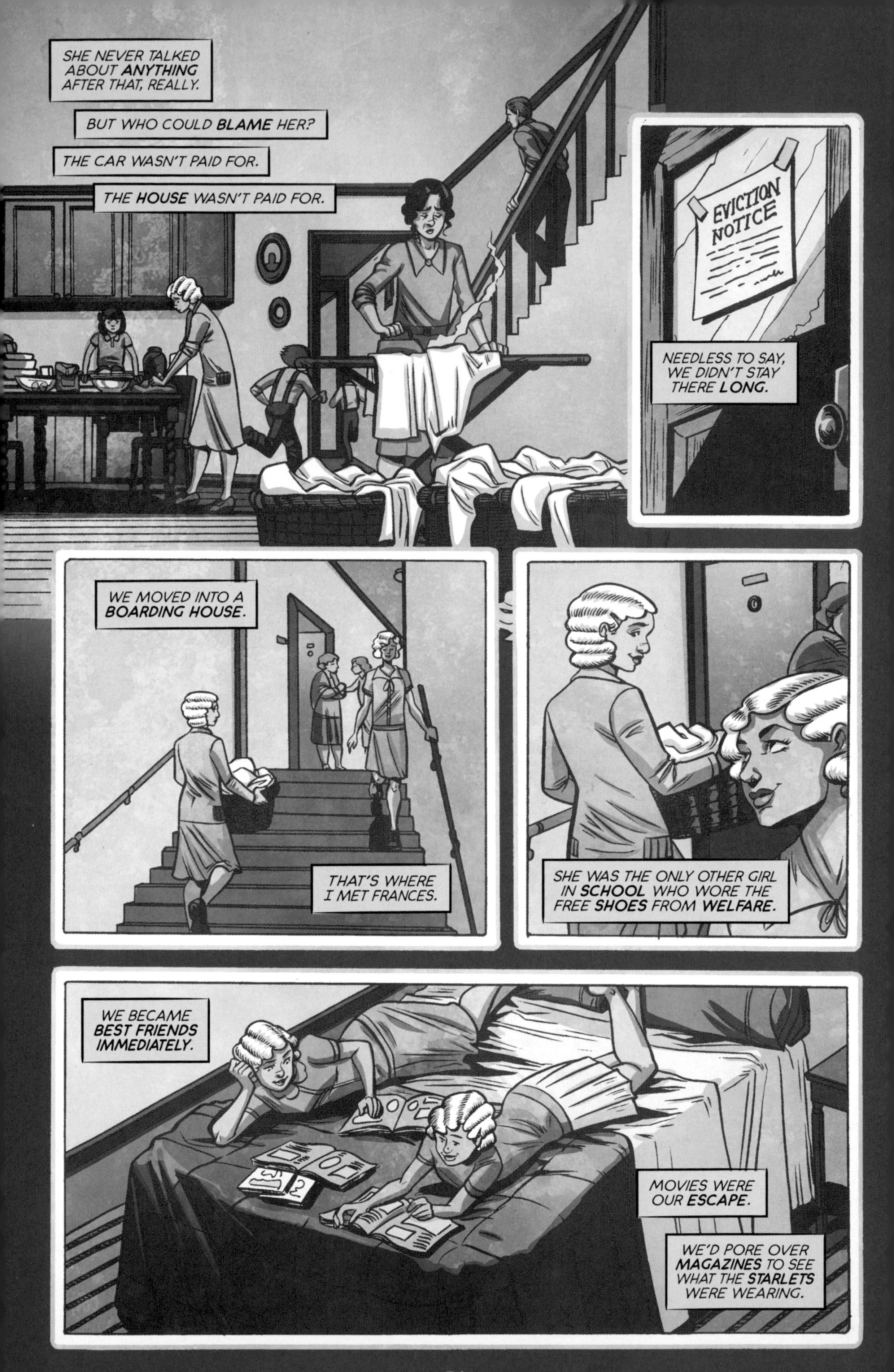
SHE NEVER TALKED ABOUT ANYTHING AFTER THAT, REALLY.
BUT WHO COULD BLAME HER?
THE CAR WASN'T PAID FOR.
THE HOUSE WASN'T PAID FOR.
EVICTION NOTICE
NEEDLESS TO SAY, WE DIDN'T STAY THERE LONG.
WE MOVED INTO A BOARDING HOUSE.
THAT'S WHERE I MET FRANCES.
SHE WAS THE ONLY OTHER GIRL IN SCHOOL WHO WORE THE FREE SHOES FROM WELFARE.
WE BECAME BEST FRIENDS IMMEDIATELY.
MOVIES WERE OUR ESCAPE.
WE'D PORE OVER MAGAZINES TO SEE WHAT THE STARLETS WERE WEARING.

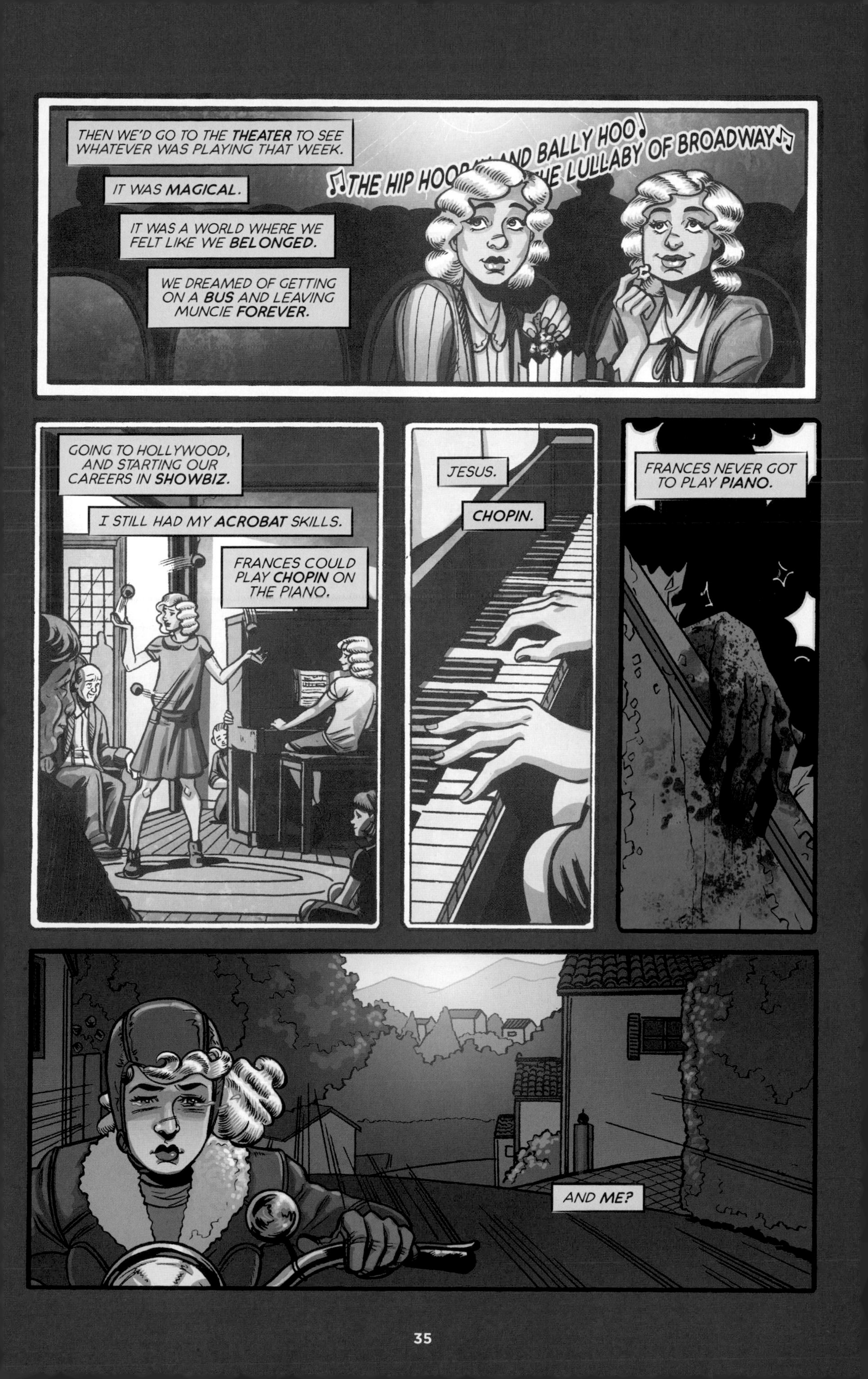
THEN WE'D GO TO THE **THEATER** TO SEE WHATEVER WAS PLAYING THAT WEEK.
IT WAS **MAGICAL**.
IT WAS A WORLD WHERE WE FELT LIKE WE **BELONGED.**
WE DREAMED OF GETTING ON A **BUS** AND LEAVING MUNCIE **FOREVER.**
♫THE HIP HOO
AND BALLY HOO♪
LULLABY OF BROADWAY♫
GOING TO HOLLYWOOD, AND STARTING OUR CAREERS IN **SHOWBIZ.**
I STILL HAD MY **ACROBAT** SKILLS.
FRANCES COULD PLAY **CHOPIN** ON THE PIANO.
JESUS.
CHOPIN.
FRANCES NEVER GOT TO PLAY **PIANO.**
AND **ME?**

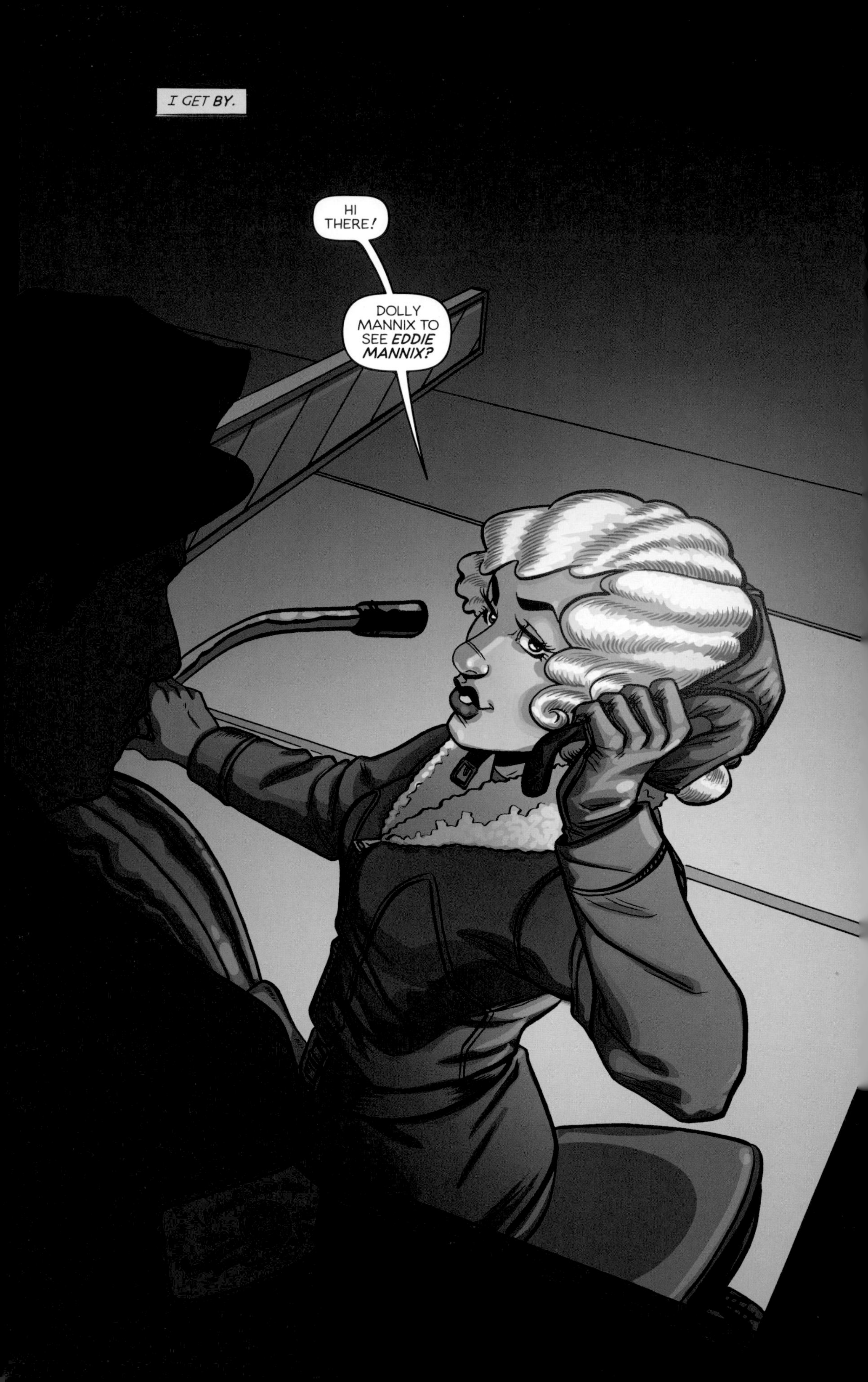
I GET BY.
HI THERE!
DOLLY MANNIX TO SEE EDDIE MANNIX?

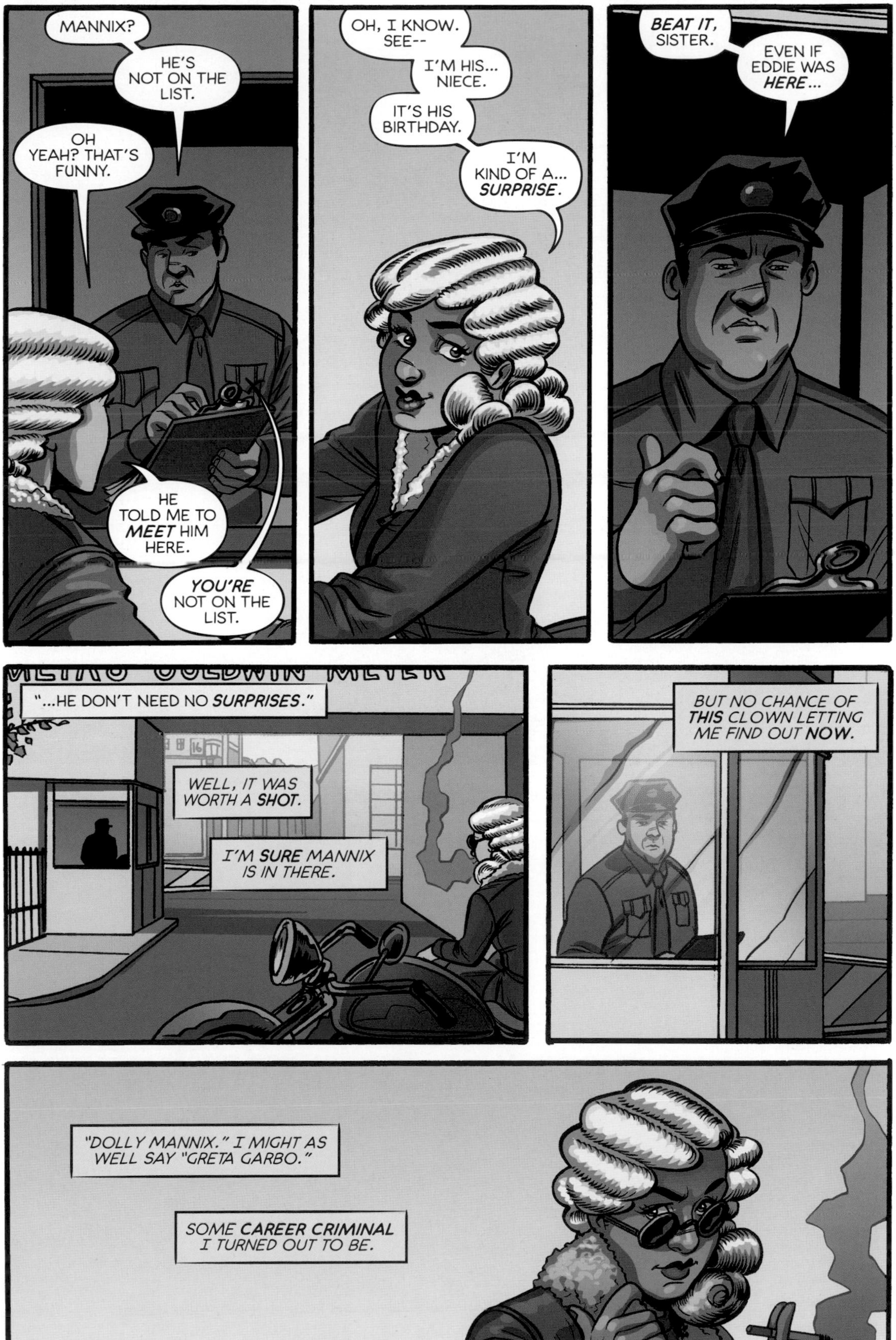
MANNIX?
HE'S NOT ON THE LIST.
OH YEAH? THAT'S FUNNY.
HE TOLD ME TO *MEET* HIM HERE.
YOU'RE NOT ON THE LIST.
OH, I KNOW. SEE--
I'M HIS... NIECE.
IT'S HIS BIRTHDAY.
I'M KIND OF A... *SURPRISE*.
BEAT IT, SISTER.
EVEN IF EDDIE WAS *HERE*...
"...HE DON'T NEED NO *SURPRISES*."
WELL, IT WAS WORTH A *SHOT*.
I'M *SURE* MANNIX IS IN THERE.
BUT NO CHANCE OF *THIS* CLOWN LETTING ME FIND OUT *NOW*.
"DOLLY MANNIX." I MIGHT AS WELL SAY "GRETA GARBO."
SOME *CAREER CRIMINAL* I TURNED OUT TO BE.

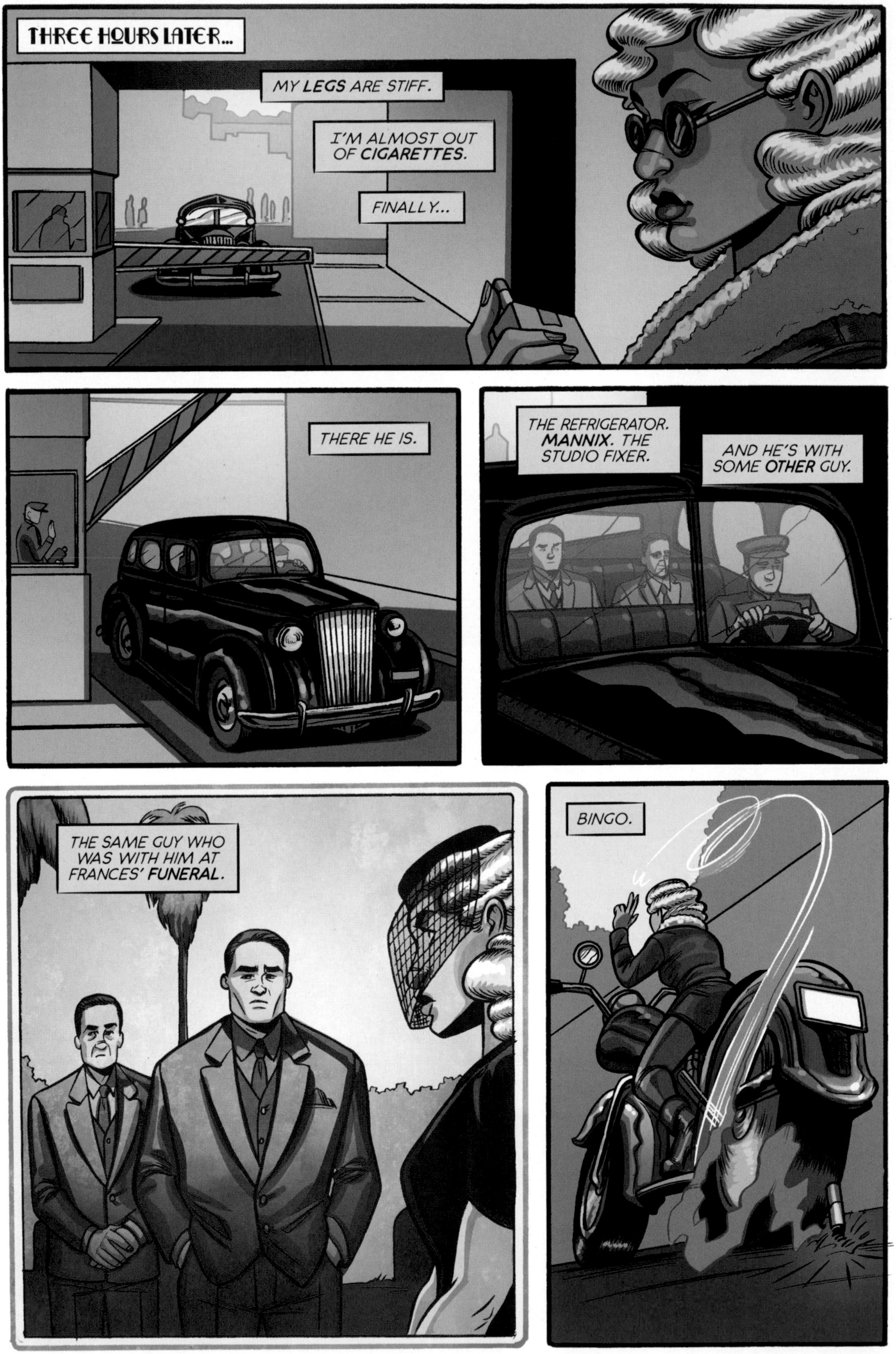
THREE HOURS LATER...
MY LEGS ARE STIFF.
I'M ALMOST OUT OF CIGARETTES.
FINALLY...
THERE HE IS.
THE REFRIGERATOR. MANNIX. THE STUDIO FIXER.
AND HE'S WITH SOME OTHER GUY.
THE SAME GUY WHO WAS WITH HIM AT FRANCES' FUNERAL.
BINGO.

THEY'RE HEADED ACROSS TOWN.

PICTURE

THE MONOGRAM LOT.

WELL, **WELL.**

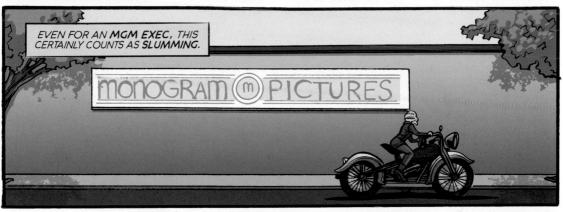

EVEN FOR AN **MGM EXEC**, THIS CERTAINLY COUNTS AS **SLUMMING.**

MONOGRAM PICTURES

I WONDER WHAT HE'S **DOING** IN THERE.

WELL, YOU KNOW WHAT THEY **SAY.**

IT PAYS TO BE **PERSISTENT.**

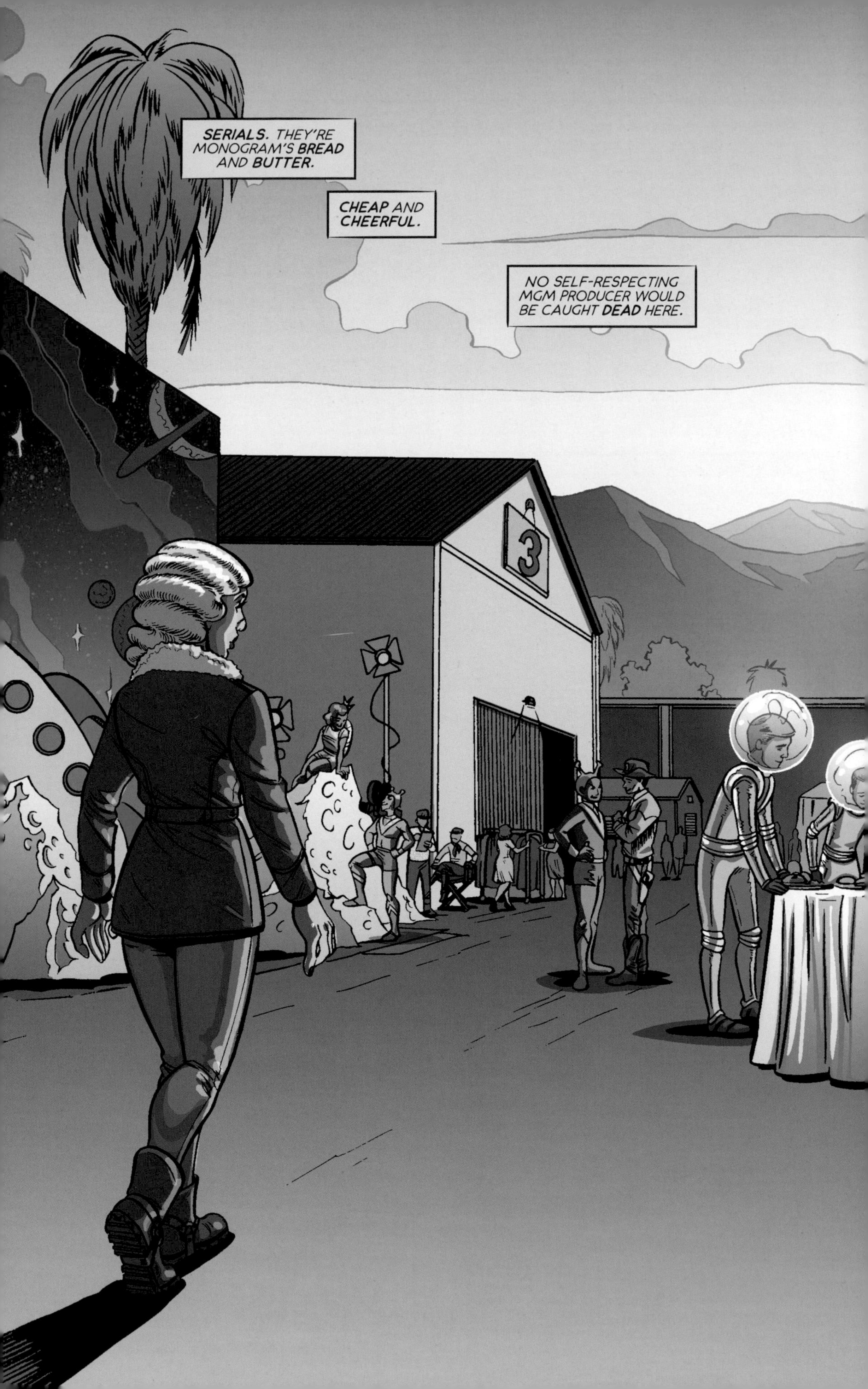
SERIALS. THEY'RE MONOGRAM'S BREAD AND BUTTER.
CHEAP AND CHEERFUL.
NO SELF-RESPECTING MGM PRODUCER WOULD BE CAUGHT DEAD HERE.
3

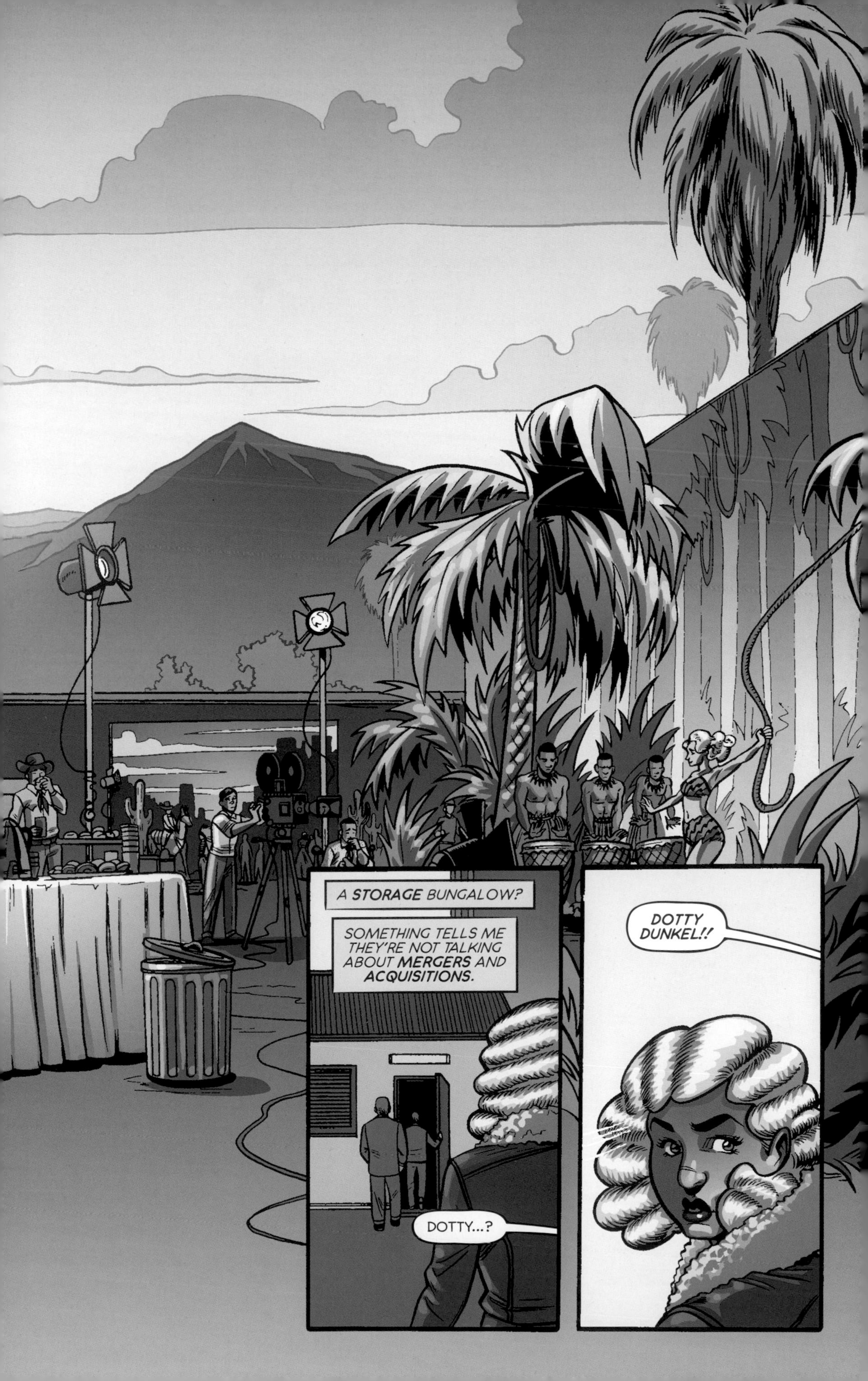
A STORAGE BUNGALOW?
SOMETHING TELLS ME THEY'RE NOT TALKING ABOUT MERGERS AND ACQUISITIONS.
DOTTY...?
DOTTY DUNKEL!!

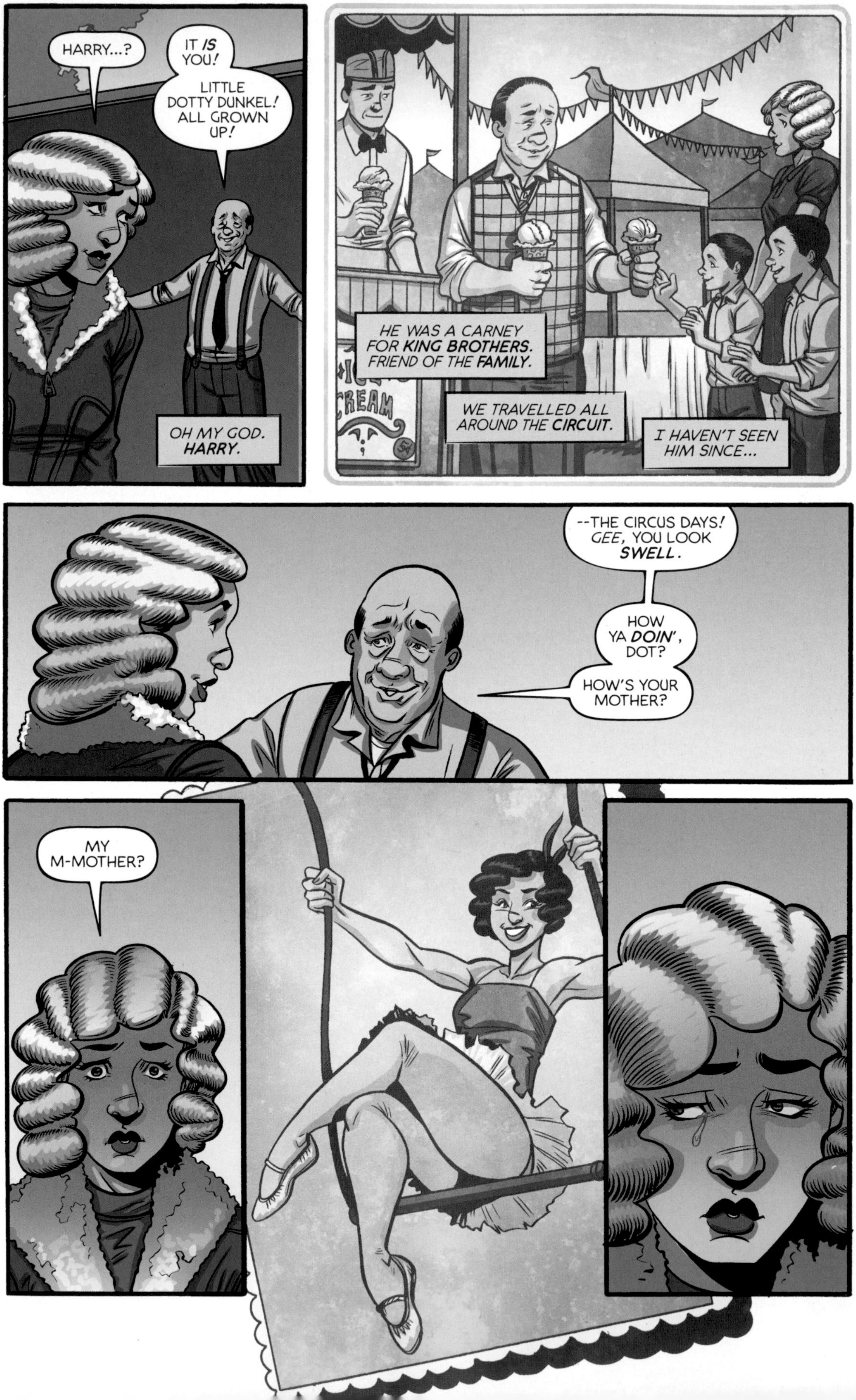
HARRY...?
IT *IS* YOU!
LITTLE DOTTY DUNKEL! ALL GROWN UP!
OH MY GOD. **HARRY.**
HE WAS A CARNEY FOR **KING BROTHERS.** FRIEND OF THE **FAMILY.**
ICE CREAM
WE TRAVELLED ALL AROUND THE **CIRCUIT.**
I HAVEN'T SEEN HIM SINCE...
--THE CIRCUS DAYS! *GEE,* YOU LOOK **SWELL**.
HOW YA ***DOIN'***, DOT?
HOW'S YOUR MOTHER?
MY M-MOTHER?

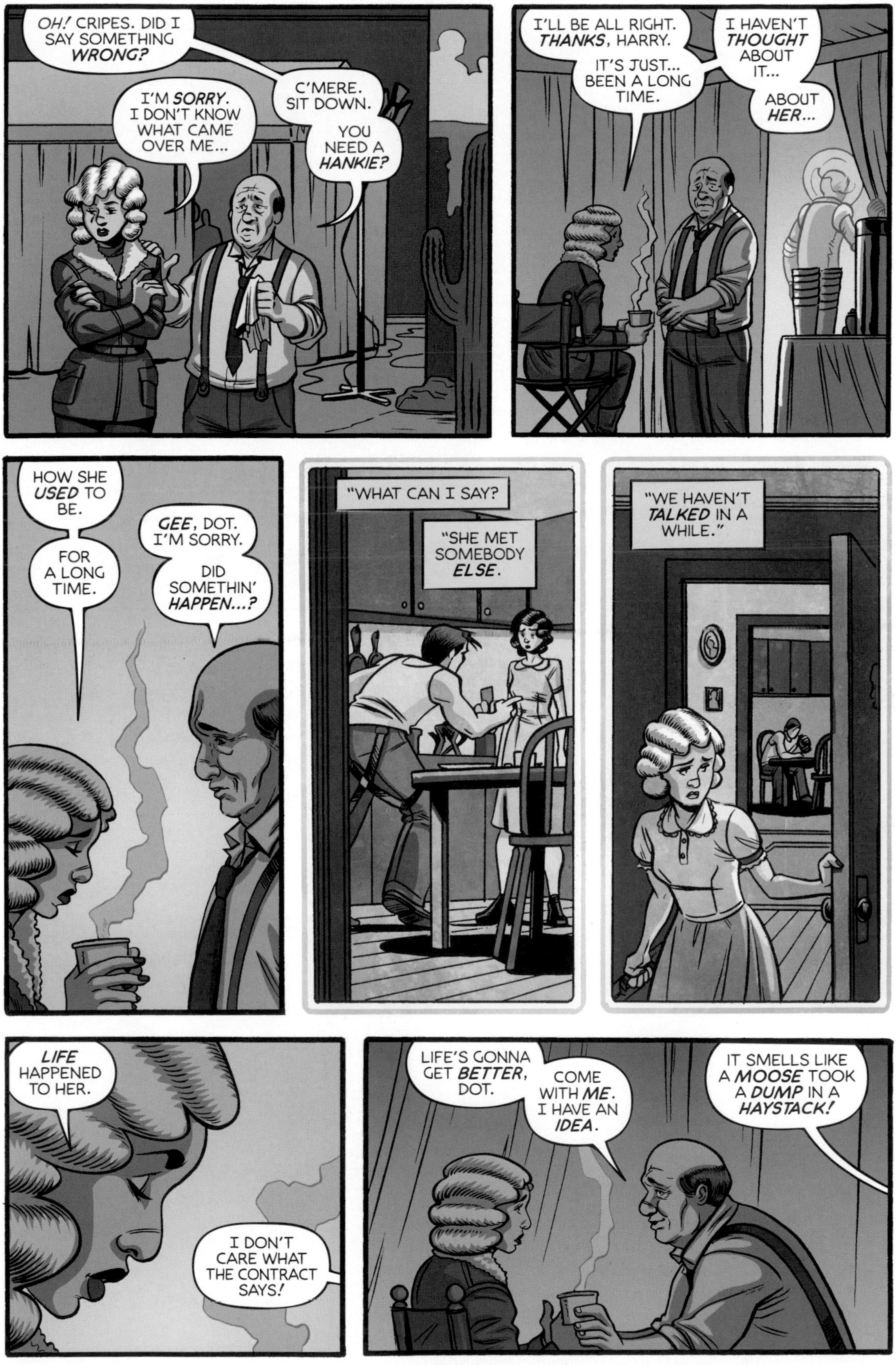
OH! CRIPES. DID I SAY SOMETHING WRONG?
I'M SORRY. I DON'T KNOW WHAT CAME OVER ME...
C'MERE. SIT DOWN.
YOU NEED A HANKIE?
I'LL BE ALL RIGHT. THANKS, HARRY.
IT'S JUST... BEEN A LONG TIME.
I HAVEN'T THOUGHT ABOUT IT...
ABOUT HER...
HOW SHE USED TO BE.
FOR A LONG TIME.
GEE, DOT. I'M SORRY.
DID SOMETHIN' HAPPEN...?
"WHAT CAN I SAY?
"SHE MET SOMEBODY ELSE.
"WE HAVEN'T TALKED IN A WHILE."
LIFE HAPPENED TO HER.
I DON'T CARE WHAT THE CONTRACT SAYS!
LIFE'S GONNA GET BETTER, DOT.
COME WITH ME. I HAVE AN IDEA.
IT SMELLS LIKE A MOOSE TOOK A DUMP IN A HAYSTACK!

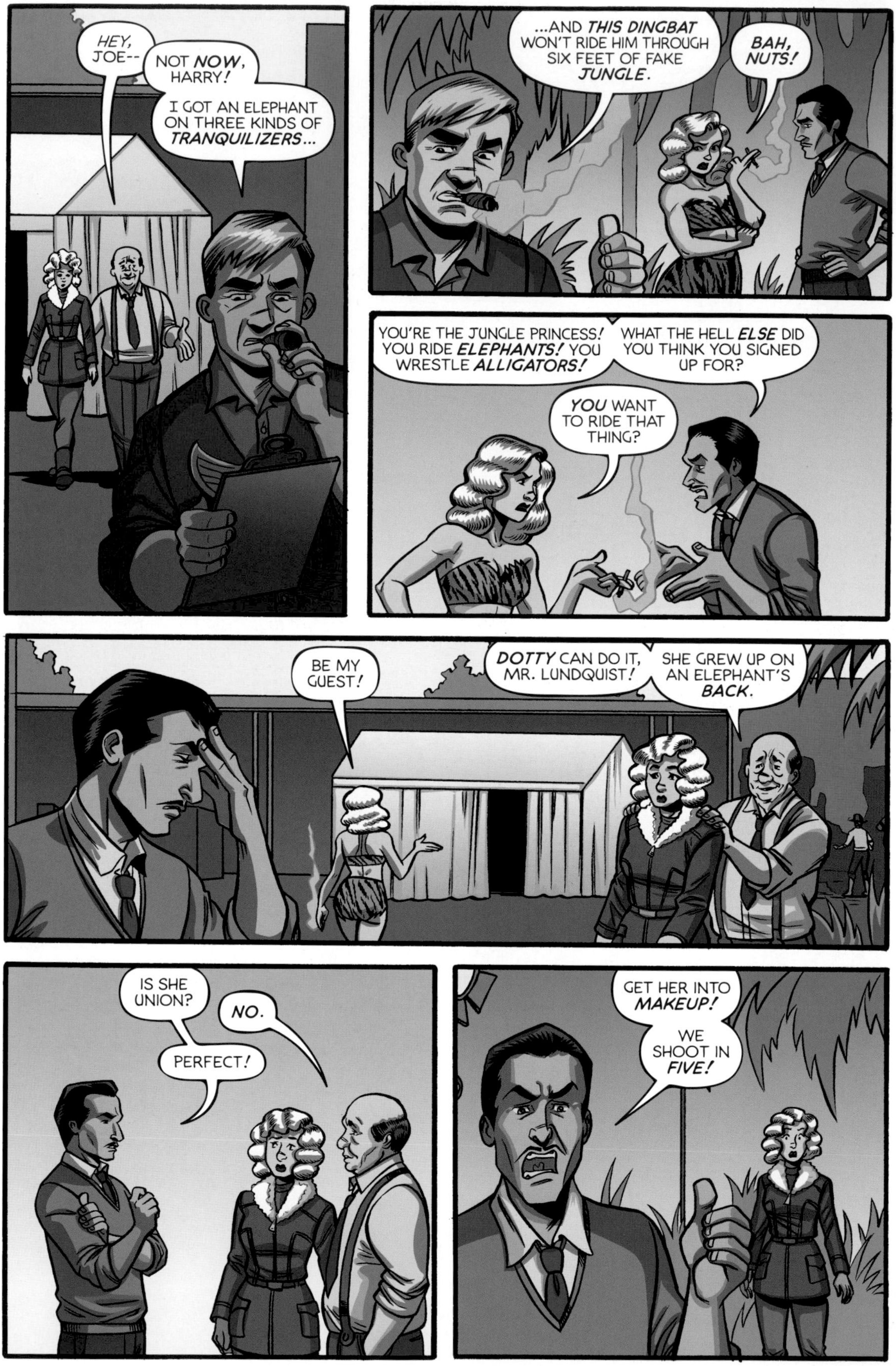
HEY, JOE--
NOT NOW, HARRY!
I GOT AN ELEPHANT ON THREE KINDS OF TRANQUILIZERS...
...AND THIS DINGBAT WON'T RIDE HIM THROUGH SIX FEET OF FAKE JUNGLE.
BAH, NUTS!
YOU'RE THE JUNGLE PRINCESS! YOU RIDE ELEPHANTS! YOU WRESTLE ALLIGATORS!
WHAT THE HELL ELSE DID YOU THINK YOU SIGNED UP FOR?
YOU WANT TO RIDE THAT THING?
BE MY GUEST!
DOTTY CAN DO IT, MR. LUNDQUIST!
SHE GREW UP ON AN ELEPHANT'S BACK.
IS SHE UNION?
NO.
PERFECT!
GET HER INTO MAKEUP!
WE SHOOT IN FIVE!

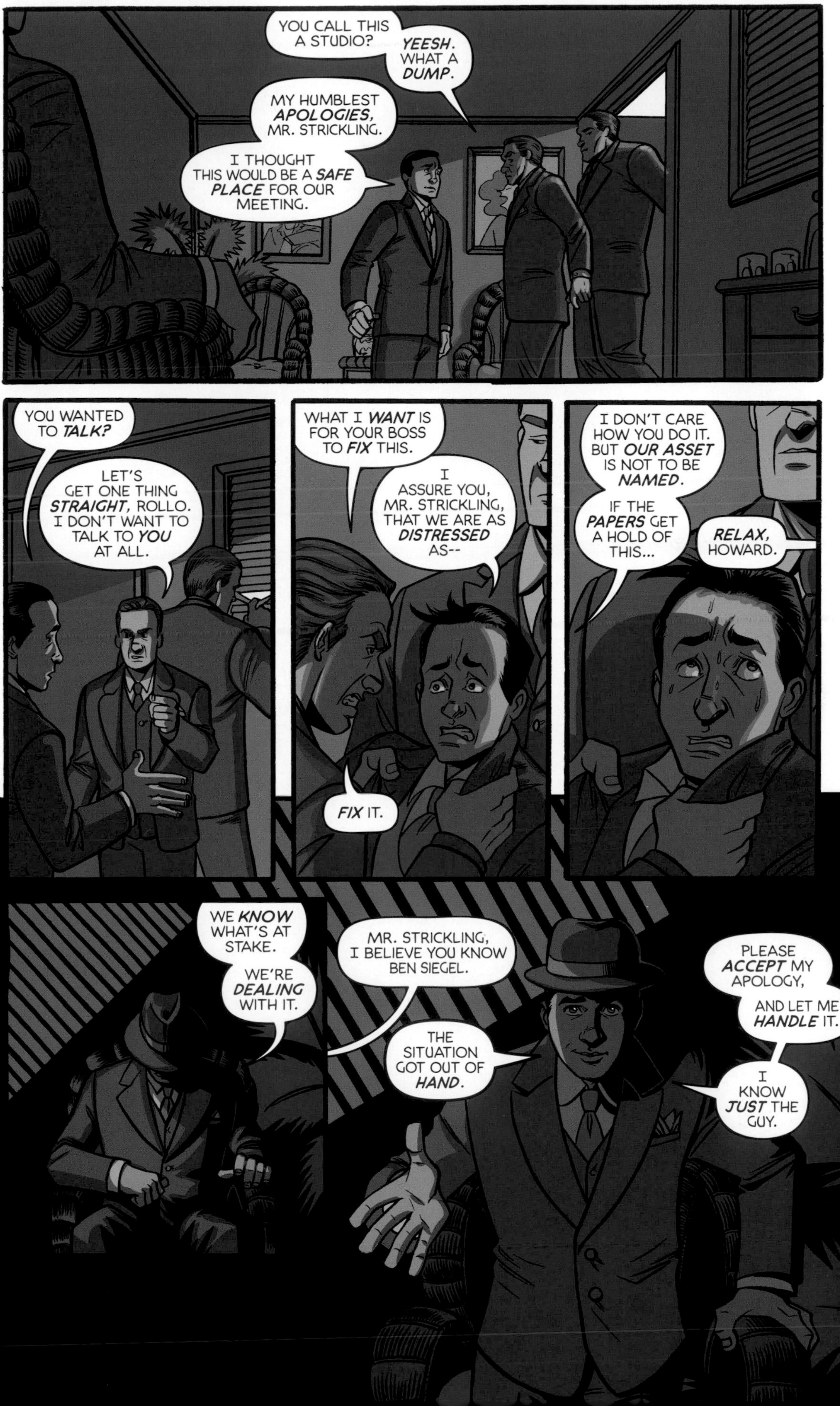

YOU CALL THIS A STUDIO?
YEESH. WHAT A DUMP.
MY HUMBLEST APOLOGIES, MR. STRICKLING.
I THOUGHT THIS WOULD BE A SAFE PLACE FOR OUR MEETING.
YOU WANTED TO TALK?
LET'S GET ONE THING STRAIGHT, ROLLO. I DON'T WANT TO TALK TO YOU AT ALL.
WHAT I WANT IS FOR YOUR BOSS TO FIX THIS.
I ASSURE YOU, MR. STRICKLING, THAT WE ARE AS DISTRESSED AS--
FIX IT.
I DON'T CARE HOW YOU DO IT. BUT OUR ASSET IS NOT TO BE NAMED.
IF THE PAPERS GET A HOLD OF THIS...
RELAX, HOWARD.
WE KNOW WHAT'S AT STAKE.
WE'RE DEALING WITH IT.
MR. STRICKLING, I BELIEVE YOU KNOW BEN SIEGEL.
THE SITUATION GOT OUT OF HAND.
PLEASE ACCEPT MY APOLOGY,
AND LET ME HANDLE IT.
I KNOW JUST THE GUY.

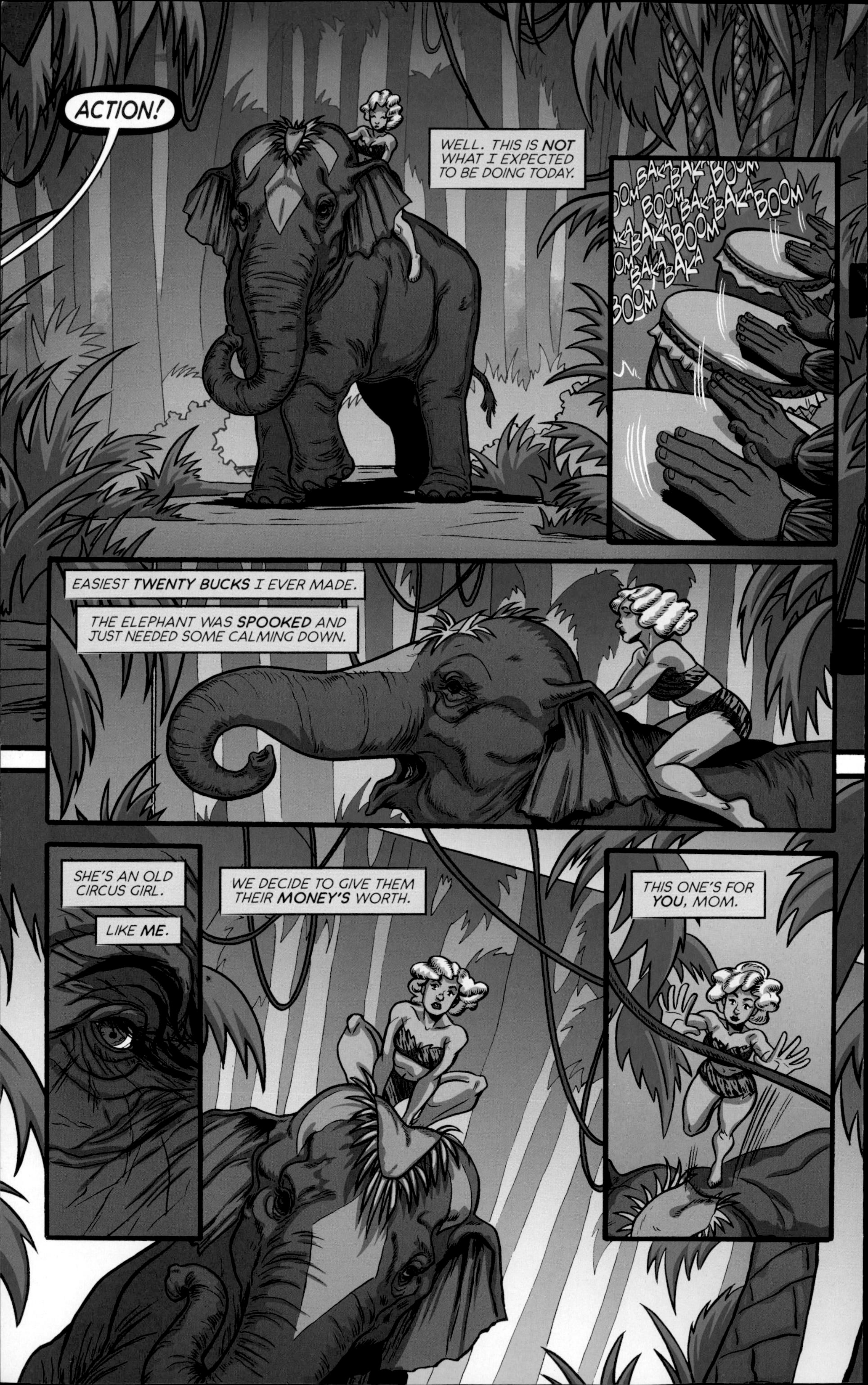
ACTION!
WELL. THIS IS NOT WHAT I EXPECTED TO BE DOING TODAY.
BOOM BAKA BAKA BOOM BAKA BOOM BAKA BAKA BOOM BAKA BOOM BAKA BOOM BAKA BAKA BOOM
EASIEST TWENTY BUCKS I EVER MADE.
THE ELEPHANT WAS SPOOKED AND JUST NEEDED SOME CALMING DOWN.
SHE'S AN OLD CIRCUS GIRL.
LIKE ME.
WE DECIDE TO GIVE THEM THEIR MONEY'S WORTH.
THIS ONE'S FOR YOU, MOM.

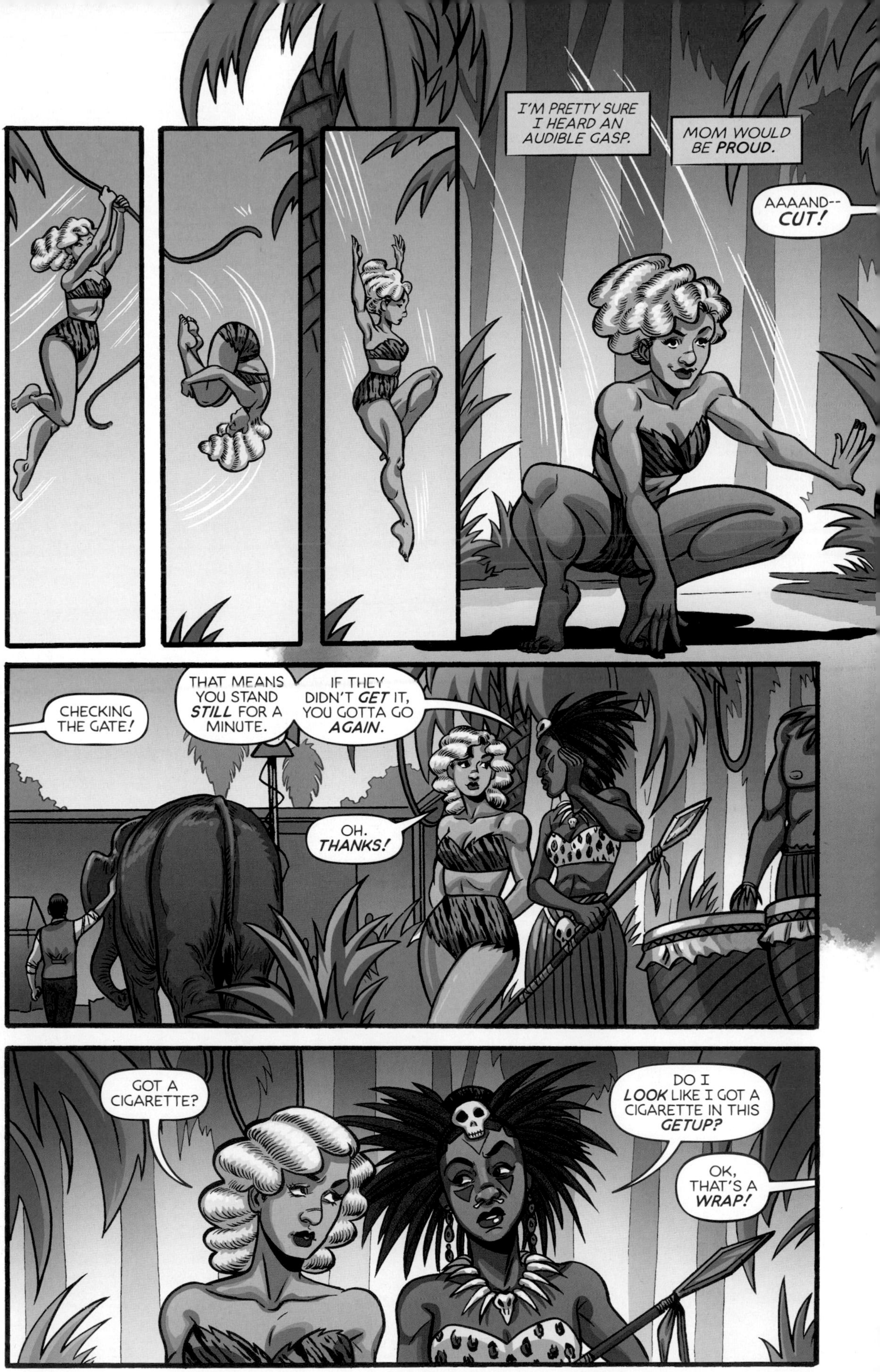
I'M PRETTY SURE I HEARD AN AUDIBLE GASP.
MOM WOULD BE PROUD.
AAAAND-- CUT!
CHECKING THE GATE!
THAT MEANS YOU STAND STILL FOR A MINUTE.
IF THEY DIDN'T GET IT, YOU GOTTA GO AGAIN.
OH. THANKS!
GOT A CIGARETTE?
DO I LOOK LIKE I GOT A CIGARETTE IN THIS GETUP?
OK, THAT'S A WRAP!

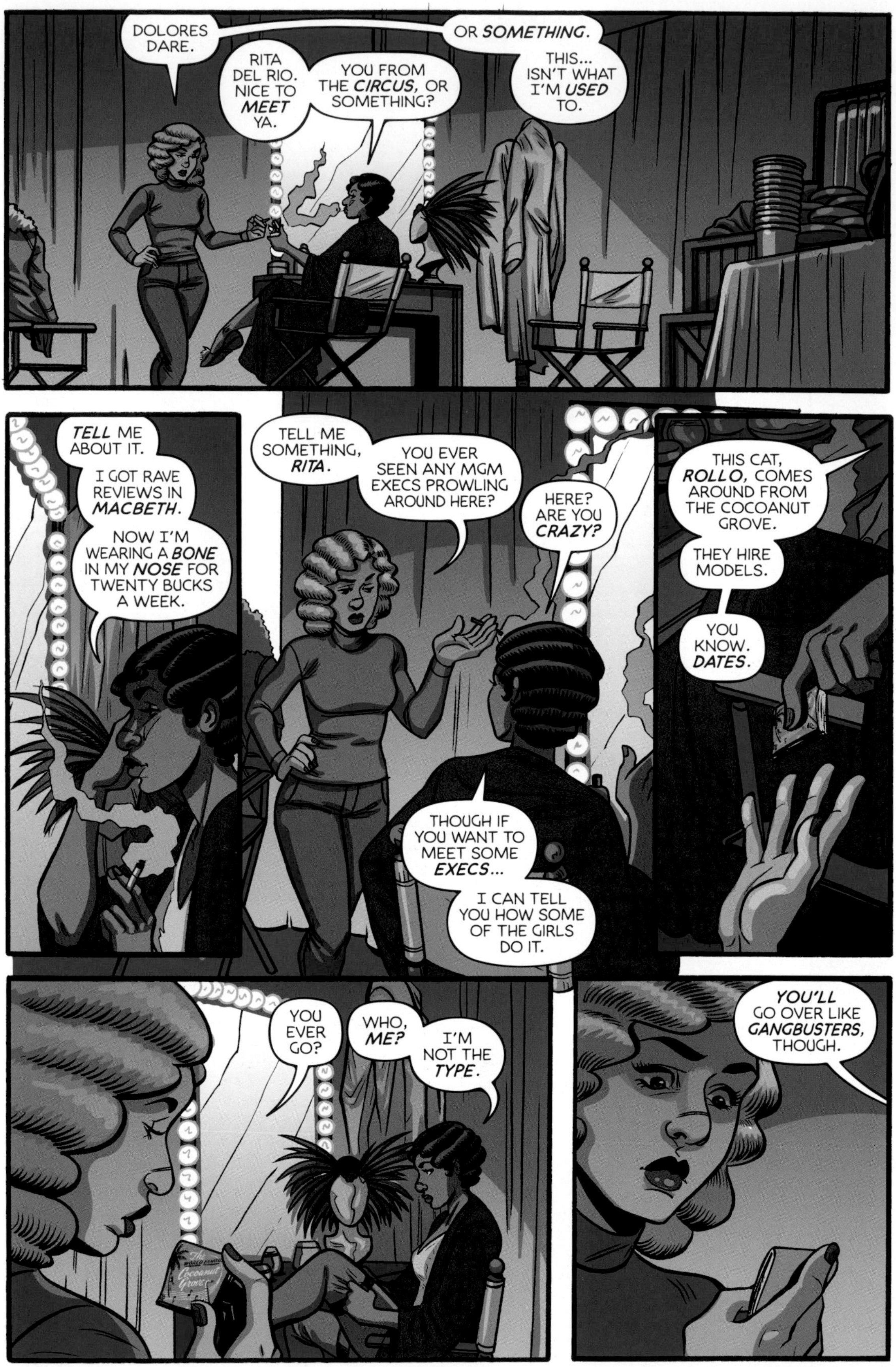
DOLORES DARE.
RITA DEL RIO. NICE TO MEET YA.
YOU FROM THE CIRCUS, OR SOMETHING?
OR SOMETHING.
THIS... ISN'T WHAT I'M USED TO.
TELL ME ABOUT IT.
I GOT RAVE REVIEWS IN MACBETH.
NOW I'M WEARING A BONE IN MY NOSE FOR TWENTY BUCKS A WEEK.
TELL ME SOMETHING, RITA.
YOU EVER SEEN ANY MGM EXECS PROWLING AROUND HERE?
HERE? ARE YOU CRAZY?
THOUGH IF YOU WANT TO MEET SOME EXECS...
I CAN TELL YOU HOW SOME OF THE GIRLS DO IT.
THIS CAT, ROLLO, COMES AROUND FROM THE COCOANUT GROVE.
THEY HIRE MODELS.
YOU KNOW. DATES.
YOU EVER GO?
WHO, ME?
I'M NOT THE TYPE.
The World Famous Cocoanut Grove
YOU'LL GO OVER LIKE GANGBUSTERS, THOUGH.

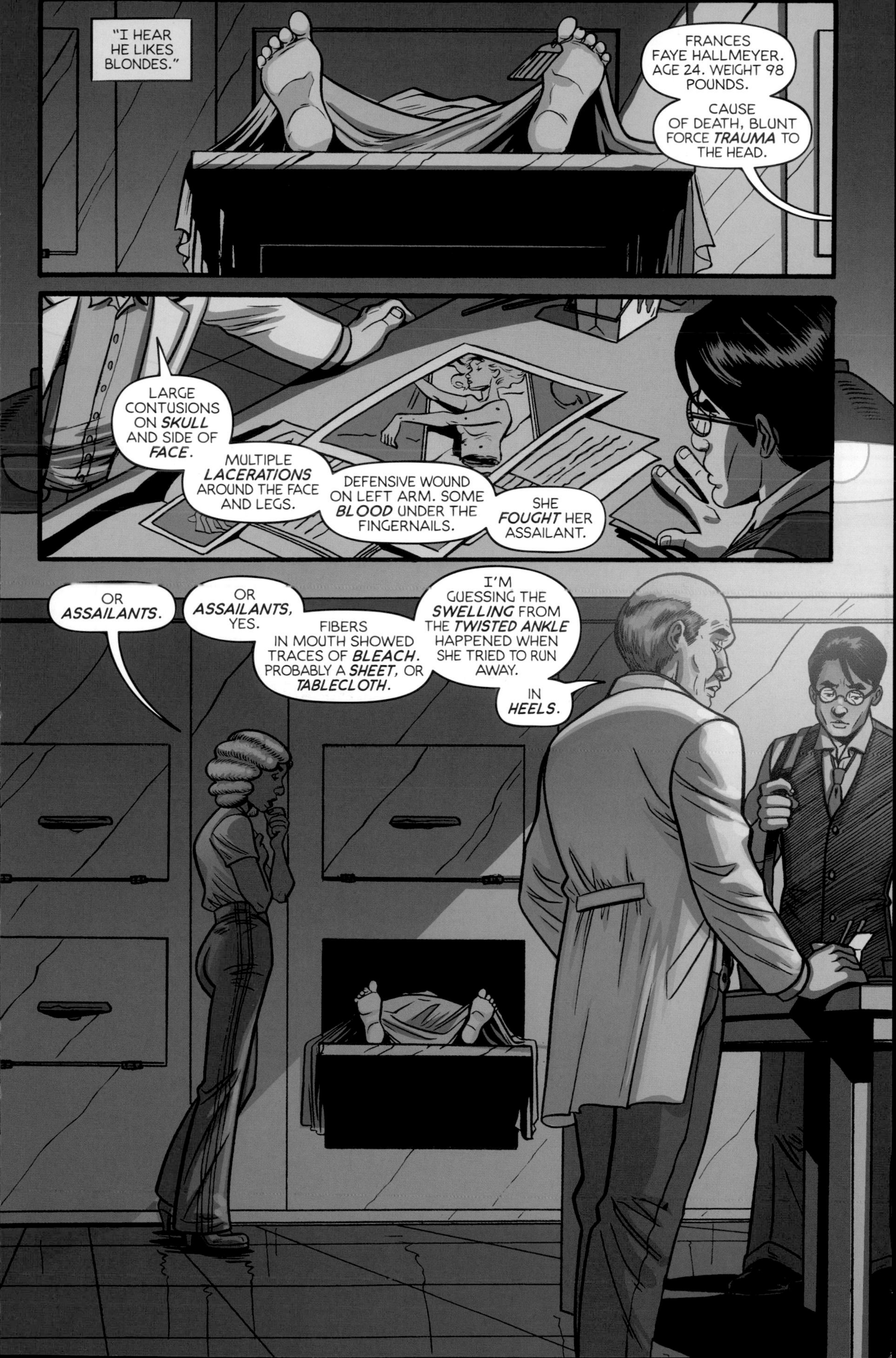
"I HEAR HE LIKES BLONDES."
FRANCES FAYE HALLMEYER. AGE 24. WEIGHT 98 POUNDS.
CAUSE OF DEATH, BLUNT FORCE *TRAUMA* TO THE HEAD.
LARGE CONTUSIONS ON *SKULL* AND SIDE OF *FACE*.
MULTIPLE *LACERATIONS* AROUND THE FACE AND LEGS.
DEFENSIVE WOUND ON LEFT ARM. SOME *BLOOD* UNDER THE FINGERNAILS.
SHE *FOUGHT* HER ASSAILANT.
OR *ASSAILANTS*.
OR *ASSAILANTS*, YES.
FIBERS IN MOUTH SHOWED TRACES OF *BLEACH*. PROBABLY A *SHEET*, OR *TABLECLOTH*.
I'M GUESSING THE *SWELLING* FROM THE *TWISTED ANKLE* HAPPENED WHEN SHE TRIED TO RUN AWAY.
IN *HEELS*.

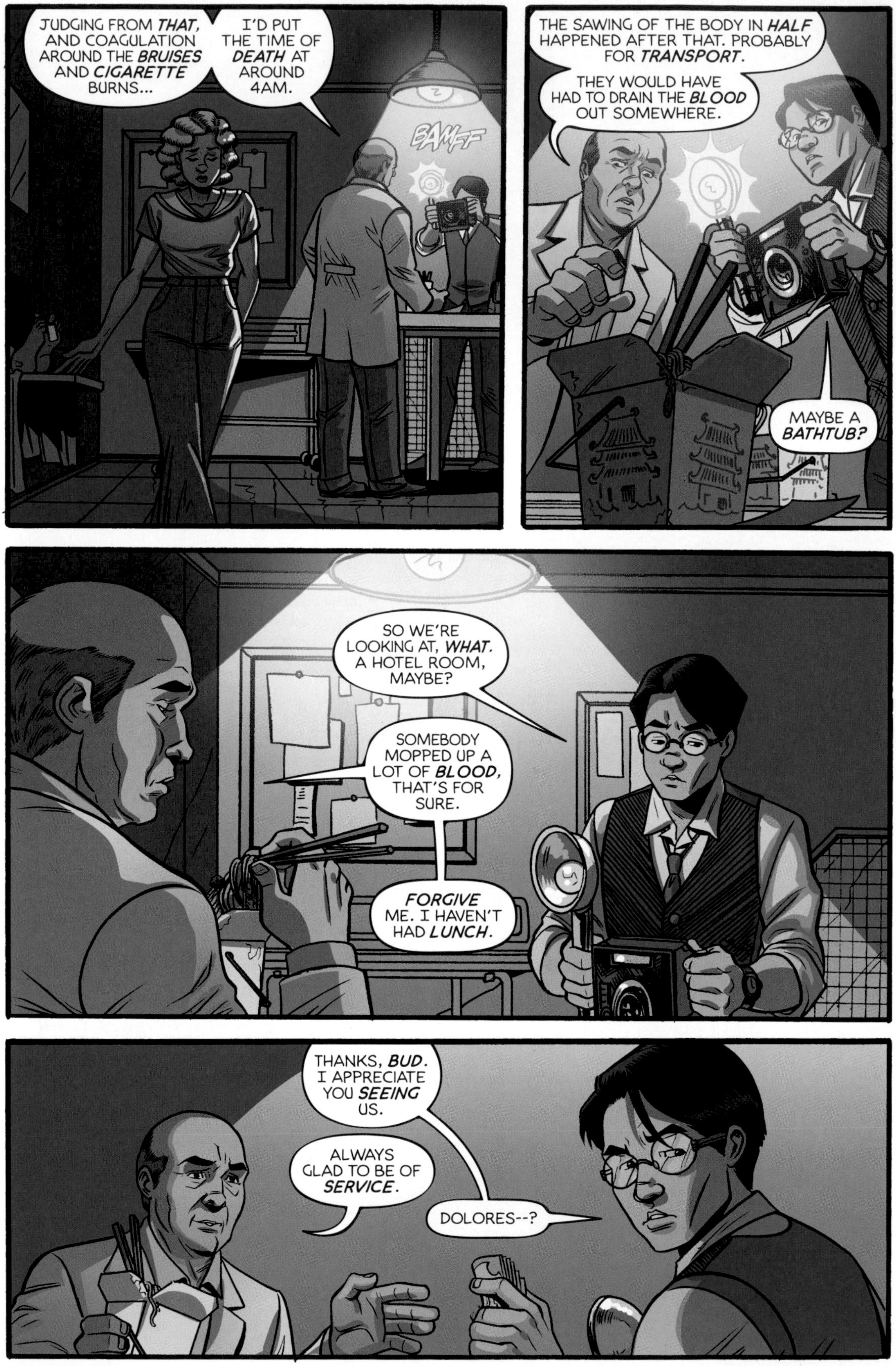
JUDGING FROM THAT, AND COAGULATION AROUND THE BRUISES AND CIGARETTE BURNS...
I'D PUT THE TIME OF DEATH AT AROUND 4AM.
BAMFF
THE SAWING OF THE BODY IN HALF HAPPENED AFTER THAT. PROBABLY FOR TRANSPORT.
THEY WOULD HAVE HAD TO DRAIN THE BLOOD OUT SOMEWHERE.
MAYBE A BATHTUB?
SO WE'RE LOOKING AT, WHAT. A HOTEL ROOM, MAYBE?
SOMEBODY MOPPED UP A LOT OF BLOOD, THAT'S FOR SURE.
FORGIVE ME. I HAVEN'T HAD LUNCH.
THANKS, BUD. I APPRECIATE YOU SEEING US.
ALWAYS GLAD TO BE OF SERVICE.
DOLORES--?

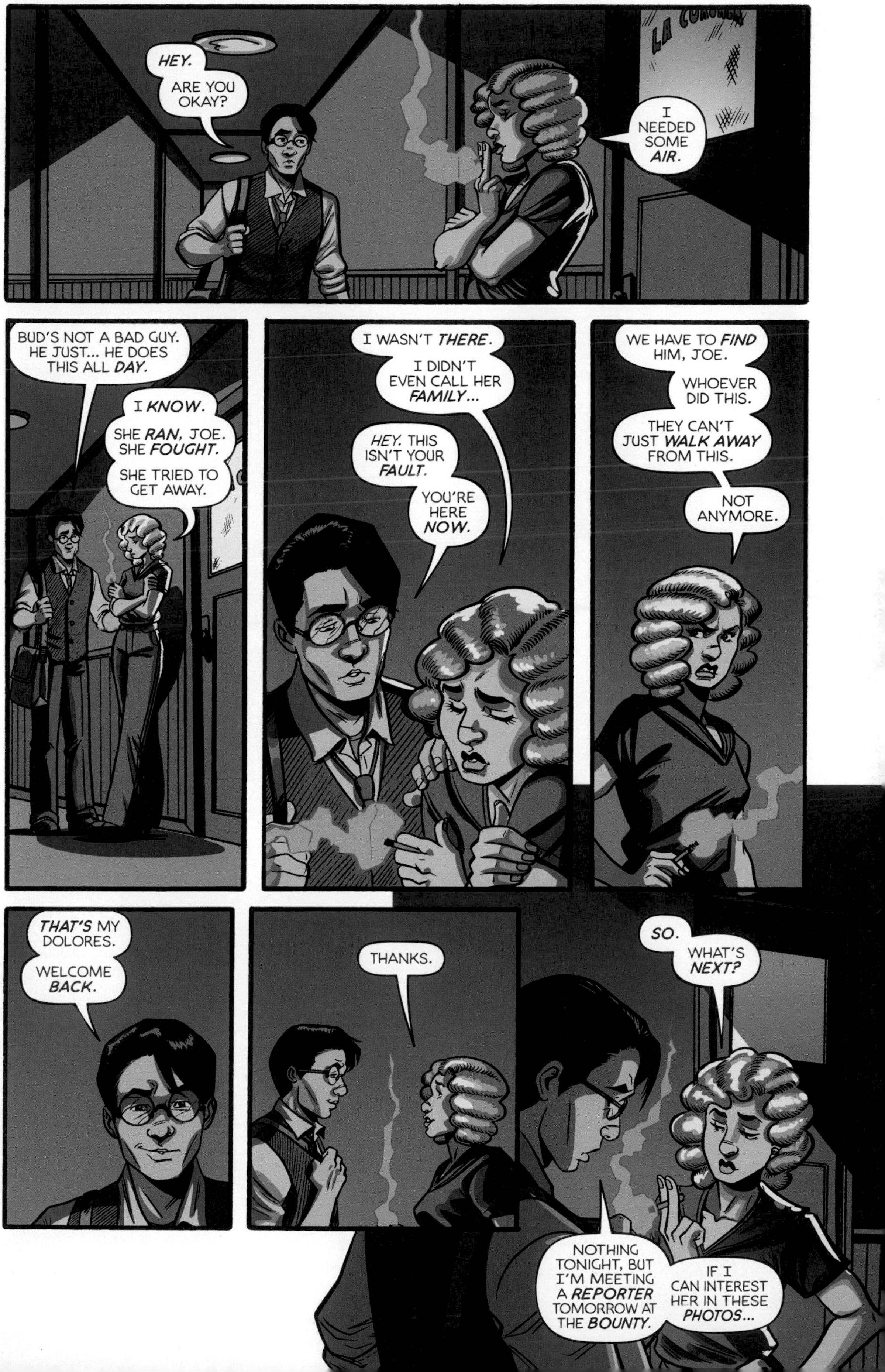
HEY.
ARE YOU OKAY?
I NEEDED SOME AIR.
LA CORONA
BUD'S NOT A BAD GUY. HE JUST... HE DOES THIS ALL DAY.
I KNOW.
SHE RAN, JOE. SHE FOUGHT.
SHE TRIED TO GET AWAY.
I WASN'T THERE.
I DIDN'T EVEN CALL HER FAMILY...
HEY. THIS ISN'T YOUR FAULT.
YOU'RE HERE NOW.
WE HAVE TO FIND HIM, JOE.
WHOEVER DID THIS.
THEY CAN'T JUST WALK AWAY FROM THIS.
NOT ANYMORE.
THAT'S MY DOLORES.
WELCOME BACK.
THANKS.
SO.
WHAT'S NEXT?
NOTHING TONIGHT, BUT I'M MEETING A REPORTER TOMORROW AT THE BOUNTY.
IF I CAN INTEREST HER IN THESE PHOTOS...

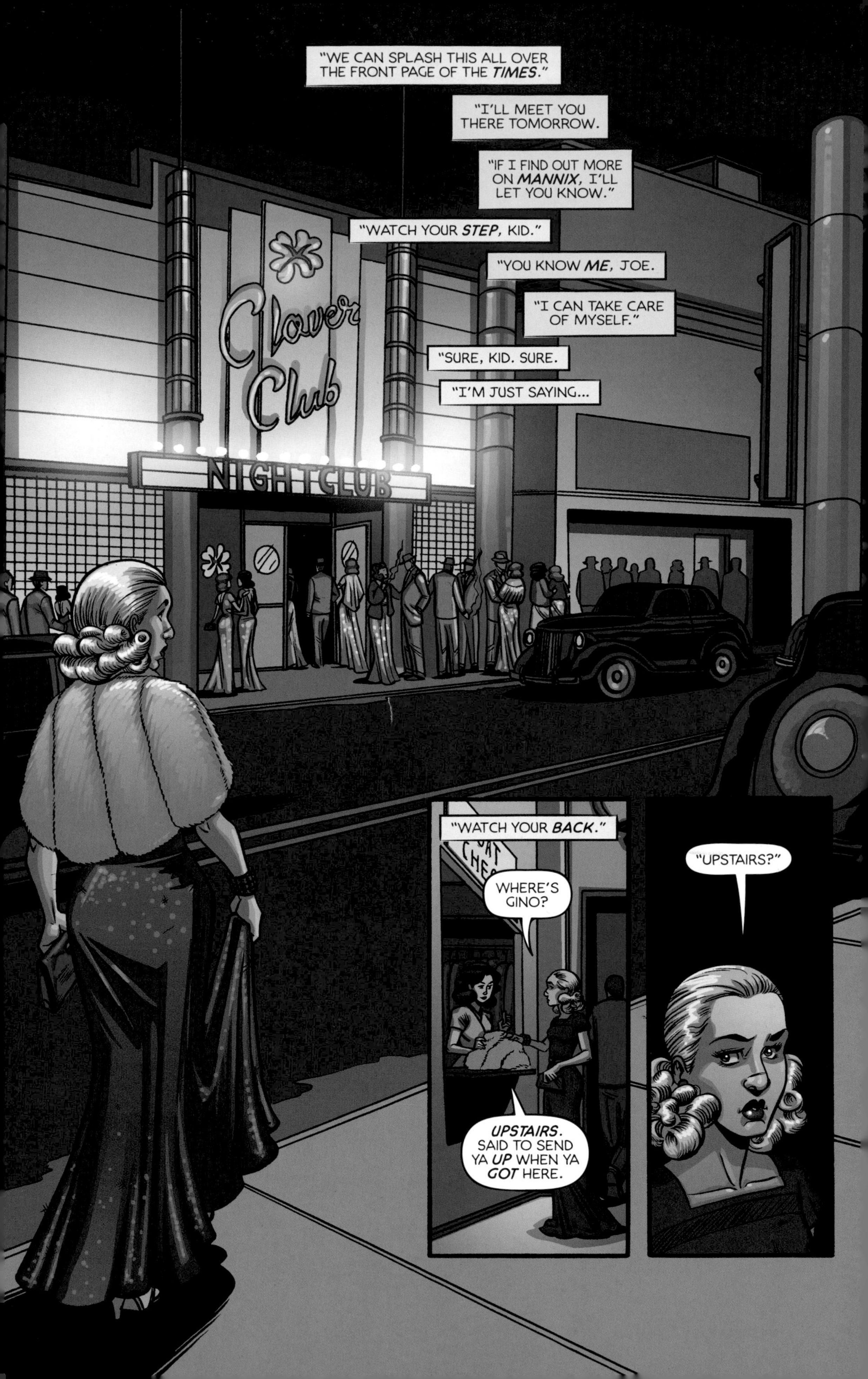
"WE CAN SPLASH THIS ALL OVER THE FRONT PAGE OF THE *TIMES*."
"I'LL MEET YOU THERE TOMORROW.
"IF I FIND OUT MORE ON *MANNIX*, I'LL LET YOU KNOW."
"WATCH YOUR *STEP*, KID."
"YOU KNOW *ME*, JOE.
"I CAN TAKE CARE OF MYSELF."
"SURE, KID. SURE.
"I'M JUST SAYING...
Clover Club
NIGHTCLUB
"WATCH YOUR *BACK*."
WHERE'S GINO?
UPSTAIRS. SAID TO SEND YA *UP* WHEN YA *GOT* HERE.
"UPSTAIRS?"

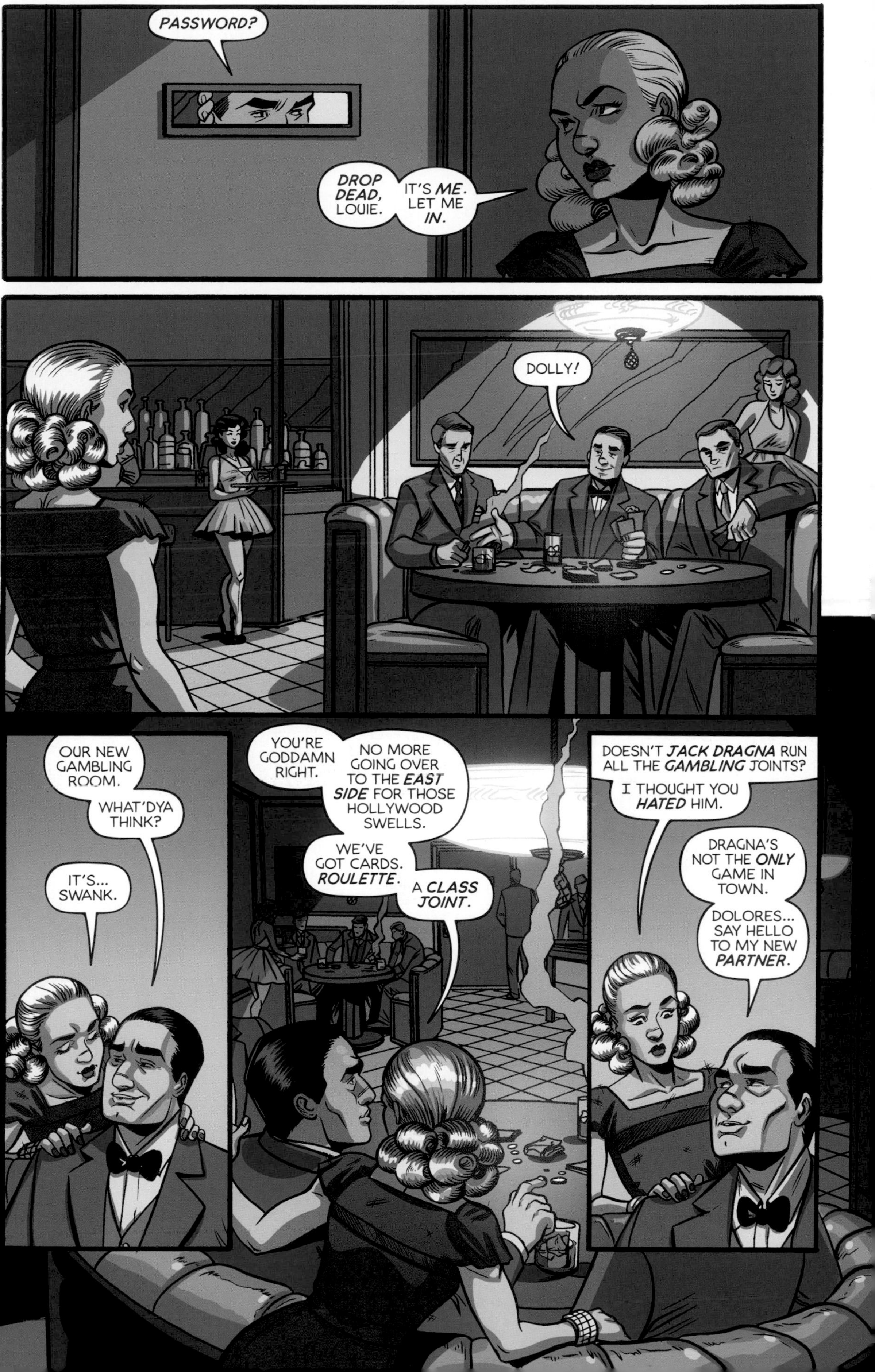
PASSWORD?
DROP DEAD, LOUIE.
IT'S ME. LET ME IN.
DOLLY!
OUR NEW GAMBLING ROOM.
WHAT'DYA THINK?
IT'S... SWANK.
YOU'RE GODDAMN RIGHT.
NO MORE GOING OVER TO THE EAST SIDE FOR THOSE HOLLYWOOD SWELLS.
WE'VE GOT CARDS. ROULETTE.
A CLASS JOINT.
DOESN'T JACK DRAGNA RUN ALL THE GAMBLING JOINTS?
I THOUGHT YOU HATED HIM.
DRAGNA'S NOT THE ONLY GAME IN TOWN.
DOLORES... SAY HELLO TO MY NEW PARTNER.

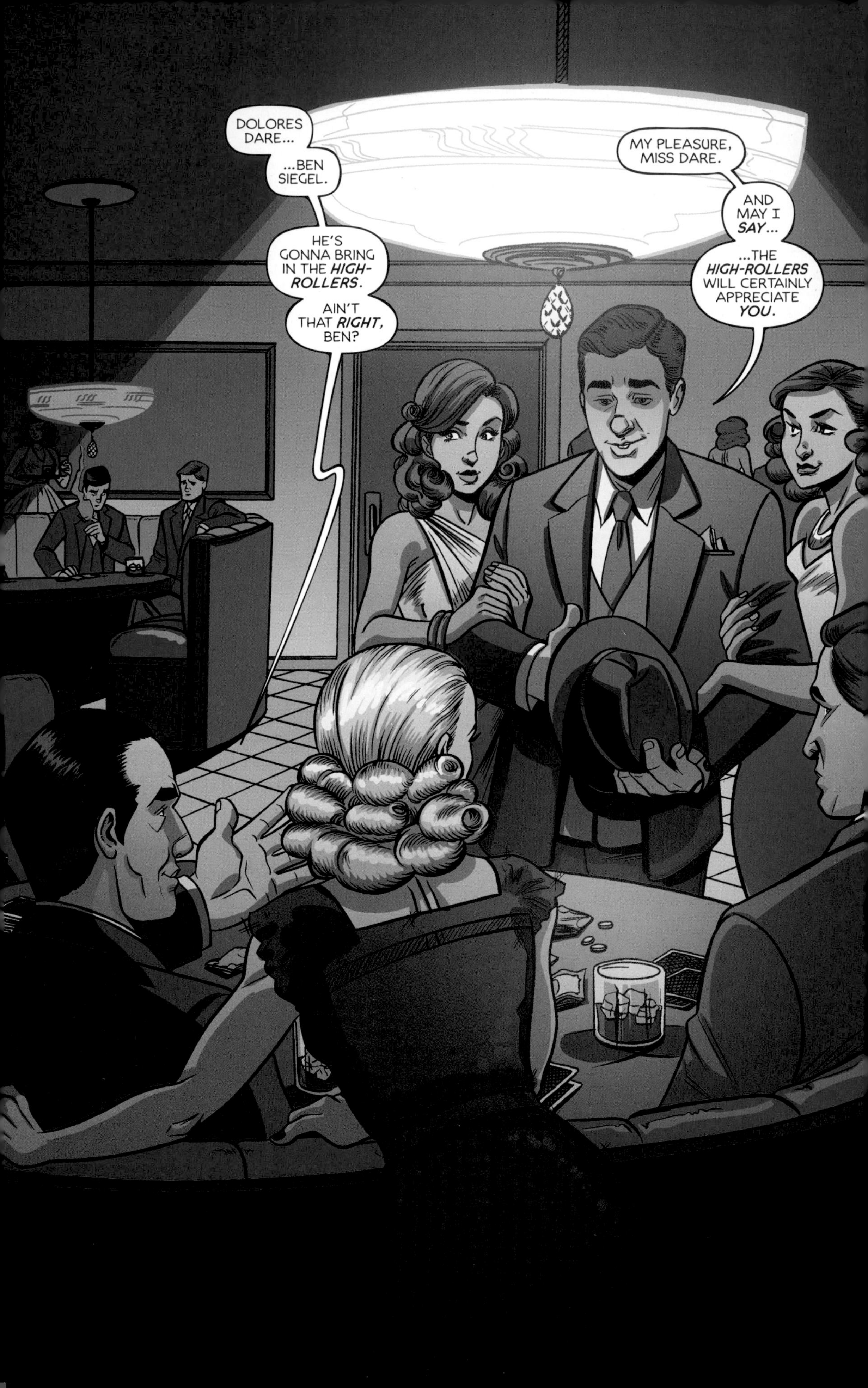
DOLORES DARE...
...BEN SIEGEL.
HE'S GONNA BRING IN THE *HIGH-ROLLERS*.
AIN'T THAT *RIGHT,* BEN?
MY PLEASURE, MISS DARE.
AND MAY I *SAY*...
...THE *HIGH-ROLLERS* WILL CERTAINLY APPRECIATE *YOU*.

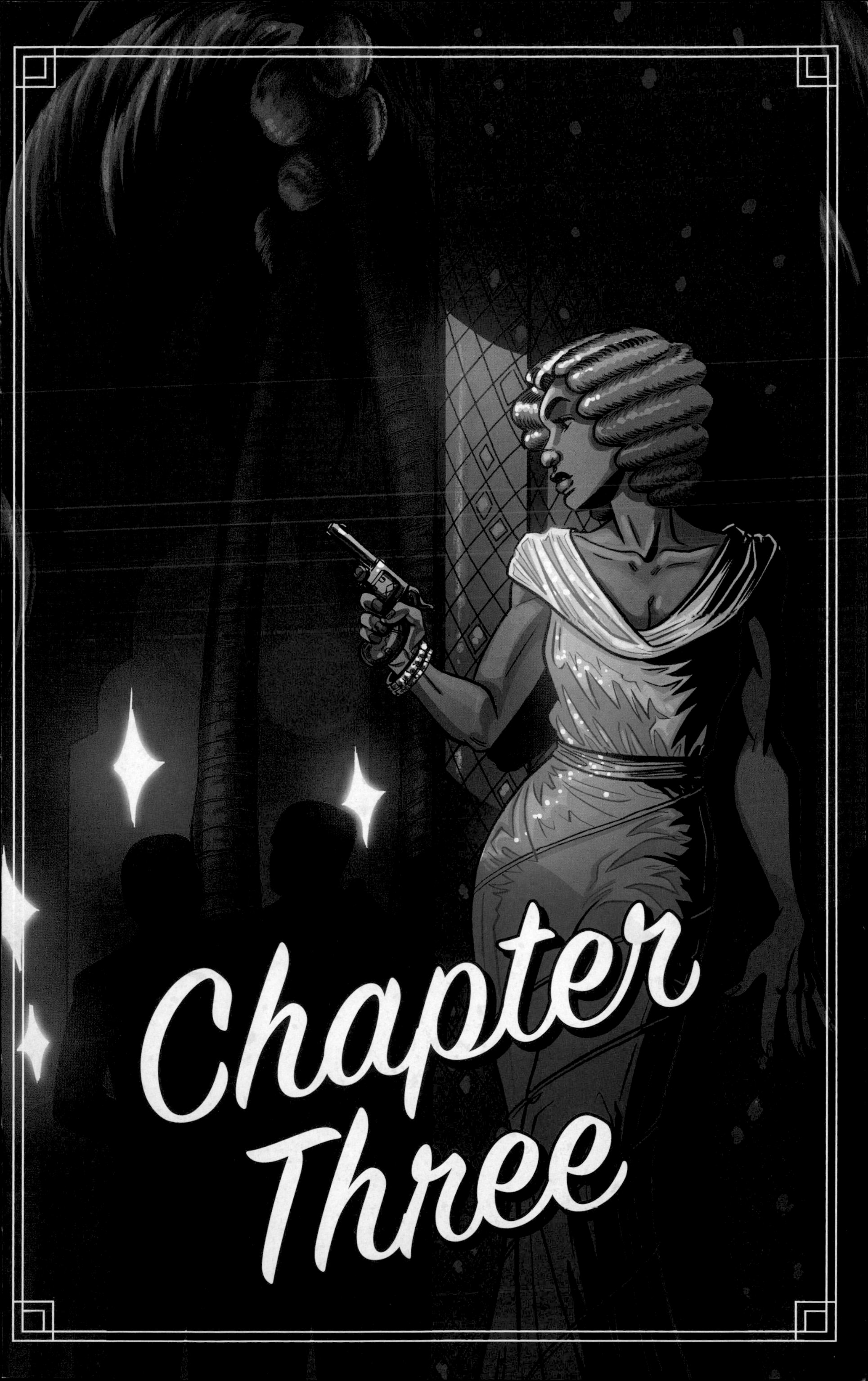
Chapter Three

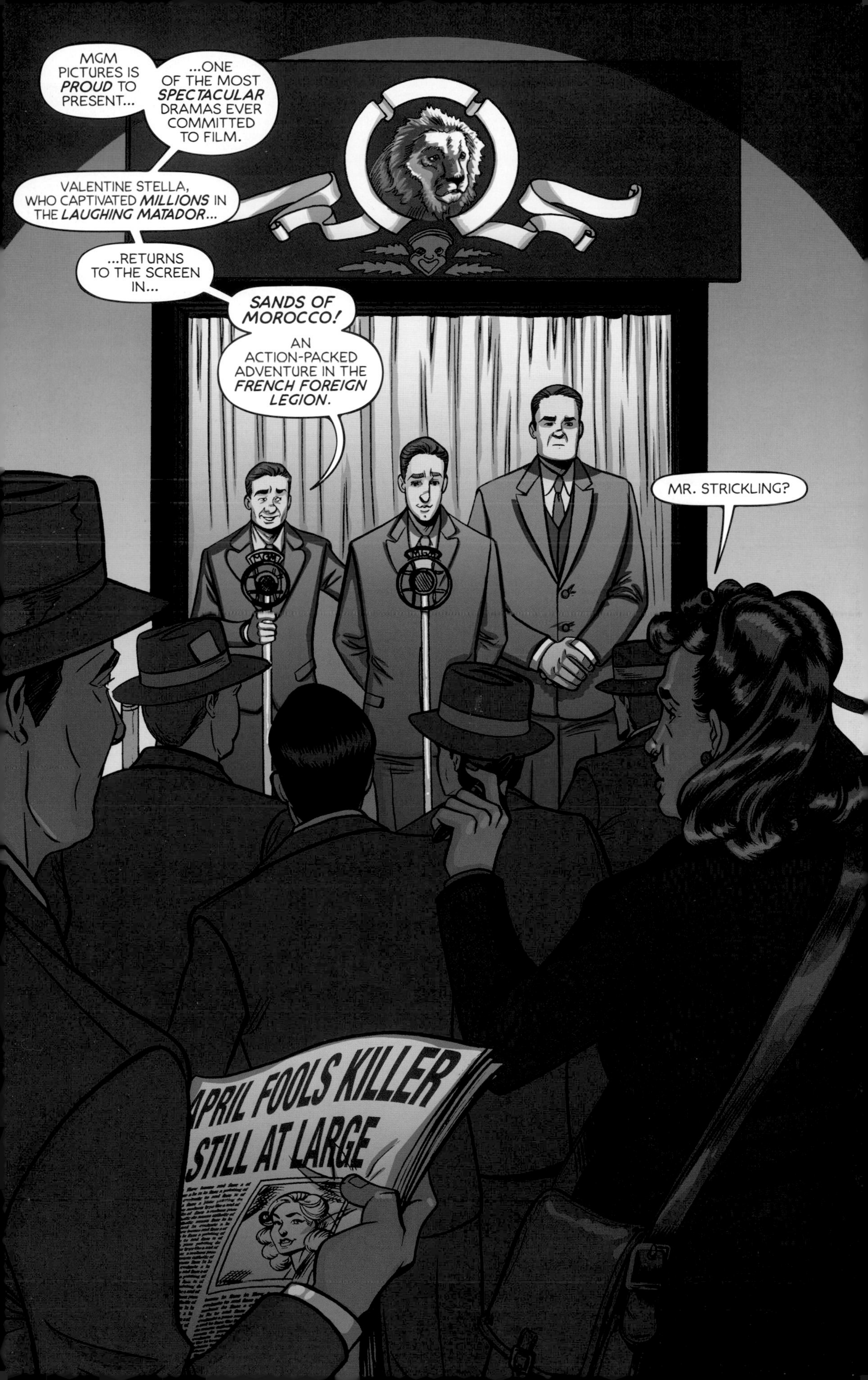
MGM PICTURES IS *PROUD* TO PRESENT...
...ONE OF THE MOST *SPECTACULAR* DRAMAS EVER COMMITTED TO FILM.
VALENTINE STELLA, WHO CAPTIVATED *MILLIONS* IN THE *LAUGHING MATADOR*...
...RETURNS TO THE SCREEN IN...
SANDS OF MOROCCO!
AN ACTION-PACKED ADVENTURE IN THE *FRENCH FOREIGN LEGION*.
MR. STRICKLING?
APRIL FOOLS KILLER STILL AT LARGE

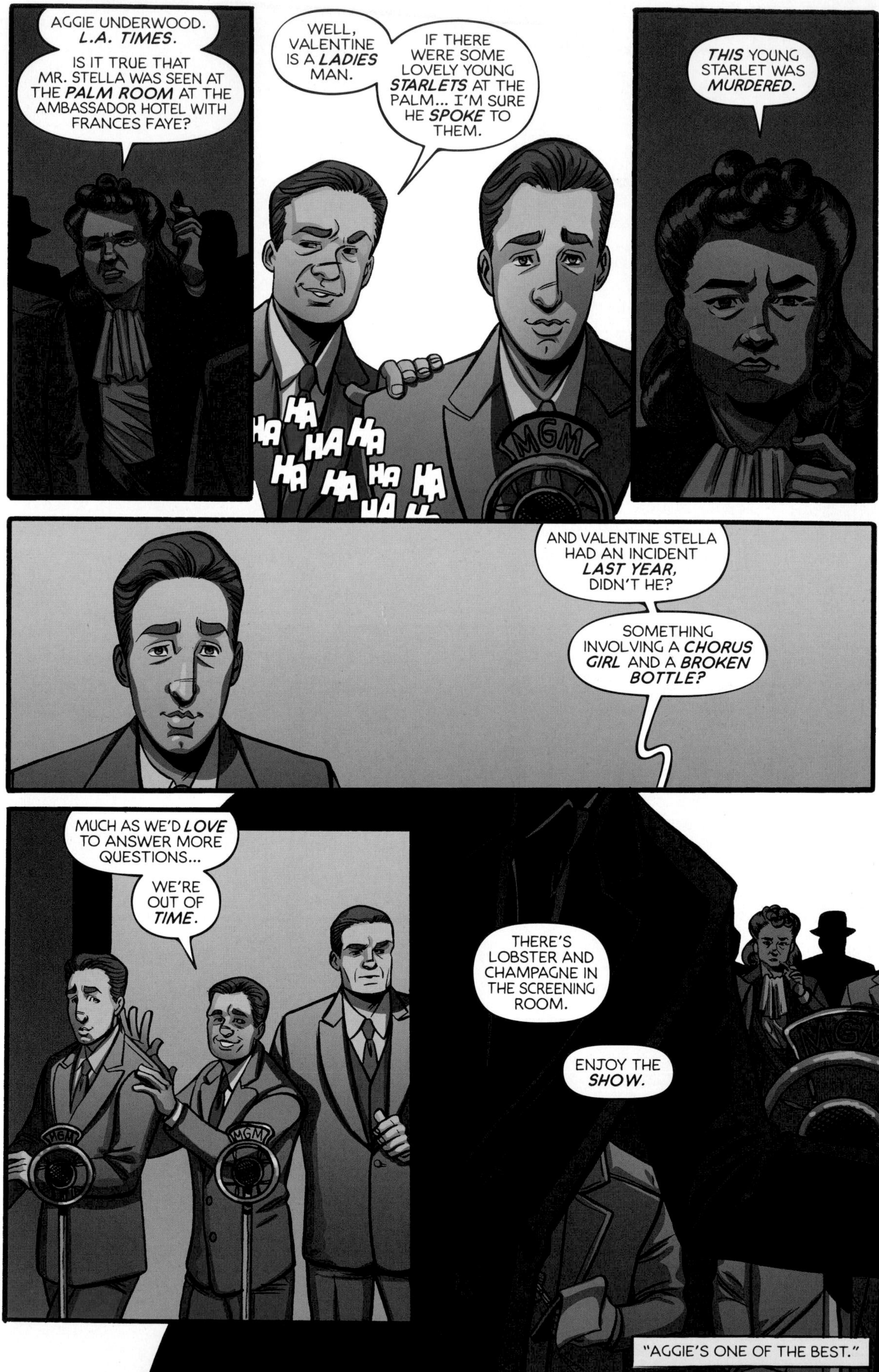
AGGIE UNDERWOOD. *L.A. TIMES*.
IS IT TRUE THAT MR. STELLA WAS SEEN AT THE *PALM ROOM* AT THE AMBASSADOR HOTEL WITH FRANCES FAYE?
WELL, VALENTINE IS A *LADIES* MAN.
IF THERE WERE SOME LOVELY YOUNG *STARLETS* AT THE PALM... I'M SURE HE *SPOKE* TO THEM.
HA HA HA HA HA HA HA HA HA
THIS YOUNG STARLET WAS *MURDERED*.
AND VALENTINE STELLA HAD AN INCIDENT *LAST YEAR*, DIDN'T HE?
SOMETHING INVOLVING A *CHORUS GIRL* AND A *BROKEN BOTTLE?*
MUCH AS WE'D *LOVE* TO ANSWER MORE QUESTIONS...
WE'RE OUT OF *TIME*.
THERE'S LOBSTER AND CHAMPAGNE IN THE SCREENING ROOM.
ENJOY THE *SHOW*.
"AGGIE'S ONE OF THE BEST."

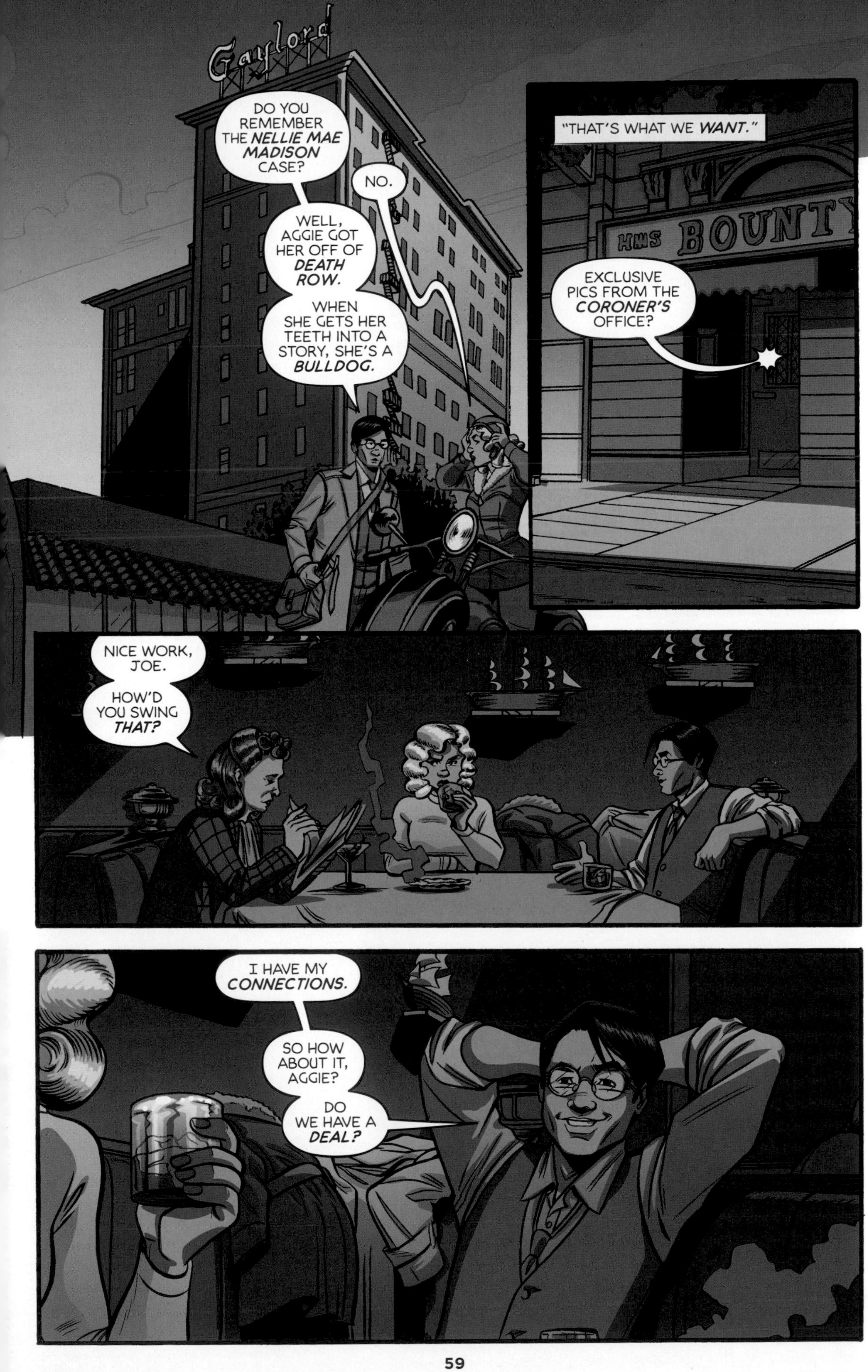
Gaylord
DO YOU REMEMBER THE *NELLIE MAE MADISON* CASE?
NO.
WELL, AGGIE GOT HER OFF OF *DEATH ROW.*
WHEN SHE GETS HER TEETH INTO A STORY, SHE'S A *BULLDOG.*
"THAT'S WHAT WE *WANT.*"
HMS BOUNTY
EXCLUSIVE PICS FROM THE *CORONER'S* OFFICE?
NICE WORK, JOE.
HOW'D YOU SWING *THAT?*
I HAVE MY *CONNECTIONS.*
SO HOW ABOUT IT, AGGIE?
DO WE HAVE A *DEAL?*

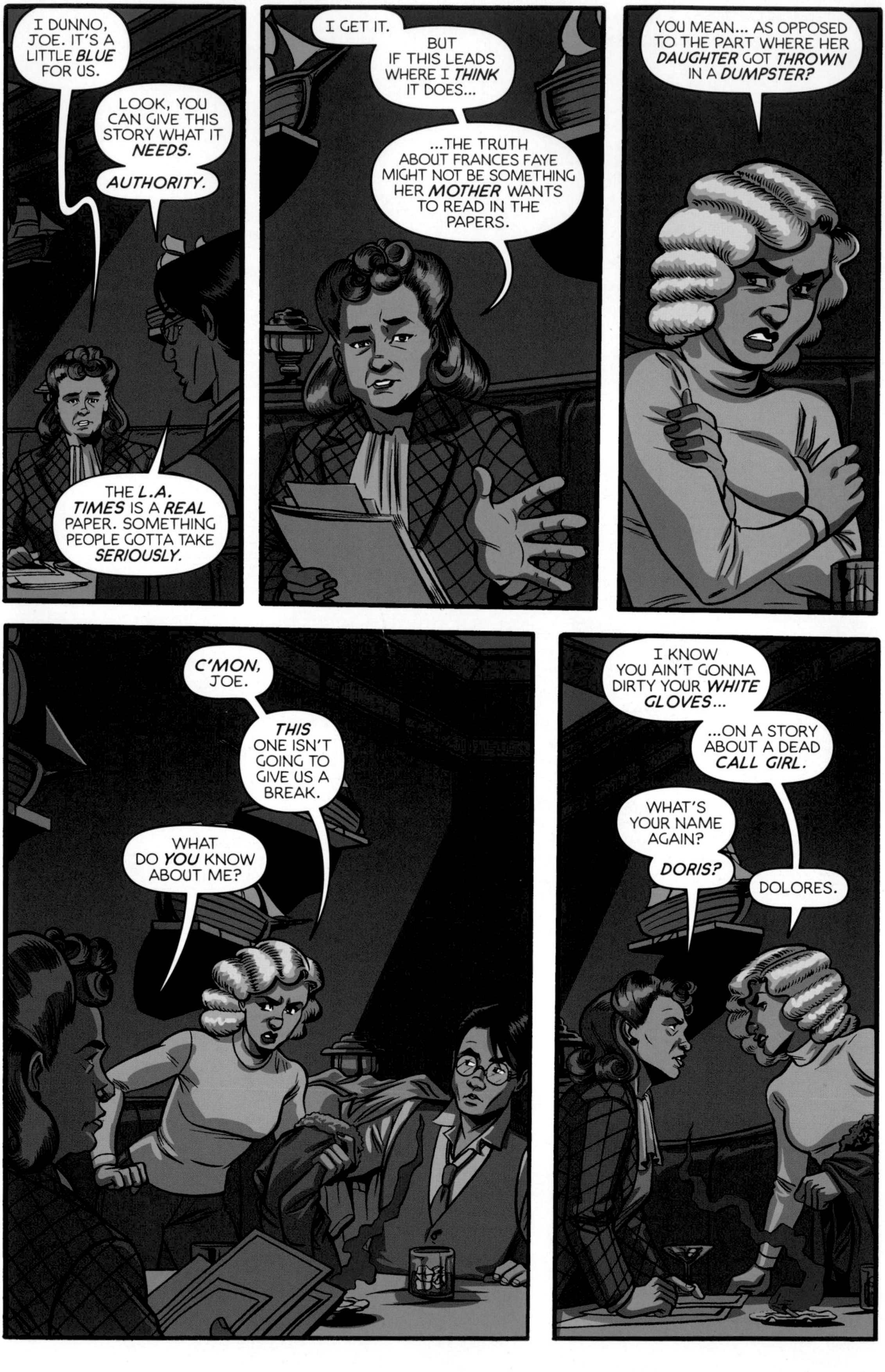
I DUNNO, JOE. IT'S A LITTLE BLUE FOR US.
LOOK, YOU CAN GIVE THIS STORY WHAT IT NEEDS.
AUTHORITY.
THE L.A. TIMES IS A REAL PAPER. SOMETHING PEOPLE GOTTA TAKE SERIOUSLY.
I GET IT.
BUT IF THIS LEADS WHERE I THINK IT DOES...
...THE TRUTH ABOUT FRANCES FAYE MIGHT NOT BE SOMETHING HER MOTHER WANTS TO READ IN THE PAPERS.
YOU MEAN... AS OPPOSED TO THE PART WHERE HER DAUGHTER GOT THROWN IN A DUMPSTER?
C'MON, JOE.
THIS ONE ISN'T GOING TO GIVE US A BREAK.
WHAT DO YOU KNOW ABOUT ME?
I KNOW YOU AIN'T GONNA DIRTY YOUR WHITE GLOVES...
...ON A STORY ABOUT A DEAD CALL GIRL.
WHAT'S YOUR NAME AGAIN?
DORIS?
DOLORES.

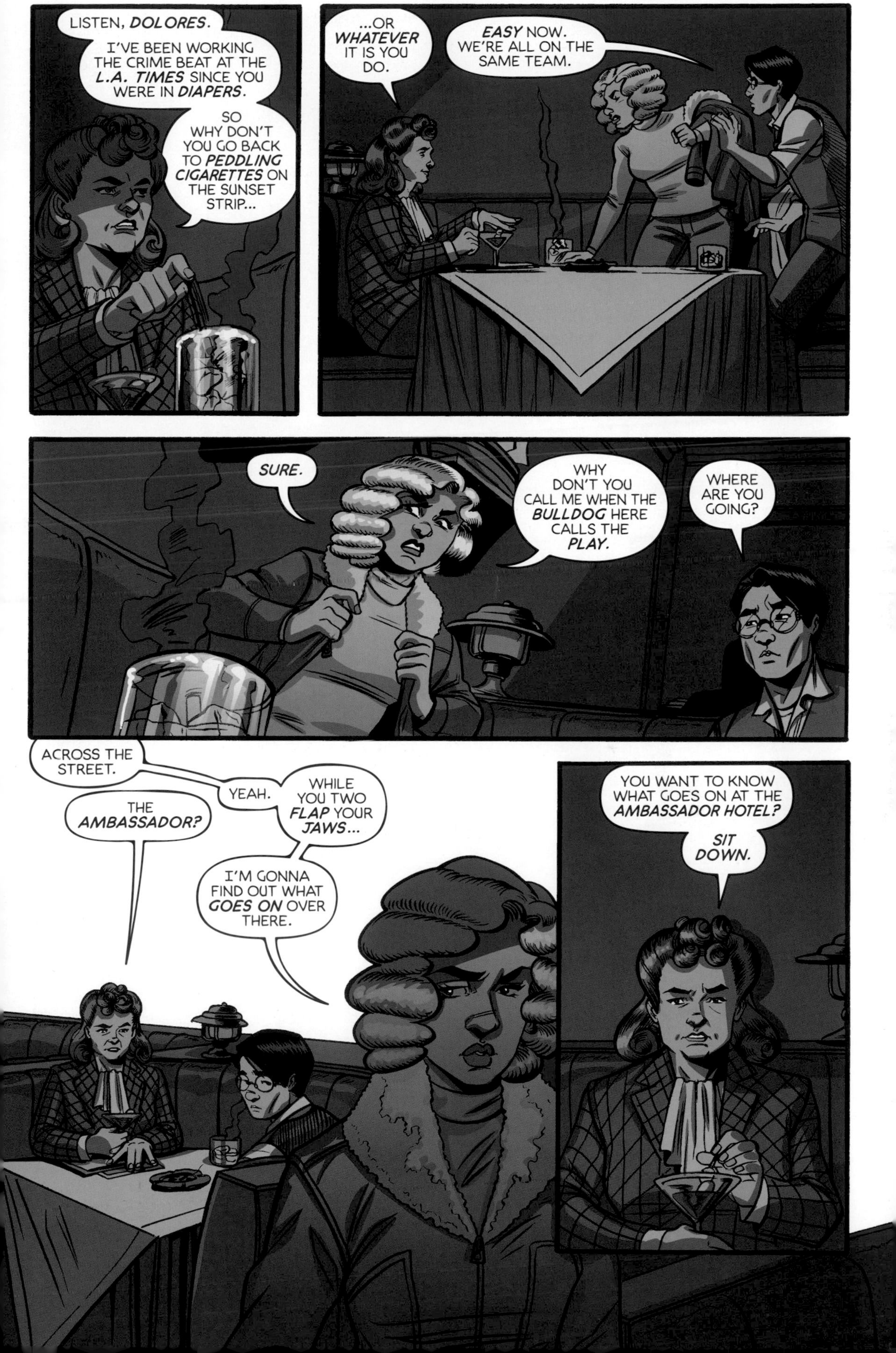
LISTEN, DOLORES.
I'VE BEEN WORKING THE CRIME BEAT AT THE L.A. TIMES SINCE YOU WERE IN DIAPERS.
SO WHY DON'T YOU GO BACK TO PEDDLING CIGARETTES ON THE SUNSET STRIP...
...OR WHATEVER IT IS YOU DO.
EASY NOW. WE'RE ALL ON THE SAME TEAM.
SURE.
WHY DON'T YOU CALL ME WHEN THE BULLDOG HERE CALLS THE PLAY.
WHERE ARE YOU GOING?
ACROSS THE STREET.
THE AMBASSADOR?
YEAH.
WHILE YOU TWO FLAP YOUR JAWS...
I'M GONNA FIND OUT WHAT GOES ON OVER THERE.
YOU WANT TO KNOW WHAT GOES ON AT THE AMBASSADOR HOTEL?
SIT DOWN.

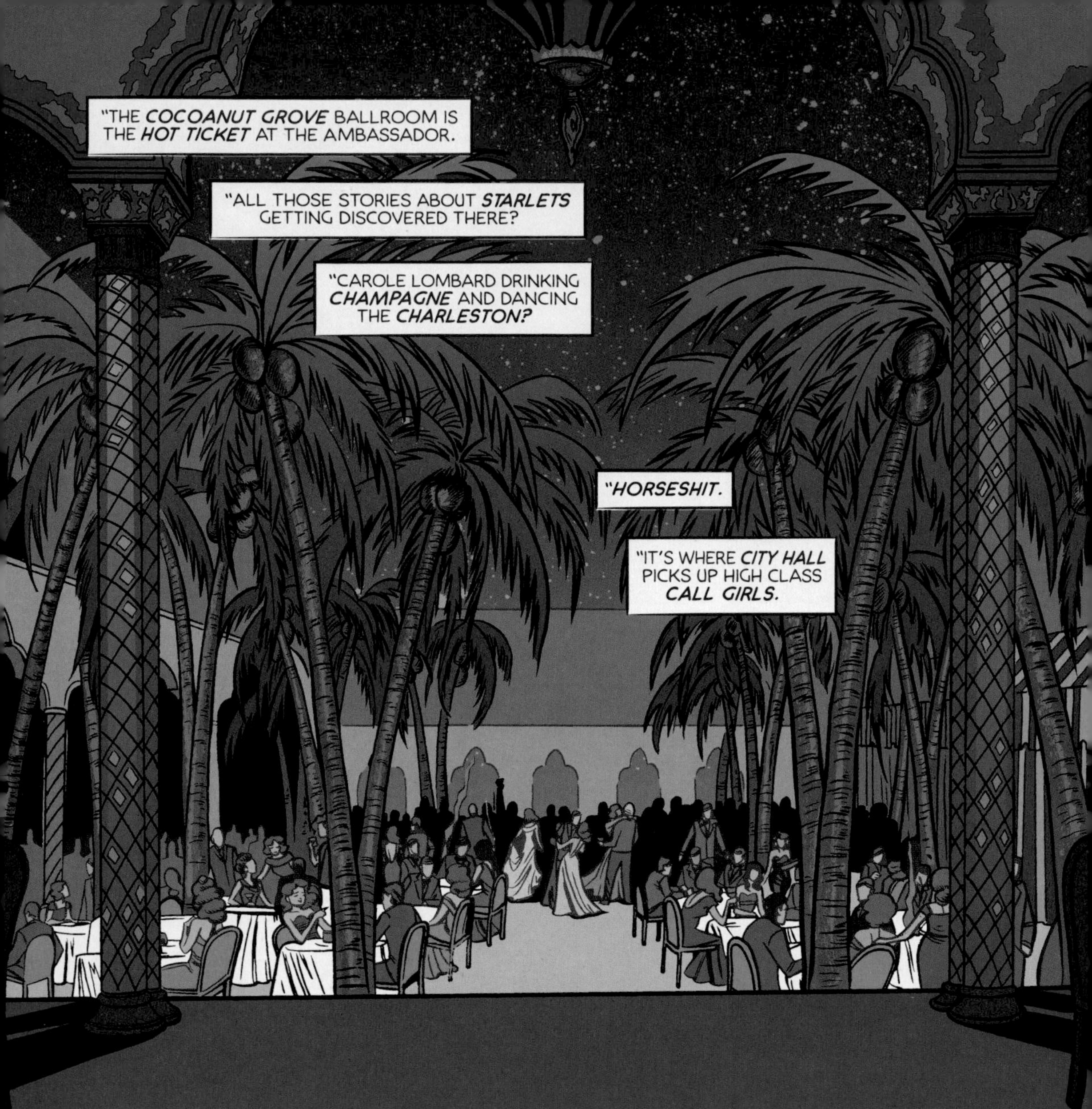
"THE *COCOANUT GROVE* BALLROOM IS THE *HOT TICKET* AT THE AMBASSADOR.
"ALL THOSE STORIES ABOUT *STARLETS* GETTING DISCOVERED THERE?
"CAROLE LOMBARD DRINKING *CHAMPAGNE* AND DANCING THE *CHARLESTON?*
"*HORSESHIT.*
"IT'S WHERE *CITY HALL* PICKS UP HIGH CLASS *CALL GIRLS.*

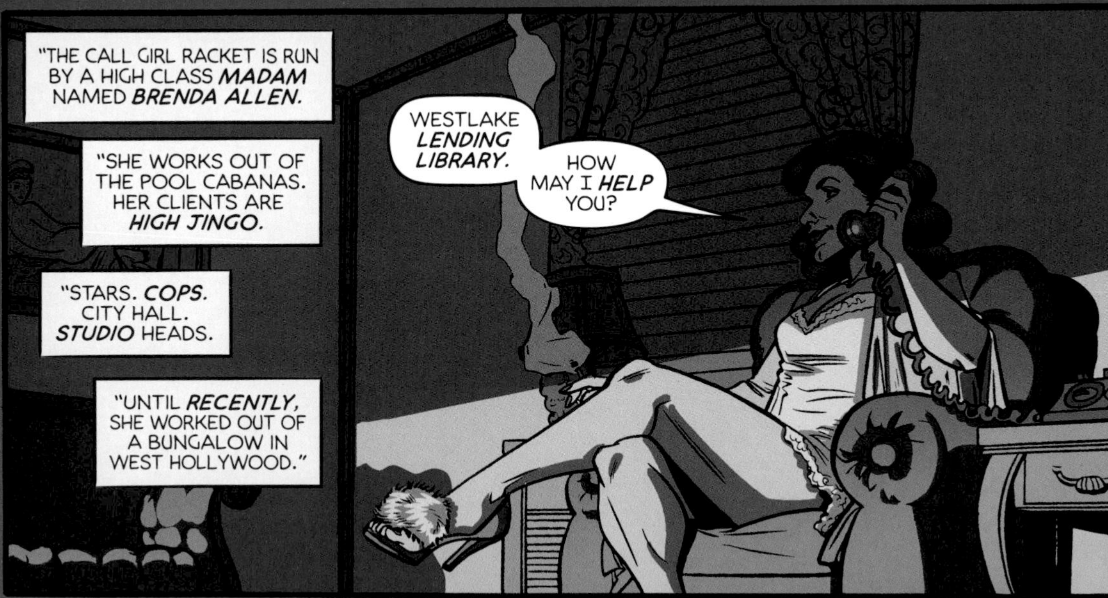
"THE CALL GIRL RACKET IS RUN BY A HIGH CLASS *MADAM* NAMED *BRENDA ALLEN.*
"SHE WORKS OUT OF THE POOL CABANAS. HER CLIENTS ARE *HIGH JINGO.*
"STARS. *COPS.* CITY HALL. *STUDIO* HEADS.
"UNTIL *RECENTLY,* SHE WORKED OUT OF A BUNGALOW IN WEST HOLLYWOOD."
WESTLAKE *LENDING LIBRARY.*
HOW MAY I *HELP* YOU?

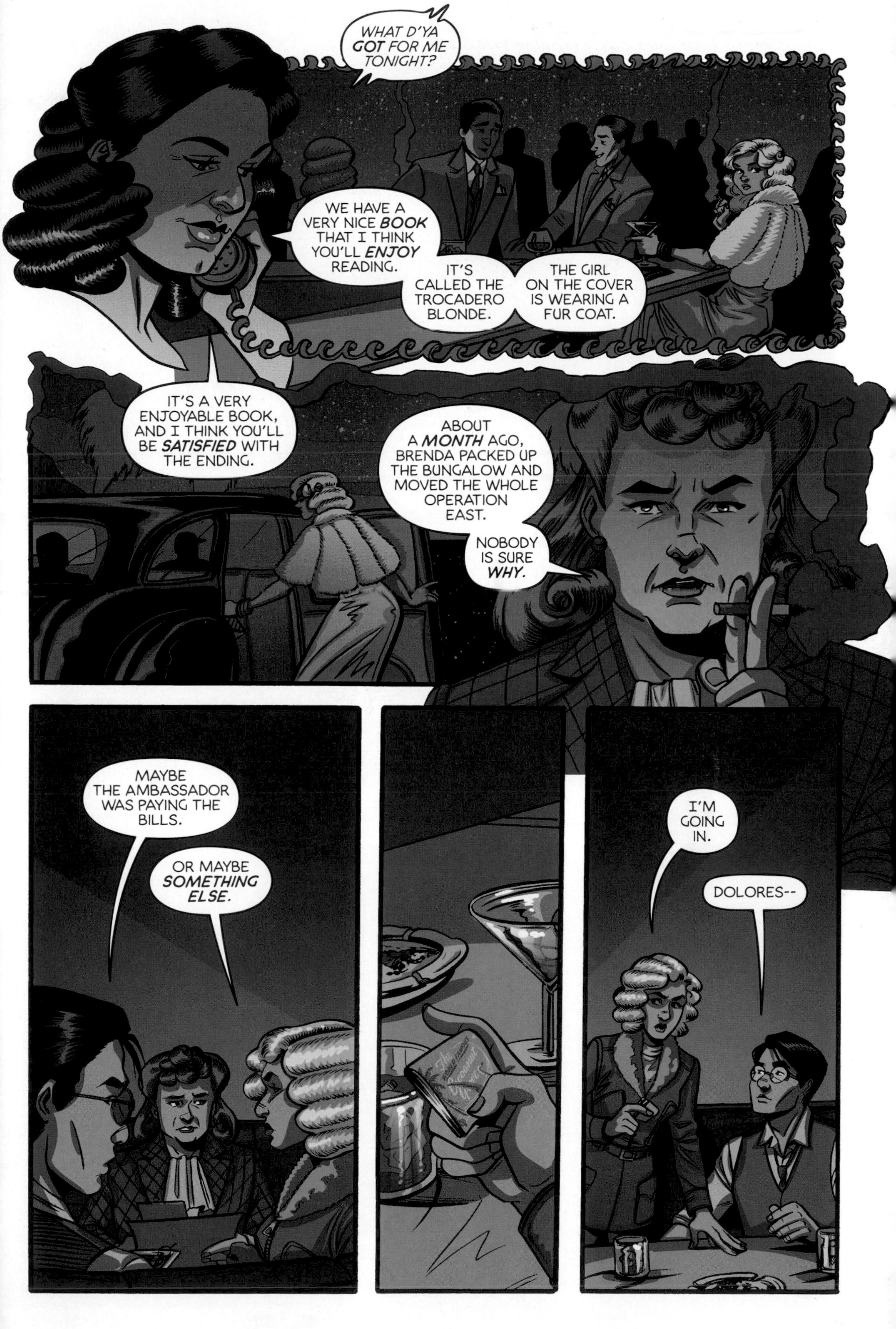
WHAT D'YA **GOT** FOR ME TONIGHT?
WE HAVE A VERY NICE **BOOK** THAT I THINK YOU'LL **ENJOY** READING.
IT'S CALLED THE TROCADERO BLONDE.
THE GIRL ON THE COVER IS WEARING A FUR COAT.
IT'S A VERY ENJOYABLE BOOK, AND I THINK YOU'LL BE **SATISFIED** WITH THE ENDING.
ABOUT A **MONTH** AGO, BRENDA PACKED UP THE BUNGALOW AND MOVED THE WHOLE OPERATION EAST.
NOBODY IS SURE **WHY.**
MAYBE THE AMBASSADOR WAS PAYING THE BILLS.
OR MAYBE **SOMETHING ELSE.**
I'M GOING IN.
DOLORES--

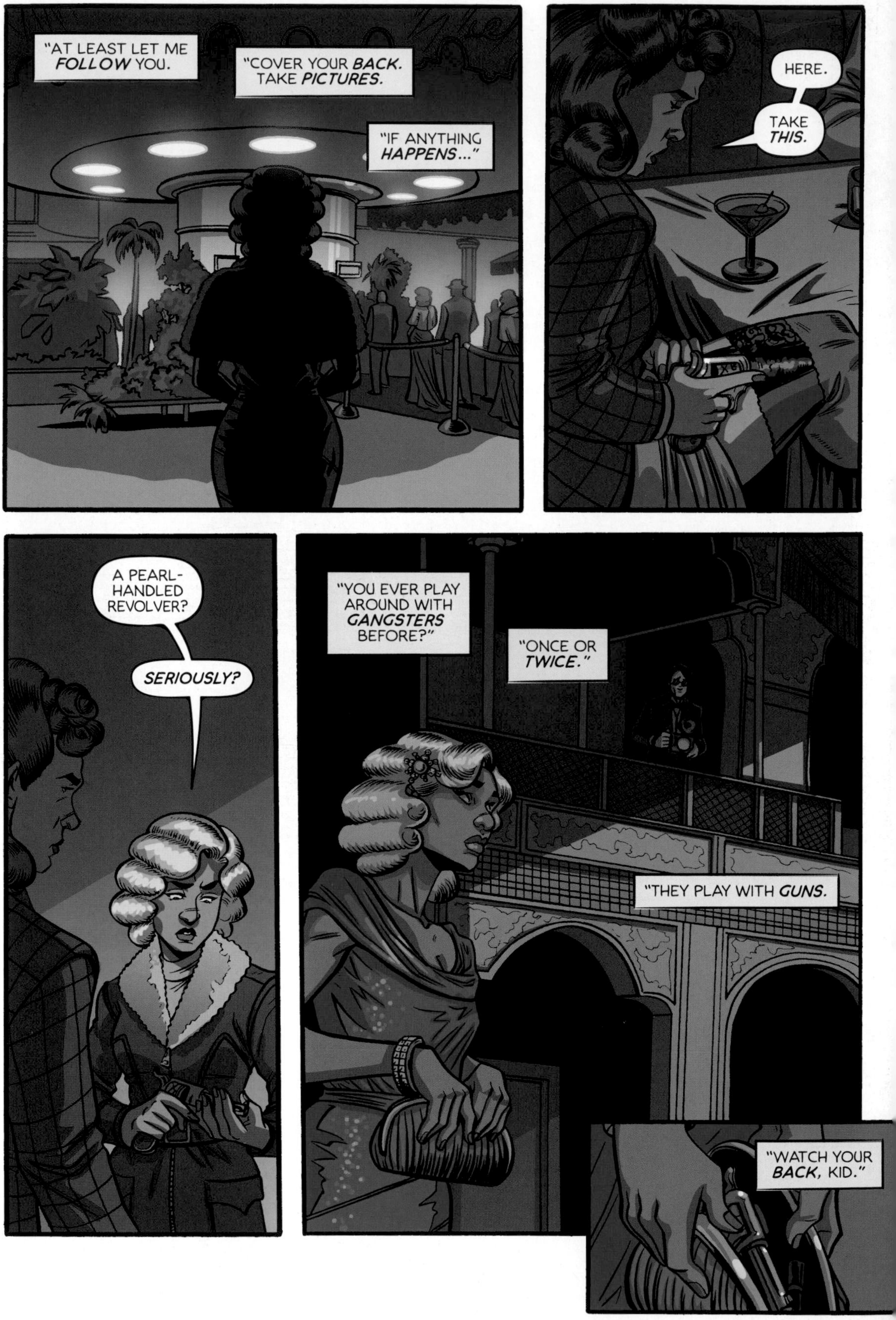
"AT LEAST LET ME *FOLLOW* YOU.
"COVER YOUR *BACK.* TAKE *PICTURES.*
"IF ANYTHING *HAPPENS...*"
HERE.
TAKE *THIS.*
A PEARL-HANDLED REVOLVER?
SERIOUSLY?
"YOU EVER PLAY AROUND WITH *GANGSTERS* BEFORE?"
"ONCE OR *TWICE.*"
"THEY PLAY WITH *GUNS.*
"WATCH YOUR *BACK,* KID."

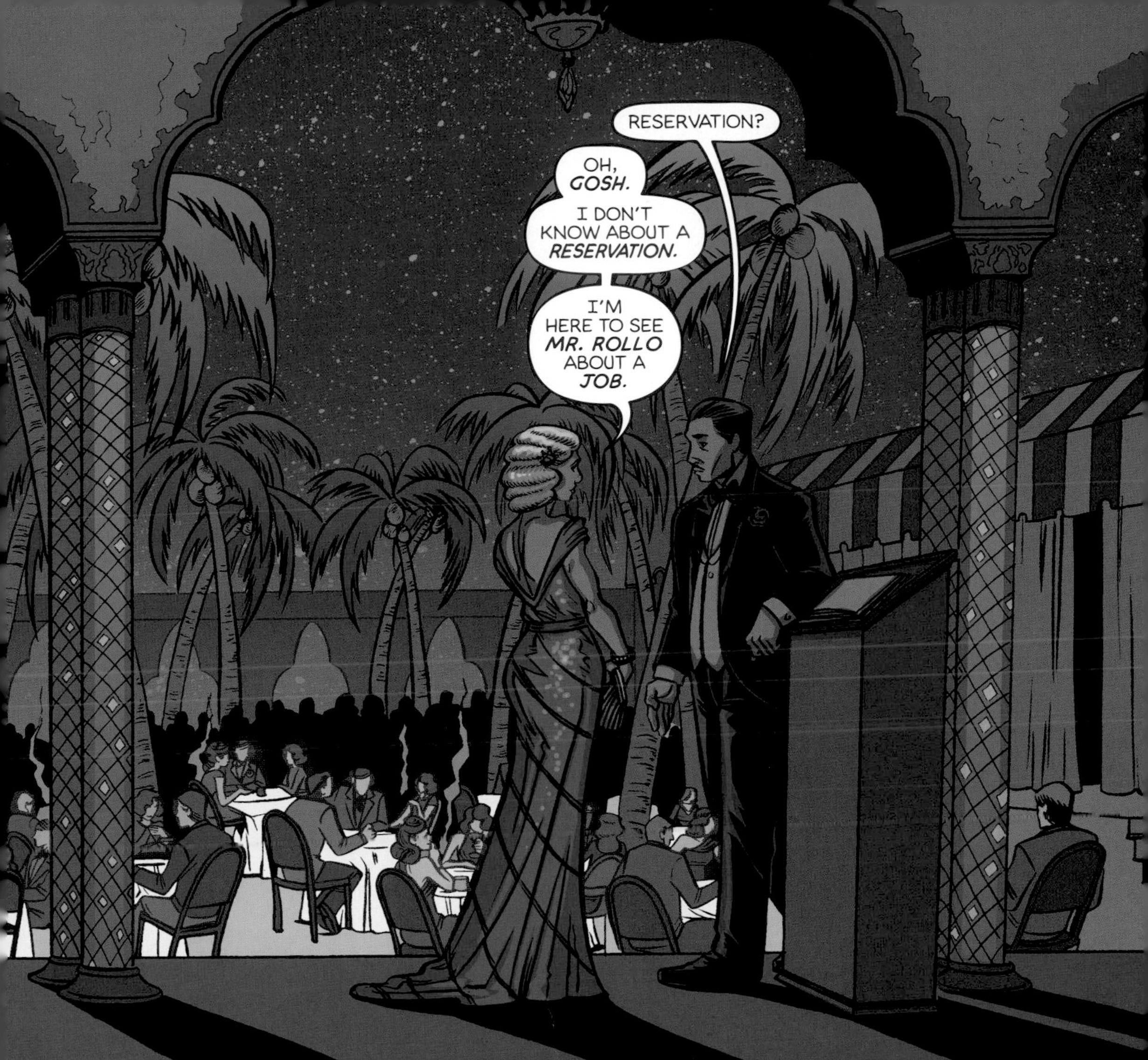
RESERVATION?
OH, *GOSH.*
I DON'T KNOW ABOUT A *RESERVATION.*
I'M HERE TO SEE *MR. ROLLO* ABOUT A *JOB.*
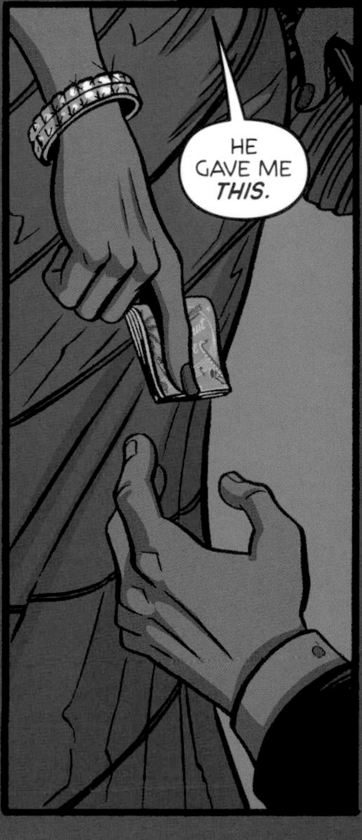
HE GAVE ME *THIS.*
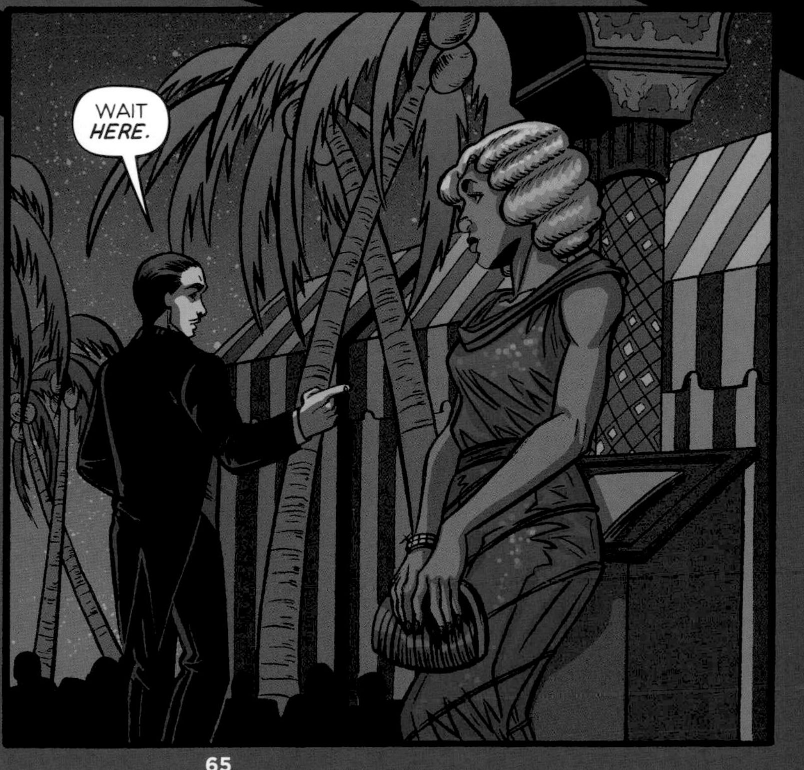
WAIT *HERE.*

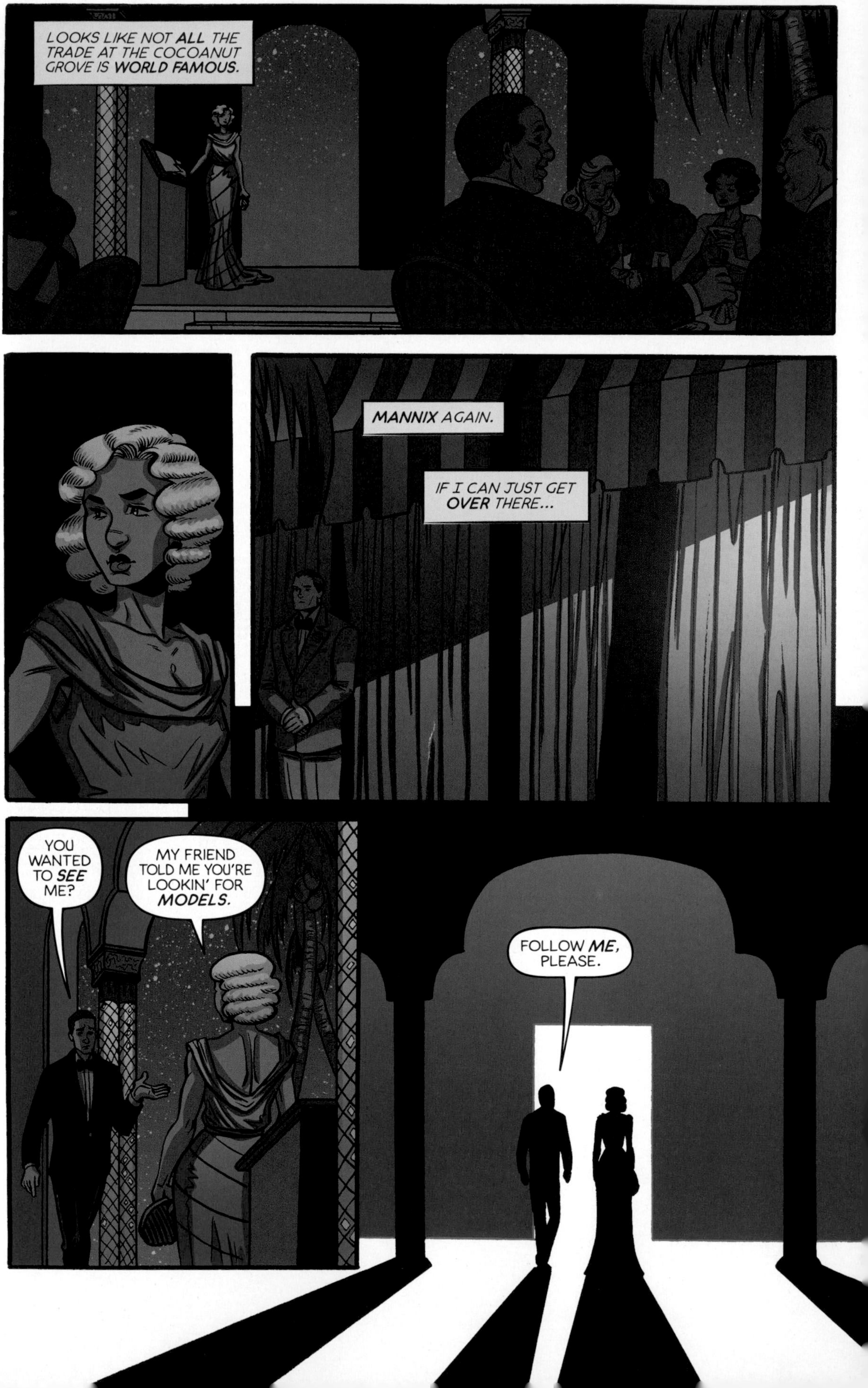
LOOKS LIKE NOT ALL THE TRADE AT THE COCOANUT GROVE IS WORLD FAMOUS.
MANNIX AGAIN.
IF I CAN JUST GET OVER THERE...
YOU WANTED TO SEE ME?
MY FRIEND TOLD ME YOU'RE LOOKIN' FOR MODELS.
FOLLOW ME, PLEASE.

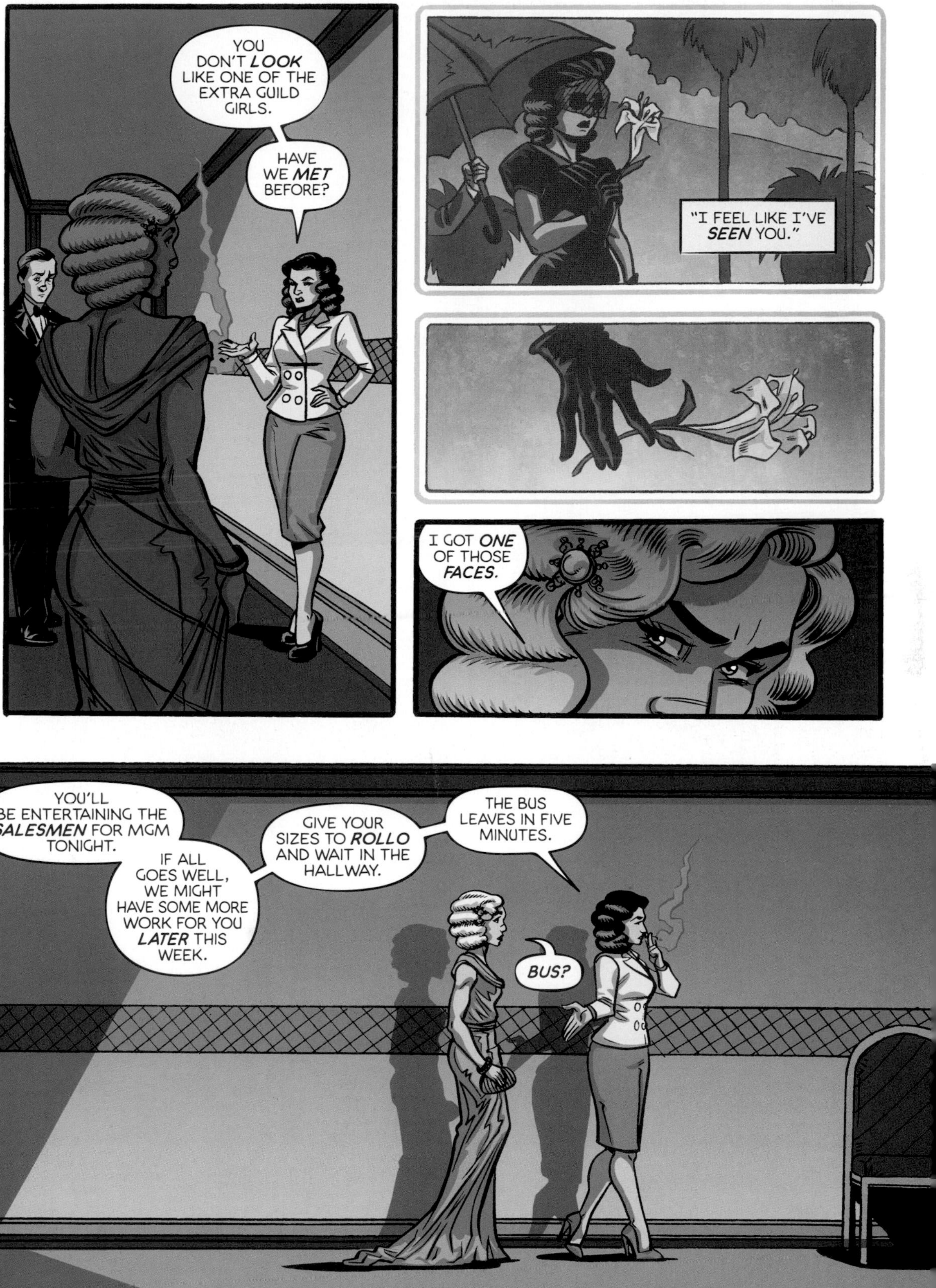
YOU DON'T ***LOOK*** LIKE ONE OF THE EXTRA GUILD GIRLS.
HAVE WE ***MET*** BEFORE?
"I FEEL LIKE I'VE ***SEEN*** YOU."
I GOT ***ONE*** OF THOSE ***FACES.***
YOU'LL BE ENTERTAINING THE ***SALESMEN*** FOR MGM TONIGHT.
IF ALL GOES WELL, WE MIGHT HAVE SOME MORE WORK FOR YOU ***LATER*** THIS WEEK.
GIVE YOUR SIZES TO ***ROLLO*** AND WAIT IN THE HALLWAY.
THE BUS LEAVES IN FIVE MINUTES.
BUS?

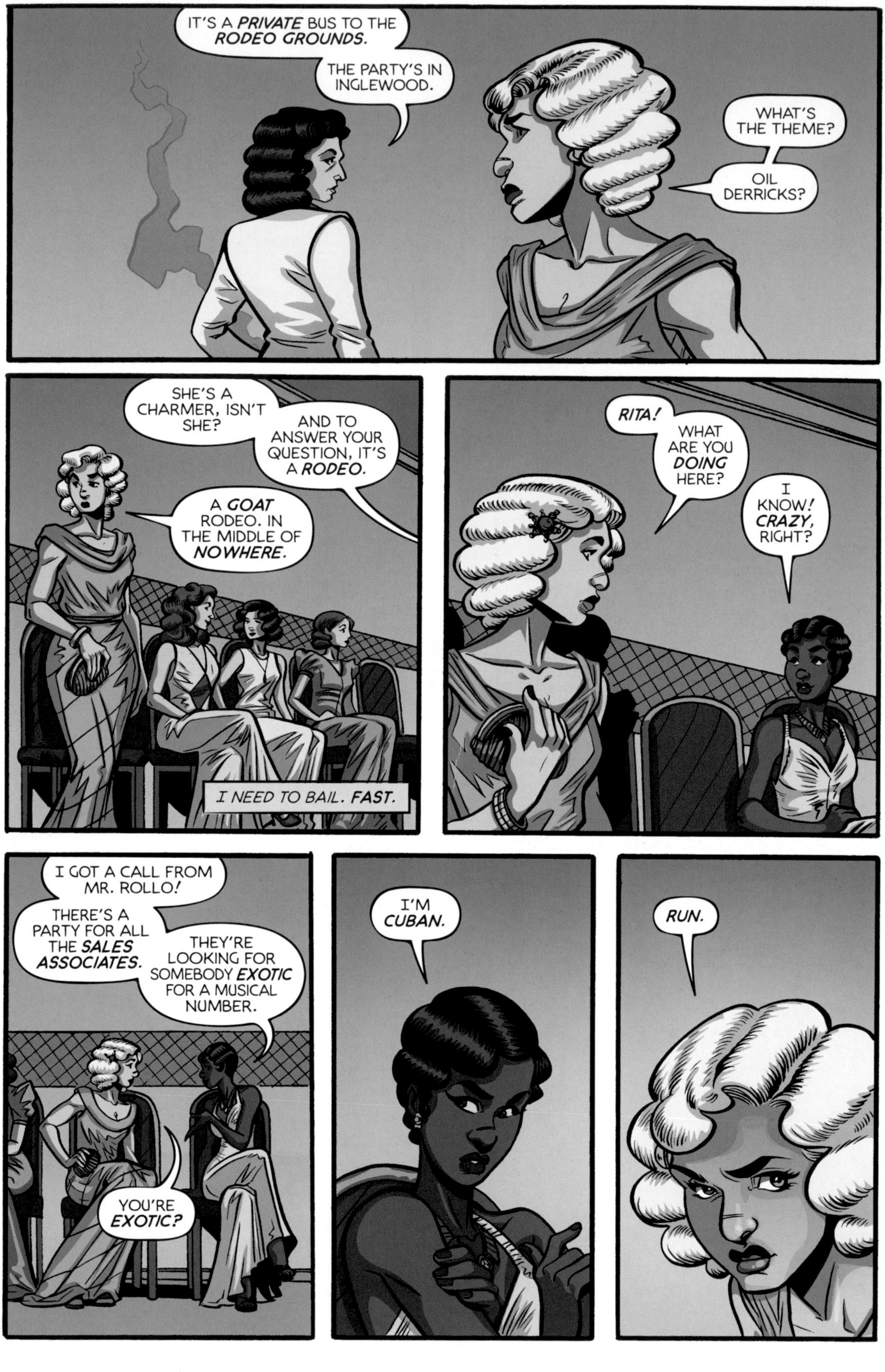
IT'S A *PRIVATE* BUS TO THE *RODEO GROUNDS.*
THE PARTY'S IN INGLEWOOD.
WHAT'S THE THEME?
OIL DERRICKS?
SHE'S A CHARMER, ISN'T SHE?
AND TO ANSWER YOUR QUESTION, IT'S A *RODEO.*
A *GOAT* RODEO. IN THE MIDDLE OF *NOWHERE.*
I NEED TO BAIL. **FAST.**
RITA!
WHAT ARE YOU *DOING* HERE?
I KNOW*!* *CRAZY,* RIGHT?
I GOT A CALL FROM MR. ROLLO*!*
THERE'S A PARTY FOR ALL THE *SALES ASSOCIATES.*
THEY'RE LOOKING FOR SOMEBODY *EXOTIC* FOR A MUSICAL NUMBER.
YOU'RE *EXOTIC?*
I'M *CUBAN.*
RUN.

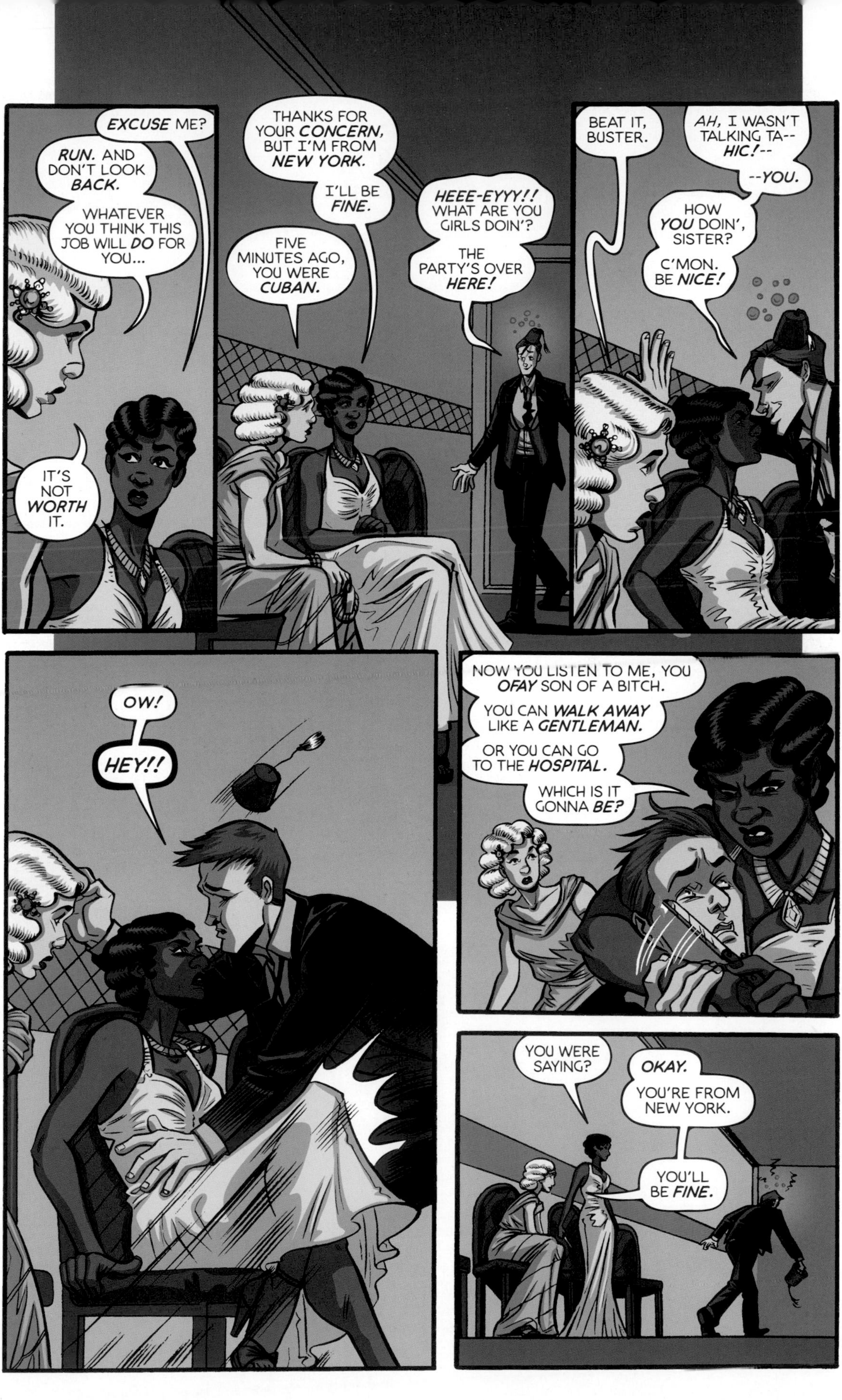
EXCUSE ME?
RUN. AND DON'T LOOK BACK.
WHATEVER YOU THINK THIS JOB WILL DO FOR YOU...
IT'S NOT WORTH IT.
THANKS FOR YOUR CONCERN, BUT I'M FROM NEW YORK.
I'LL BE FINE.
FIVE MINUTES AGO, YOU WERE CUBAN.
HEEE-EYYY!! WHAT ARE YOU GIRLS DOIN'?
THE PARTY'S OVER HERE!
BEAT IT, BUSTER.
AH, I WASN'T TALKING TA-- HIC!--
--YOU.
HOW YOU DOIN', SISTER?
C'MON. BE NICE!
OW!
HEY!!
NOW YOU LISTEN TO ME, YOU OFAY SON OF A BITCH.
YOU CAN WALK AWAY LIKE A GENTLEMAN.
OR YOU CAN GO TO THE HOSPITAL.
WHICH IS IT GONNA BE?
YOU WERE SAYING?
OKAY.
YOU'RE FROM NEW YORK.
YOU'LL BE FINE.

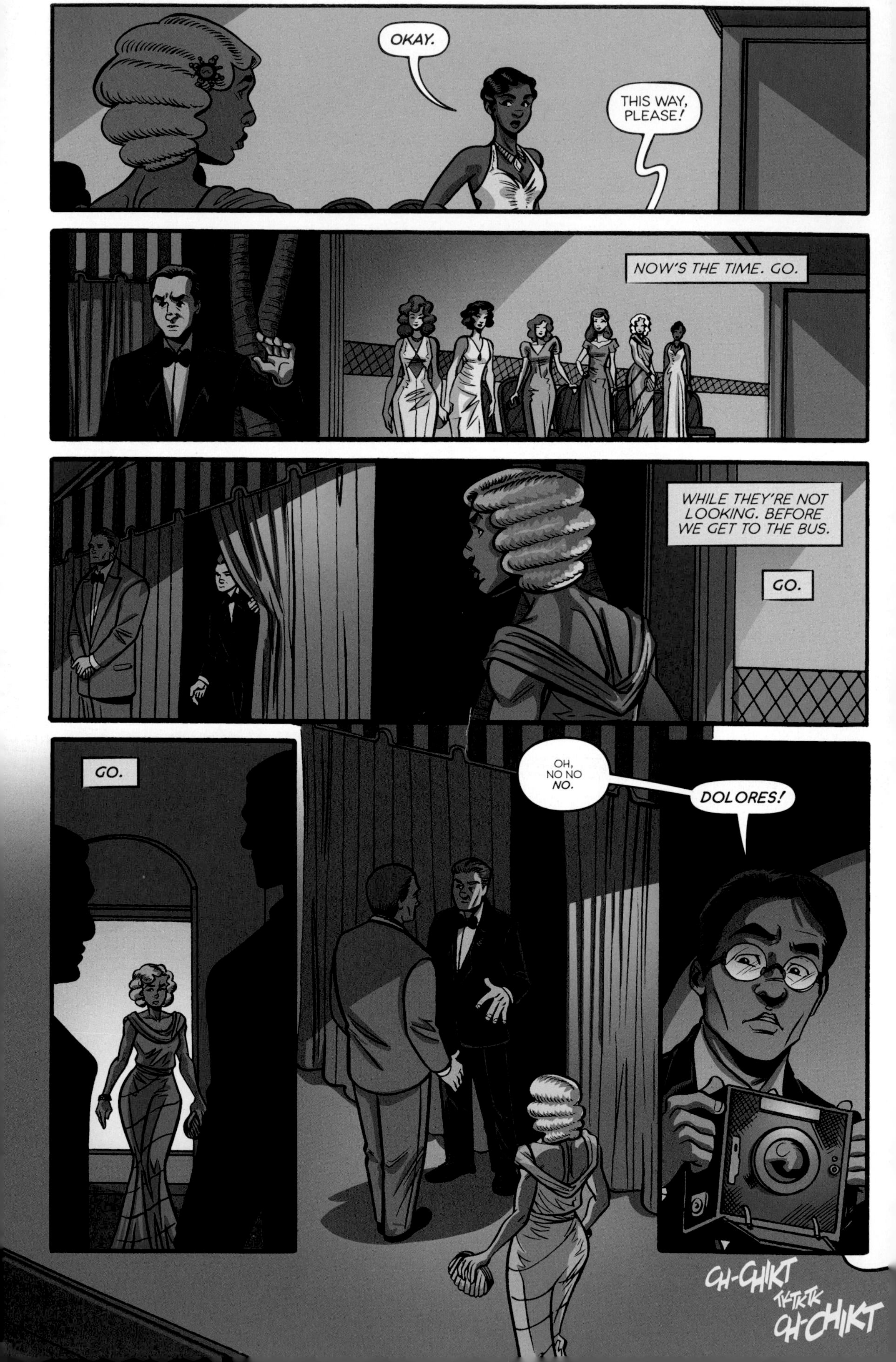
OKAY.
THIS WAY, PLEASE!
NOW'S THE TIME. GO.
WHILE THEY'RE NOT LOOKING. BEFORE WE GET TO THE BUS.
GO.
GO.
OH, NO NO NO.
DOLORES!
CH-CHIKT
TKTKTK
CH-CHIKT

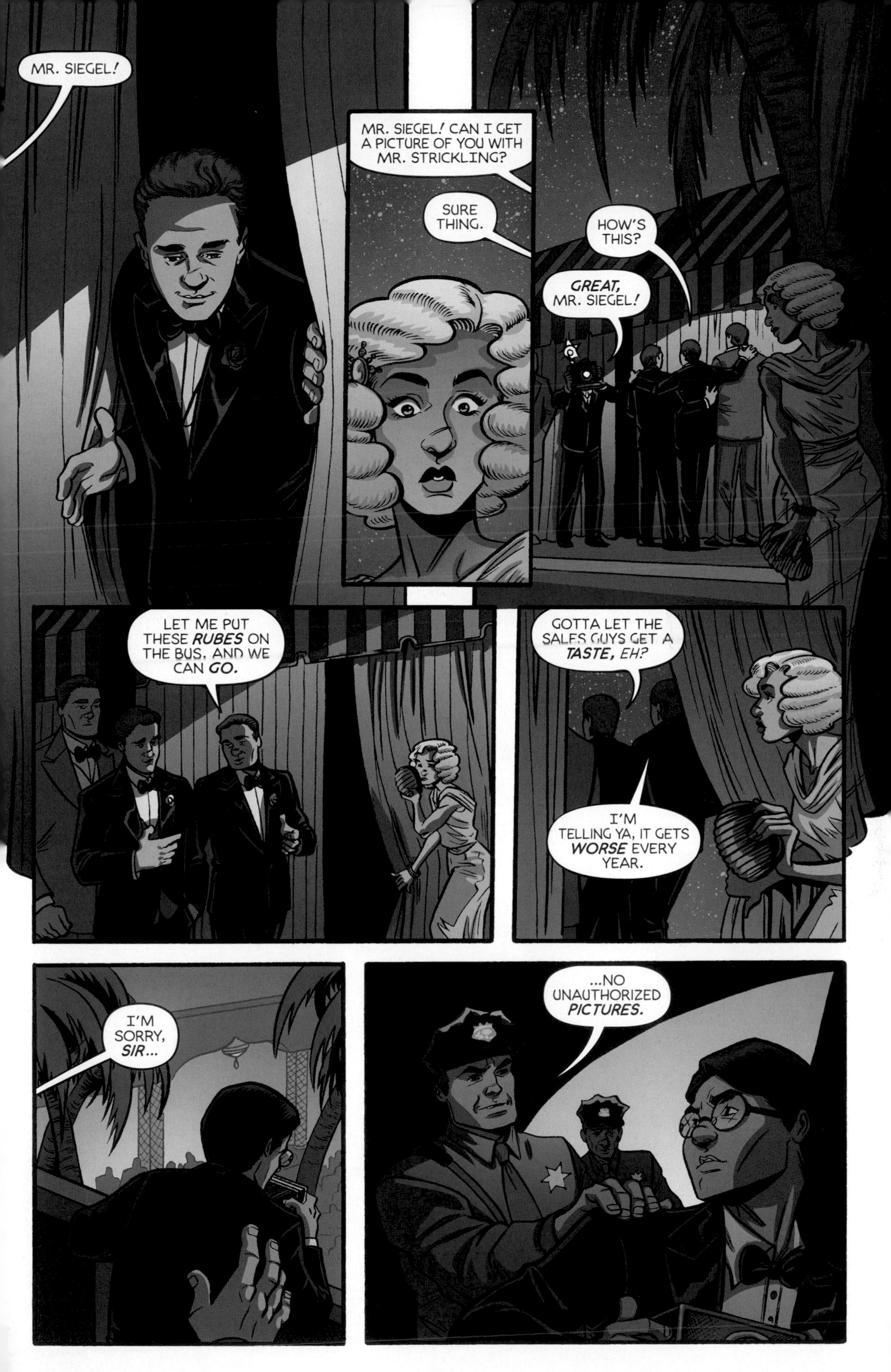
MR. SIEGEL!
MR. SIEGEL! CAN I GET A PICTURE OF YOU WITH MR. STRICKLING?
SURE THING.
HOW'S THIS?
GREAT, MR. SIEGEL!
LET ME PUT THESE RUBES ON THE BUS, AND WE CAN GO.
GOTTA LET THE SALES GUYS GET A TASTE, EH?
I'M TELLING YA, IT GETS WORSE EVERY YEAR.
I'M SORRY, SIR...
...NO UNAUTHORIZED PICTURES.

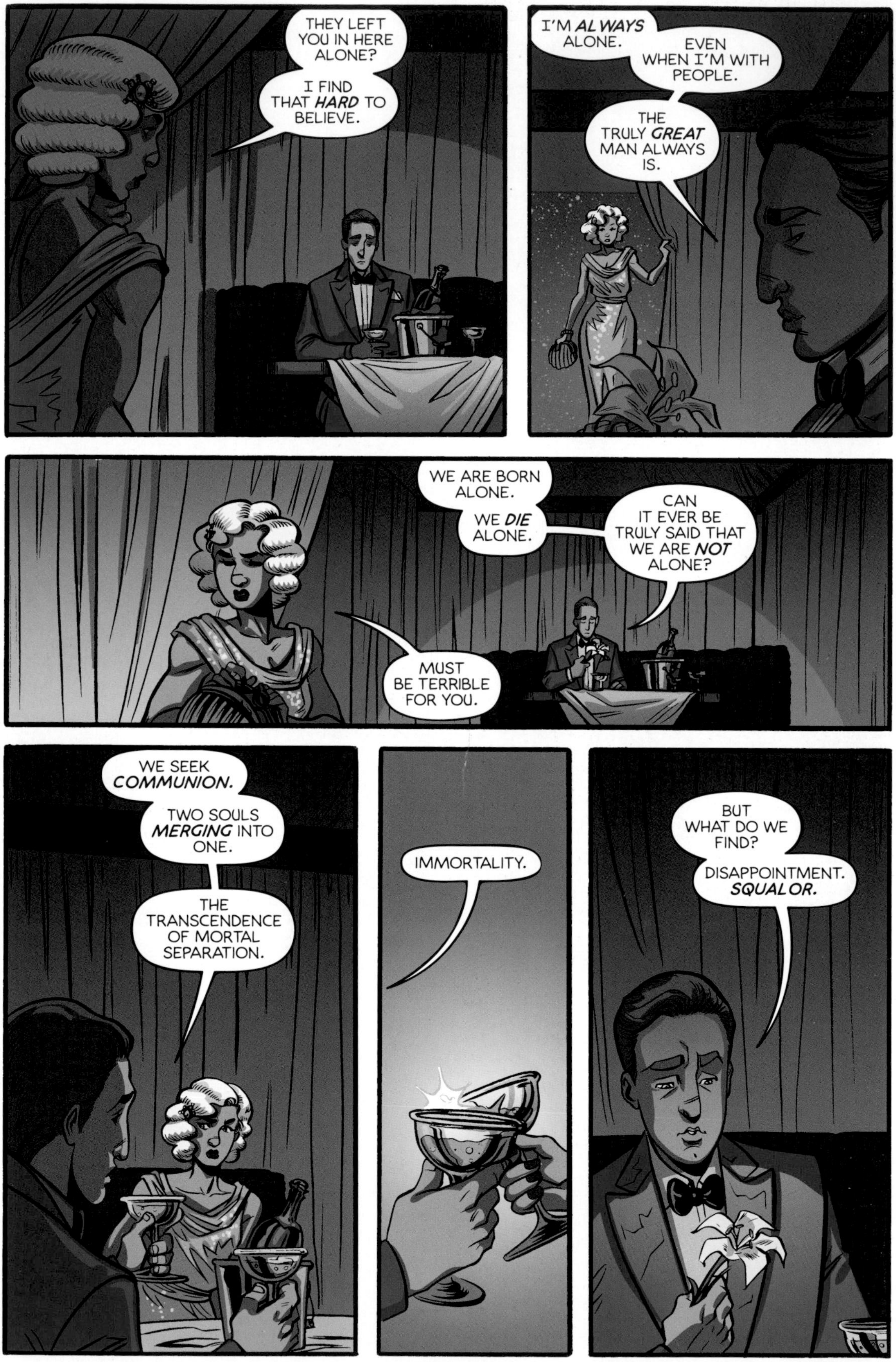
THEY LEFT YOU IN HERE ALONE?
I FIND THAT **HARD** TO BELIEVE.
I'M **ALWAYS** ALONE.
EVEN WHEN I'M WITH PEOPLE.
THE TRULY **GREAT** MAN ALWAYS IS.
MUST BE TERRIBLE FOR YOU.
WE ARE BORN ALONE.
WE **DIE** ALONE.
CAN IT EVER BE TRULY SAID THAT WE ARE **NOT** ALONE?
WE SEEK **COMMUNION.**
TWO SOULS **MERGING** INTO ONE.
THE TRANSCENDENCE OF MORTAL SEPARATION.
IMMORTALITY.
BUT WHAT DO WE FIND?
DISAPPOINTMENT. **SQUALOR.**

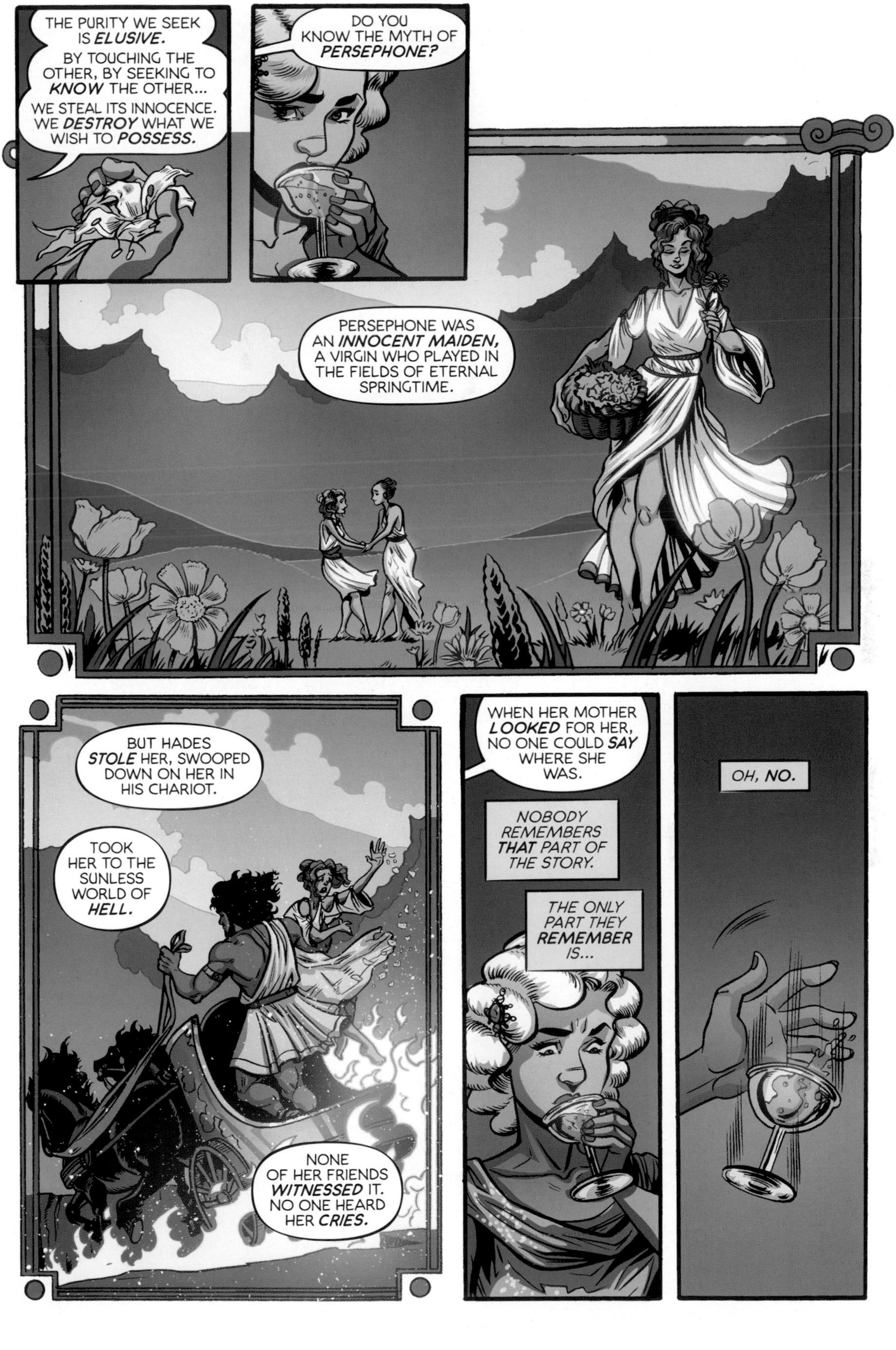
THE PURITY WE SEEK IS *ELUSIVE.*
BY TOUCHING THE OTHER, BY SEEKING TO *KNOW* THE OTHER...
WE STEAL ITS INNOCENCE. WE *DESTROY* WHAT WE WISH TO *POSSESS.*
DO YOU KNOW THE MYTH OF *PERSEPHONE?*
PERSEPHONE WAS AN *INNOCENT MAIDEN,* A VIRGIN WHO PLAYED IN THE FIELDS OF ETERNAL SPRINGTIME.
BUT HADES *STOLE* HER, SWOOPED DOWN ON HER IN HIS CHARIOT.
TOOK HER TO THE SUNLESS WORLD OF *HELL.*
NONE OF HER FRIENDS *WITNESSED* IT. NO ONE HEARD HER *CRIES.*
WHEN HER MOTHER *LOOKED* FOR HER, NO ONE COULD *SAY* WHERE SHE WAS.
NOBODY REMEMBERS *THAT* PART OF THE STORY.
THE ONLY PART THEY *REMEMBER* IS...
OH, *NO.*

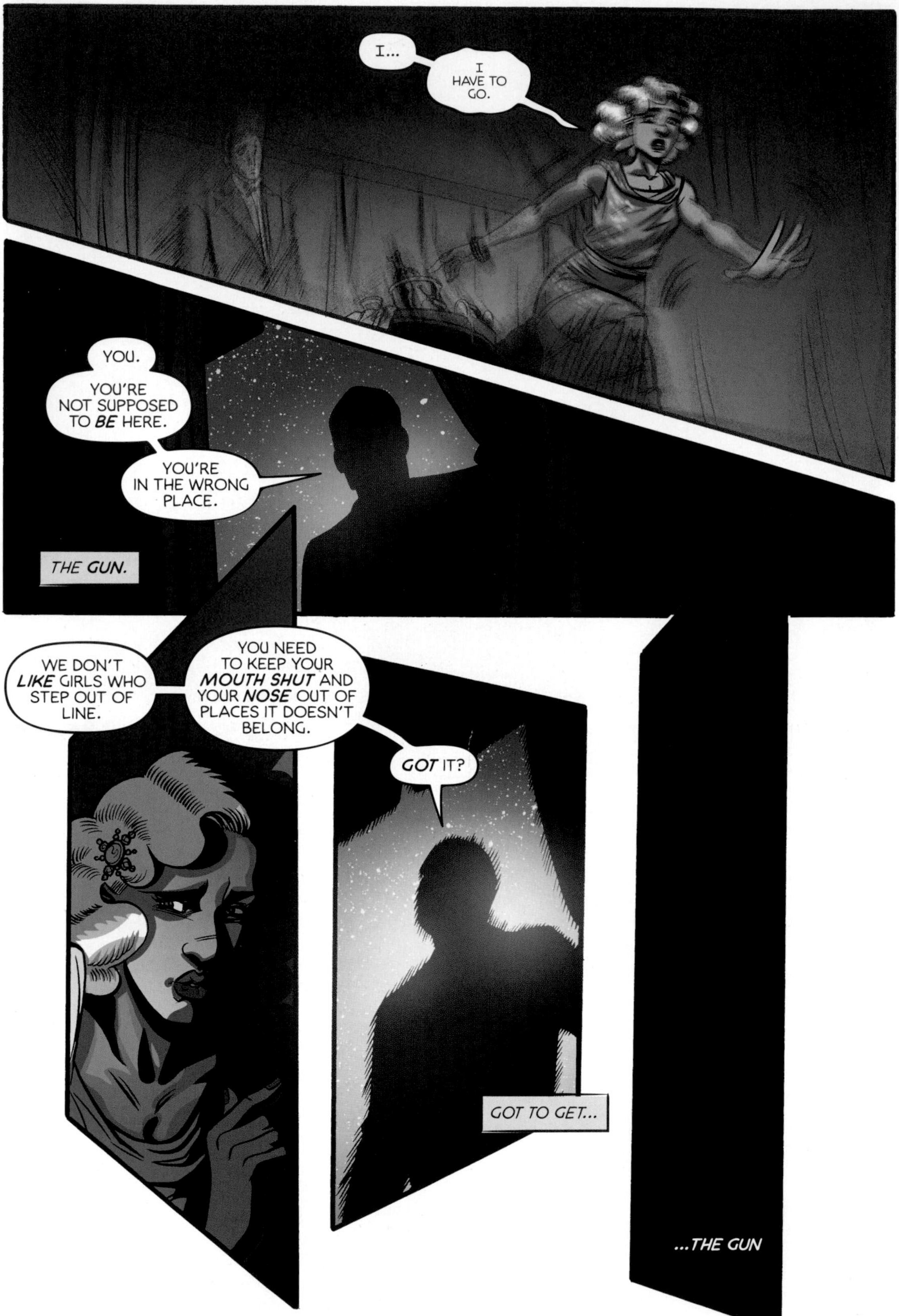
I...
I HAVE TO GO.
YOU.
YOU'RE NOT SUPPOSED TO *BE* HERE.
YOU'RE IN THE WRONG PLACE.
THE *GUN.*
WE DON'T *LIKE* GIRLS WHO STEP OUT OF LINE.
YOU NEED TO KEEP YOUR *MOUTH SHUT* AND YOUR *NOSE* OUT OF PLACES IT DOESN'T BELONG.
GOT IT?
GOT TO GET...
...THE GUN

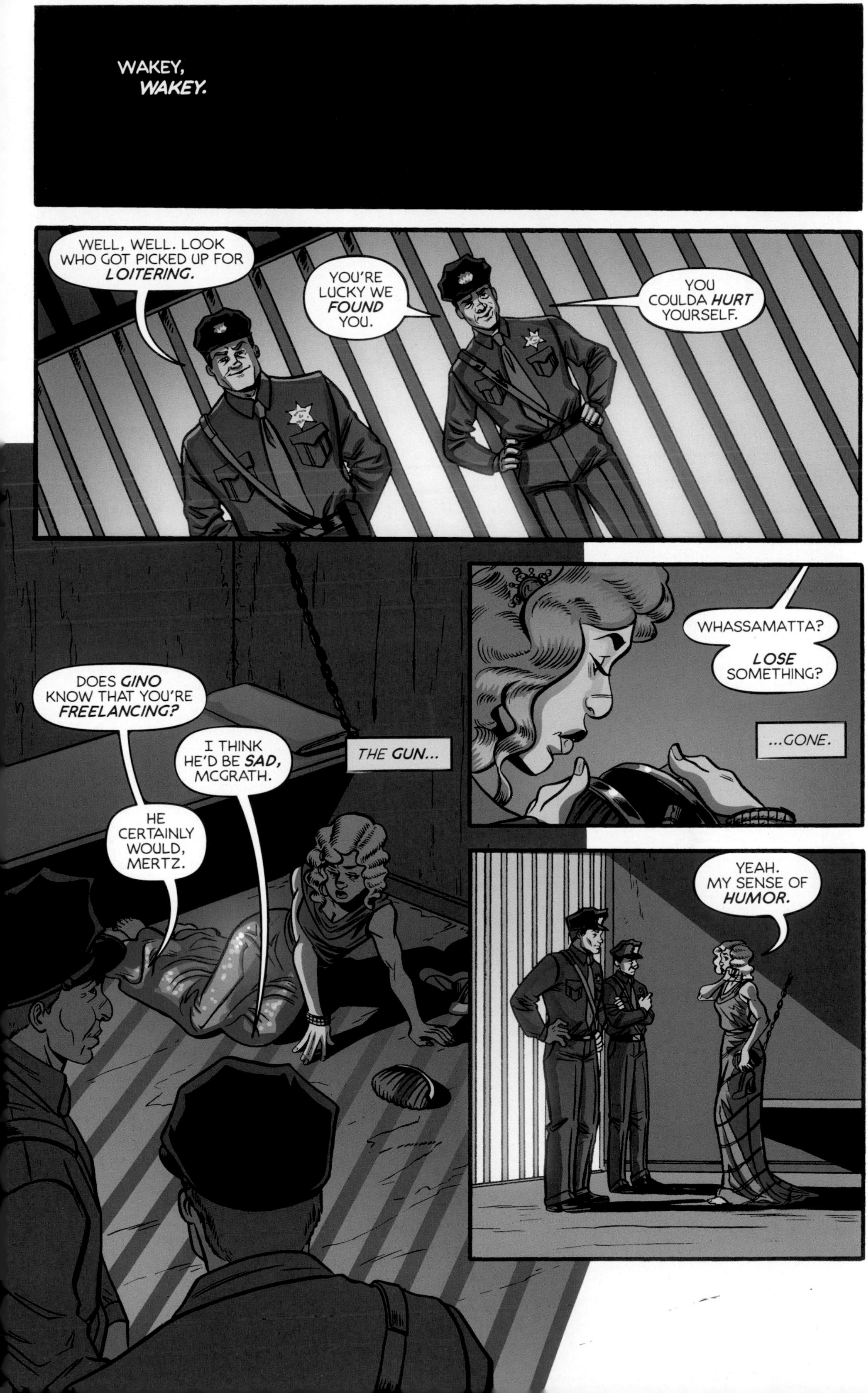
WAKEY, *WAKEY.*
WELL, WELL. LOOK WHO GOT PICKED UP FOR *LOITERING.*
YOU'RE LUCKY WE *FOUND* YOU.
YOU COULDA *HURT* YOURSELF.
DOES *GINO* KNOW THAT YOU'RE *FREELANCING?*
I THINK HE'D BE *SAD,* MCGRATH.
HE CERTAINLY WOULD, MERTZ.
THE GUN...
WHASSAMATTA?
LOSE SOMETHING?
...GONE.
YEAH. MY SENSE OF *HUMOR.*

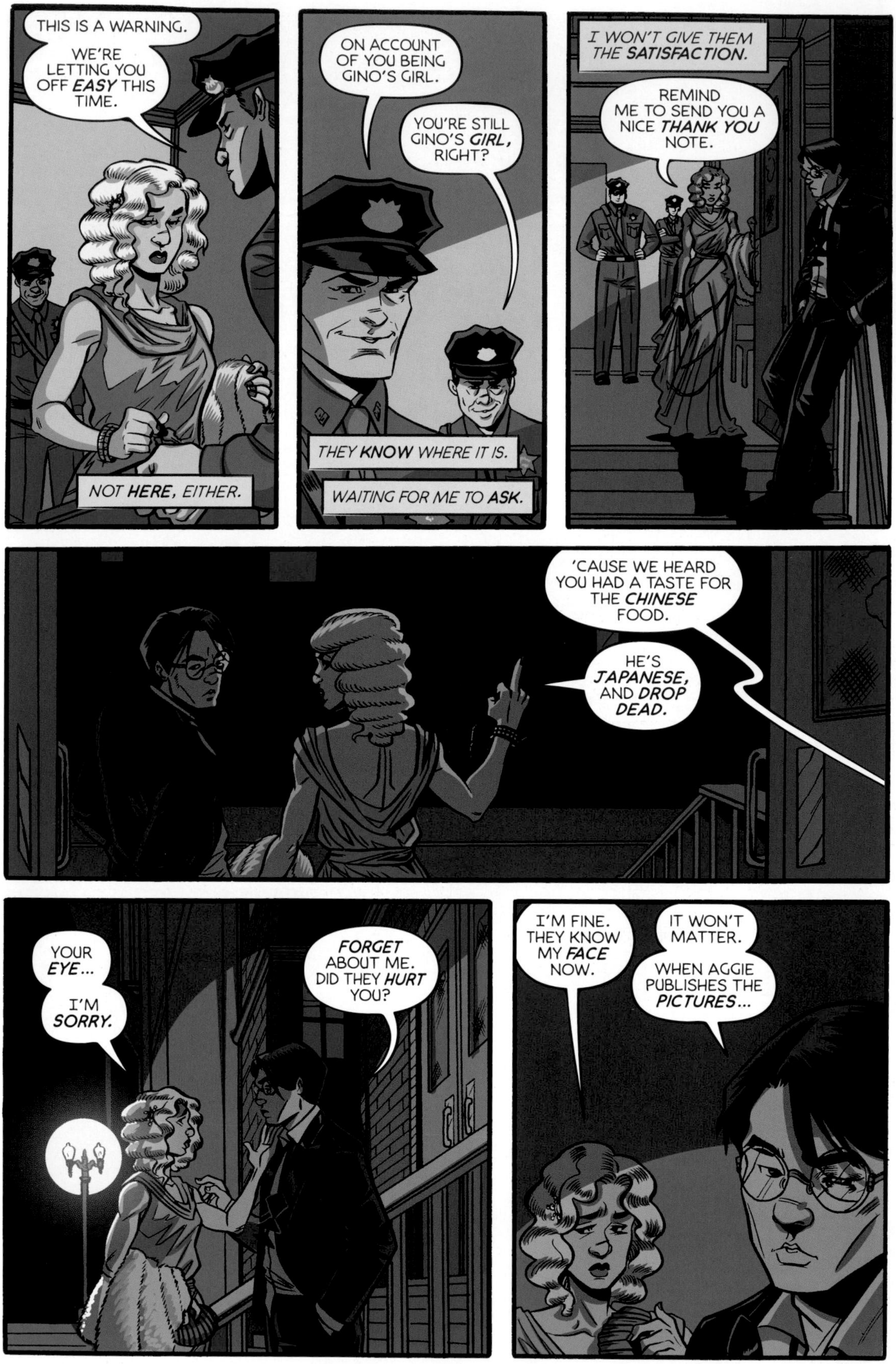
THIS IS A WARNING.
WE'RE LETTING YOU OFF *EASY* THIS TIME.
NOT **HERE**, EITHER.
ON ACCOUNT OF YOU BEING GINO'S GIRL.
YOU'RE STILL GINO'S *GIRL*, RIGHT?
THEY **KNOW** WHERE IT IS.
WAITING FOR ME TO **ASK**.
I WON'T GIVE THEM THE **SATISFACTION**.
REMIND ME TO SEND YOU A NICE *THANK YOU* NOTE.
'CAUSE WE HEARD YOU HAD A TASTE FOR THE *CHINESE* FOOD.
HE'S *JAPANESE*, AND *DROP DEAD*.
YOUR *EYE*...
I'M *SORRY*.
FORGET ABOUT ME. DID THEY *HURT* YOU?
I'M FINE. THEY KNOW MY *FACE* NOW.
IT WON'T MATTER.
WHEN AGGIE PUBLISHES THE *PICTURES*...

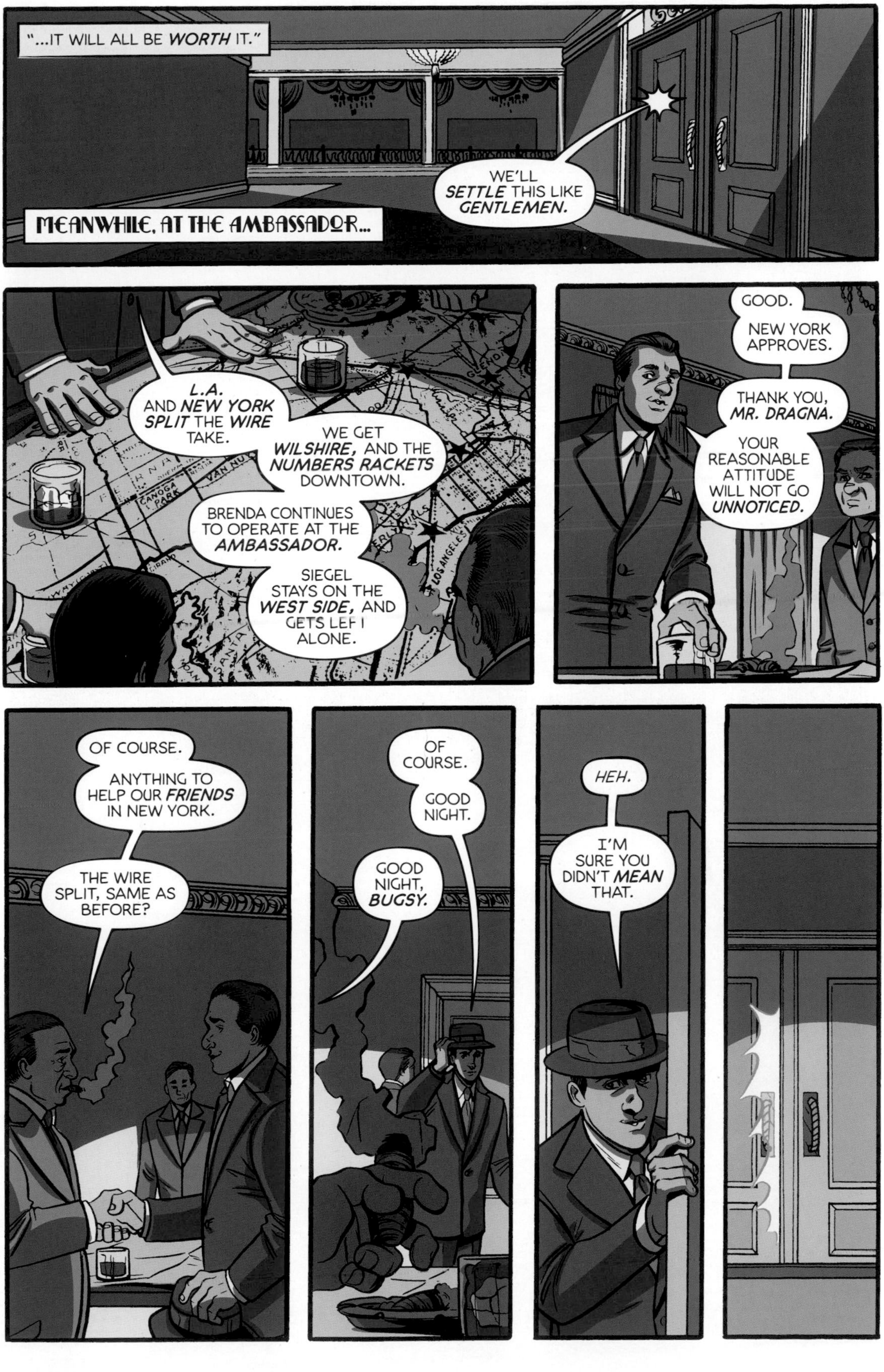
"...IT WILL ALL BE WORTH IT."
MEANWHILE, AT THE AMBASSADOR...
WE'LL SETTLE THIS LIKE GENTLEMEN.
L.A. AND NEW YORK SPLIT THE WIRE TAKE.
WE GET WILSHIRE, AND THE NUMBERS RACKETS DOWNTOWN.
BRENDA CONTINUES TO OPERATE AT THE AMBASSADOR.
SIEGEL STAYS ON THE WEST SIDE, AND GETS LEFT ALONE.
GOOD.
NEW YORK APPROVES.
THANK YOU, MR. DRAGNA.
YOUR REASONABLE ATTITUDE WILL NOT GO UNNOTICED.
OF COURSE.
ANYTHING TO HELP OUR FRIENDS IN NEW YORK.
THE WIRE SPLIT, SAME AS BEFORE?
OF COURSE.
GOOD NIGHT.
GOOD NIGHT, BUGSY.
HEH.
I'M SURE YOU DIDN'T MEAN THAT.

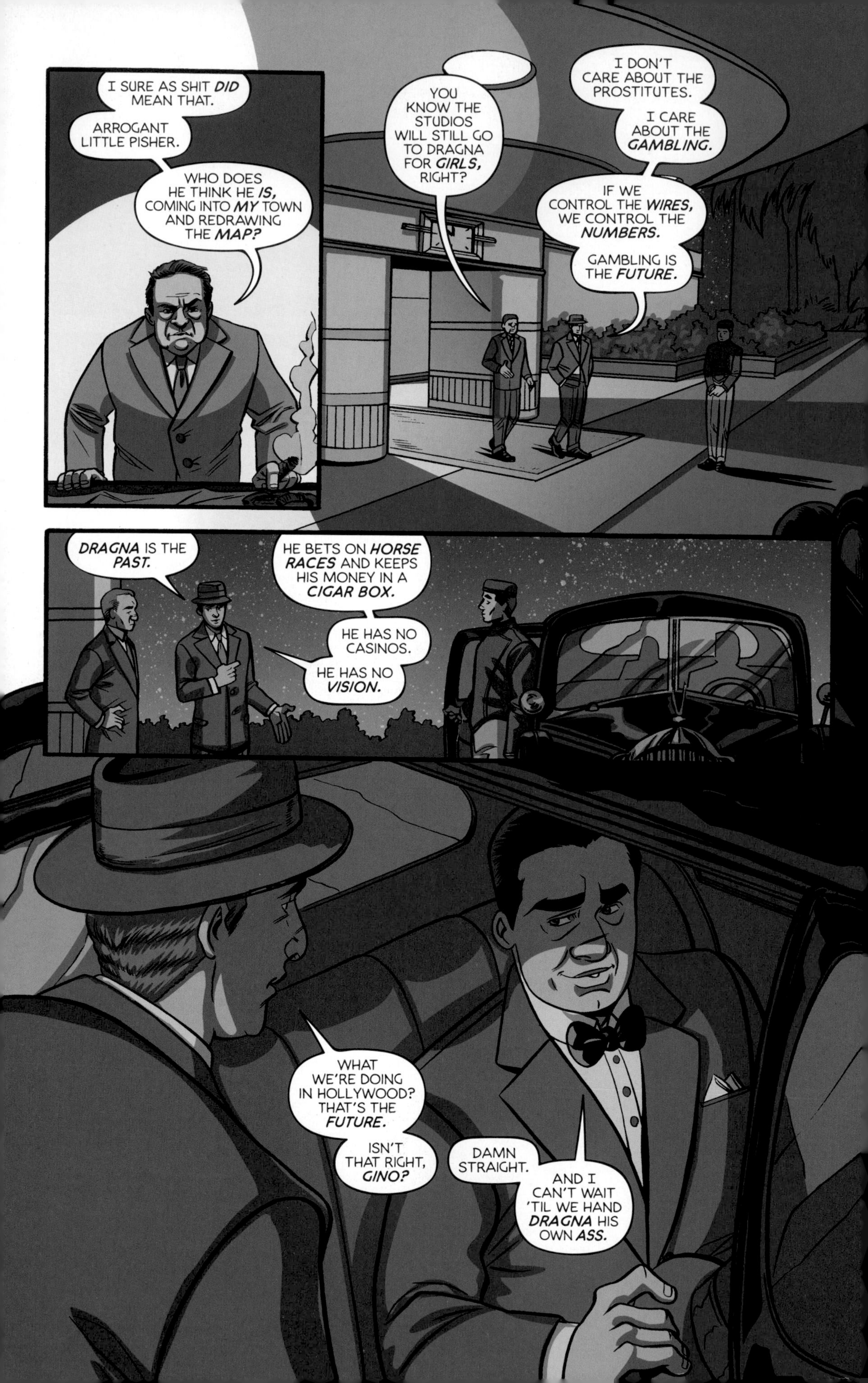
I SURE AS SHIT *DID* MEAN THAT.
ARROGANT LITTLE PISHER.
WHO DOES HE THINK HE *IS,* COMING INTO *MY* TOWN AND REDRAWING THE *MAP?*
YOU KNOW THE STUDIOS WILL STILL GO TO DRAGNA FOR *GIRLS,* RIGHT?
I DON'T CARE ABOUT THE PROSTITUTES.
I CARE ABOUT THE *GAMBLING.*
IF WE CONTROL THE *WIRES,* WE CONTROL THE *NUMBERS.*
GAMBLING IS THE *FUTURE.*
DRAGNA IS THE *PAST.*
HE BETS ON *HORSE RACES* AND KEEPS HIS MONEY IN A *CIGAR BOX.*
HE HAS NO CASINOS.
HE HAS NO *VISION.*
WHAT WE'RE DOING IN HOLLYWOOD? THAT'S THE *FUTURE.*
ISN'T THAT RIGHT, *GINO?*
DAMN STRAIGHT.
AND I CAN'T WAIT 'TIL WE HAND *DRAGNA* HIS OWN *ASS.*

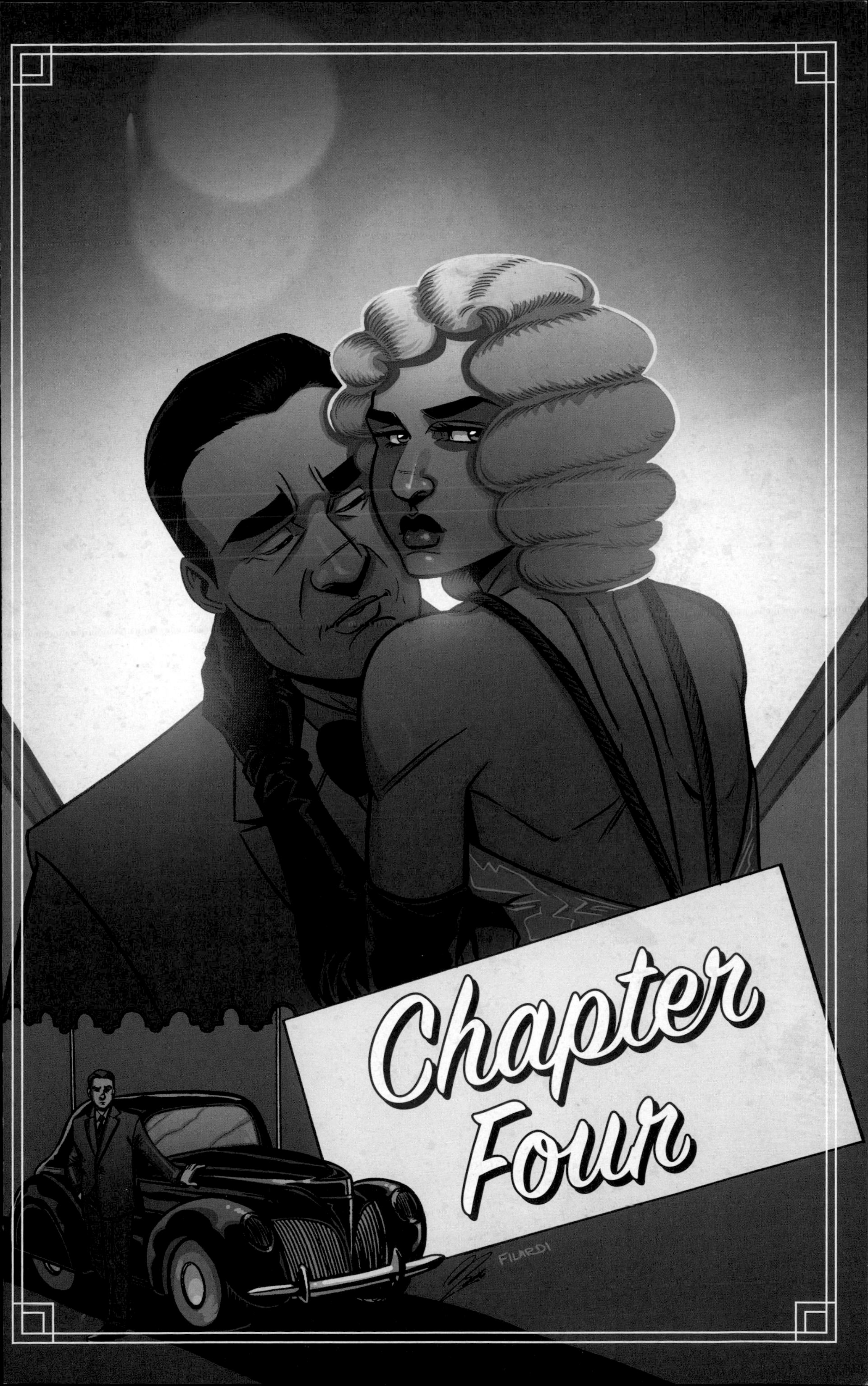
Chapter Four
FILARDI

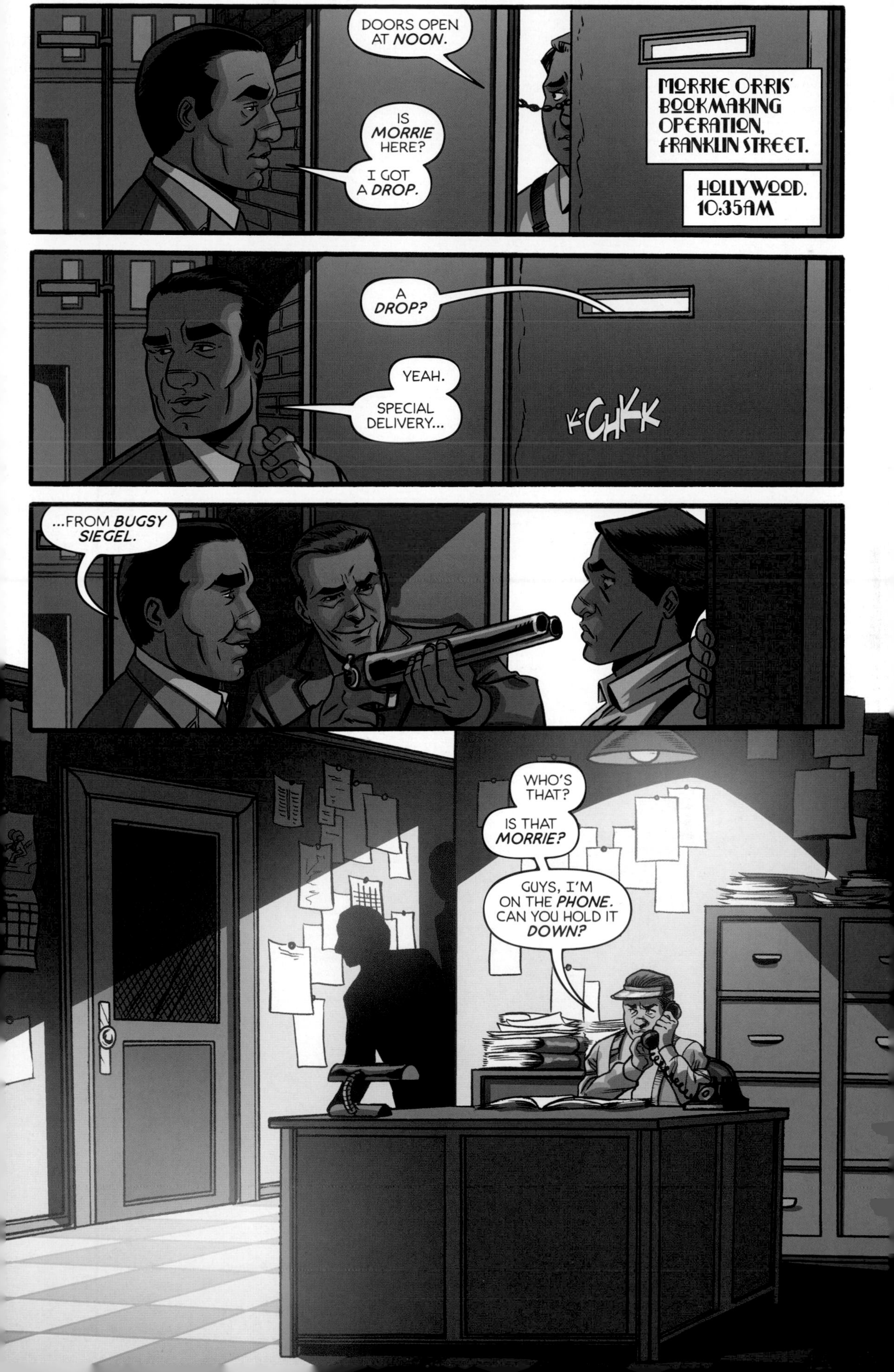
MORRIE ORRIS' BOOKMAKING OPERATION, FRANKLIN STREET.
HOLLYWOOD. 10:35AM
IS MORRIE HERE?
I GOT A DROP.
DOORS OPEN AT NOON.
A DROP?
YEAH.
SPECIAL DELIVERY...
K-CHKK
...FROM BUGSY SIEGEL.
WHO'S THAT?
IS THAT MORRIE?
GUYS, I'M ON THE PHONE. CAN YOU HOLD IT DOWN?

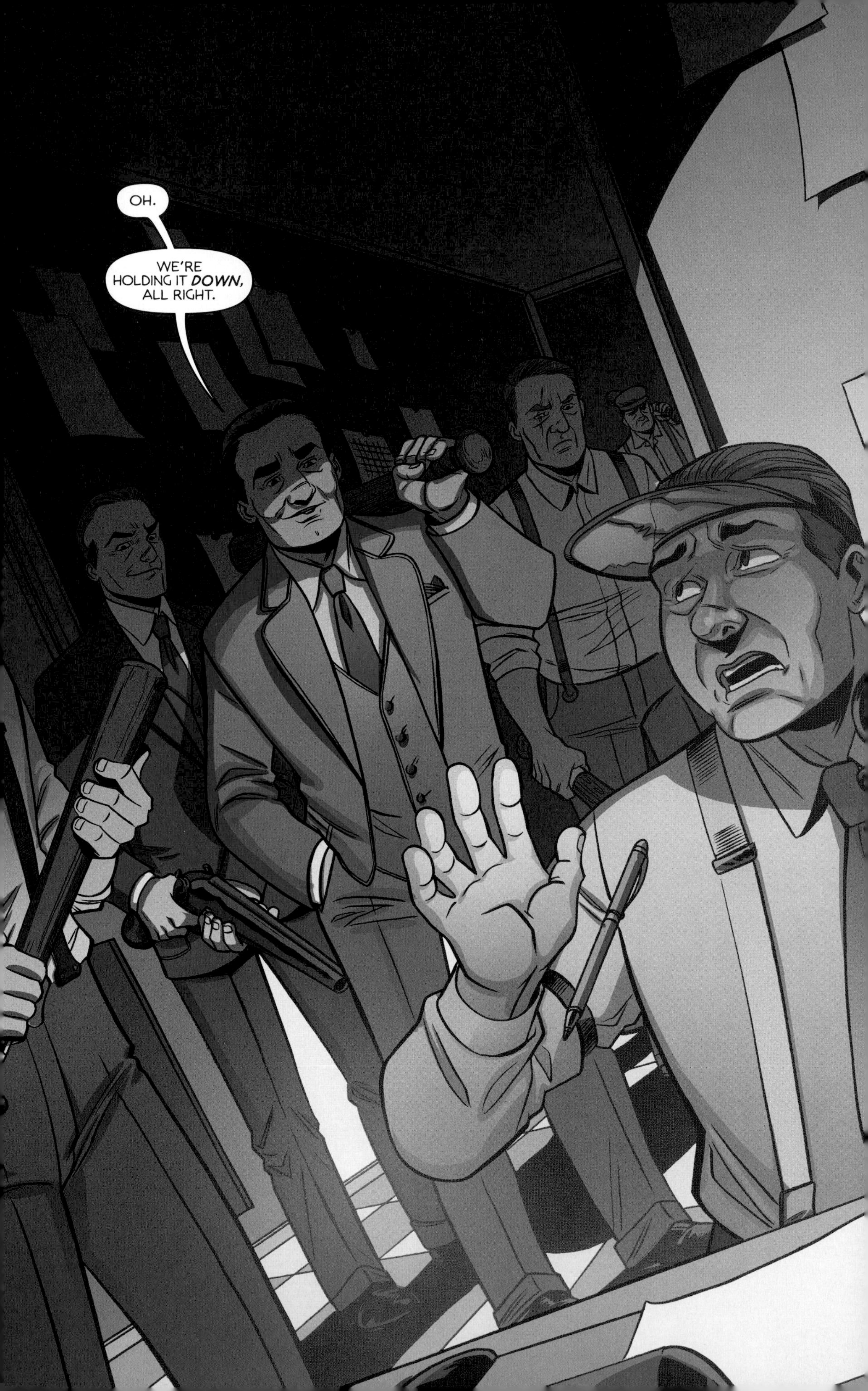
OH.
WE'RE HOLDING IT *DOWN,* ALL RIGHT.

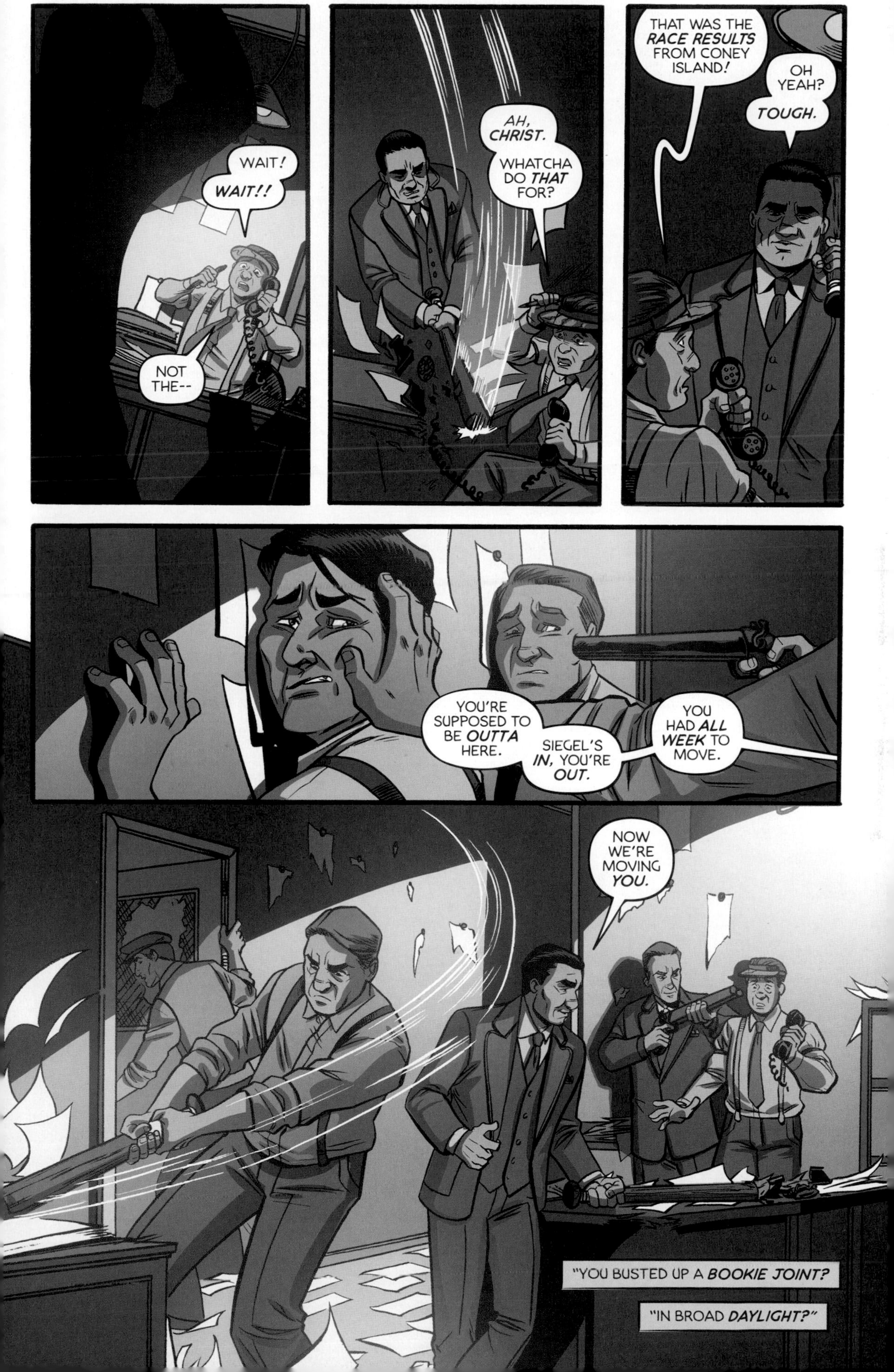
WAIT! WAIT!!
NOT THE--
AH, CHRIST.
WHATCHA DO THAT FOR?
THAT WAS THE RACE RESULTS FROM CONEY ISLAND!
OH YEAH? TOUGH.
YOU'RE SUPPOSED TO BE OUTTA HERE.
SIEGEL'S IN, YOU'RE OUT.
YOU HAD ALL WEEK TO MOVE.
NOW WE'RE MOVING YOU.
"YOU BUSTED UP A BOOKIE JOINT?
"IN BROAD DAYLIGHT?"

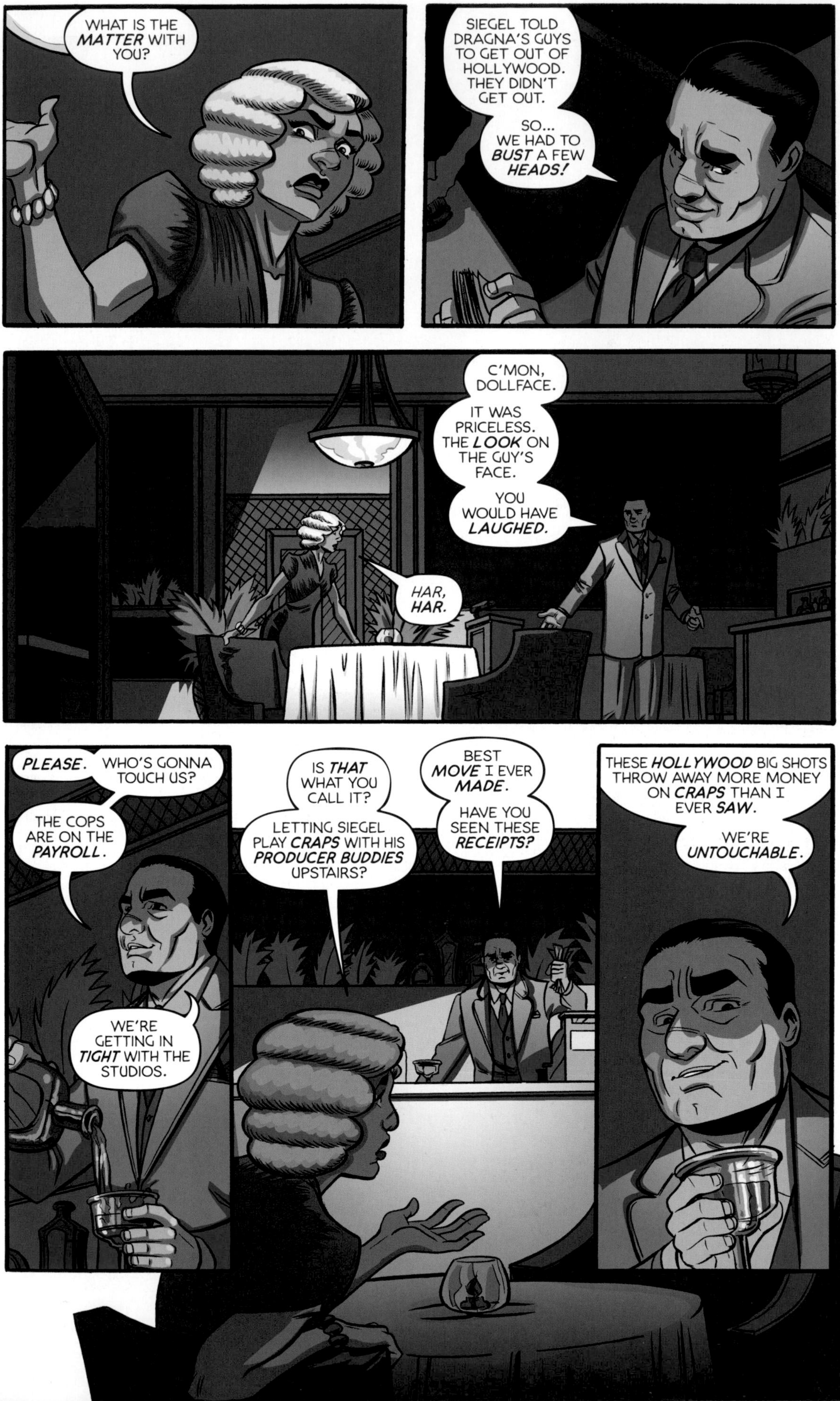

WHAT IS THE *MATTER* WITH YOU?
SIEGEL TOLD DRAGNA'S GUYS TO GET OUT OF HOLLYWOOD. THEY DIDN'T GET OUT.
SO... WE HAD TO *BUST* A FEW *HEADS!*
C'MON, DOLLFACE.
IT WAS PRICELESS. THE *LOOK* ON THE GUY'S FACE.
YOU WOULD HAVE *LAUGHED.*
HAR, HAR.
PLEASE.
WHO'S GONNA TOUCH US?
THE COPS ARE ON THE *PAYROLL*.
WE'RE GETTING IN *TIGHT* WITH THE STUDIOS.
IS *THAT* WHAT YOU CALL IT?
LETTING SIEGEL PLAY *CRAPS* WITH HIS *PRODUCER BUDDIES* UPSTAIRS?
BEST *MOVE* I EVER *MADE*.
HAVE YOU SEEN THESE *RECEIPTS?*
THESE *HOLLYWOOD* BIG SHOTS THROW AWAY MORE MONEY ON *CRAPS* THAN I EVER *SAW*.
WE'RE *UNTOUCHABLE*.

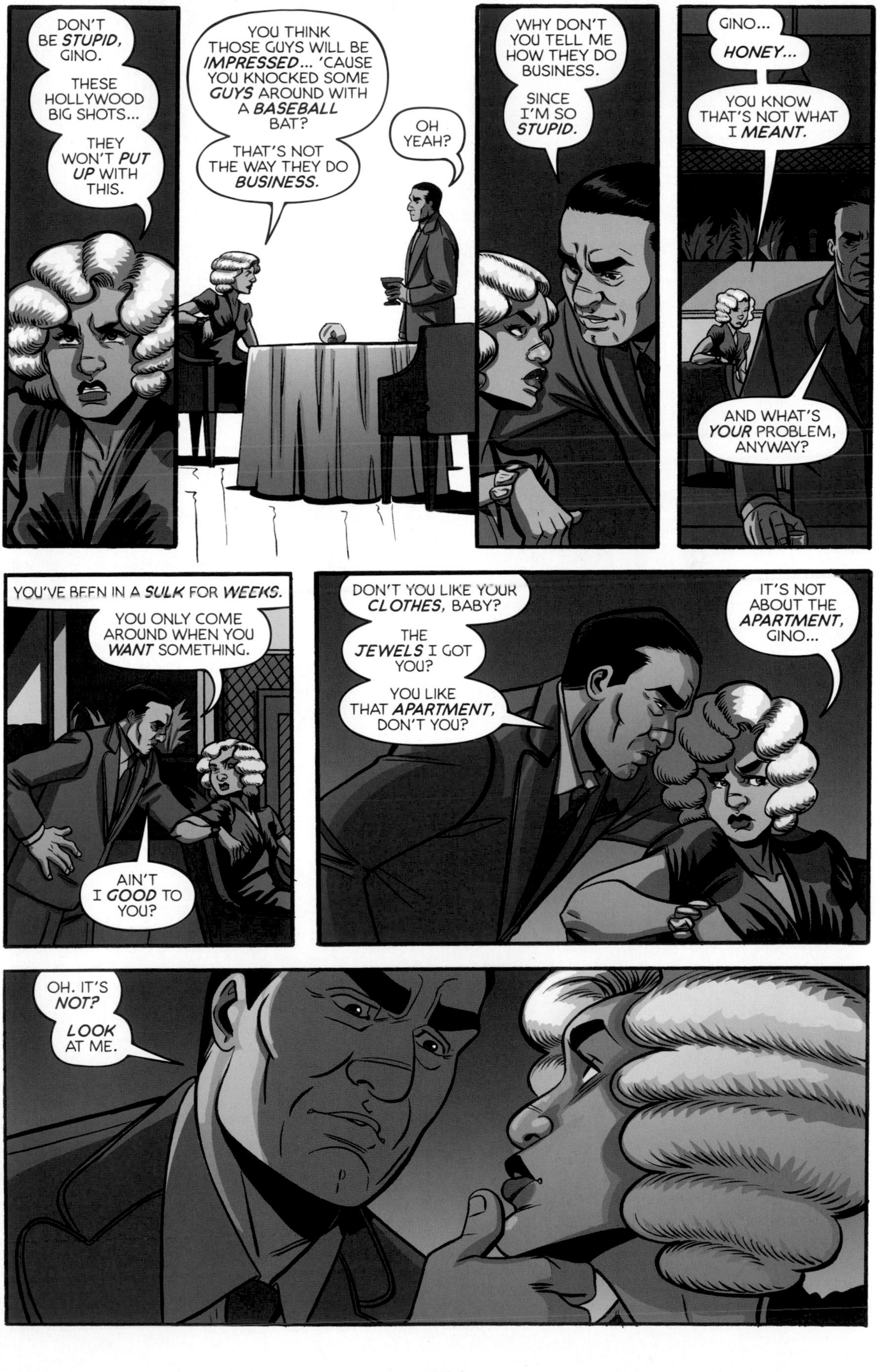
DON'T BE *STUPID*, GINO.
THESE HOLLYWOOD BIG SHOTS...
THEY WON'T *PUT UP* WITH THIS.
YOU THINK THOSE GUYS WILL BE *IMPRESSED*... 'CAUSE YOU KNOCKED SOME *GUYS* AROUND WITH A *BASEBALL* BAT?
THAT'S NOT THE WAY THEY DO *BUSINESS*.
OH YEAH?
WHY DON'T YOU TELL ME HOW THEY DO BUSINESS.
SINCE I'M SO *STUPID*.
GINO...
HONEY...
YOU KNOW THAT'S NOT WHAT I *MEANT*.
AND WHAT'S *YOUR* PROBLEM, ANYWAY?
YOU'VE BEEN IN A *SULK* FOR *WEEKS*.
YOU ONLY COME AROUND WHEN YOU *WANT* SOMETHING.
AIN'T I *GOOD* TO YOU?
DON'T YOU LIKE YOUR *CLOTHES*, BABY?
THE *JEWELS* I GOT YOU?
YOU LIKE THAT *APARTMENT*, DON'T YOU?
IT'S NOT ABOUT THE *APARTMENT*, GINO...
OH. IT'S *NOT?*
LOOK AT ME.

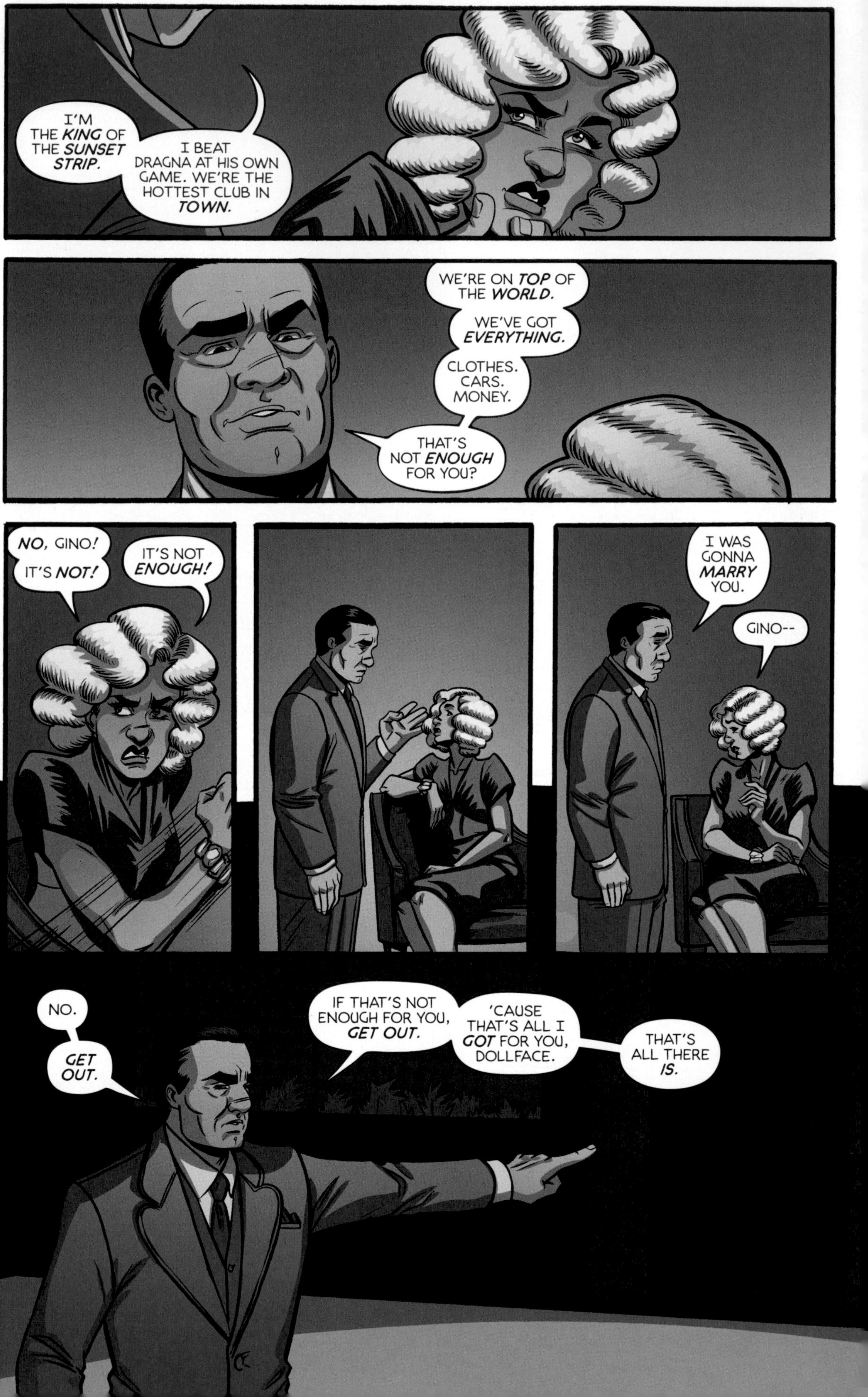
I'M THE KING OF THE SUNSET STRIP.
I BEAT DRAGNA AT HIS OWN GAME. WE'RE THE HOTTEST CLUB IN TOWN.
WE'RE ON TOP OF THE WORLD.
WE'VE GOT EVERYTHING.
CLOTHES. CARS. MONEY.
THAT'S NOT ENOUGH FOR YOU?
NO, GINO!
IT'S NOT!
IT'S NOT ENOUGH!
I WAS GONNA MARRY YOU.
GINO--
NO.
GET OUT.
IF THAT'S NOT ENOUGH FOR YOU, GET OUT.
'CAUSE THAT'S ALL I GOT FOR YOU, DOLLFACE.
THAT'S ALL THERE IS.

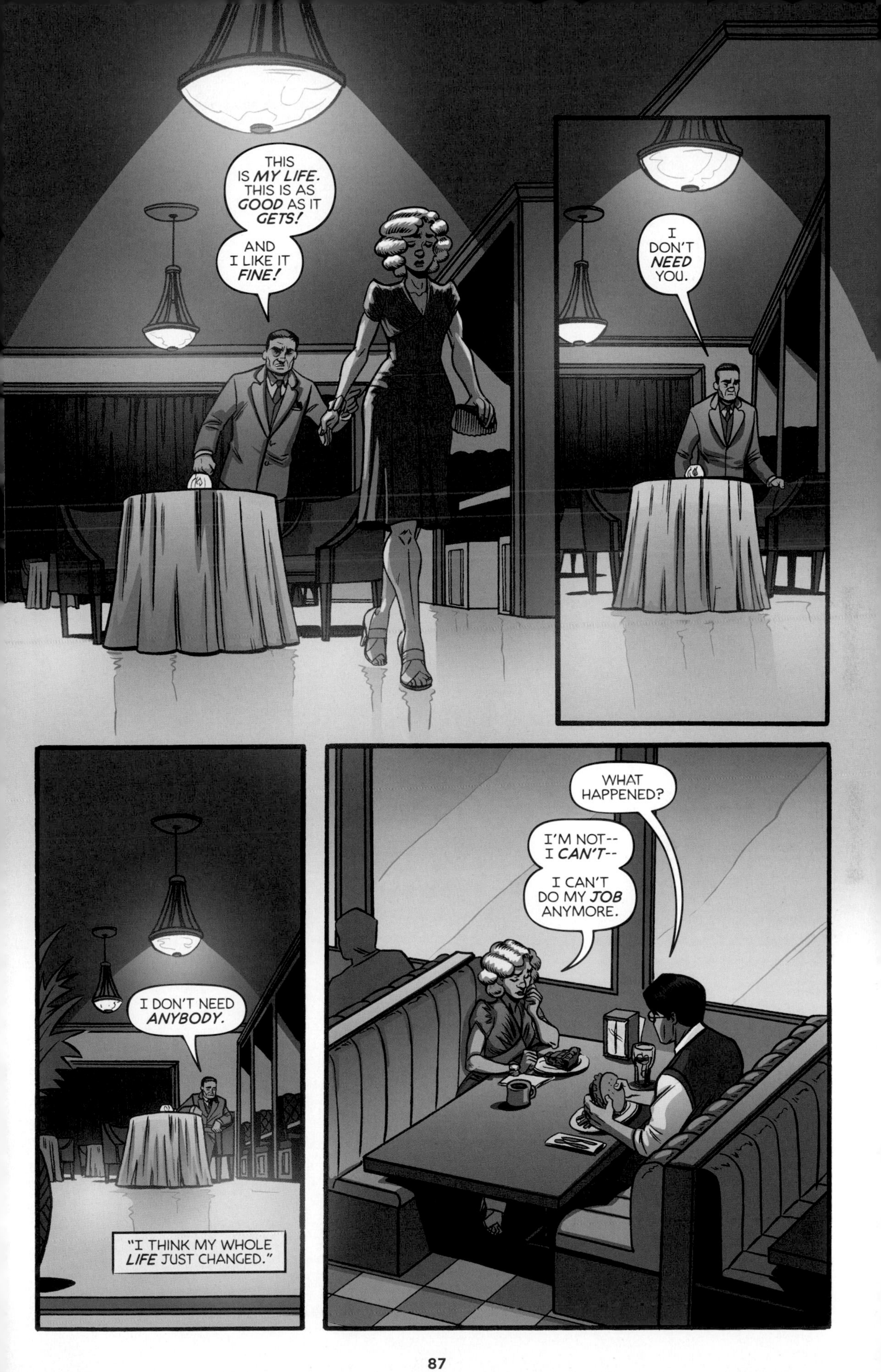
THIS IS MY LIFE. THIS IS AS GOOD AS IT GETS!
AND I LIKE IT FINE!
I DON'T NEED YOU.
I DON'T NEED ANYBODY.
"I THINK MY WHOLE LIFE JUST CHANGED."
WHAT HAPPENED?
I'M NOT-- I CAN'T--
I CAN'T DO MY JOB ANYMORE.

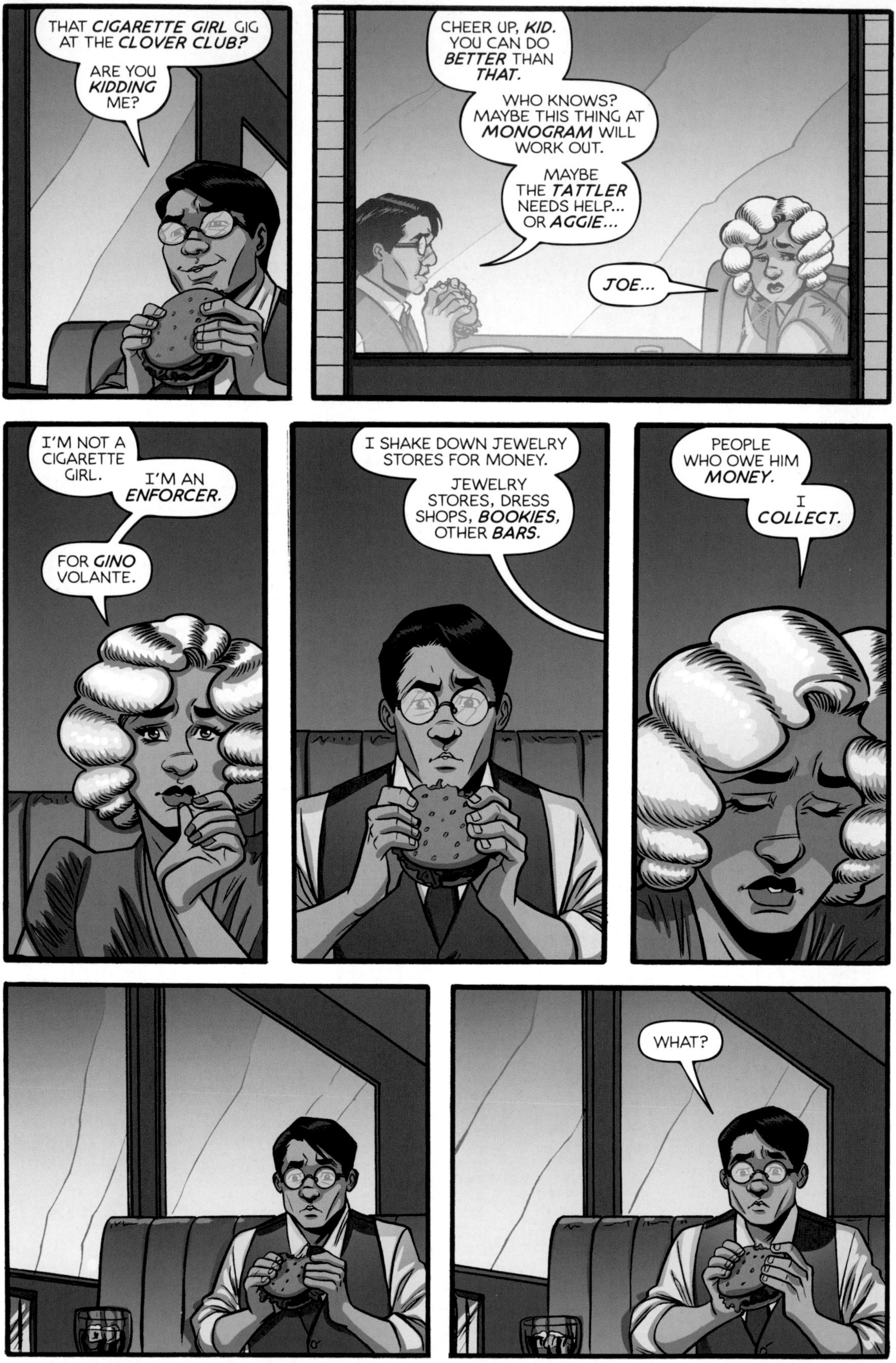
THAT CIGARETTE GIRL GIG AT THE CLOVER CLUB?
ARE YOU KIDDING ME?
CHEER UP, KID. YOU CAN DO BETTER THAN THAT.
WHO KNOWS? MAYBE THIS THING AT MONOGRAM WILL WORK OUT.
MAYBE THE TATTLER NEEDS HELP... OR AGGIE...
JOE...
I'M NOT A CIGARETTE GIRL.
I'M AN ENFORCER.
FOR GINO VOLANTE.
I SHAKE DOWN JEWELRY STORES FOR MONEY.
JEWELRY STORES, DRESS SHOPS, BOOKIES, OTHER BARS.
PEOPLE WHO OWE HIM MONEY.
I COLLECT.
WHAT?

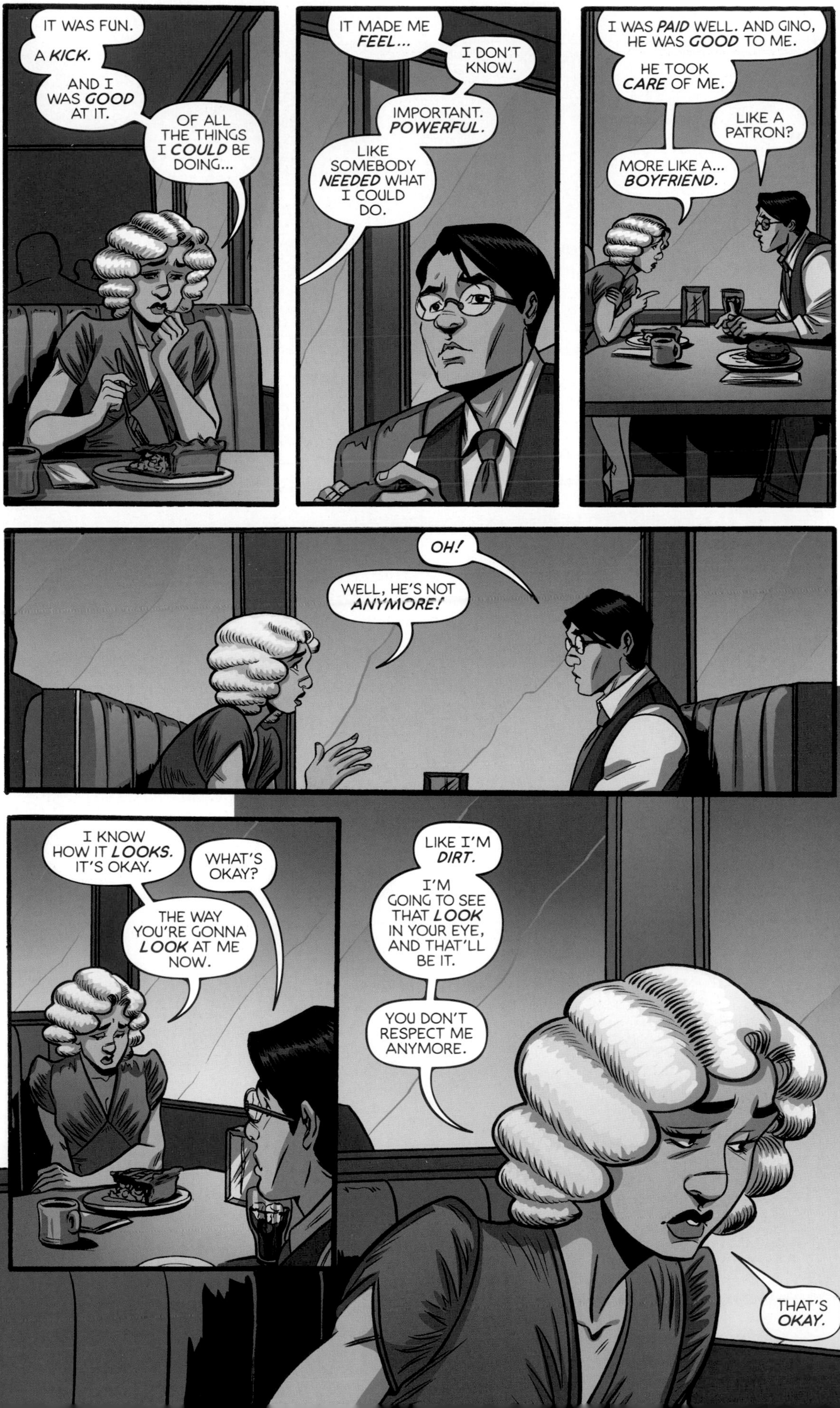

IT WAS FUN.
A KICK.
AND I WAS GOOD AT IT.
OF ALL THE THINGS I COULD BE DOING...
IT MADE ME FEEL...
I DON'T KNOW.
IMPORTANT. POWERFUL.
LIKE SOMEBODY NEEDED WHAT I COULD DO.
I WAS PAID WELL. AND GINO, HE WAS GOOD TO ME.
HE TOOK CARE OF ME.
LIKE A PATRON?
MORE LIKE A... BOYFRIEND.
OH!
WELL, HE'S NOT ANYMORE!
I KNOW HOW IT LOOKS. IT'S OKAY.
WHAT'S OKAY?
THE WAY YOU'RE GONNA LOOK AT ME NOW.
LIKE I'M DIRT.
I'M GOING TO SEE THAT LOOK IN YOUR EYE, AND THAT'LL BE IT.
YOU DON'T RESPECT ME ANYMORE.
THAT'S OKAY.

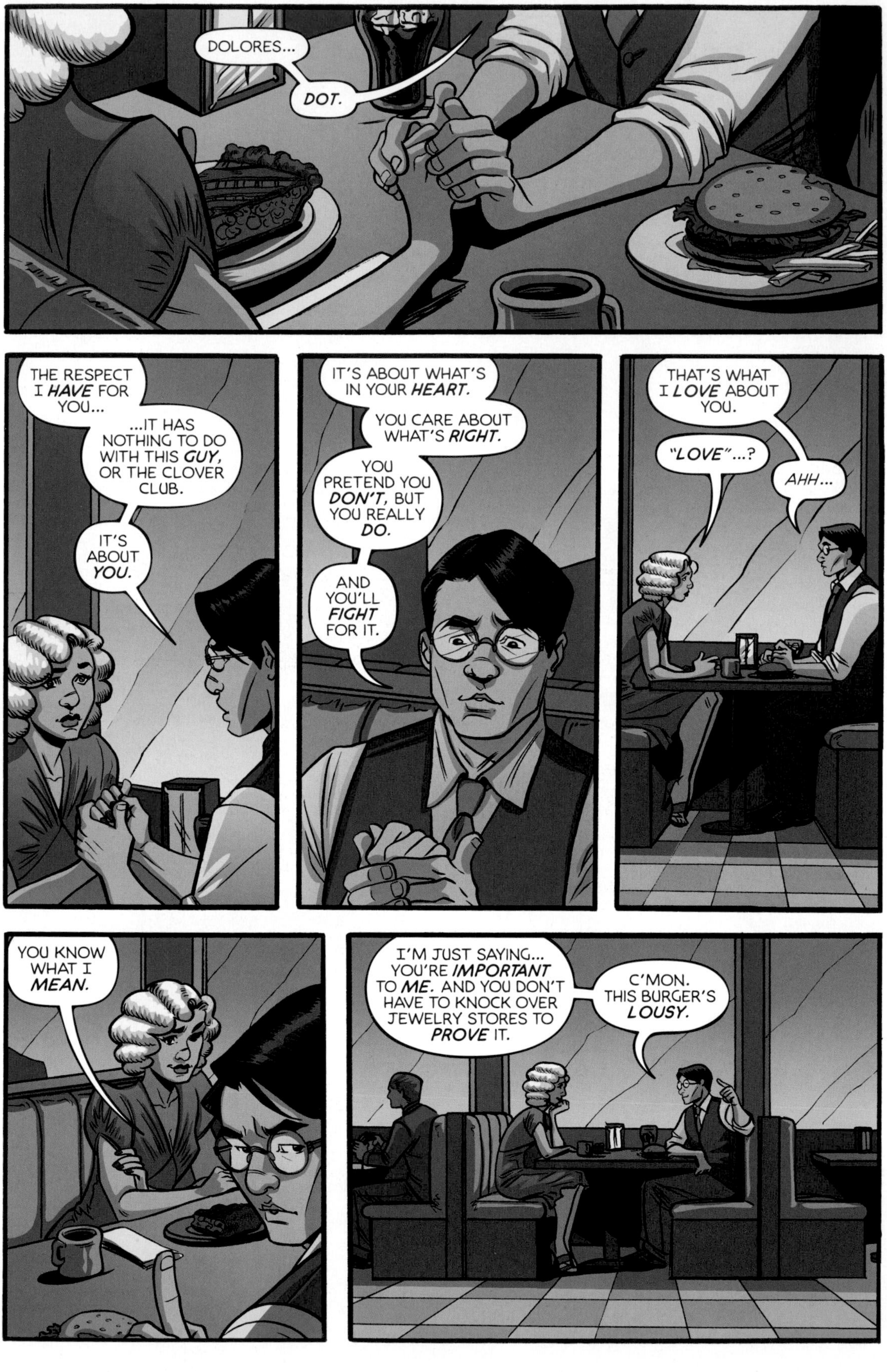
DOLORES...
DOT.
THE RESPECT I HAVE FOR YOU...
...IT HAS NOTHING TO DO WITH THIS GUY, OR THE CLOVER CLUB.
IT'S ABOUT YOU.
IT'S ABOUT WHAT'S IN YOUR HEART.
YOU CARE ABOUT WHAT'S RIGHT.
YOU PRETEND YOU DON'T, BUT YOU REALLY DO.
AND YOU'LL FIGHT FOR IT.
THAT'S WHAT I LOVE ABOUT YOU.
"LOVE"...?
AHH...
YOU KNOW WHAT I MEAN.
I'M JUST SAYING... YOU'RE IMPORTANT TO ME. AND YOU DON'T HAVE TO KNOCK OVER JEWELRY STORES TO PROVE IT.
C'MON. THIS BURGER'S LOUSY.

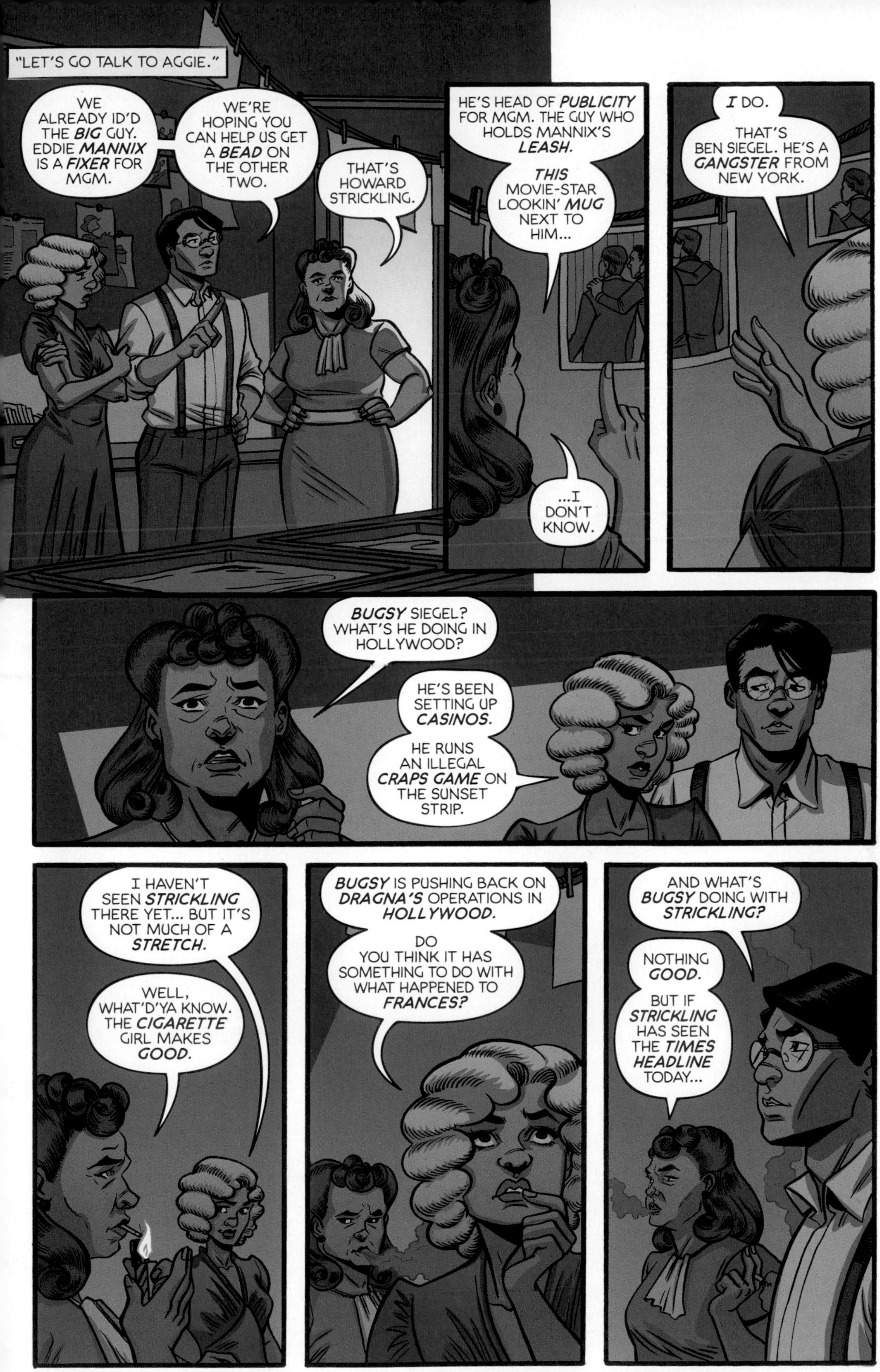
"LET'S GO TALK TO AGGIE."
WE ALREADY ID'D THE BIG GUY. EDDIE MANNIX IS A FIXER FOR MGM.
WE'RE HOPING YOU CAN HELP US GET A BEAD ON THE OTHER TWO.
THAT'S HOWARD STRICKLING.
HE'S HEAD OF PUBLICITY FOR MGM. THE GUY WHO HOLDS MANNIX'S LEASH.
THIS MOVIE-STAR LOOKIN' MUG NEXT TO HIM...
...I DON'T KNOW.
I DO.
THAT'S BEN SIEGEL. HE'S A GANGSTER FROM NEW YORK.
BUGSY SIEGEL? WHAT'S HE DOING IN HOLLYWOOD?
HE'S BEEN SETTING UP CASINOS.
HE RUNS AN ILLEGAL CRAPS GAME ON THE SUNSET STRIP.
I HAVEN'T SEEN STRICKLING THERE YET... BUT IT'S NOT MUCH OF A STRETCH.
WELL, WHAT'D'YA KNOW. THE CIGARETTE GIRL MAKES GOOD.
BUGSY IS PUSHING BACK ON DRAGNA'S OPERATIONS IN HOLLYWOOD.
DO YOU THINK IT HAS SOMETHING TO DO WITH WHAT HAPPENED TO FRANCES?
AND WHAT'S BUGSY DOING WITH STRICKLING?
NOTHING GOOD.
BUT IF STRICKLING HAS SEEN THE TIMES HEADLINE TODAY...

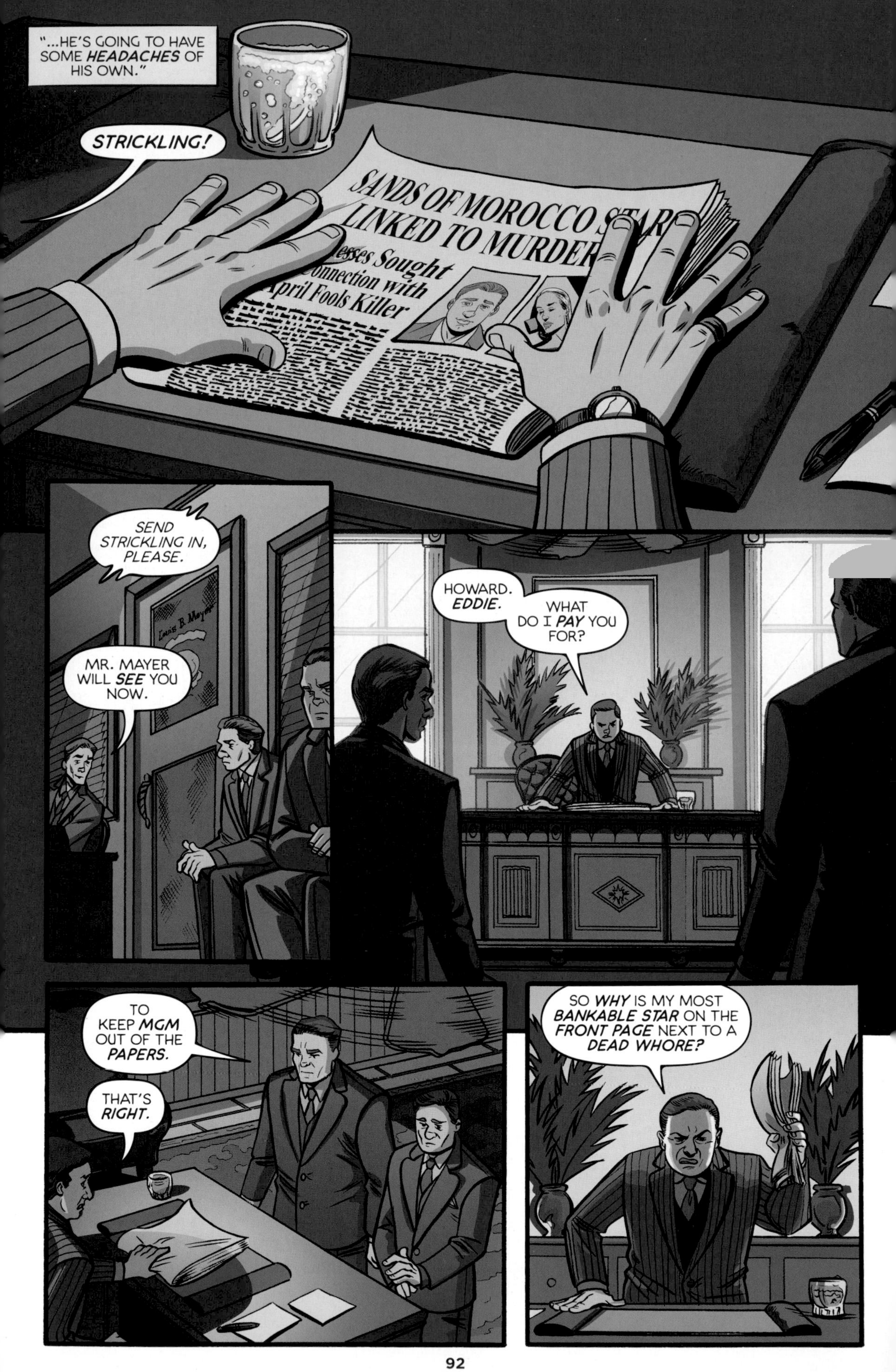
"...HE'S GOING TO HAVE SOME *HEADACHES* OF HIS OWN."
STRICKLING!
SANDS OF MOROCCO STAR
LINKED TO MURDER
Connection with
April Fools Killer
SEND STRICKLING IN, PLEASE.
MR. MAYER WILL *SEE* YOU NOW.
HOWARD. *EDDIE.*
WHAT DO I *PAY* YOU FOR?
TO KEEP *MGM* OUT OF THE *PAPERS.*
THAT'S *RIGHT.*
SO *WHY* IS MY MOST *BANKABLE STAR* ON THE *FRONT PAGE* NEXT TO A *DEAD WHORE?*

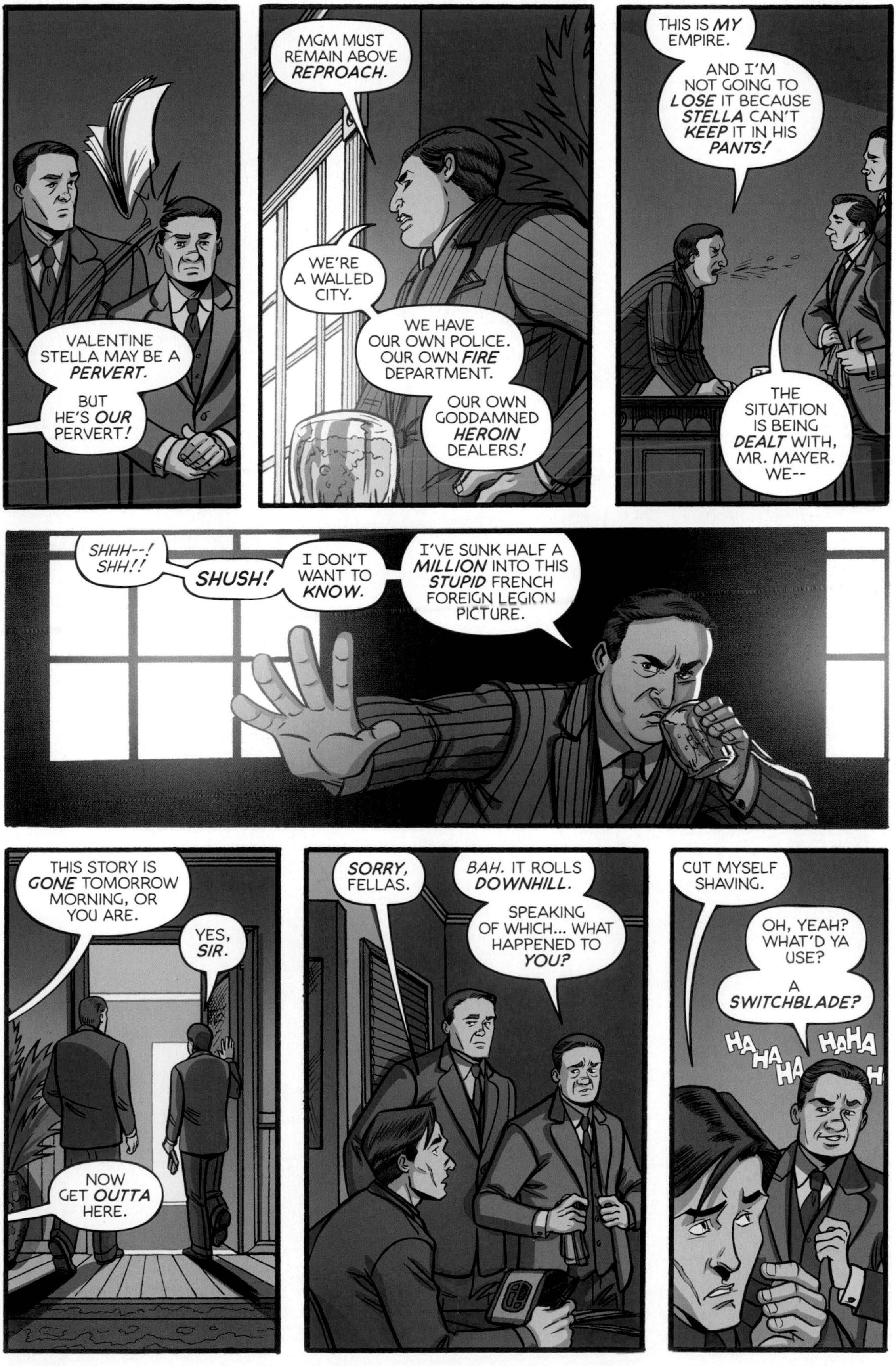
VALENTINE STELLA MAY BE A PERVERT.
BUT HE'S OUR PERVERT!
MGM MUST REMAIN ABOVE REPROACH.
WE'RE A WALLED CITY.
WE HAVE OUR OWN POLICE. OUR OWN FIRE DEPARTMENT.
OUR OWN GODDAMNED HEROIN DEALERS!
THIS IS MY EMPIRE.
AND I'M NOT GOING TO LOSE IT BECAUSE STELLA CAN'T KEEP IT IN HIS PANTS!
THE SITUATION IS BEING DEALT WITH, MR. MAYER. WE--
SHHH--! SHH!!
SHUSH!
I DON'T WANT TO KNOW.
I'VE SUNK HALF A MILLION INTO THIS STUPID FRENCH FOREIGN LEGION PICTURE.
THIS STORY IS GONE TOMORROW MORNING, OR YOU ARE.
YES, SIR.
NOW GET OUTTA HERE.
SORRY, FELLAS.
BAH. IT ROLLS DOWNHILL.
SPEAKING OF WHICH... WHAT HAPPENED TO YOU?
CUT MYSELF SHAVING.
OH, YEAH? WHAT'D YA USE?
A SWITCHBLADE?
HAHA HA HAHA

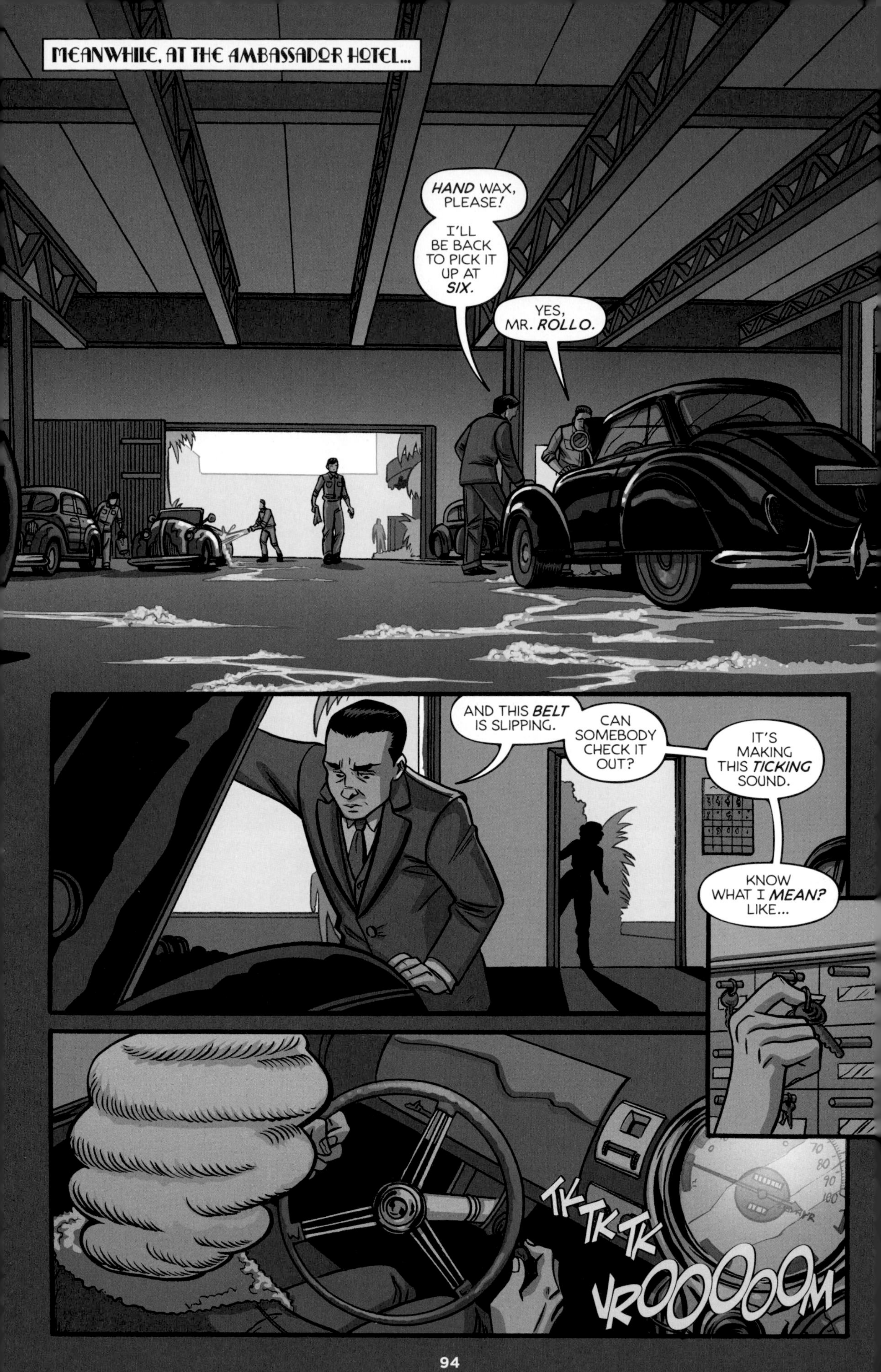
MEANWHILE, AT THE AMBASSADOR HOTEL...
HAND WAX, PLEASE!
I'LL BE BACK TO PICK IT UP AT SIX.
YES, MR. ROLLO.
AND THIS BELT IS SLIPPING.
CAN SOMEBODY CHECK IT OUT?
IT'S MAKING THIS TICKING SOUND.
KNOW WHAT I MEAN? LIKE...
TK TK TK
VROOOOOOM

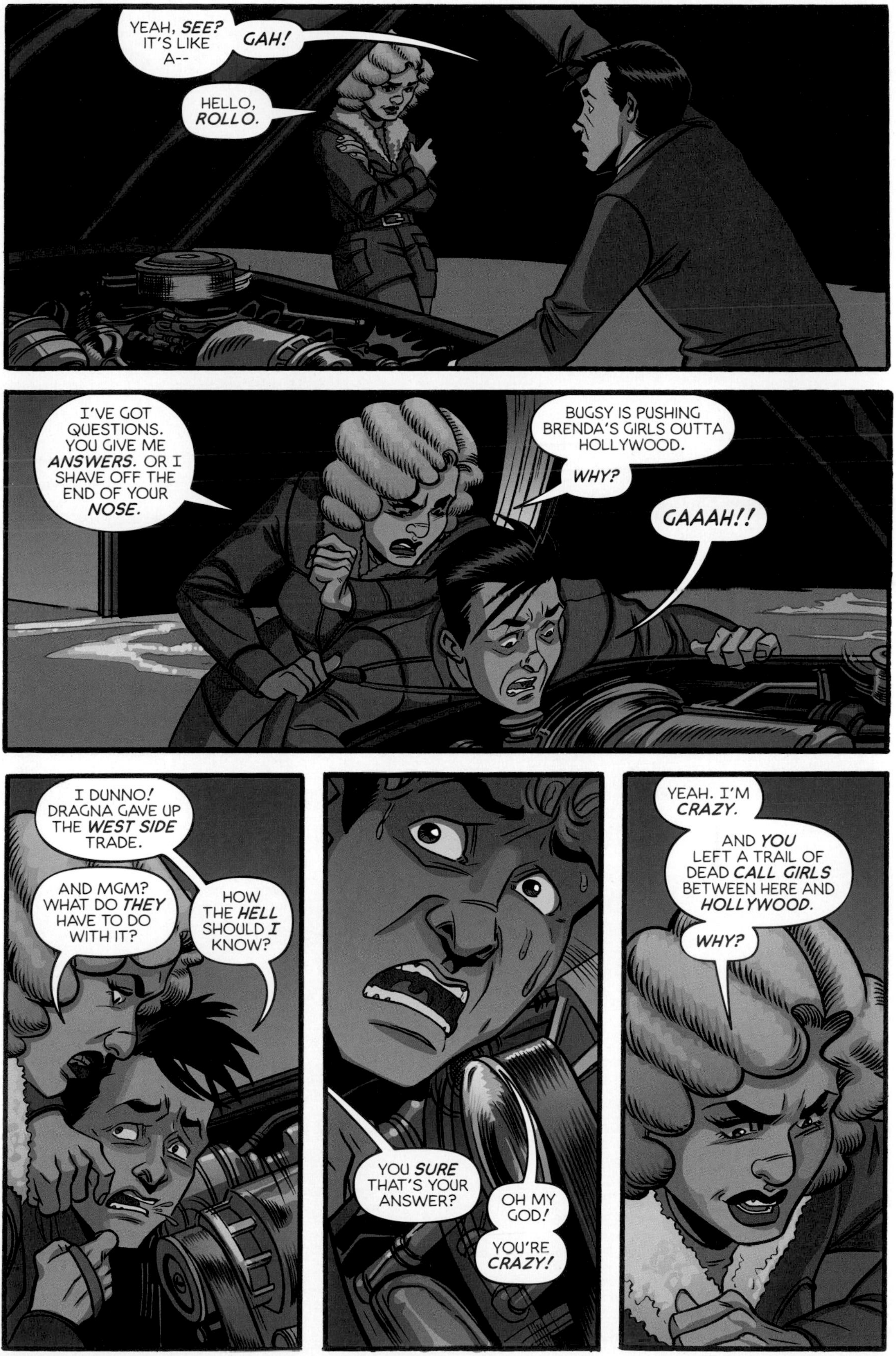
YEAH, SEE? IT'S LIKE A--
GAH!
HELLO, ROLLO.
I'VE GOT QUESTIONS. YOU GIVE ME ANSWERS. OR I SHAVE OFF THE END OF YOUR NOSE.
BUGSY IS PUSHING BRENDA'S GIRLS OUTTA HOLLYWOOD.
WHY?
GAAAH!!
I DUNNO! DRAGNA GAVE UP THE WEST SIDE TRADE.
AND MGM? WHAT DO THEY HAVE TO DO WITH IT?
HOW THE HELL SHOULD I KNOW?
YOU SURE THAT'S YOUR ANSWER?
OH MY GOD!
YOU'RE CRAZY!
YEAH. I'M CRAZY.
AND YOU LEFT A TRAIL OF DEAD CALL GIRLS BETWEEN HERE AND HOLLYWOOD.
WHY?

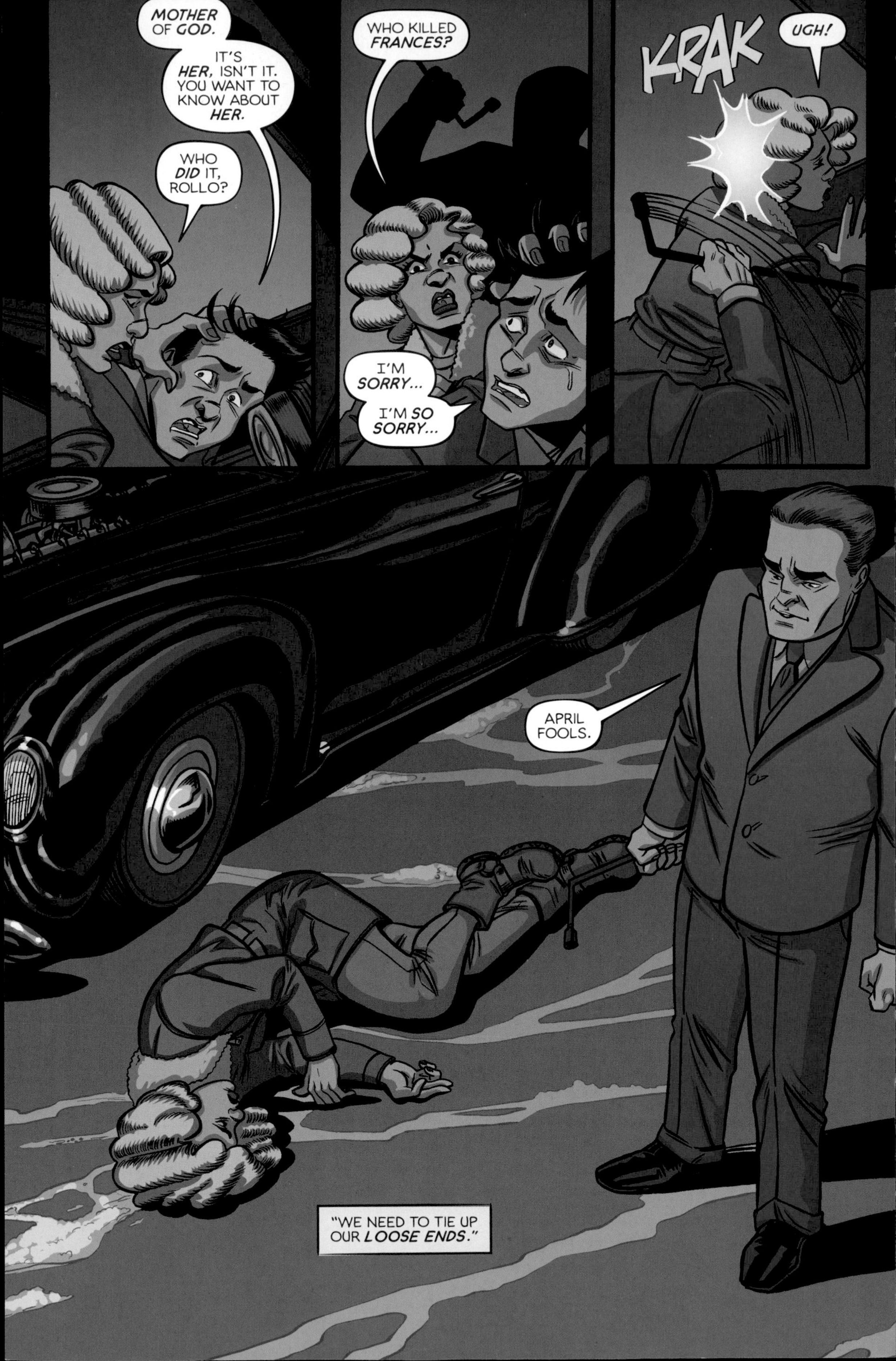
MOTHER OF GOD.
IT'S HER, ISN'T IT. YOU WANT TO KNOW ABOUT HER.
WHO DID IT, ROLLO?
WHO KILLED FRANCES?
I'M SORRY...
I'M SO SORRY...
KRAK
UGH!
APRIL FOOLS.
"WE NEED TO TIE UP OUR LOOSE ENDS."

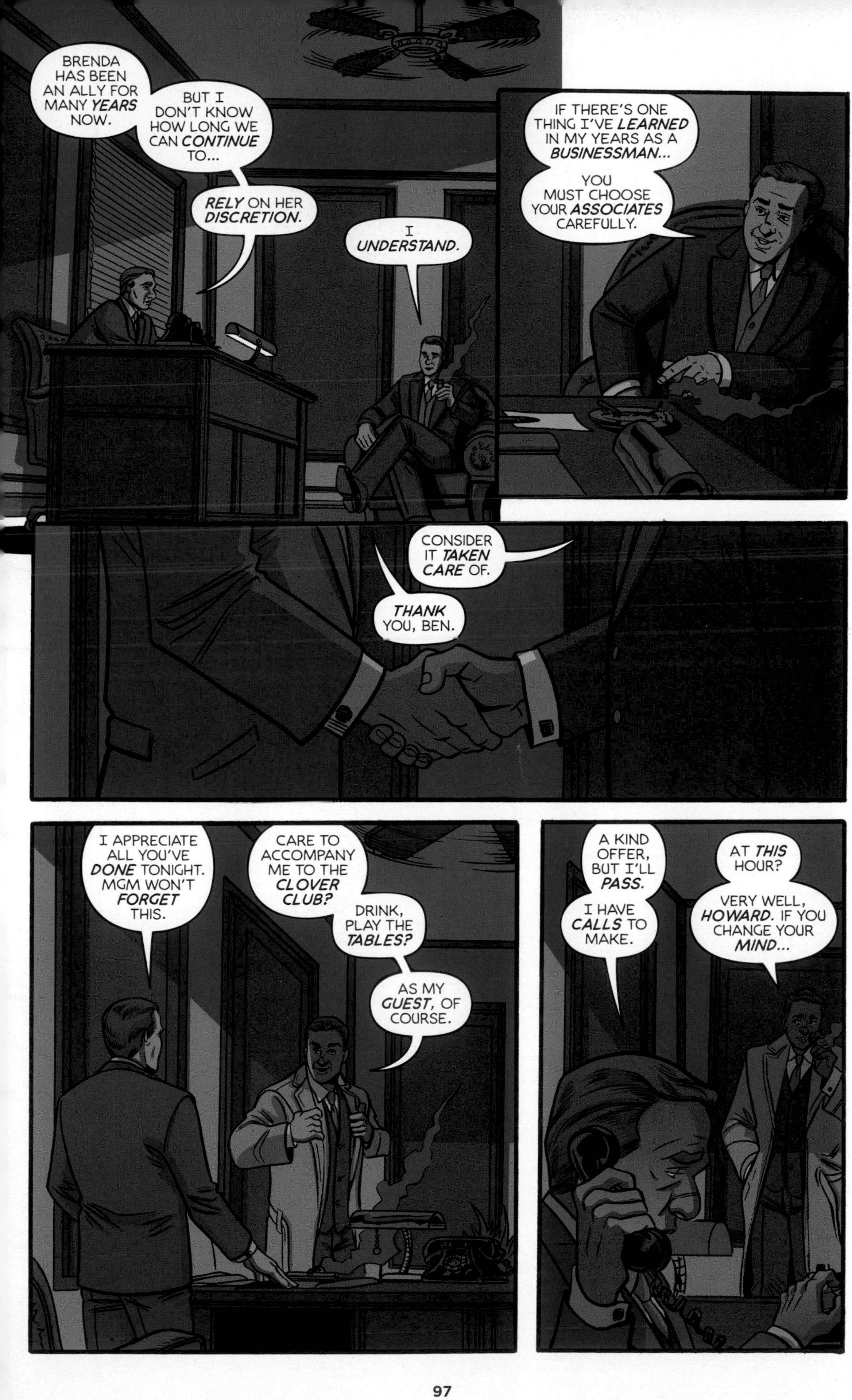
BRENDA HAS BEEN AN ALLY FOR MANY *YEARS* NOW.
BUT I DON'T KNOW HOW LONG WE CAN *CONTINUE* TO...
RELY ON HER *DISCRETION.*
I *UNDERSTAND.*
IF THERE'S ONE THING I'VE *LEARNED* IN MY YEARS AS A *BUSINESSMAN...*
YOU MUST CHOOSE YOUR *ASSOCIATES* CAREFULLY.
CONSIDER IT *TAKEN CARE* OF.
THANK YOU, BEN.
I APPRECIATE ALL YOU'VE *DONE* TONIGHT. MGM WON'T *FORGET* THIS.
CARE TO ACCOMPANY ME TO THE *CLOVER CLUB?*
DRINK, PLAY THE *TABLES?*
AS MY *GUEST*, OF COURSE.
A KIND OFFER, BUT I'LL *PASS.*
I HAVE *CALLS* TO MAKE.
AT *THIS* HOUR?
VERY WELL, *HOWARD.* IF YOU CHANGE YOUR *MIND...*

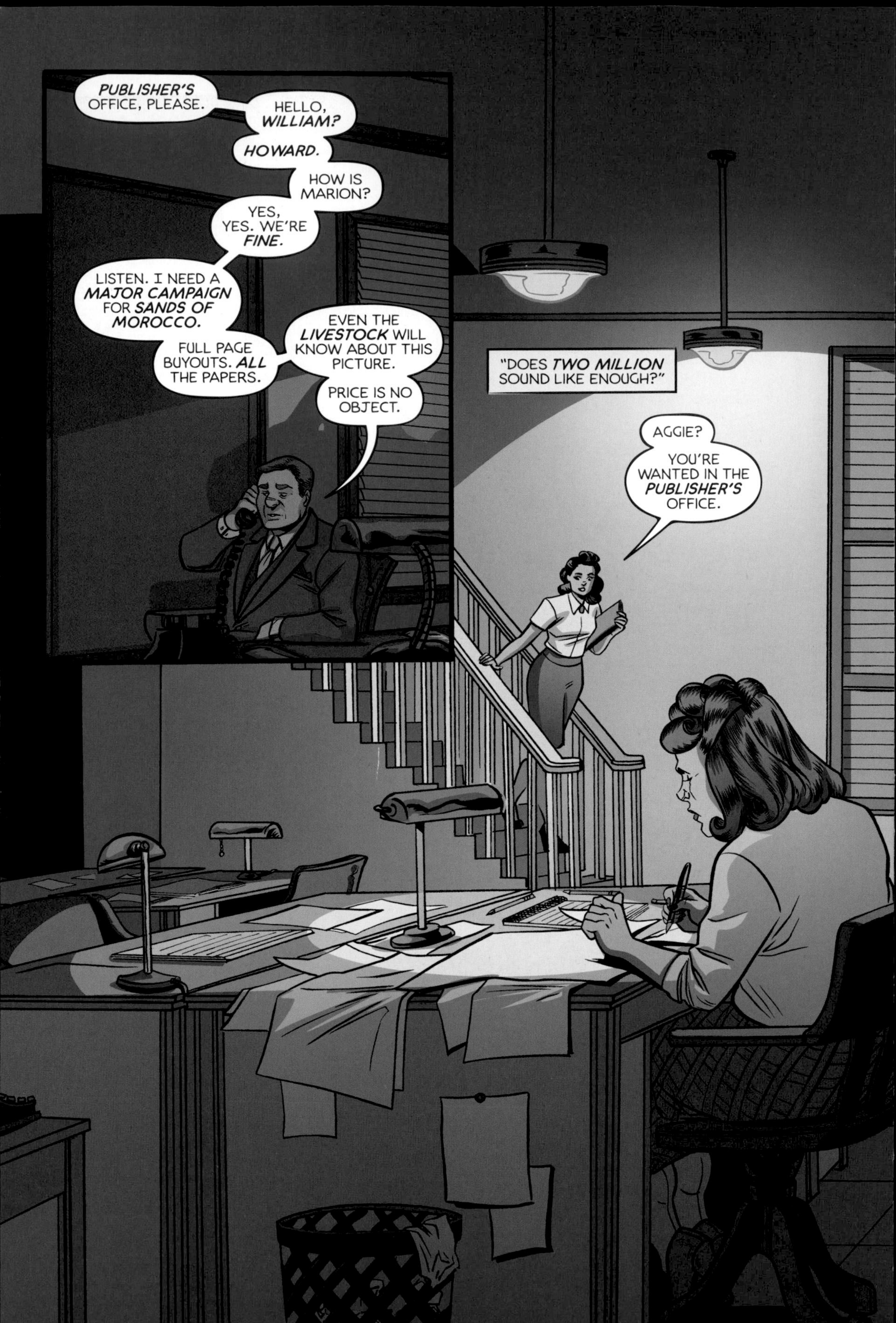
PUBLISHER'S OFFICE, PLEASE.
HELLO, WILLIAM?
HOWARD.
HOW IS MARION?
YES, YES. WE'RE FINE.
LISTEN. I NEED A MAJOR CAMPAIGN FOR SANDS OF MOROCCO.
FULL PAGE BUYOUTS. ALL THE PAPERS.
EVEN THE LIVESTOCK WILL KNOW ABOUT THIS PICTURE.
PRICE IS NO OBJECT.
"DOES TWO MILLION SOUND LIKE ENOUGH?"
AGGIE?
YOU'RE WANTED IN THE PUBLISHER'S OFFICE.

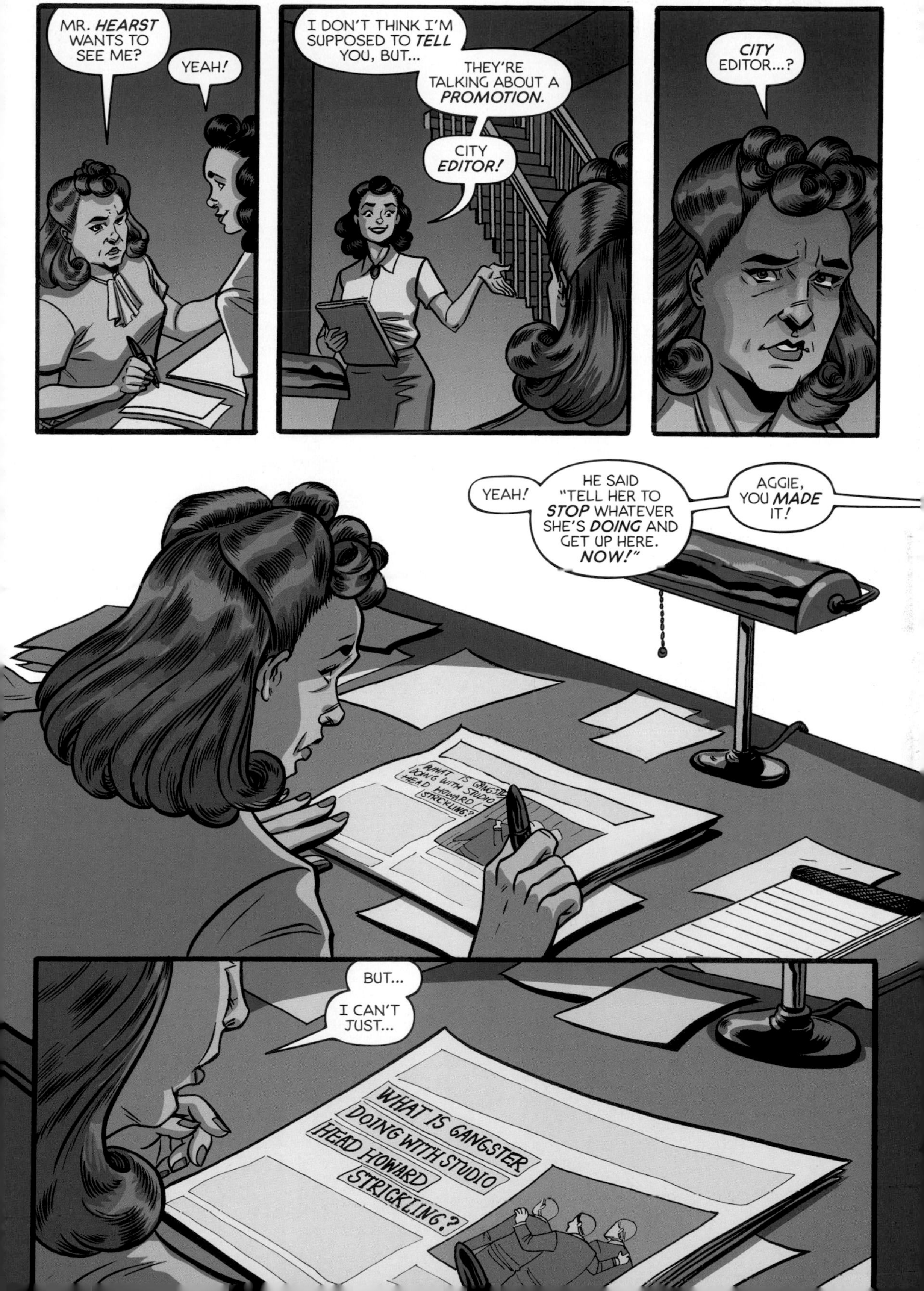

MR. HEARST WANTS TO SEE ME?
YEAH!
I DON'T THINK I'M SUPPOSED TO TELL YOU, BUT...
THEY'RE TALKING ABOUT A PROMOTION.
CITY EDITOR!
CITY EDITOR...?
YEAH!
HE SAID "TELL HER TO STOP WHATEVER SHE'S DOING AND GET UP HERE. NOW!"
AGGIE, YOU MADE IT!
WHAT IS GANGSTER DOING WITH STUDIO HEAD HOWARD STRICKLING?
BUT...
I CAN'T JUST...
WHAT IS GANGSTER DOING WITH STUDIO HEAD HOWARD STRICKLING?

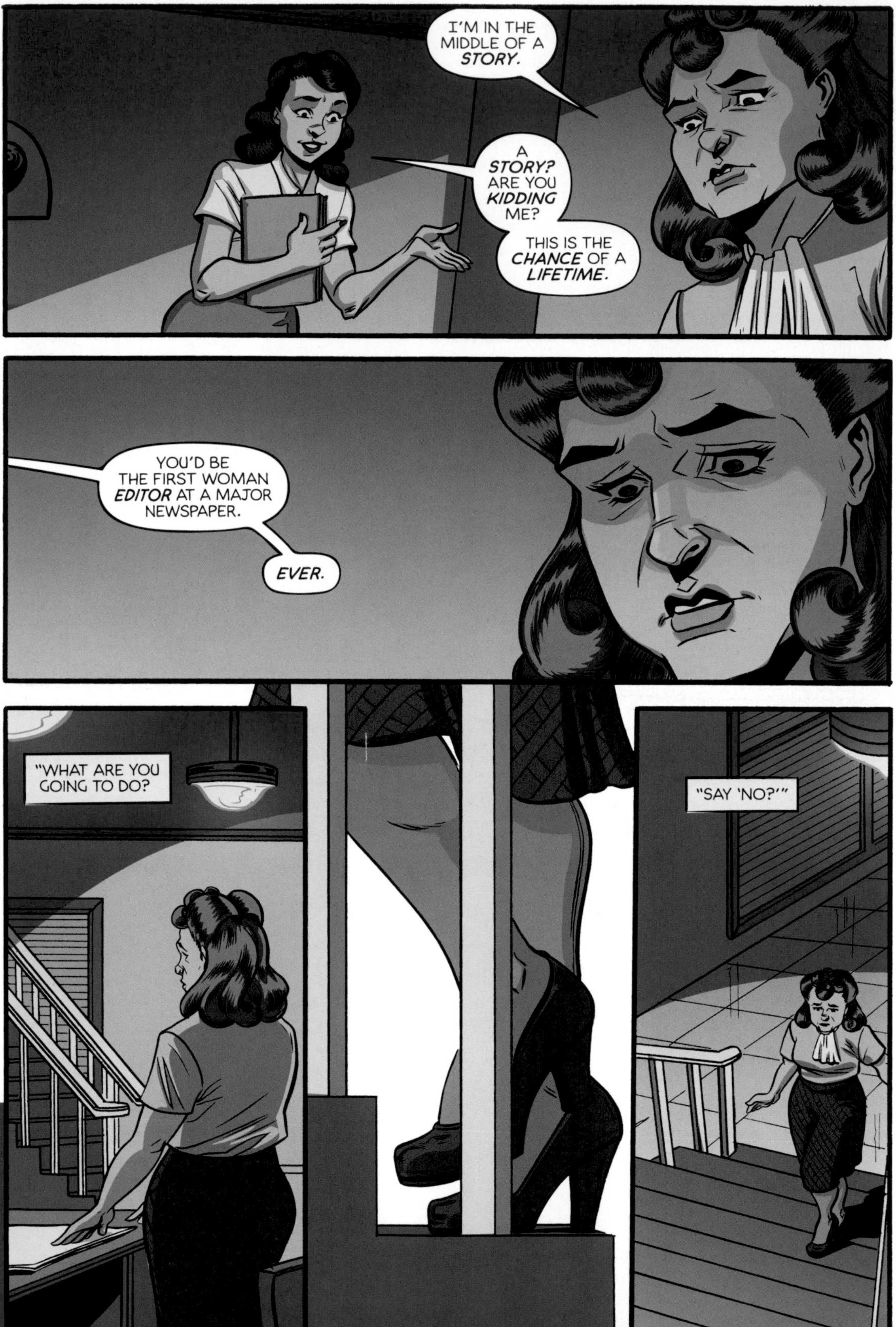
I'M IN THE MIDDLE OF A *STORY.*
A *STORY?* ARE YOU *KIDDING* ME?
THIS IS THE *CHANCE* OF A *LIFETIME.*
YOU'D BE THE FIRST WOMAN *EDITOR* AT A MAJOR NEWSPAPER.
EVER.
"WHAT ARE YOU GOING TO DO?
"SAY 'NO?'"

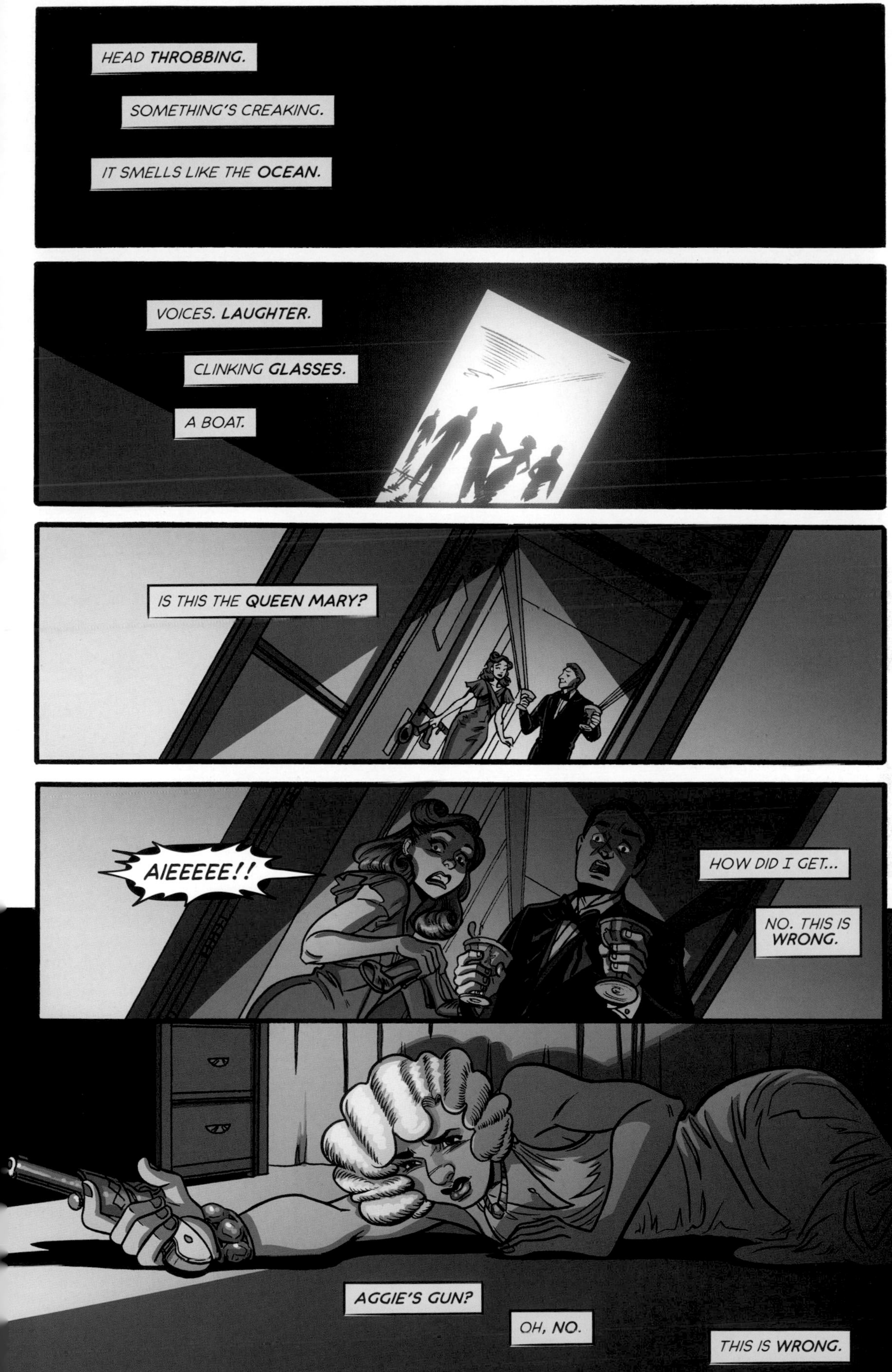
HEAD THROBBING.
SOMETHING'S CREAKING.
IT SMELLS LIKE THE OCEAN.
VOICES. LAUGHTER.
CLINKING GLASSES.
A BOAT.
IS THIS THE QUEEN MARY?
AIEEEEE!!
HOW DID I GET...
NO. THIS IS WRONG.
AGGIE'S GUN?
OH, NO.
THIS IS WRONG.

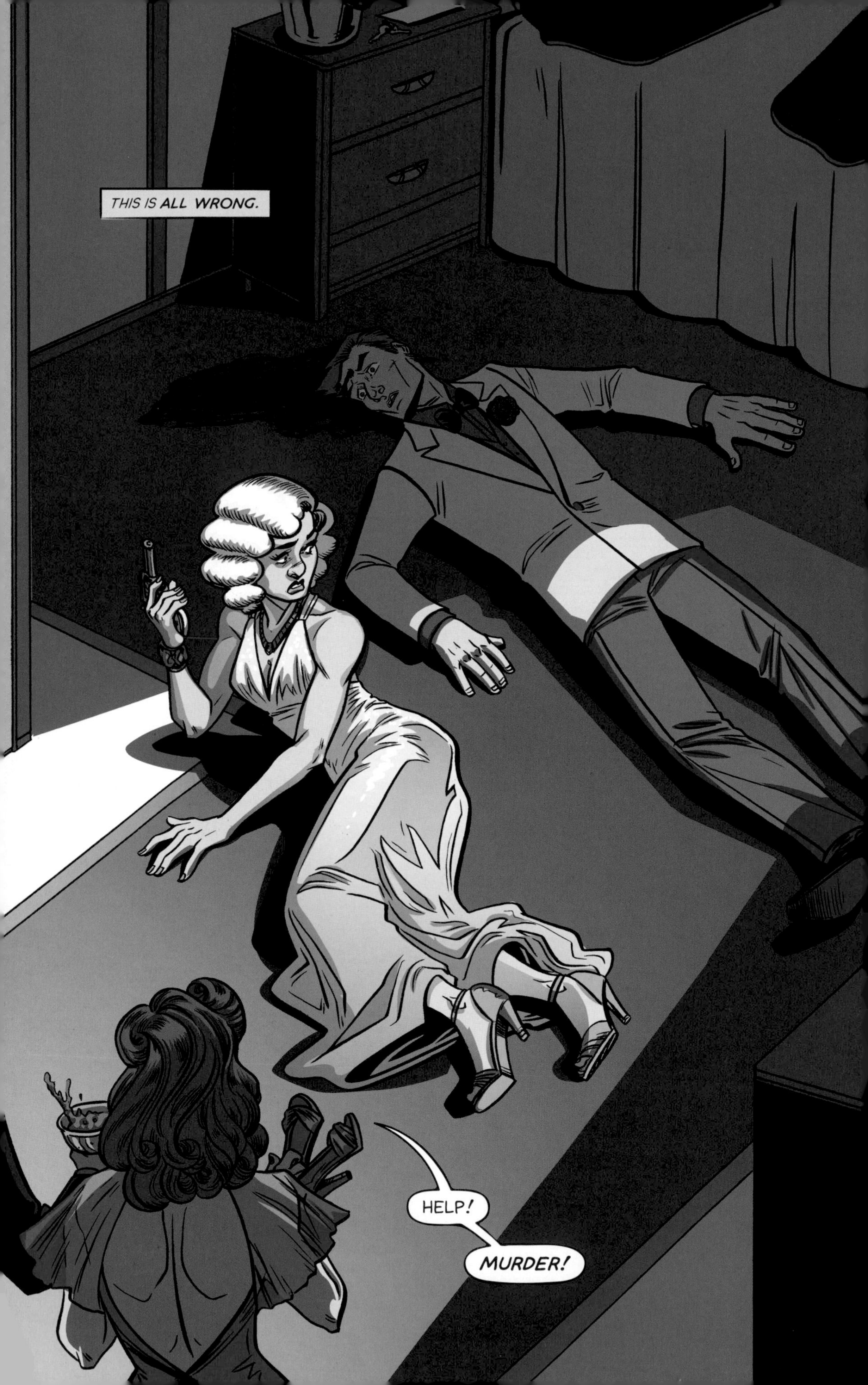
THIS IS ALL WRONG.
HELP!
MURDER!

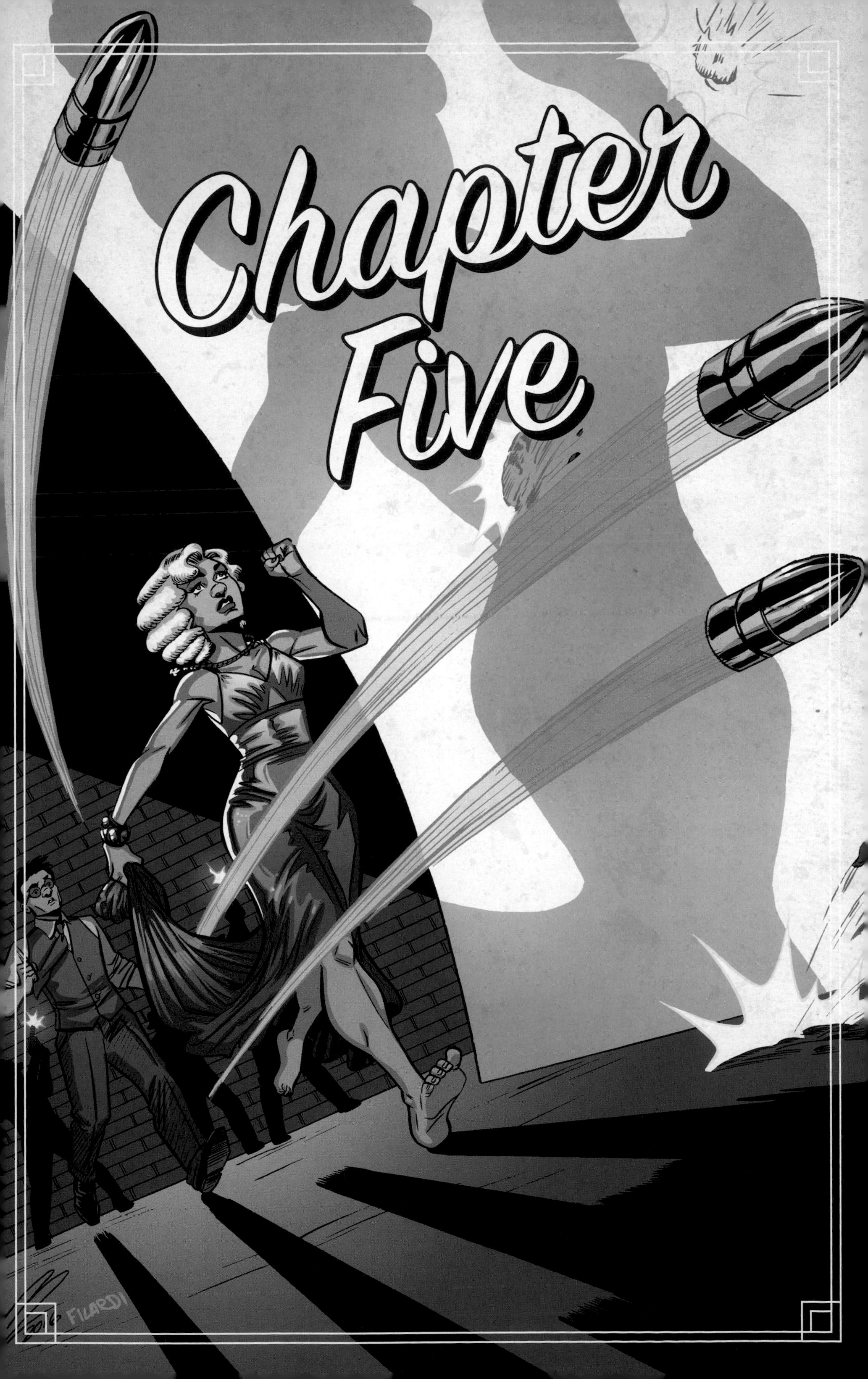
Chapter
Five
FILARDI

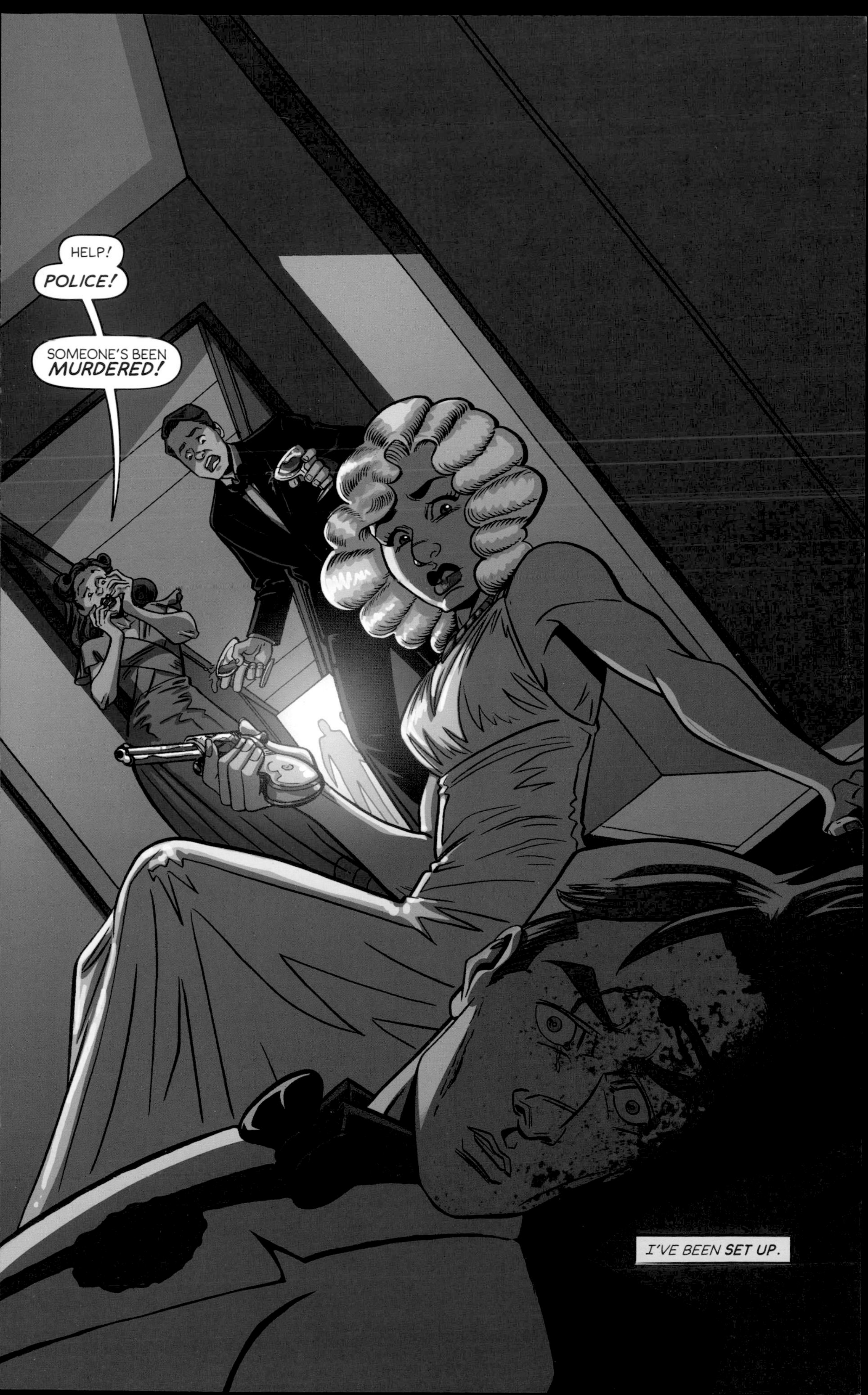
HELP! POLICE!
SOMEONE'S BEEN MURDERED!
I'VE BEEN SET UP.

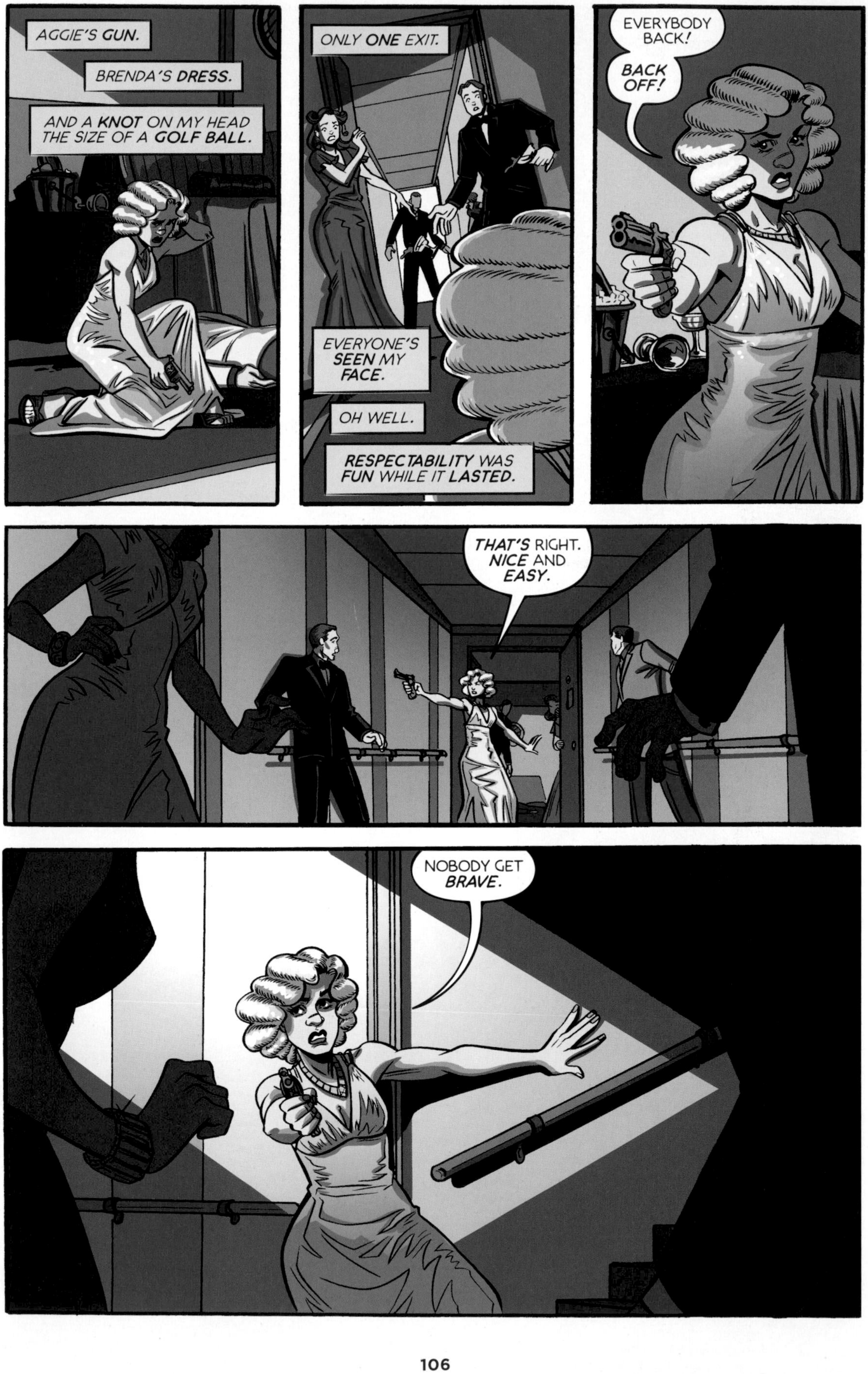
AGGIE'S **GUN**.
BRENDA'S **DRESS**.
AND A **KNOT** ON MY HEAD THE SIZE OF A **GOLF BALL**.
ONLY **ONE** EXIT.
EVERYONE'S **SEEN** MY **FACE**.
OH WELL.
RESPECTABILITY WAS **FUN** WHILE IT **LASTED**.
EVERYBODY BACK! **BACK OFF!**
THAT'S RIGHT. **NICE** AND **EASY**.
NOBODY GET **BRAVE**.

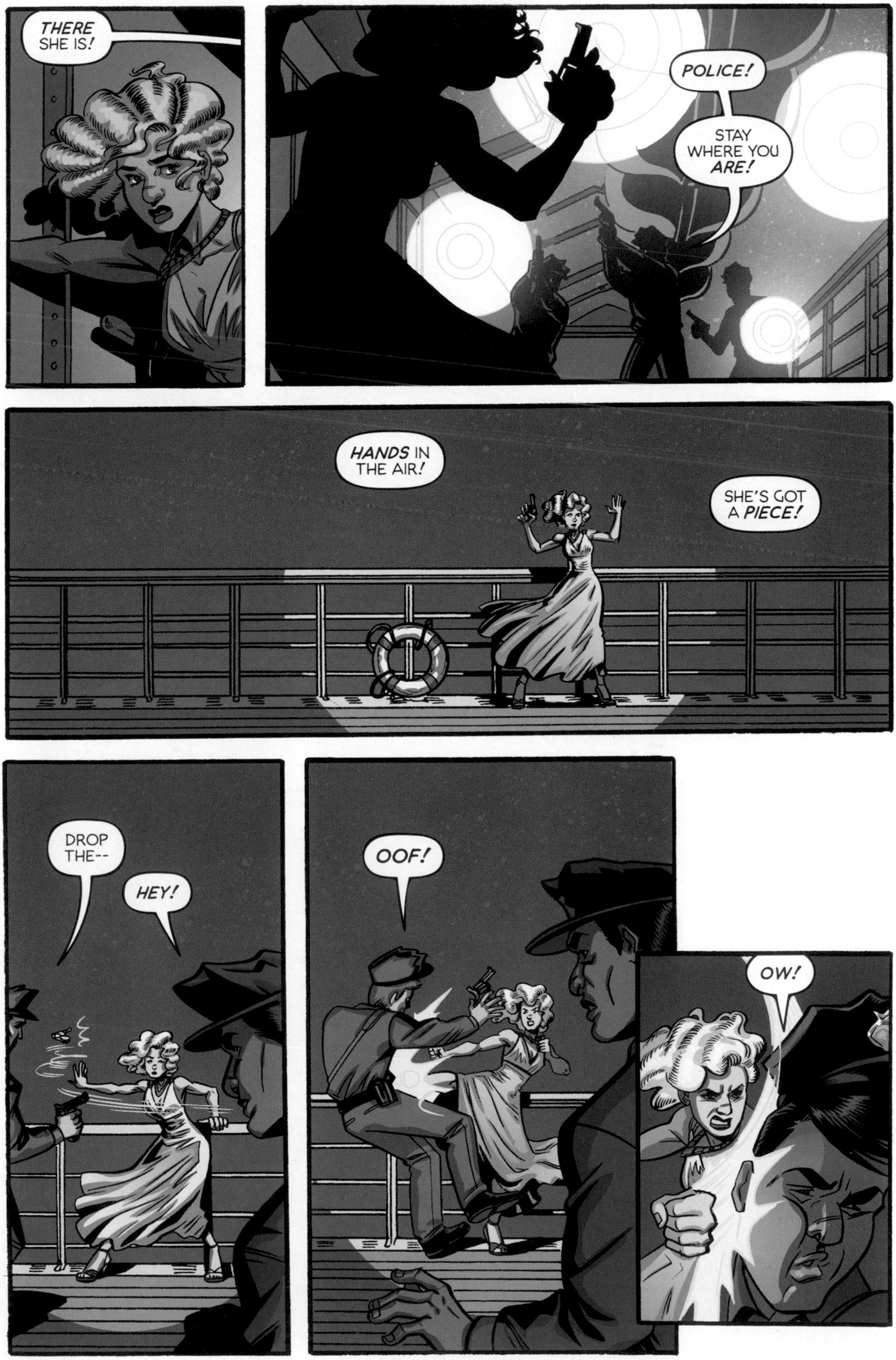
THERE SHE IS!
POLICE!
STAY WHERE YOU ARE!
HANDS IN THE AIR!
SHE'S GOT A PIECE!
DROP THE--
HEY!
OOF!
OW!

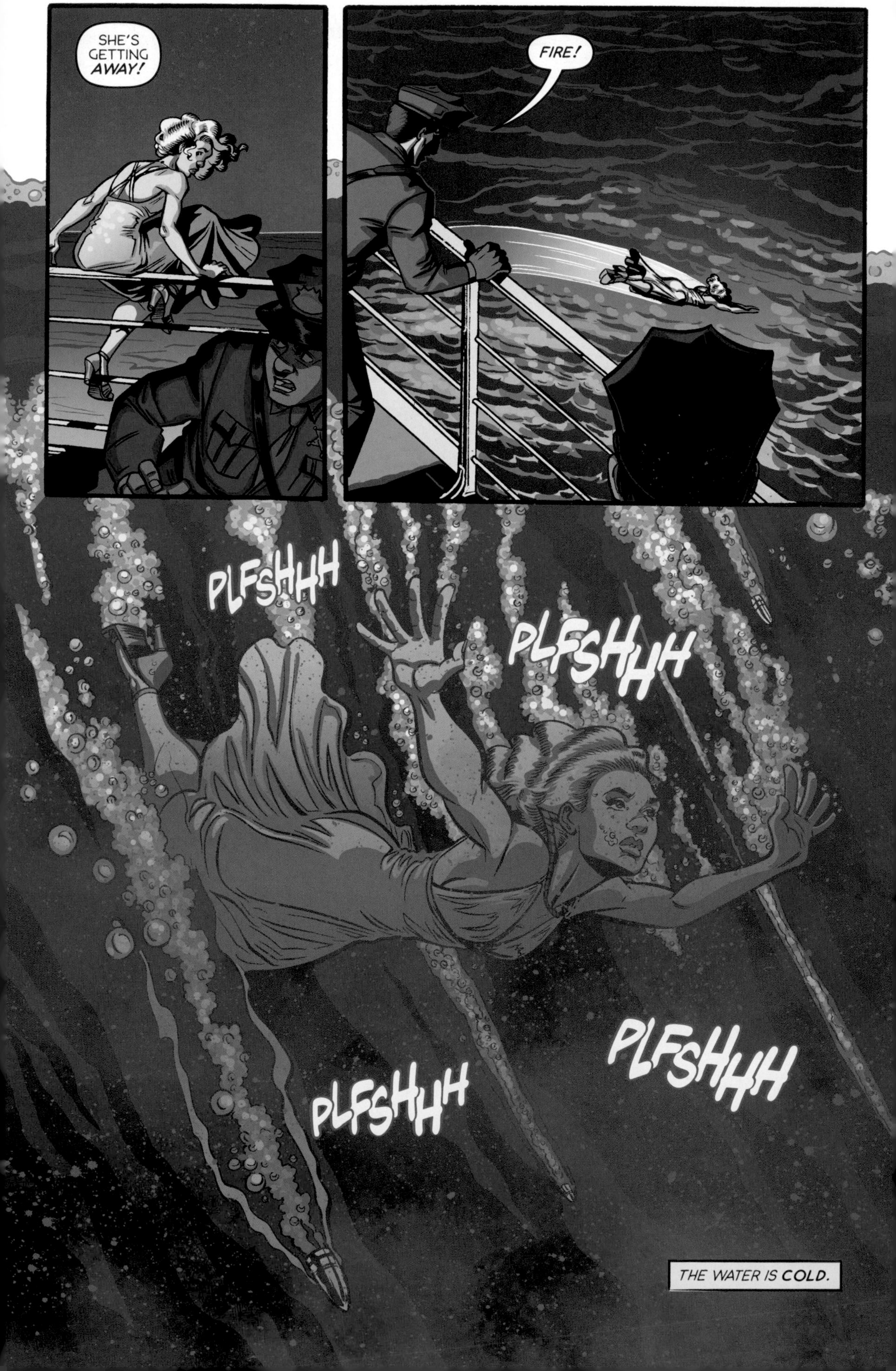
SHE'S GETTING AWAY!
FIRE!
PLFSHHH
PLFSHHH
PLFSHHH
PLFSHHH
THE WATER IS COLD.

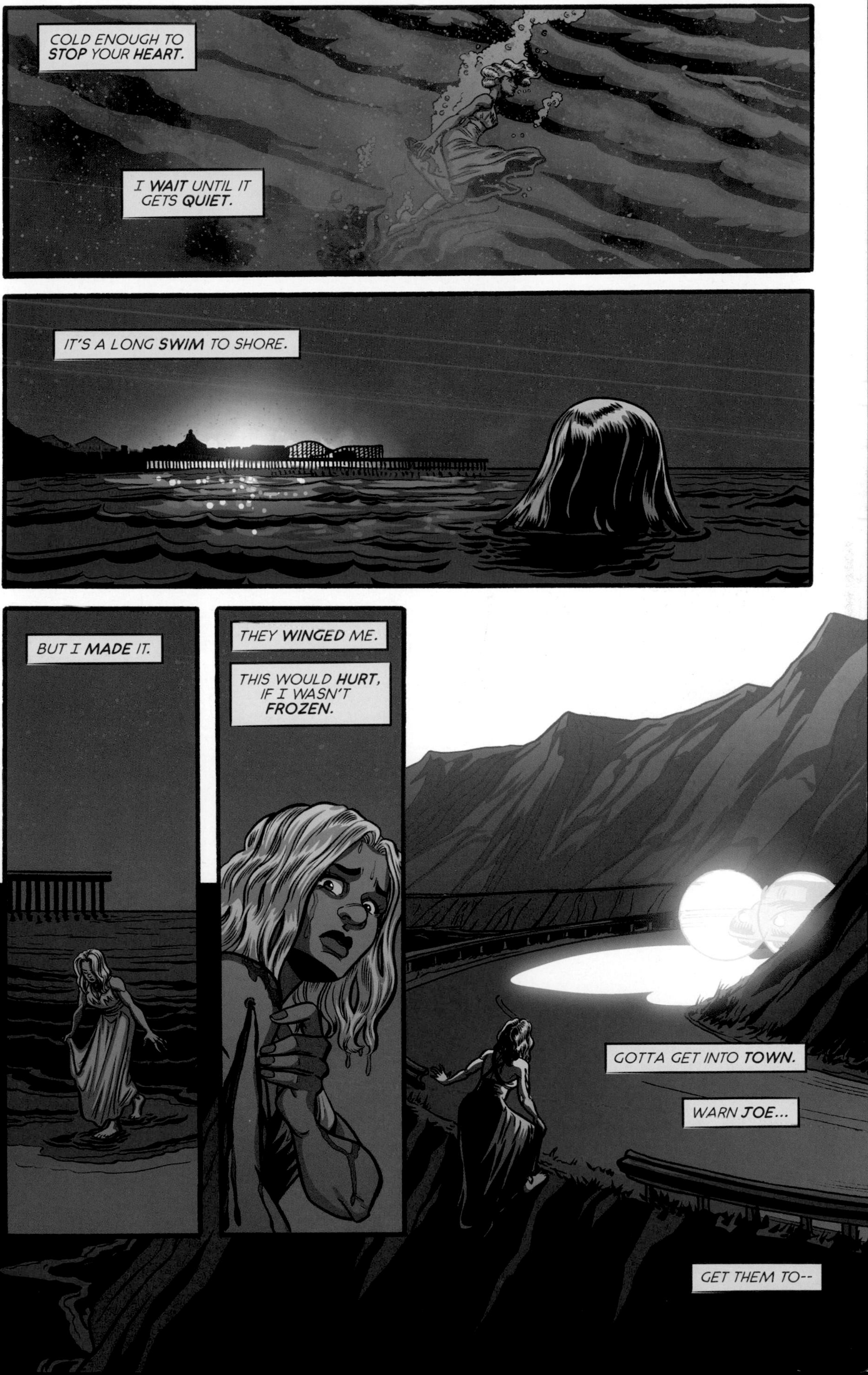
COLD ENOUGH TO STOP YOUR HEART.
I WAIT UNTIL IT GETS QUIET.
IT'S A LONG SWIM TO SHORE.
BUT I MADE IT.
THEY WINGED ME.
THIS WOULD HURT, IF I WASN'T FROZEN.
GOTTA GET INTO TOWN.
WARN JOE...
GET THEM TO--

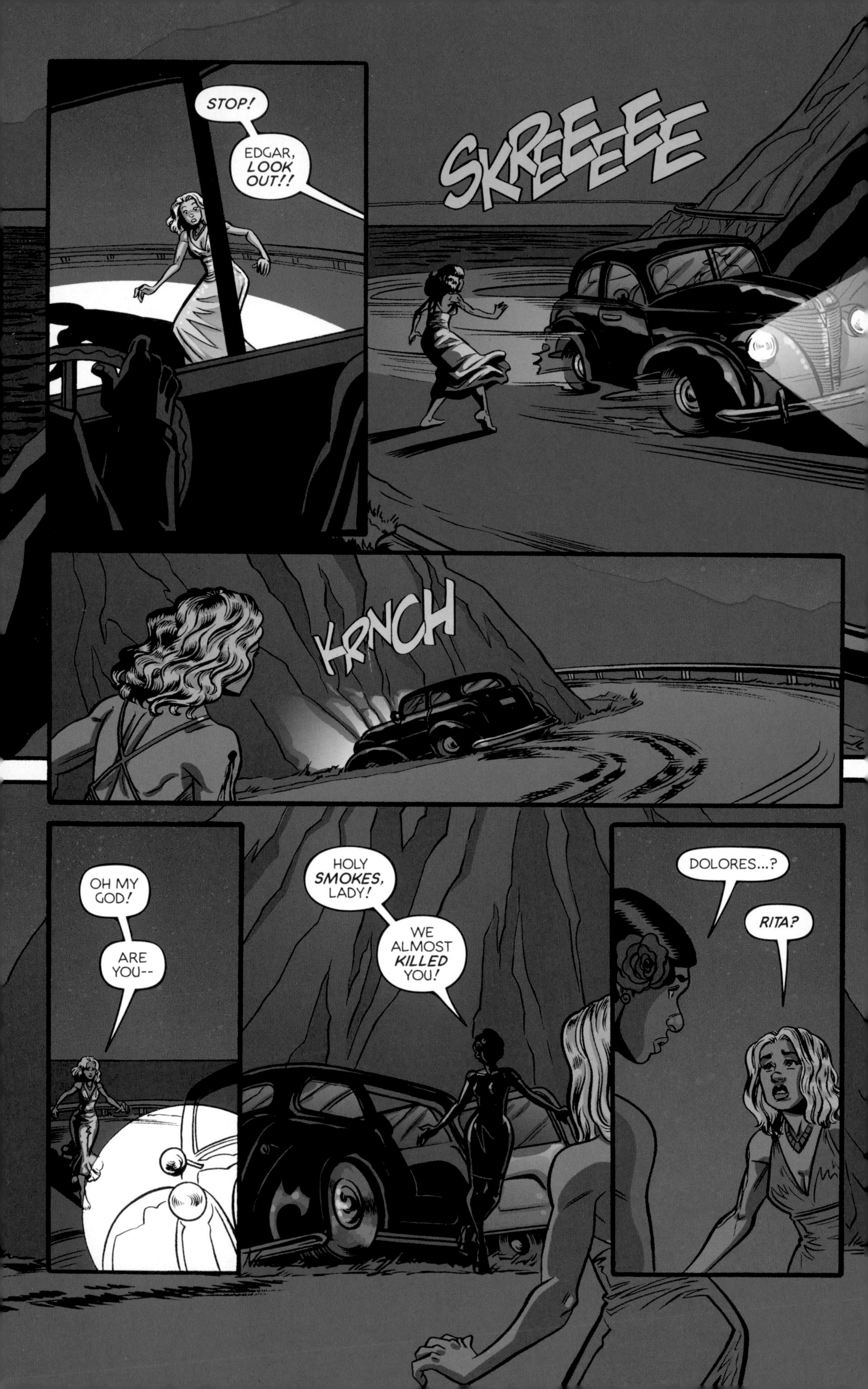
STOP!
EDGAR, LOOK OUT!!
SKREEEEEE
KRNCH
OH MY GOD!
ARE YOU--
HOLY SMOKES, LADY!
WE ALMOST KILLED YOU!
DOLORES...?
RITA?

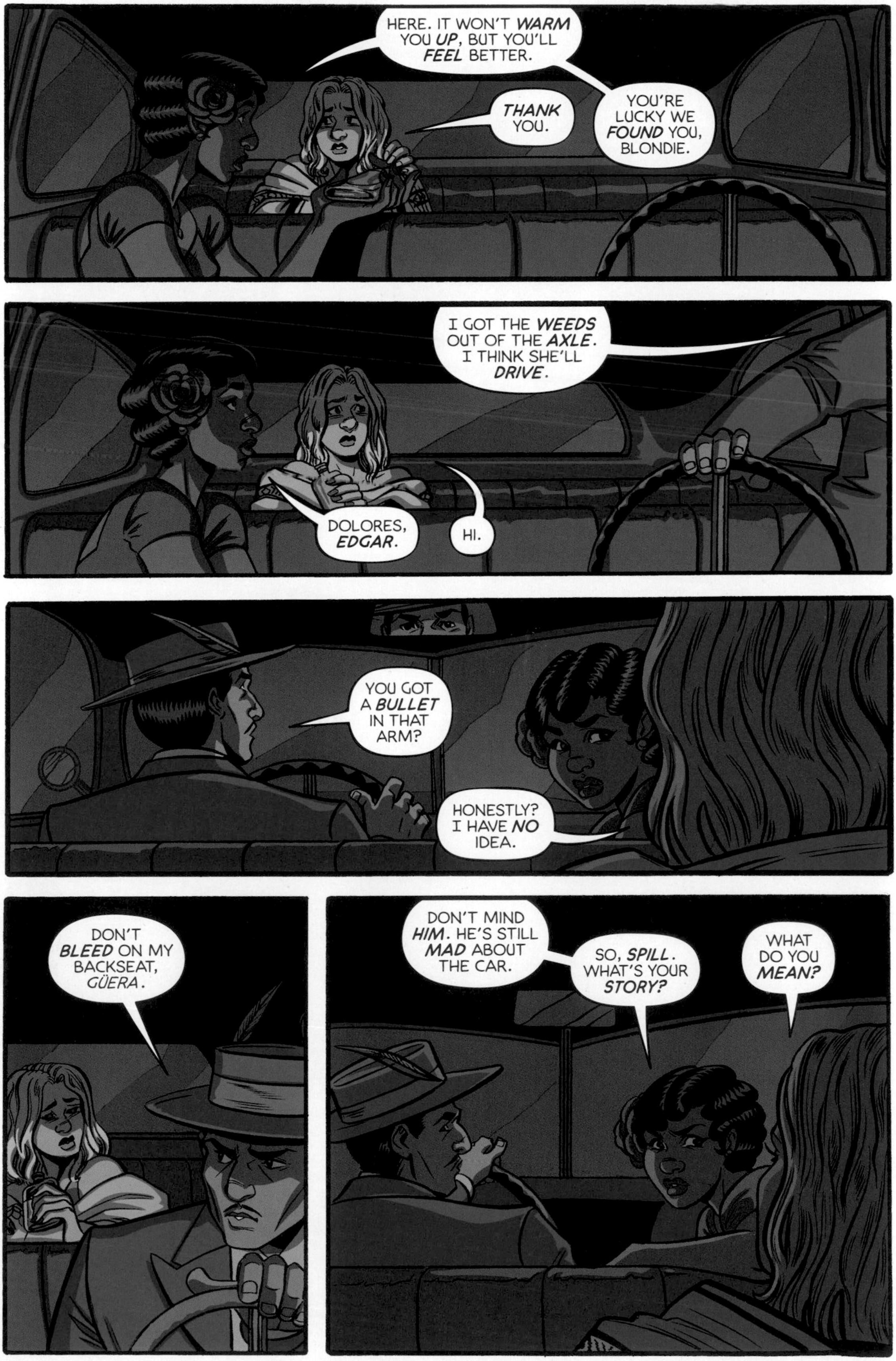
HERE. IT WON'T *WARM* YOU *UP*, BUT YOU'LL *FEEL* BETTER.
THANK YOU.
YOU'RE LUCKY WE *FOUND* YOU, BLONDIE.
I GOT THE *WEEDS* OUT OF THE *AXLE*. I THINK SHE'LL *DRIVE*.
DOLORES, *EDGAR*.
HI.
YOU GOT A *BULLET* IN THAT ARM?
HONESTLY? I HAVE *NO* IDEA.
DON'T *BLEED* ON MY BACKSEAT, *GÜERA*.
DON'T MIND *HIM*. HE'S STILL *MAD* ABOUT THE CAR.
SO, *SPILL*. WHAT'S YOUR *STORY?*
WHAT DO YOU *MEAN?*

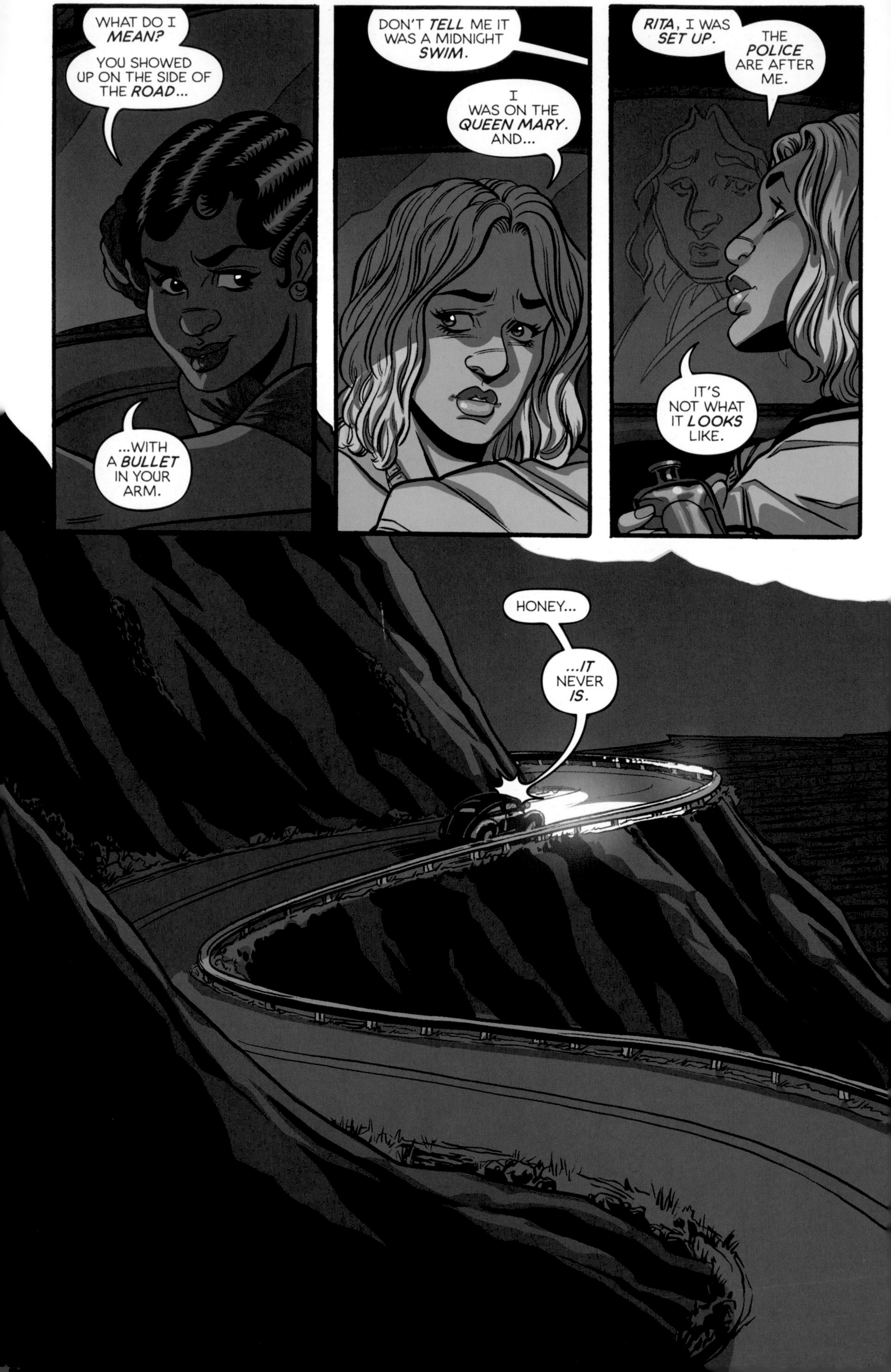
WHAT DO I MEAN?
YOU SHOWED UP ON THE SIDE OF THE ROAD...
...WITH A BULLET IN YOUR ARM.
DON'T TELL ME IT WAS A MIDNIGHT SWIM.
I WAS ON THE QUEEN MARY. AND...
RITA, I WAS SET UP.
THE POLICE ARE AFTER ME.
IT'S NOT WHAT IT LOOKS LIKE.
HONEY...
...IT NEVER IS.

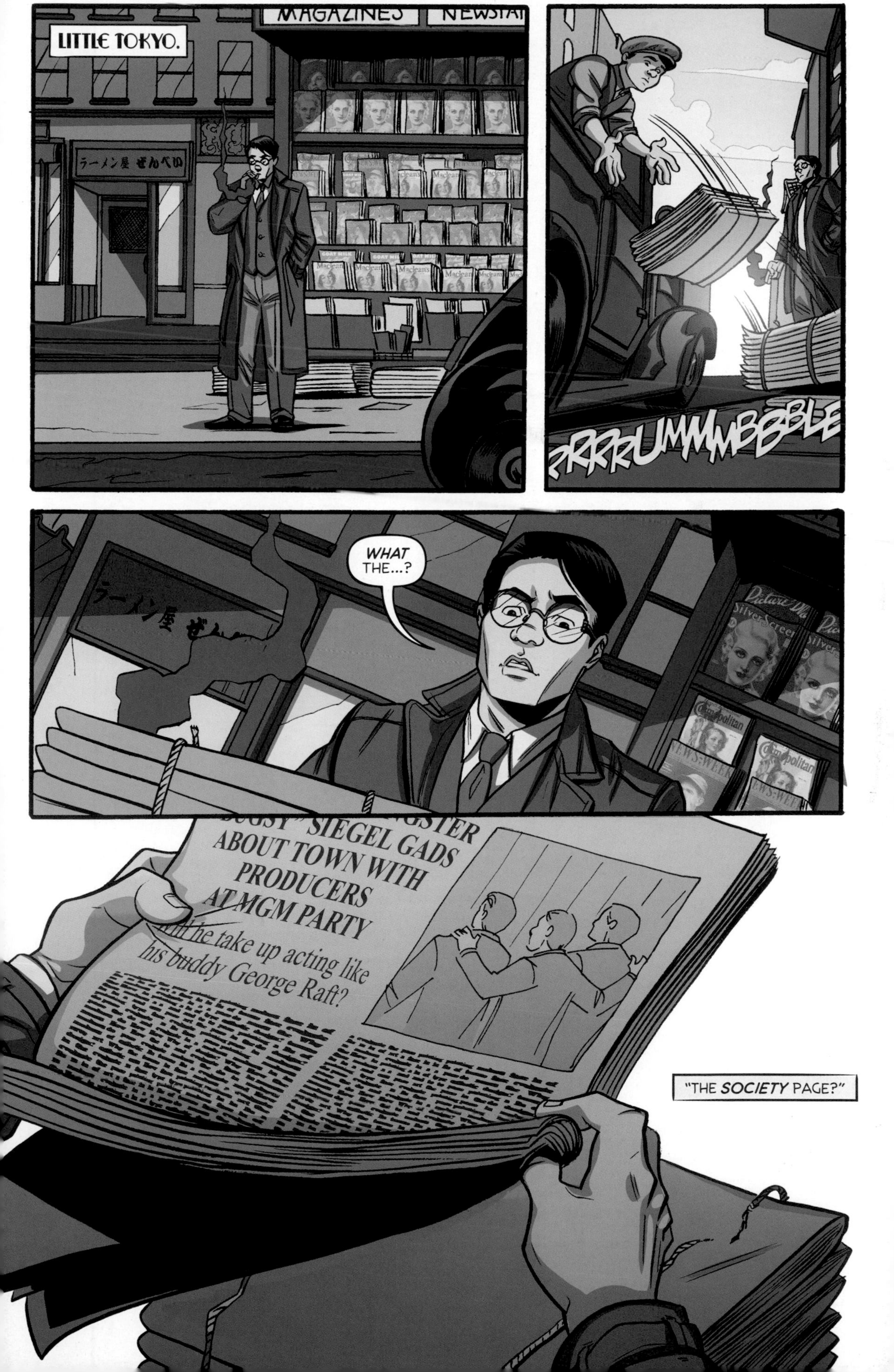
LITTLE TOKYO.
MAGAZINES
ラーメン屋
RRRRUMMMBBBLE
WHAT THE...?
SIEGEL GADS
ABOUT TOWN WITH
PRODUCERS
AT MGM PARTY
take up acting like
his buddy George Raft?
"THE SOCIETY PAGE?"

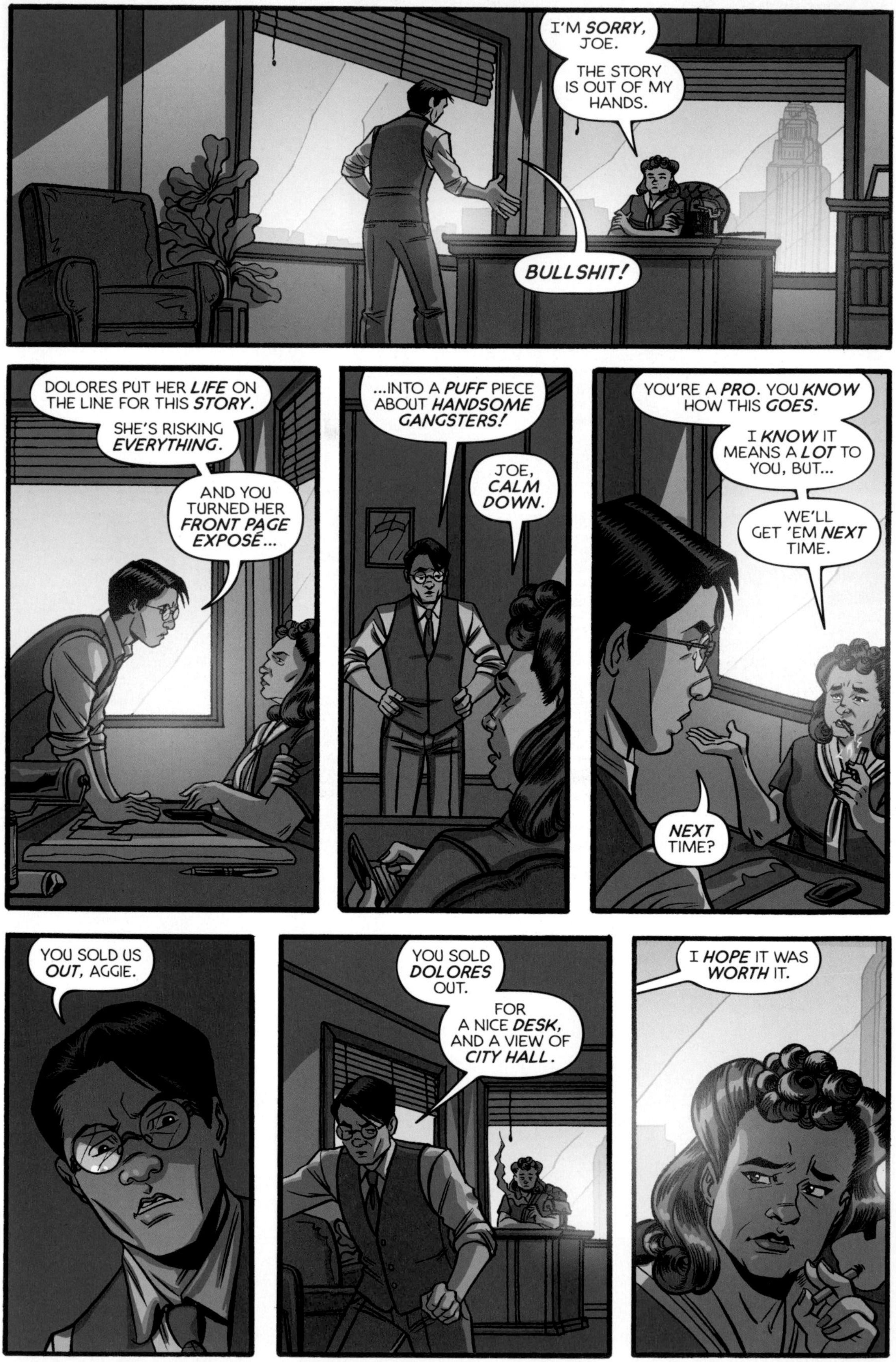
I'M SORRY, JOE.
THE STORY IS OUT OF MY HANDS.
BULLSHIT!
DOLORES PUT HER LIFE ON THE LINE FOR THIS STORY.
SHE'S RISKING EVERYTHING.
AND YOU TURNED HER FRONT PAGE EXPOSÉ...
...INTO A PUFF PIECE ABOUT HANDSOME GANGSTERS!
JOE, CALM DOWN.
YOU'RE A PRO. YOU KNOW HOW THIS GOES.
I KNOW IT MEANS A LOT TO YOU, BUT...
WE'LL GET 'EM NEXT TIME.
NEXT TIME?
YOU SOLD US OUT, AGGIE.
YOU SOLD DOLORES OUT.
FOR A NICE DESK, AND A VIEW OF CITY HALL.
I HOPE IT WAS WORTH IT.

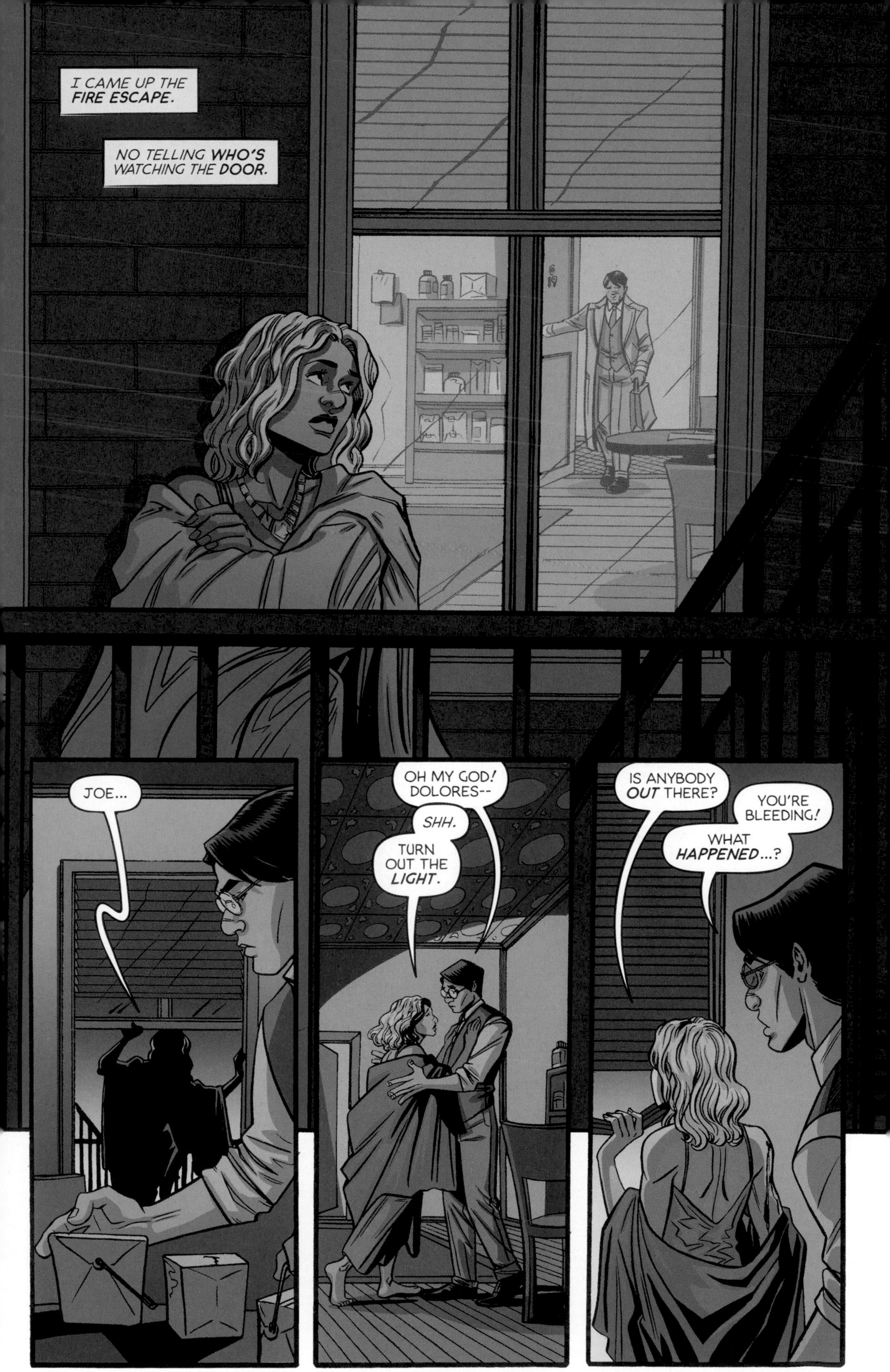
I CAME UP THE FIRE ESCAPE.
NO TELLING WHO'S WATCHING THE DOOR.
JOE...
OH MY GOD! DOLORES--
SHH.
TURN OUT THE LIGHT.
IS ANYBODY OUT THERE?
YOU'RE BLEEDING!
WHAT HAPPENED...?

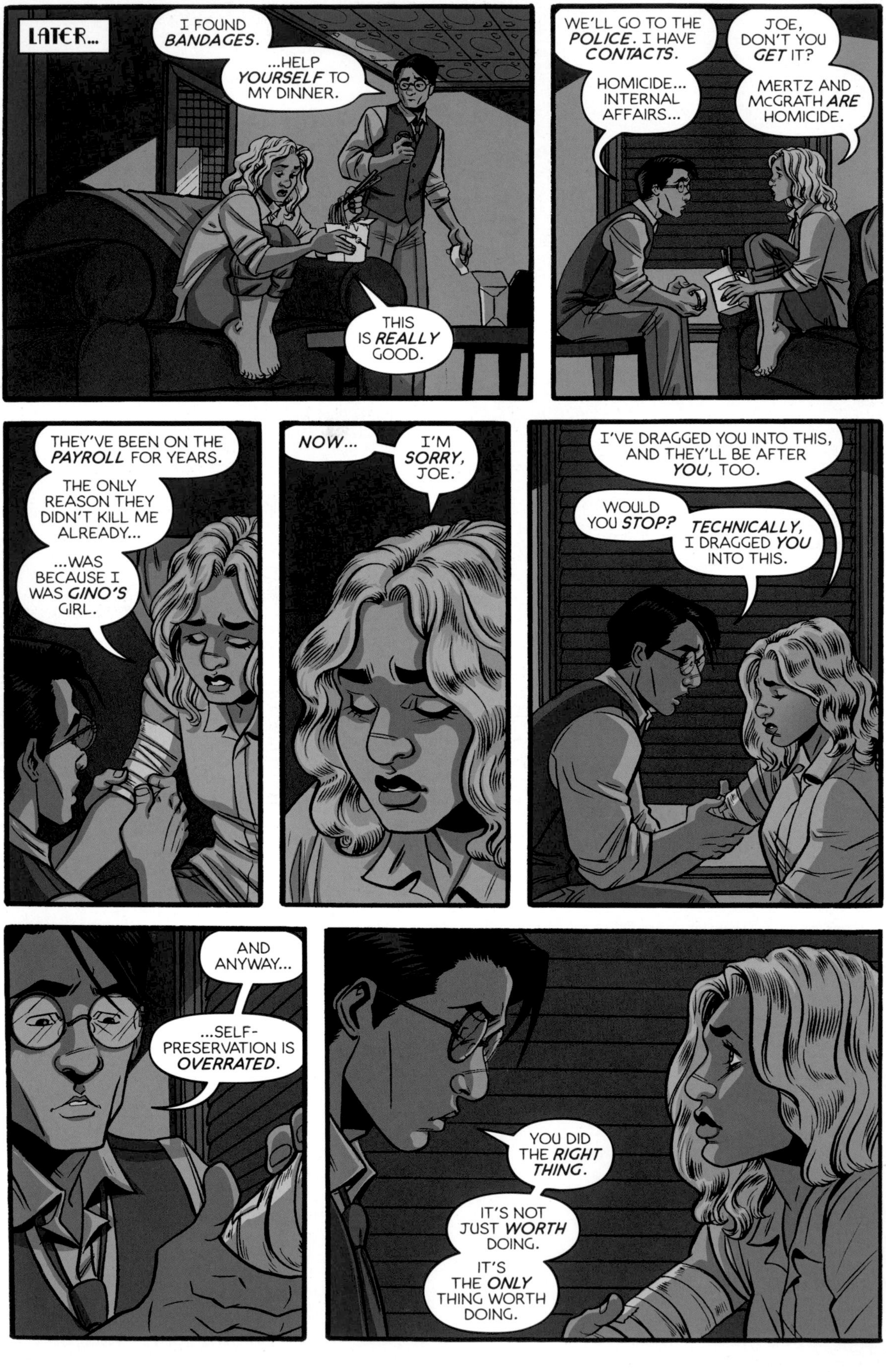
LATER...
I FOUND BANDAGES.
...HELP YOURSELF TO MY DINNER.
THIS IS REALLY GOOD.
WE'LL GO TO THE POLICE. I HAVE CONTACTS.
HOMICIDE... INTERNAL AFFAIRS...
JOE, DON'T YOU GET IT?
MERTZ AND McGRATH ARE HOMICIDE.
THEY'VE BEEN ON THE PAYROLL FOR YEARS.
THE ONLY REASON THEY DIDN'T KILL ME ALREADY...
...WAS BECAUSE I WAS GINO'S GIRL.
NOW...
I'M SORRY, JOE.
I'VE DRAGGED YOU INTO THIS, AND THEY'LL BE AFTER YOU, TOO.
WOULD YOU STOP?
TECHNICALLY, I DRAGGED YOU INTO THIS.
AND ANYWAY...
...SELF-PRESERVATION IS OVERRATED.
YOU DID THE RIGHT THING.
IT'S NOT JUST WORTH DOING.
IT'S THE ONLY THING WORTH DOING.

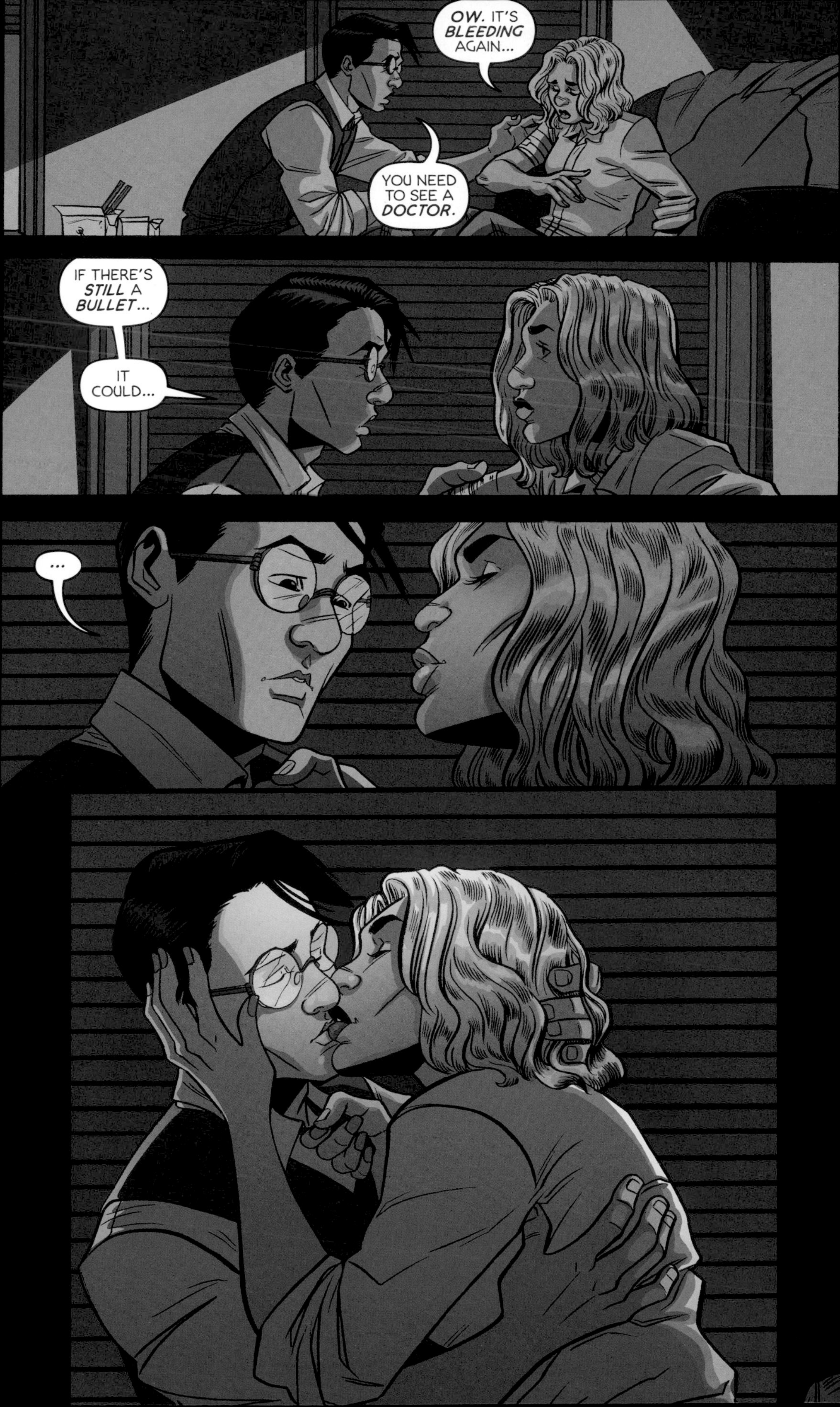
OW. IT'S BLEEDING AGAIN...
YOU NEED TO SEE A DOCTOR.
IF THERE'S STILL A BULLET...
IT COULD...
...

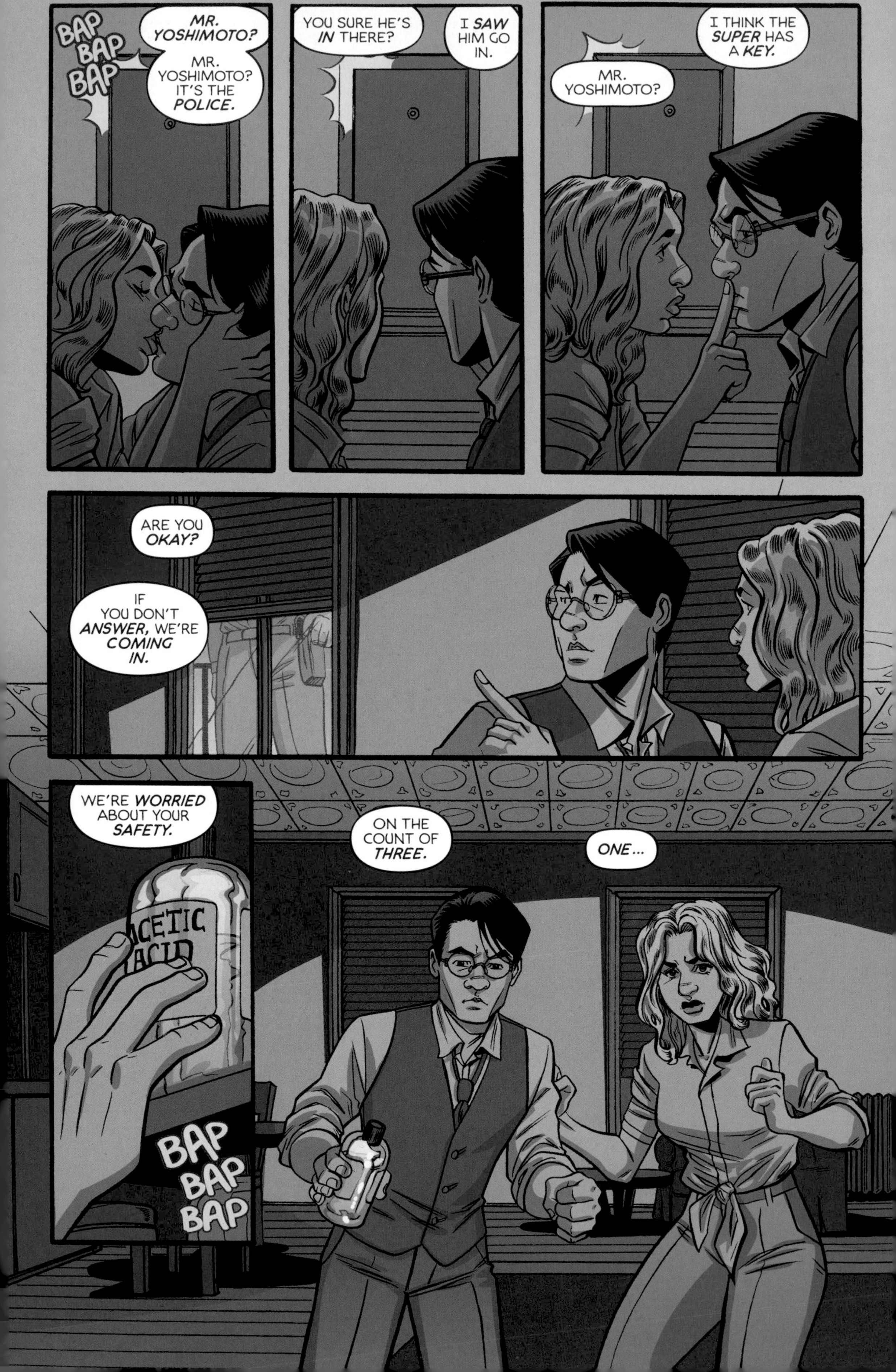
BAP BAP BAP
MR. YOSHIMOTO?
MR. YOSHIMOTO? IT'S THE POLICE.
YOU SURE HE'S IN THERE?
I SAW HIM GO IN.
MR. YOSHIMOTO?
I THINK THE SUPER HAS A KEY.
ARE YOU OKAY?
IF YOU DON'T ANSWER, WE'RE COMING IN.
WE'RE WORRIED ABOUT YOUR SAFETY.
ACETIC ACID
BAP BAP BAP
ON THE COUNT OF THREE.
ONE...

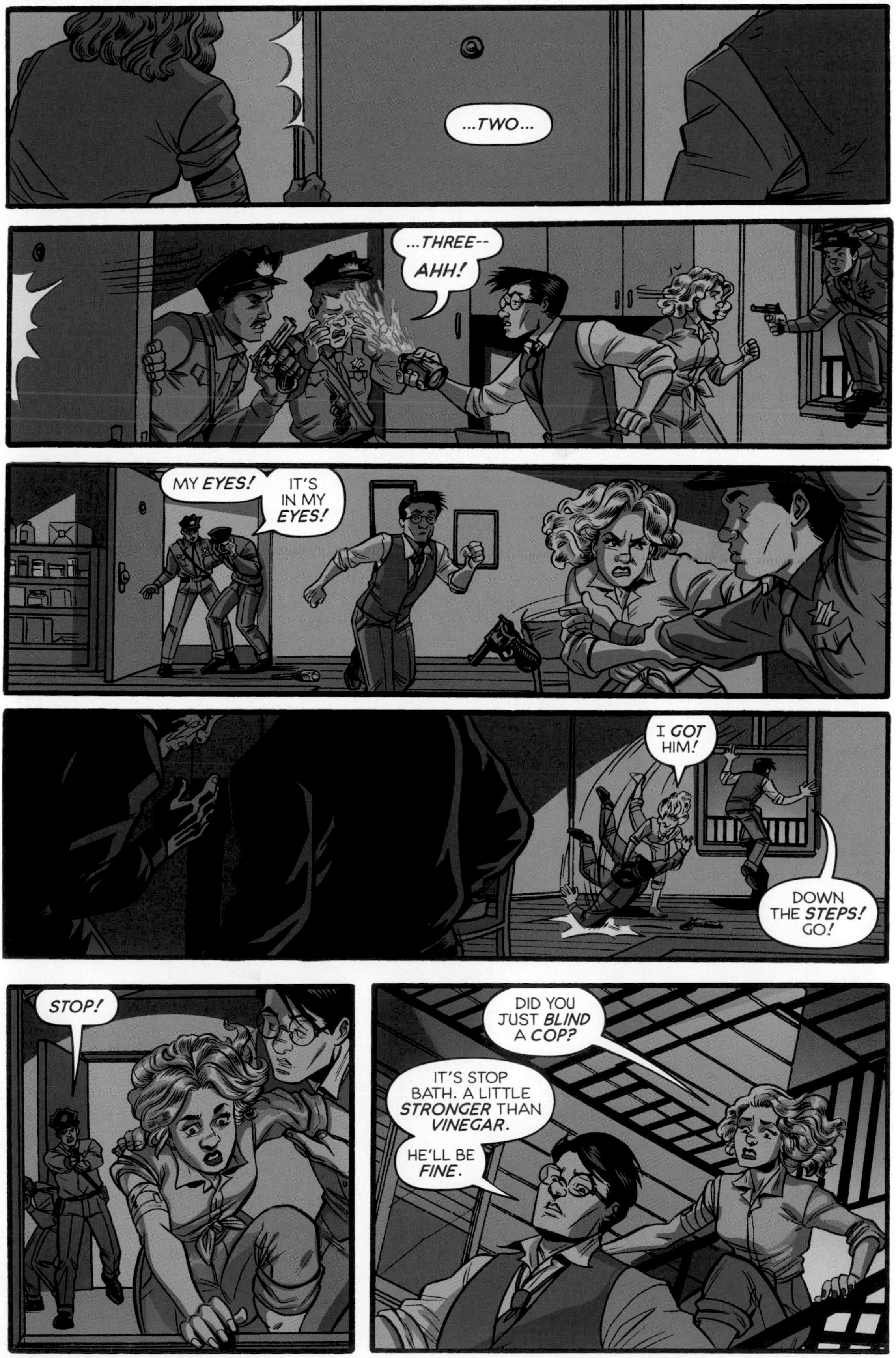
...TWO...
...THREE--
AHH!
MY EYES!
IT'S IN MY EYES!
I GOT HIM!
DOWN THE STEPS! GO!
STOP!
DID YOU JUST BLIND A COP?
IT'S STOP BATH. A LITTLE STRONGER THAN VINEGAR.
HE'LL BE FINE.

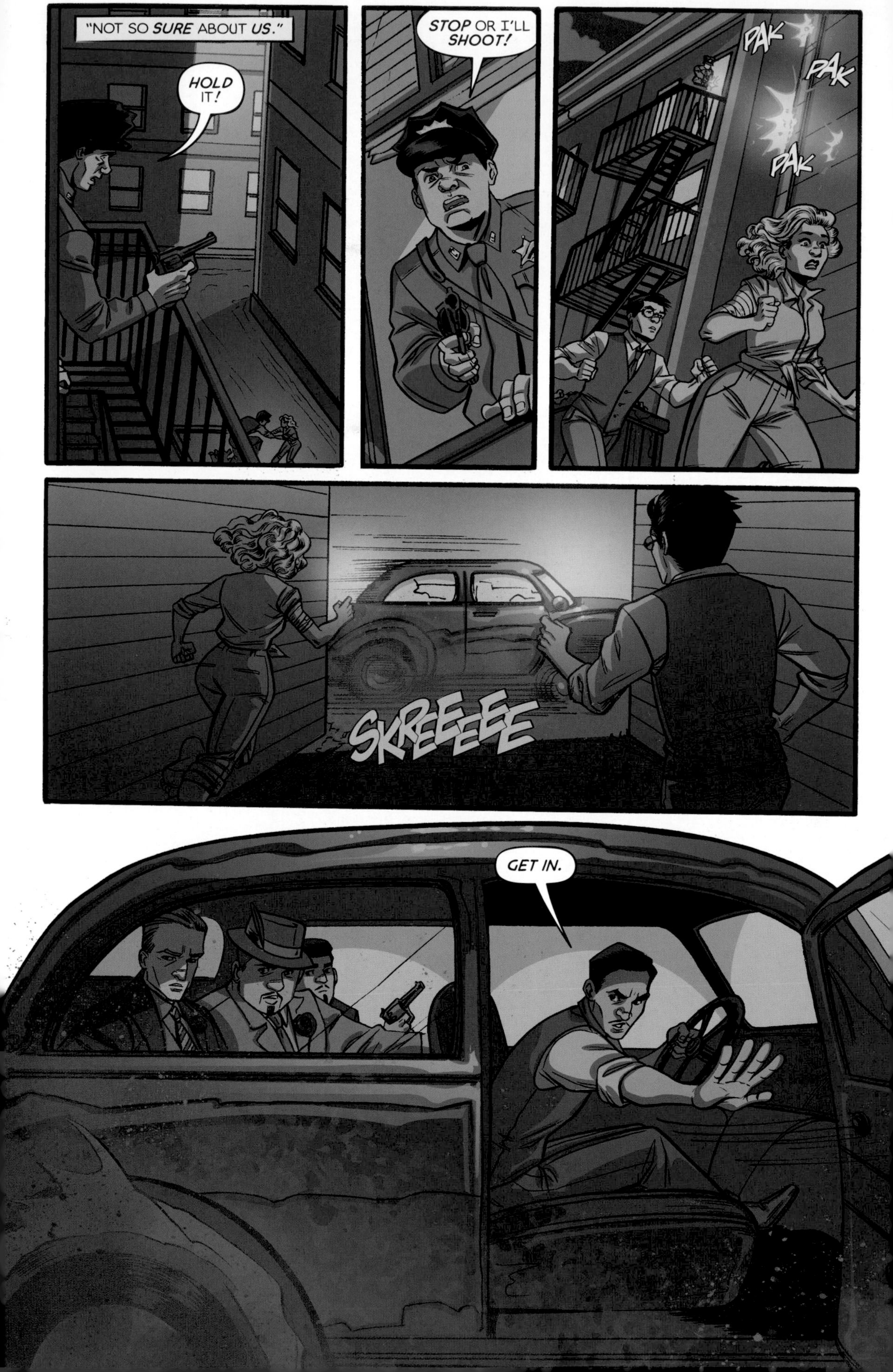
"NOT SO SURE ABOUT US."
HOLD IT!
STOP OR I'LL SHOOT!
PAK
PAK
PAK
SKREEEEEE
GET IN.

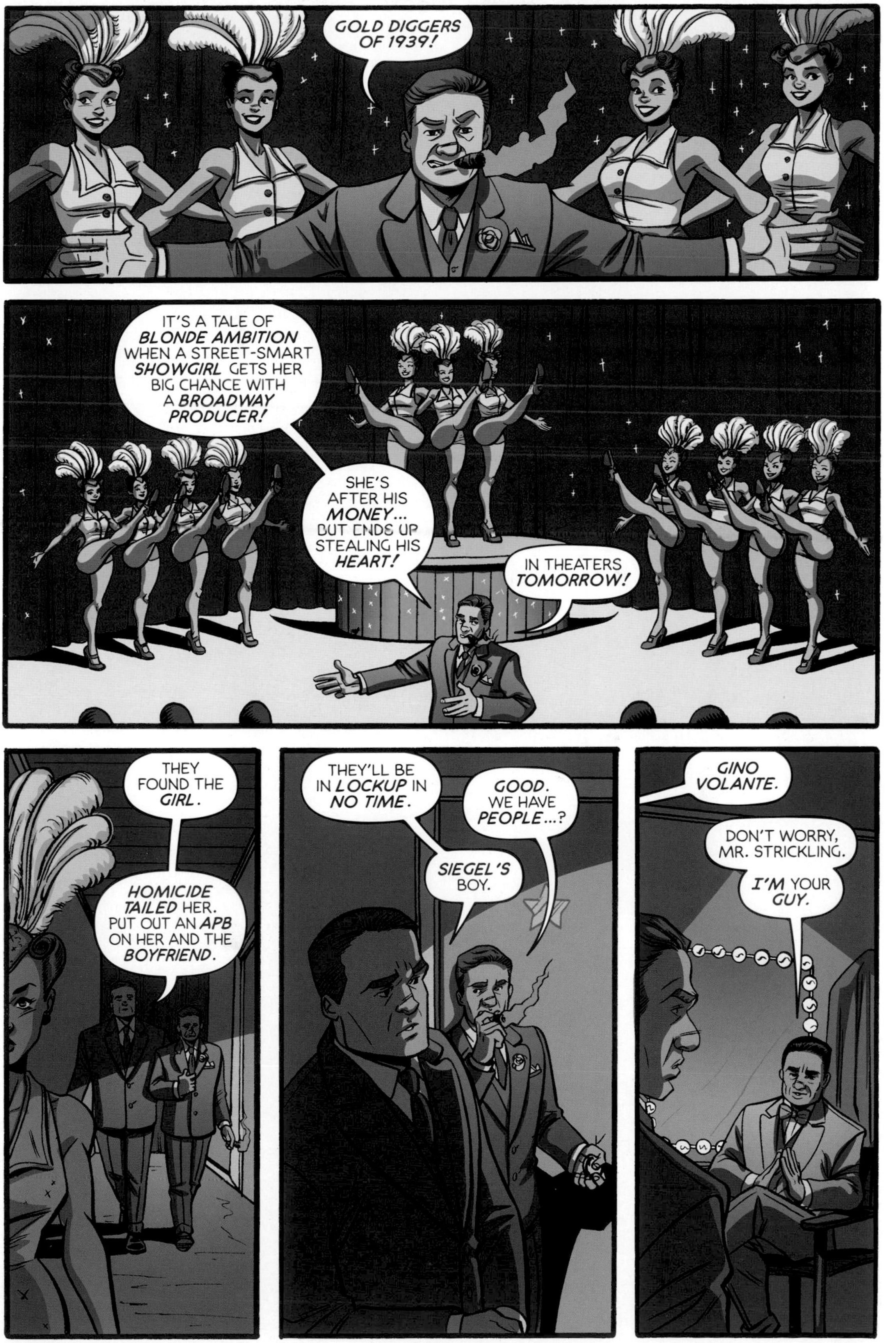
GOLD DIGGERS OF 1939!
IT'S A TALE OF BLONDE AMBITION WHEN A STREET-SMART SHOWGIRL GETS HER BIG CHANCE WITH A BROADWAY PRODUCER!
SHE'S AFTER HIS MONEY... BUT ENDS UP STEALING HIS HEART!
IN THEATERS TOMORROW!
THEY FOUND THE GIRL.
HOMICIDE TAILED HER. PUT OUT AN APB ON HER AND THE BOYFRIEND.
THEY'LL BE IN LOCKUP IN NO TIME.
GOOD. WE HAVE PEOPLE...?
SIEGEL'S BOY.
GINO VOLANTE.
DON'T WORRY, MR. STRICKLING.
I'M YOUR GUY.

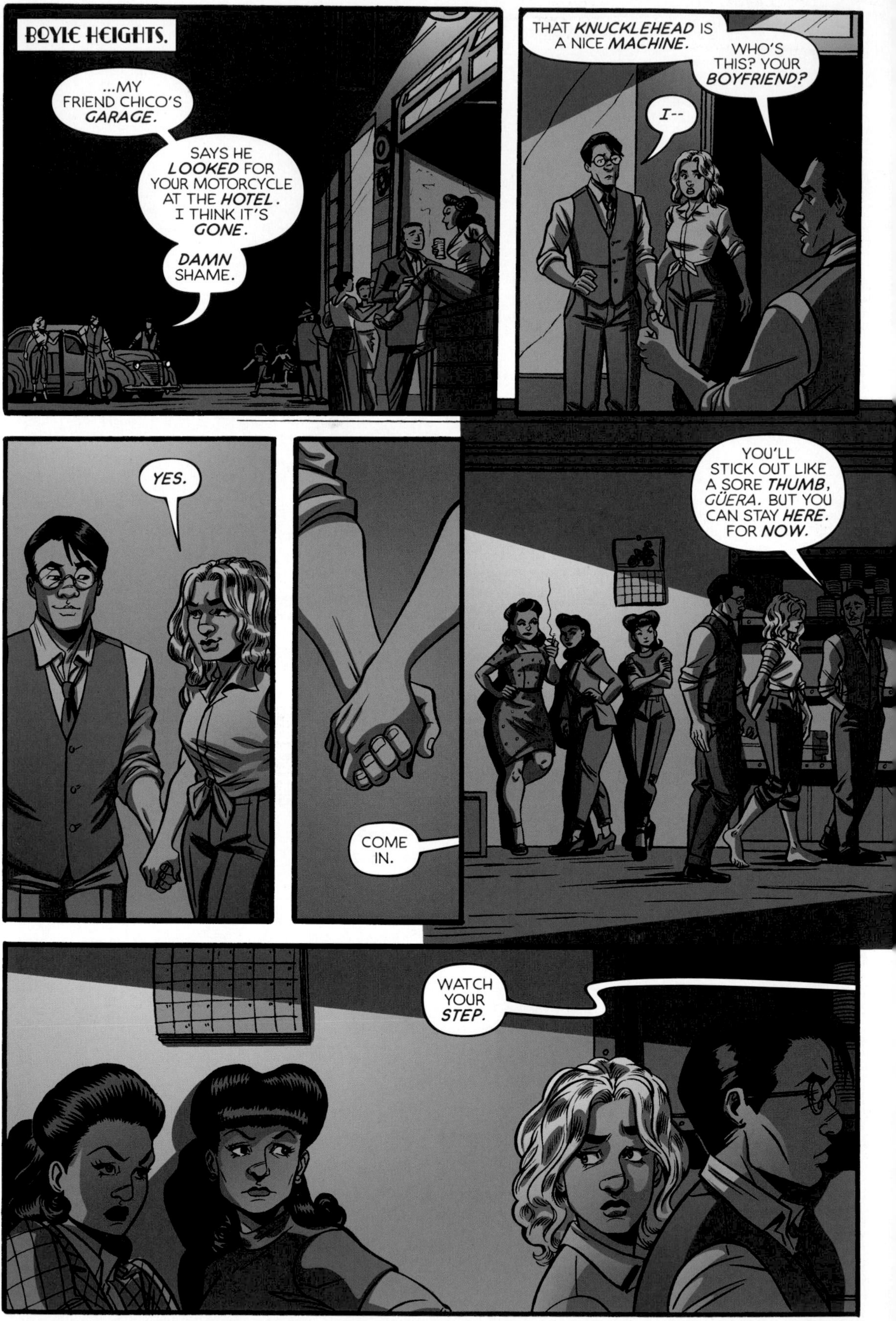
BOYLE HEIGHTS.
...MY FRIEND CHICO'S *GARAGE*.
SAYS HE *LOOKED* FOR YOUR MOTORCYCLE AT THE *HOTEL*. I THINK IT'S *GONE*.
DAMN SHAME.
THAT *KNUCKLEHEAD* IS A NICE *MACHINE*.
WHO'S THIS? YOUR *BOYFRIEND?*
I--
YES.
COME IN.
YOU'LL STICK OUT LIKE A SORE *THUMB*, *GÜERA*. BUT YOU CAN STAY *HERE*. FOR *NOW*.
WATCH YOUR *STEP*.

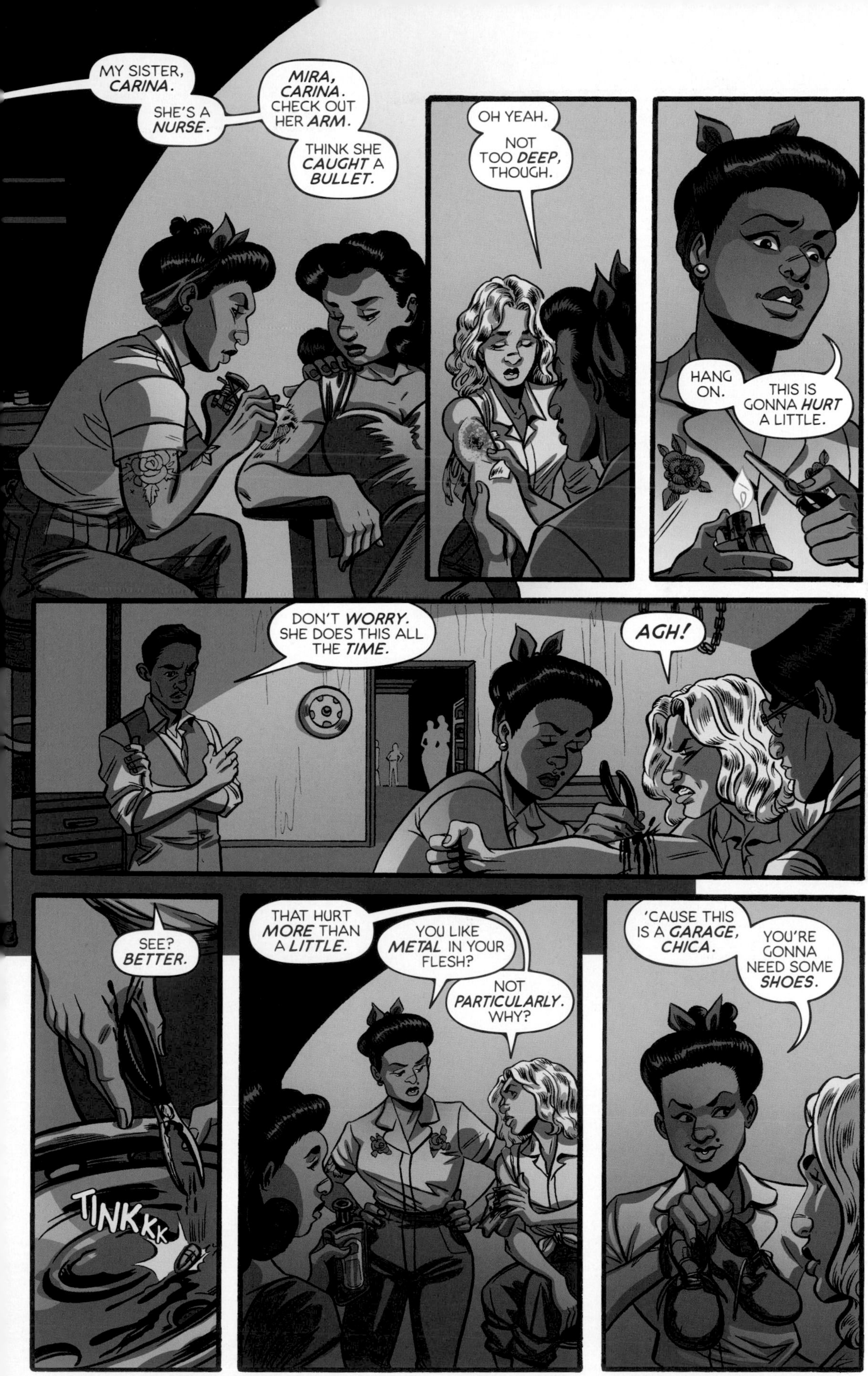
MY SISTER, CARINA.
SHE'S A NURSE.
MIRA, CARINA. CHECK OUT HER ARM.
THINK SHE CAUGHT A BULLET.
OH YEAH.
NOT TOO DEEP, THOUGH.
HANG ON.
THIS IS GONNA HURT A LITTLE.
DON'T WORRY. SHE DOES THIS ALL THE TIME.
AGH!
SEE? BETTER.
TINKKK
THAT HURT MORE THAN A LITTLE.
YOU LIKE METAL IN YOUR FLESH?
NOT PARTICULARLY. WHY?
'CAUSE THIS IS A GARAGE, CHICA.
YOU'RE GONNA NEED SOME SHOES.

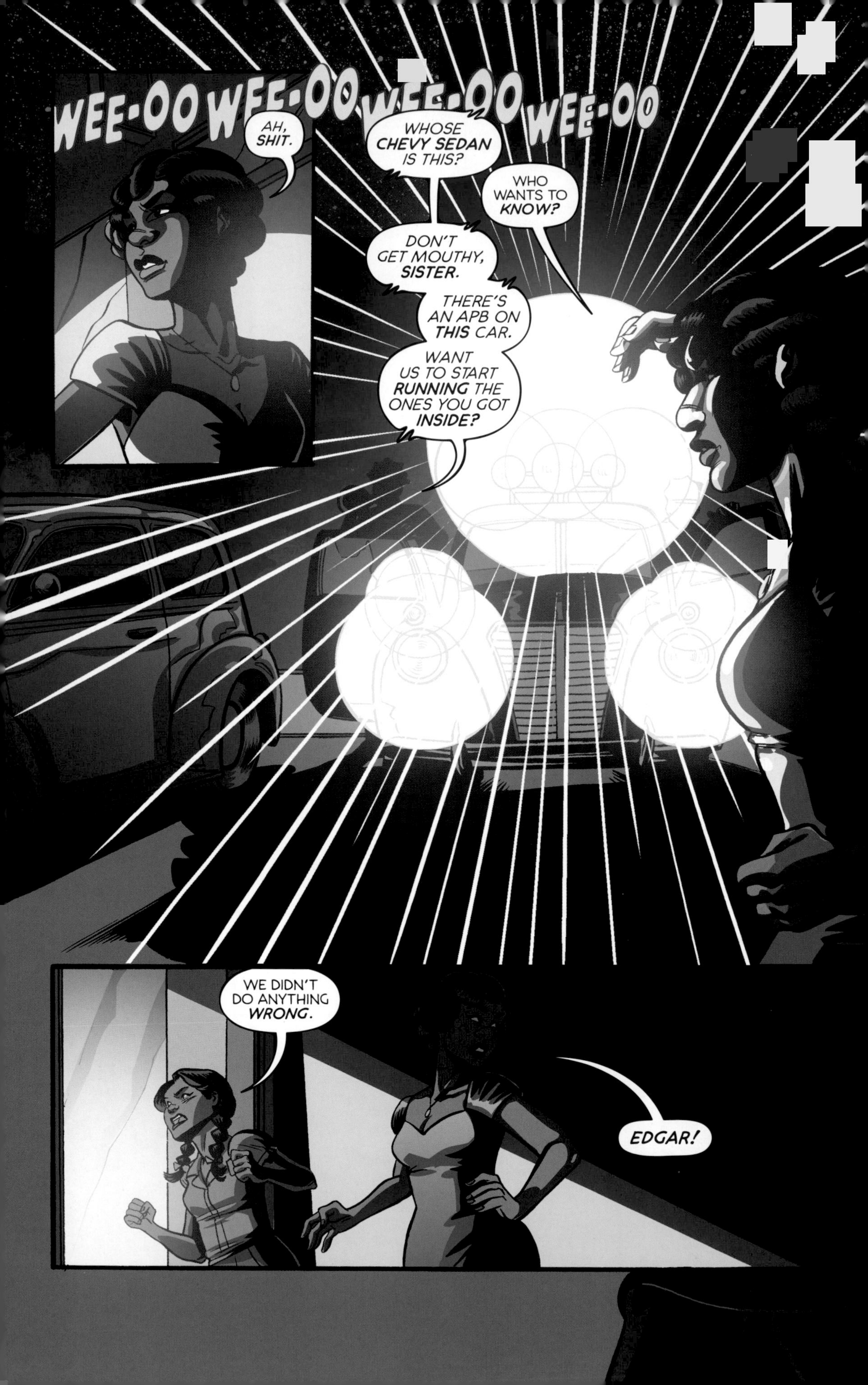
WEE-OO WEE-OO WEE-OO WEE-OO
AH, SHIT.
WHOSE CHEVY SEDAN IS THIS?
DON'T GET MOUTHY, SISTER.
THERE'S AN APB ON THIS CAR.
WANT US TO START RUNNING THE ONES YOU GOT INSIDE?
WHO WANTS TO KNOW?
WE DIDN'T DO ANYTHING WRONG.
EDGAR!

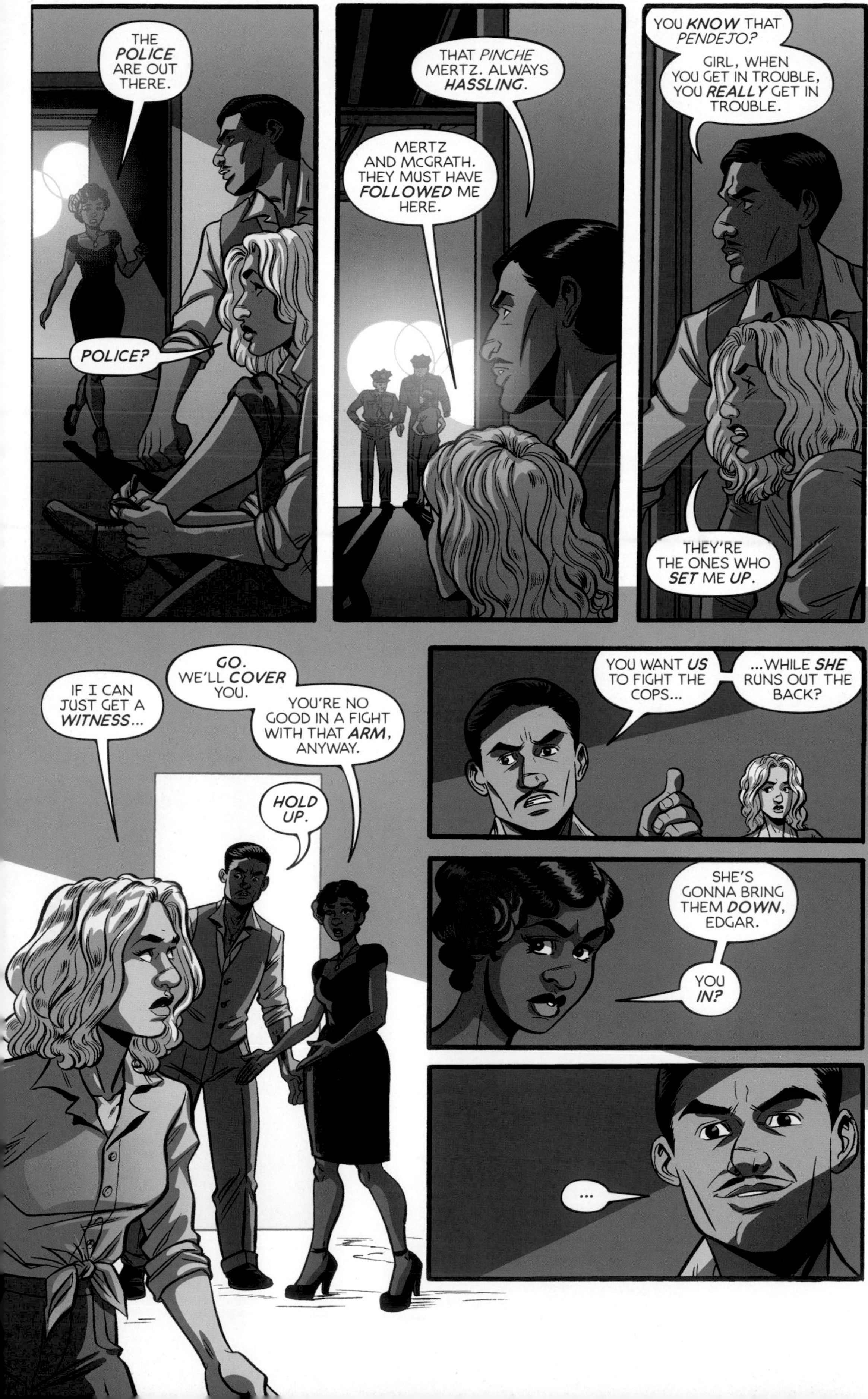
THE POLICE ARE OUT THERE.
POLICE?
THAT PINCHE MERTZ. ALWAYS HASSLING.
MERTZ AND McGRATH. THEY MUST HAVE FOLLOWED ME HERE.
YOU KNOW THAT PENDEJO?
GIRL, WHEN YOU GET IN TROUBLE, YOU REALLY GET IN TROUBLE.
THEY'RE THE ONES WHO SET ME UP.
IF I CAN JUST GET A WITNESS...
GO. WE'LL COVER YOU.
YOU'RE NO GOOD IN A FIGHT WITH THAT ARM, ANYWAY.
HOLD UP.
YOU WANT US TO FIGHT THE COPS...
...WHILE SHE RUNS OUT THE BACK?
SHE'S GONNA BRING THEM DOWN, EDGAR.
YOU IN?
...

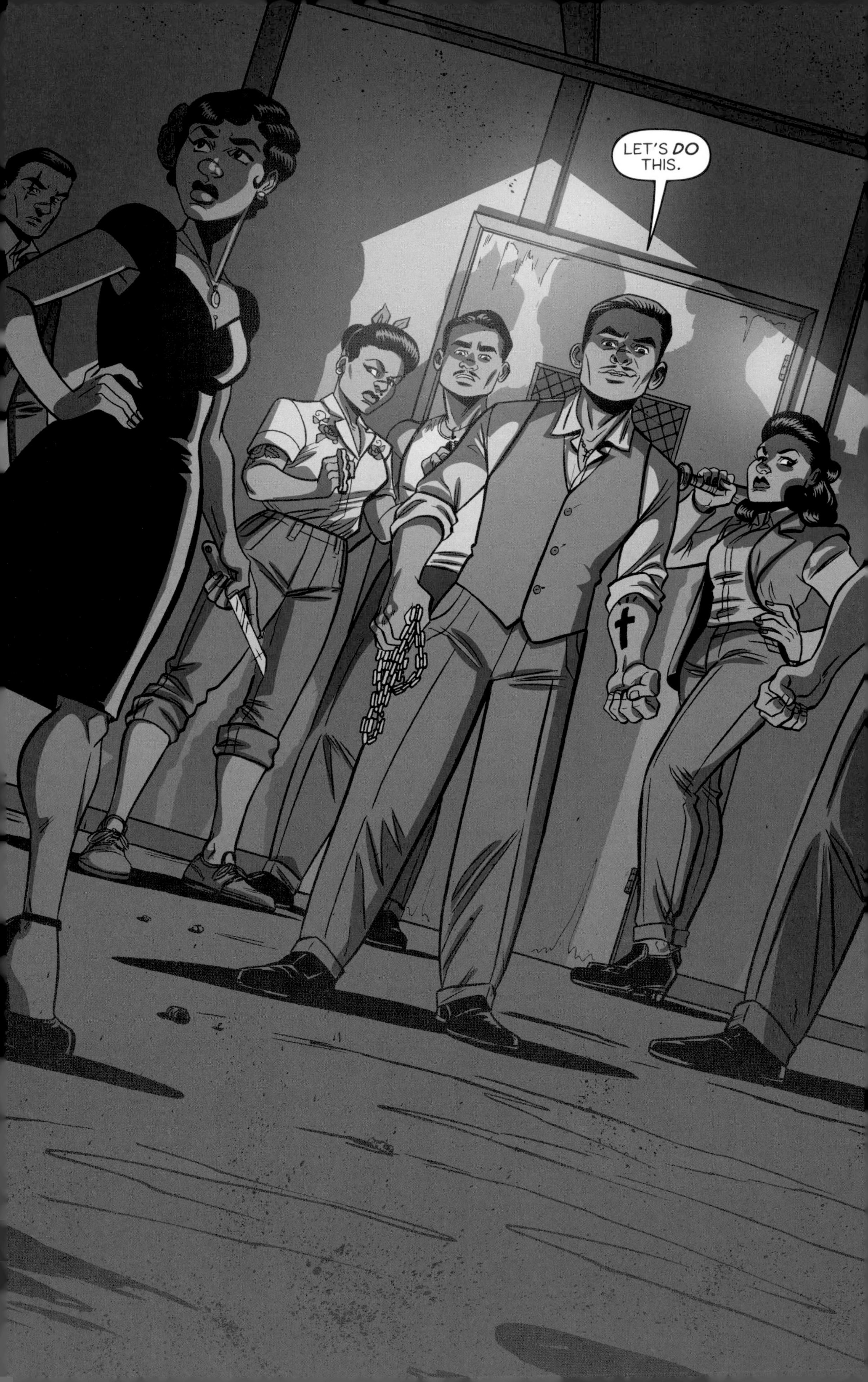
LET'S DO THIS.

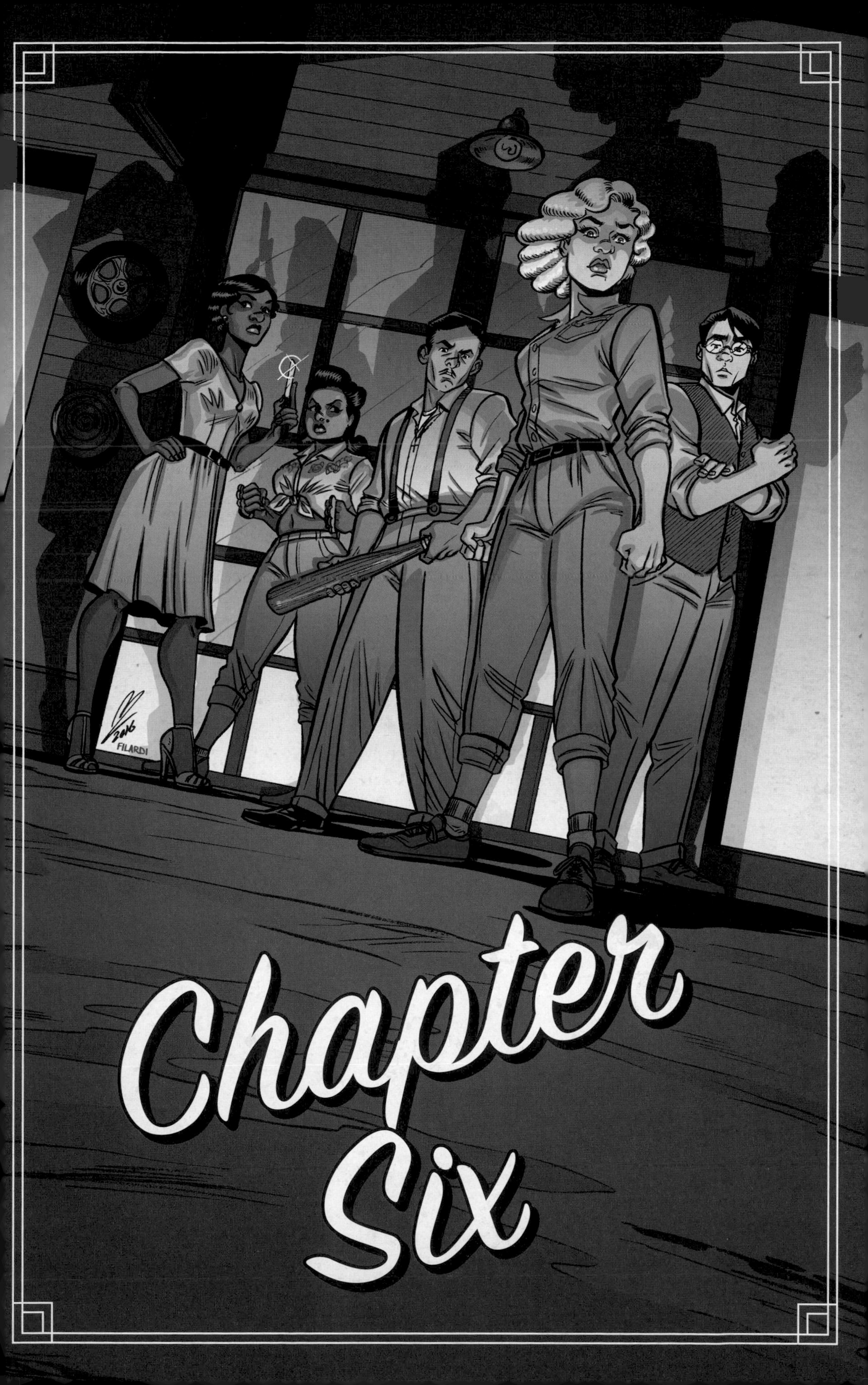
FILARDI

Chapter Six

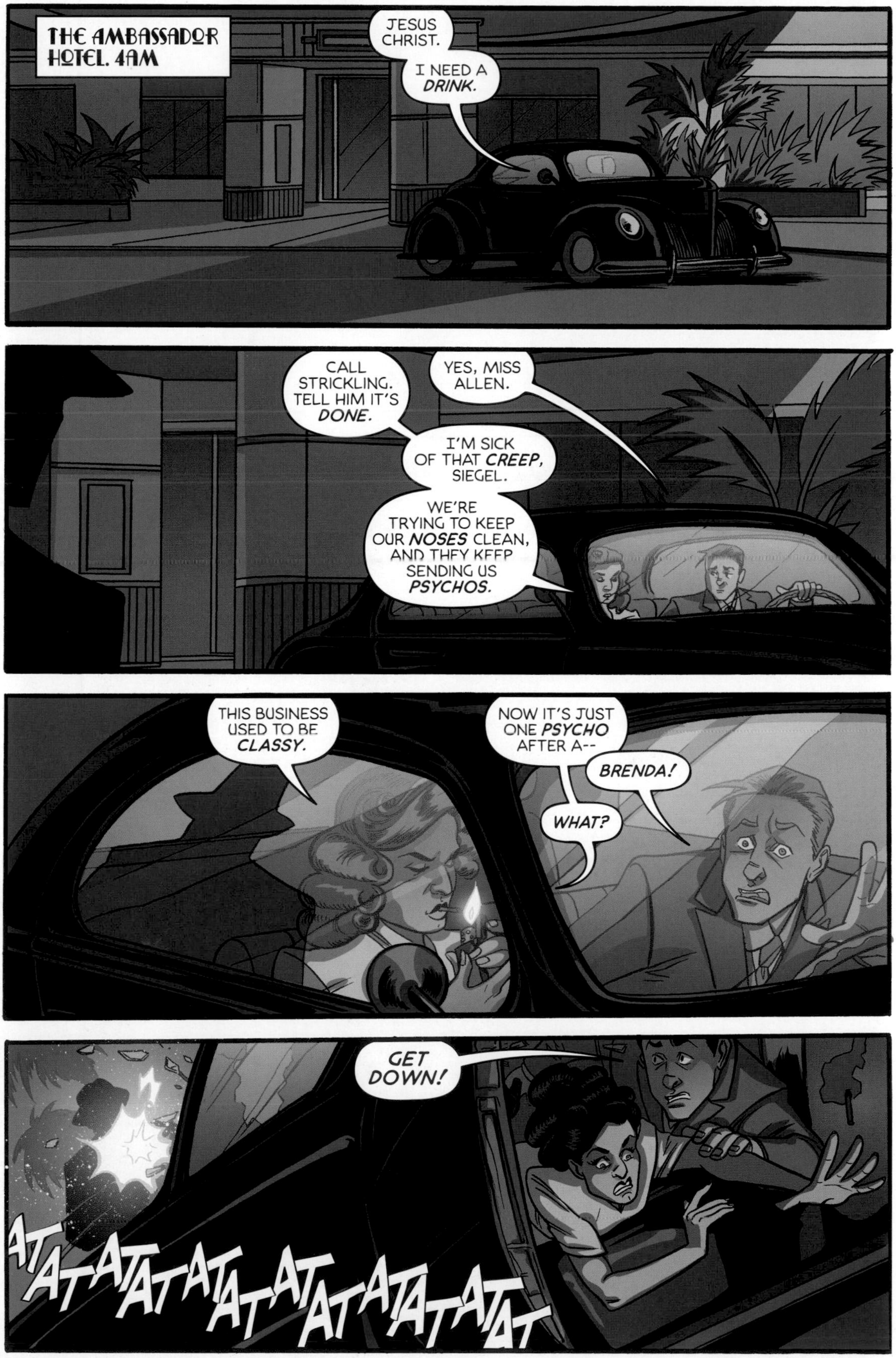
THE AMBASSADOR HOTEL. 4AM
JESUS CHRIST.
I NEED A *DRINK.*
CALL STRICKLING. TELL HIM IT'S *DONE.*
YES, MISS ALLEN.
I'M SICK OF THAT *CREEP,* SIEGEL.
WE'RE TRYING TO KEEP OUR *NOSES* CLEAN, AND THEY KEEP SENDING US *PSYCHOS.*
THIS BUSINESS USED TO BE *CLASSY.*
NOW IT'S JUST ONE *PSYCHO* AFTER A--
BRENDA!
WHAT?
GET DOWN!
ATATATATATATATATATATATATATAT

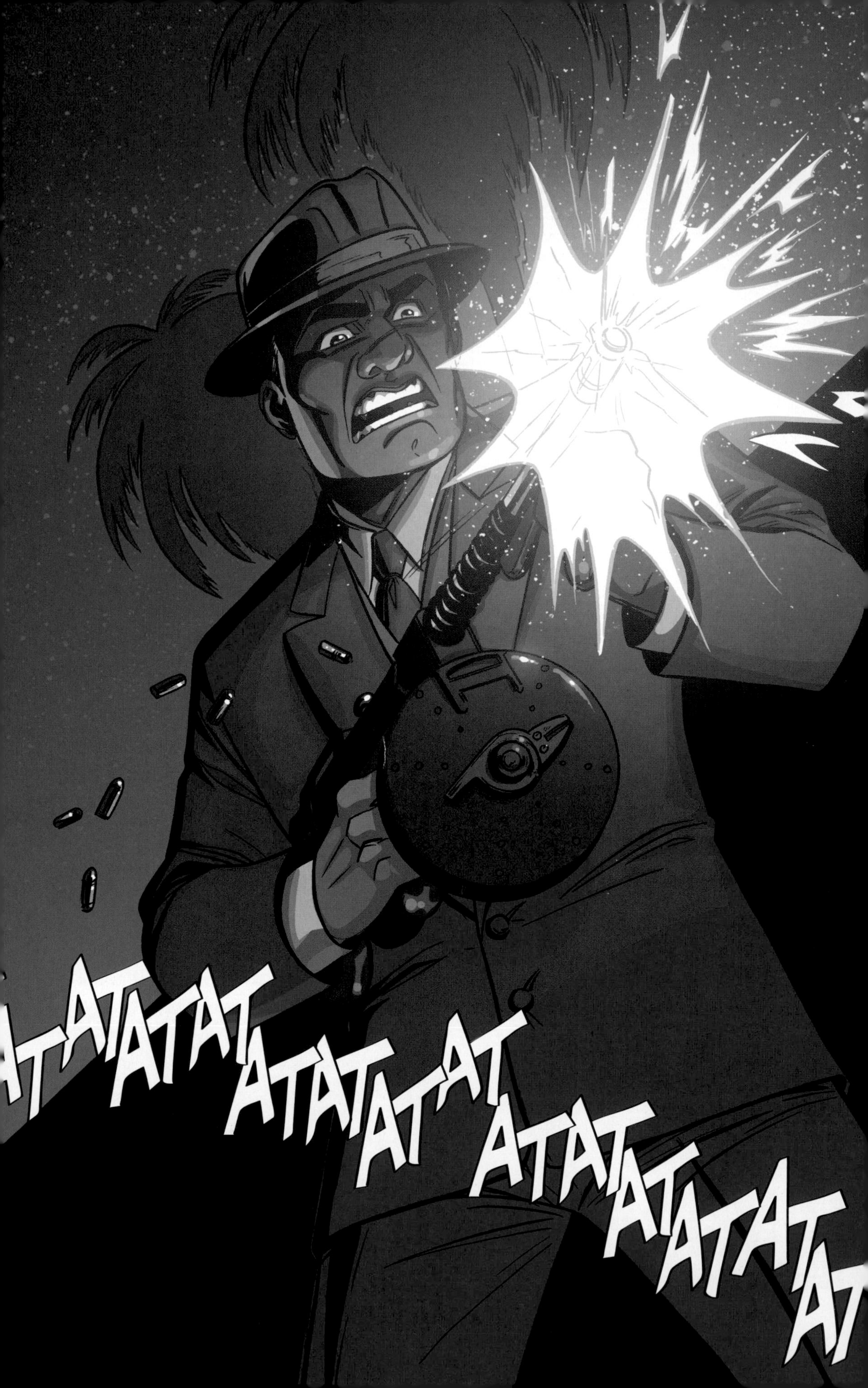
ATATATAT
ATATATAT
ATATATATATAT

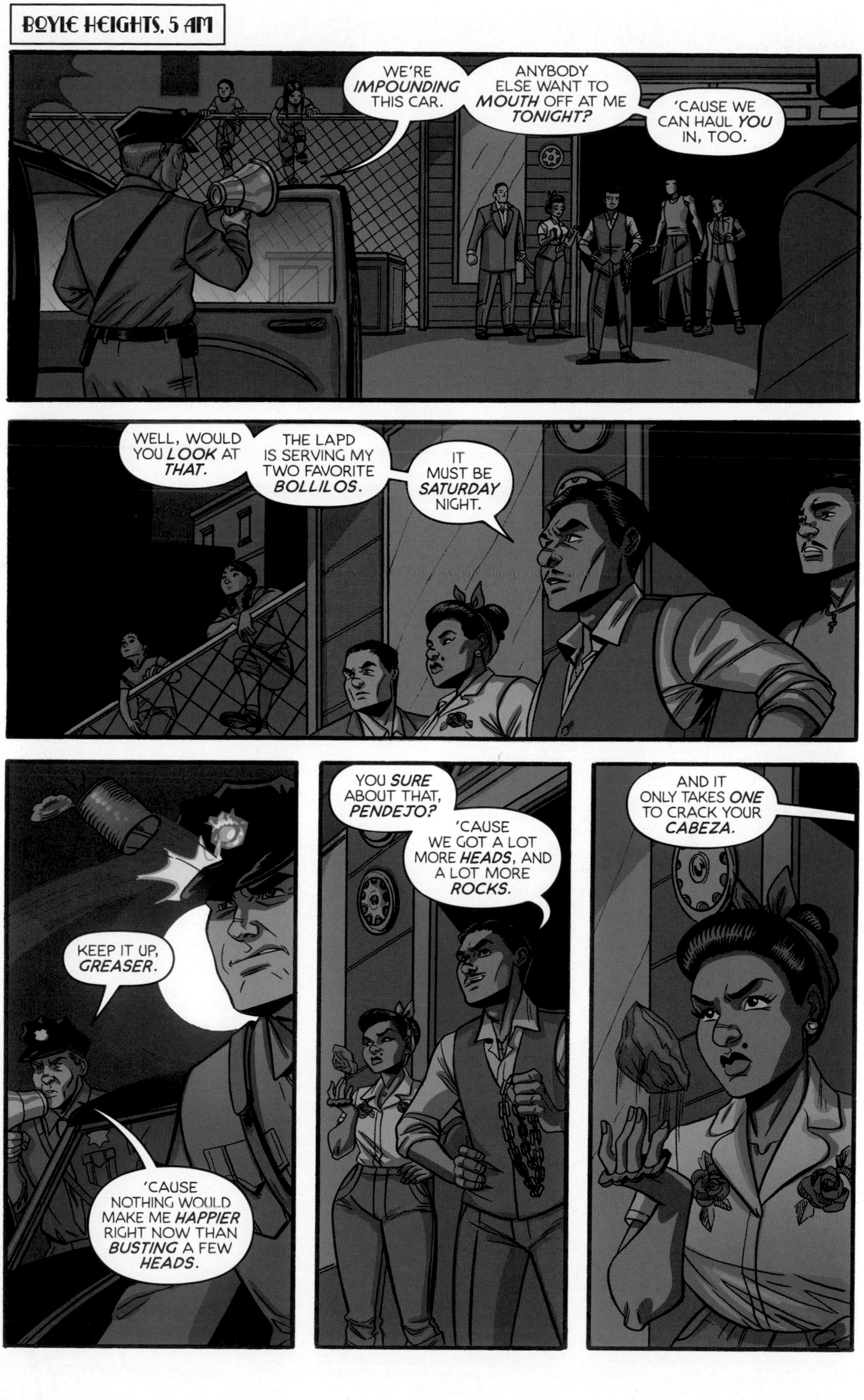
BOYLE HEIGHTS, 5 AM
WE'RE IMPOUNDING THIS CAR.
ANYBODY ELSE WANT TO MOUTH OFF AT ME TONIGHT?
'CAUSE WE CAN HAUL YOU IN, TOO.
WELL, WOULD YOU LOOK AT THAT.
THE LAPD IS SERVING MY TWO FAVORITE BOLLILOS.
IT MUST BE SATURDAY NIGHT.
KEEP IT UP, GREASER.
'CAUSE NOTHING WOULD MAKE ME HAPPIER RIGHT NOW THAN BUSTING A FEW HEADS.
YOU SURE ABOUT THAT, PENDEJO?
'CAUSE WE GOT A LOT MORE HEADS, AND A LOT MORE ROCKS.
AND IT ONLY TAKES ONE TO CRACK YOUR CABEZA.

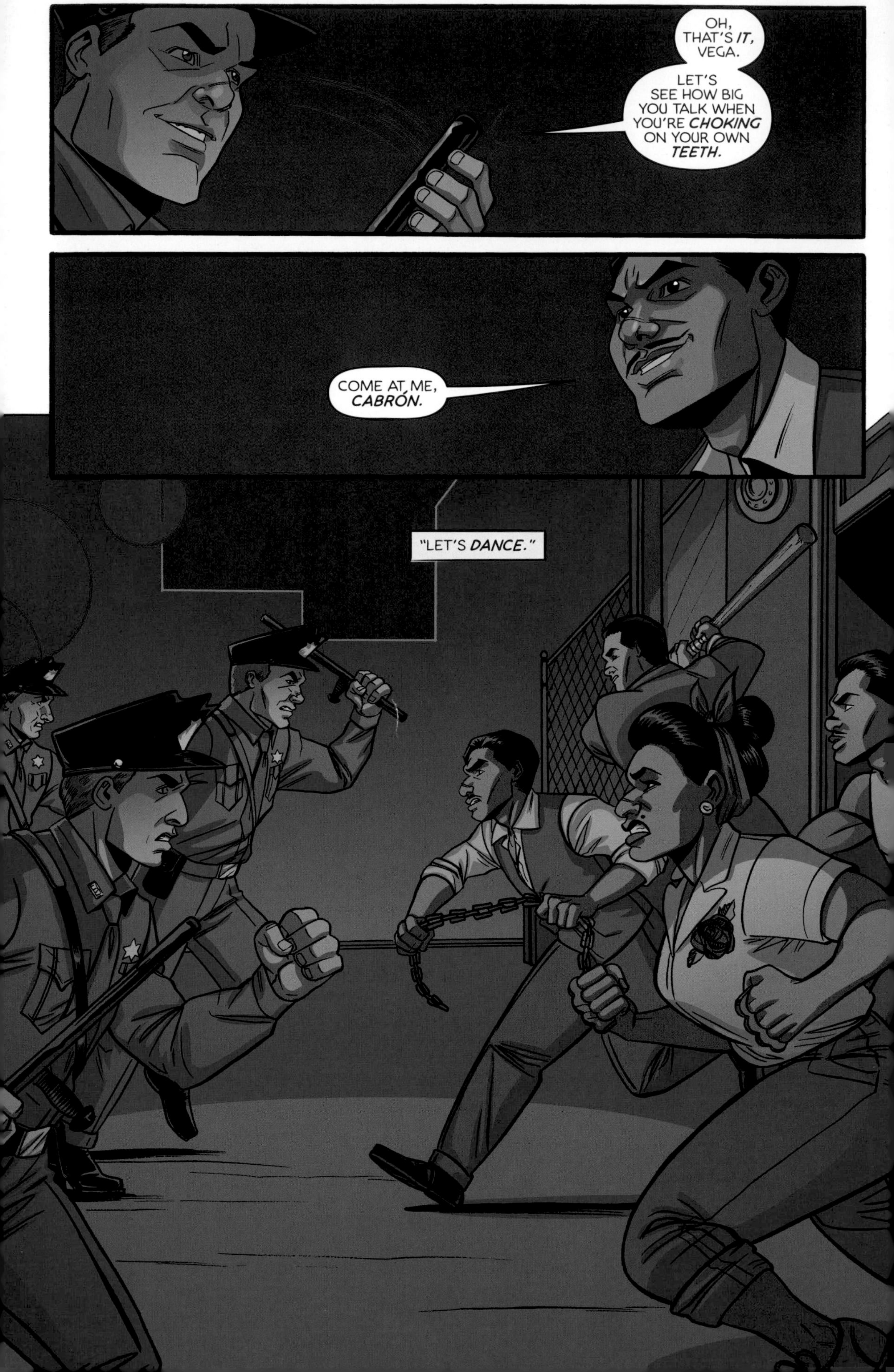
OH, THAT'S *IT*, VEGA.
LET'S SEE HOW BIG YOU TALK WHEN YOU'RE ***CHOKING*** ON YOUR OWN ***TEETH***.
COME AT ME, ***CABRÓN***.
"LET'S *DANCE*."

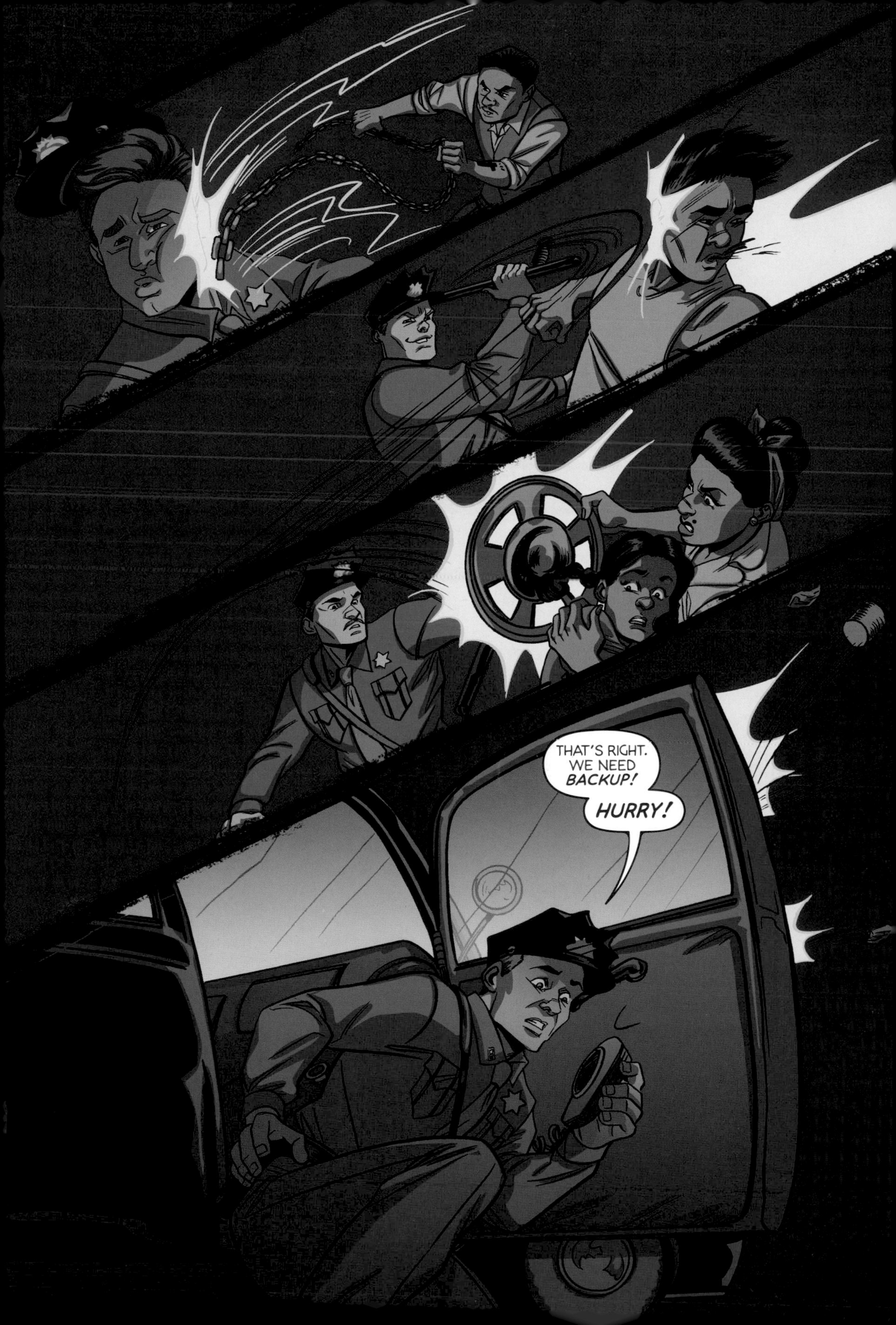
THAT'S RIGHT. WE NEED *BACKUP!*
HURRY!

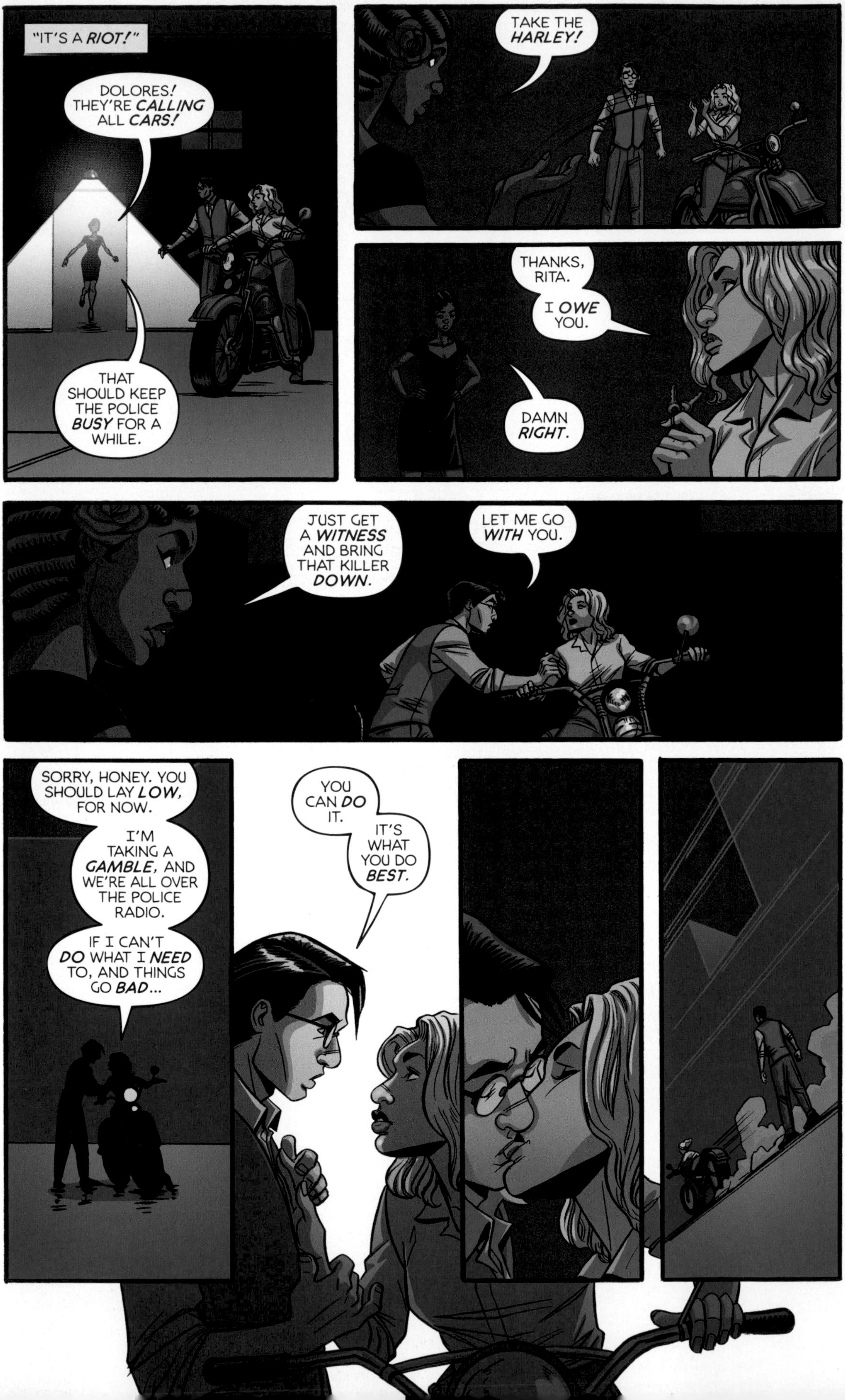
"IT'S A *RIOT!*"
DOLORES! THEY'RE *CALLING* ALL *CARS!*
THAT SHOULD KEEP THE POLICE *BUSY* FOR A WHILE.
TAKE THE *HARLEY!*
THANKS, RITA.
I *OWE* YOU.
DAMN *RIGHT*.
JUST GET A *WITNESS* AND BRING THAT KILLER *DOWN*.
LET ME GO *WITH* YOU.
SORRY, HONEY. YOU SHOULD LAY *LOW,* FOR NOW.
I'M TAKING A *GAMBLE,* AND WE'RE ALL OVER THE POLICE RADIO.
IF I CAN'T *DO* WHAT I *NEED* TO, AND THINGS GO *BAD*...
YOU CAN *DO* IT.
IT'S WHAT YOU DO *BEST*.

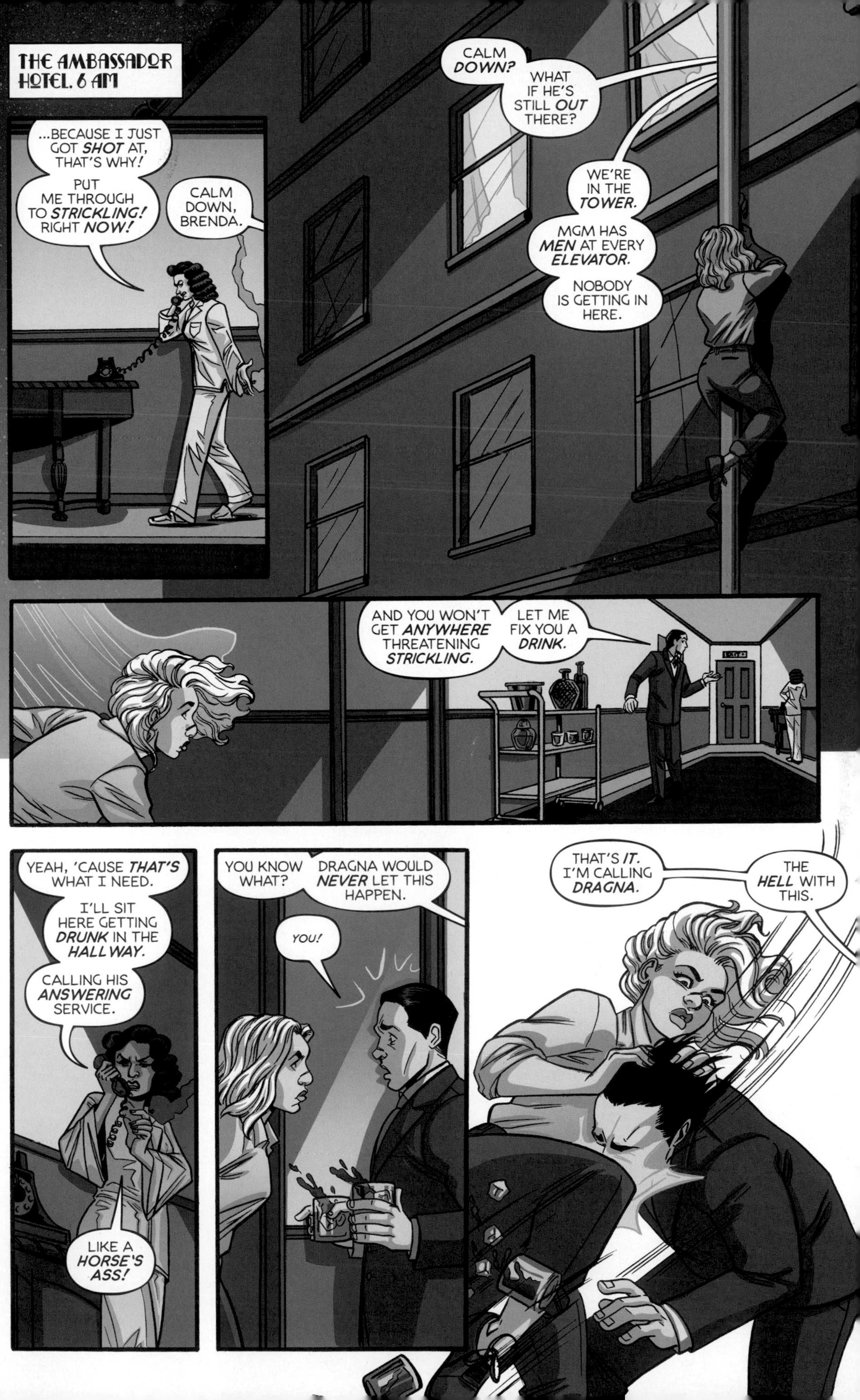
THE AMBASSADOR HOTEL. 6 AM
...BECAUSE I JUST GOT *SHOT* AT, THAT'S WHY!
PUT ME THROUGH TO *STRICKLING!* RIGHT *NOW!*
CALM DOWN, BRENDA.
CALM *DOWN?*
WHAT IF HE'S STILL *OUT* THERE?
WE'RE IN THE *TOWER.*
MGM HAS *MEN* AT EVERY *ELEVATOR.*
NOBODY IS GETTING IN HERE.
AND YOU WON'T GET *ANYWHERE* THREATENING *STRICKLING.*
LET ME FIX YOU A *DRINK.*
YEAH, 'CAUSE *THAT'S* WHAT I NEED.
I'LL SIT HERE GETTING *DRUNK* IN THE *HALLWAY.*
CALLING HIS *ANSWERING* SERVICE.
LIKE A *HORSE'S ASS!*
YOU KNOW WHAT?
DRAGNA WOULD *NEVER* LET THIS HAPPEN.
YOU!
THAT'S *IT.* I'M CALLING *DRAGNA.*
THE *HELL* WITH THIS.

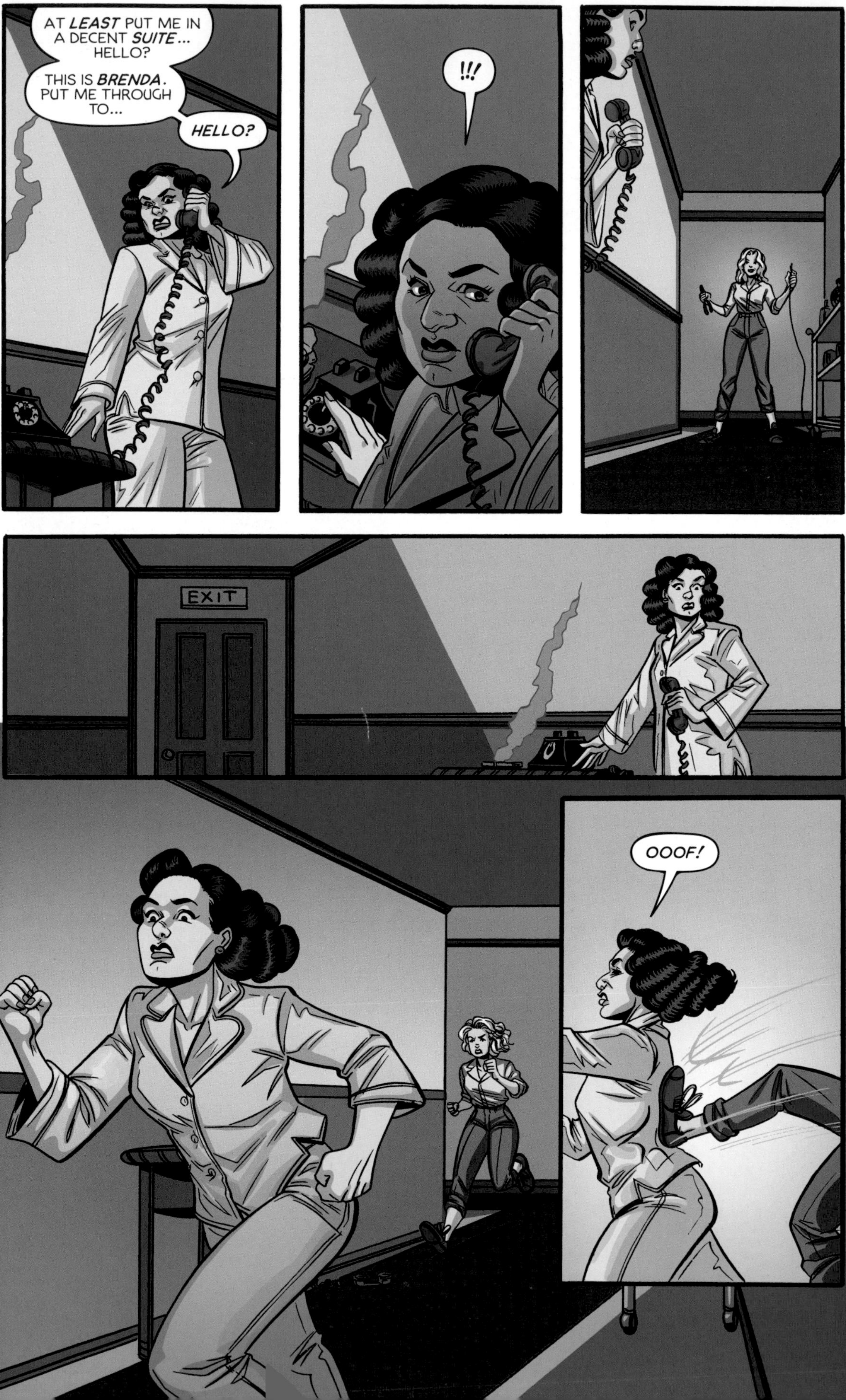
AT *LEAST* PUT ME IN A DECENT *SUITE*... HELLO?
THIS IS *BRENDA*. PUT ME THROUGH TO...
HELLO?
!!!
EXIT
OOOF!

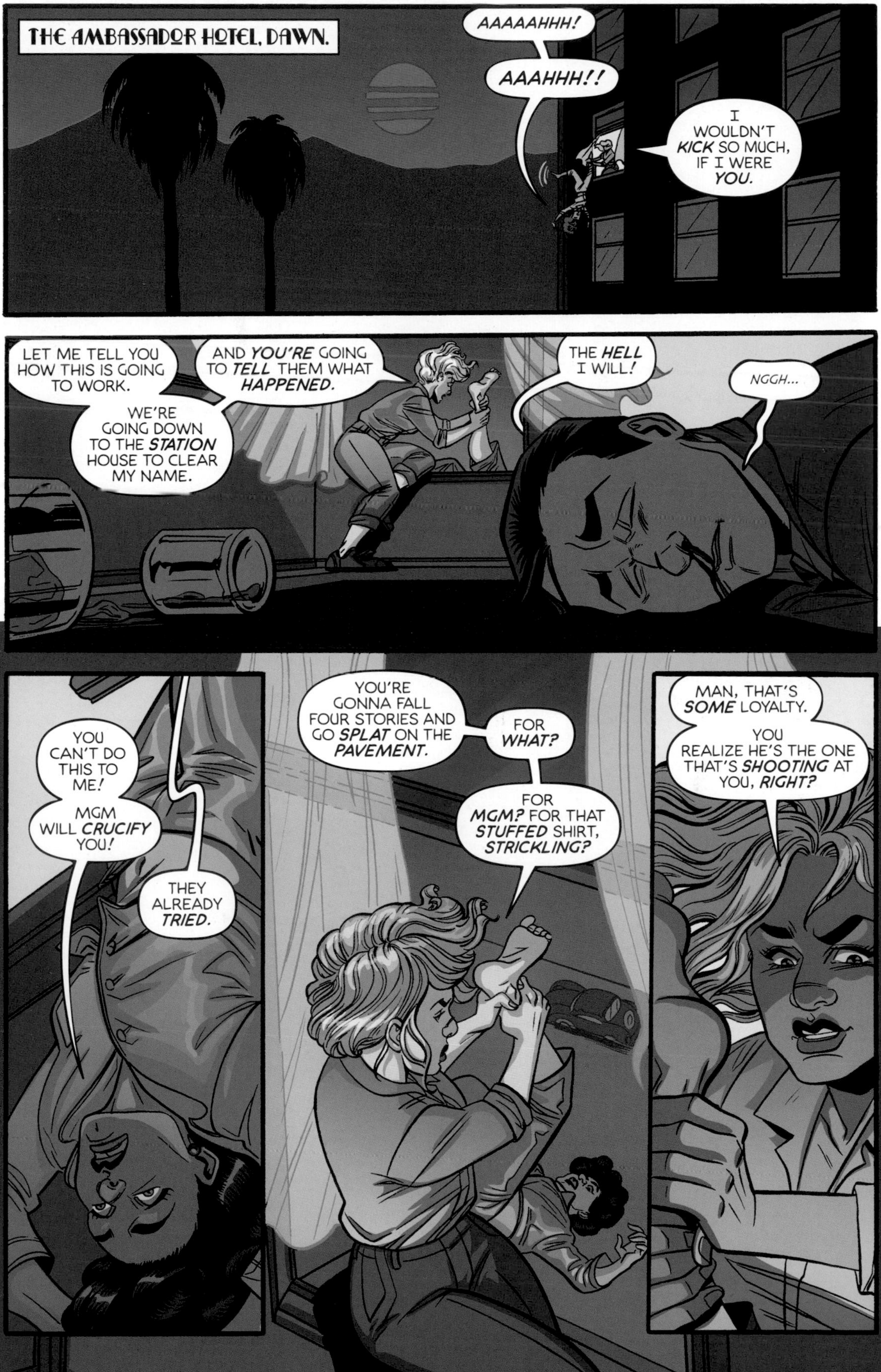
THE AMBASSADOR HOTEL, DAWN.
AAAAAHHH!
AAAHHH!!
I WOULDN'T KICK SO MUCH, IF I WERE YOU.
LET ME TELL YOU HOW THIS IS GOING TO WORK.
WE'RE GOING DOWN TO THE STATION HOUSE TO CLEAR MY NAME.
AND YOU'RE GOING TO TELL THEM WHAT HAPPENED.
THE HELL I WILL!
NGGH...
YOU CAN'T DO THIS TO ME!
MGM WILL CRUCIFY YOU!
THEY ALREADY TRIED.
YOU'RE GONNA FALL FOUR STORIES AND GO SPLAT ON THE PAVEMENT.
FOR WHAT?
FOR MGM? FOR THAT STUFFED SHIRT, STRICKLING?
MAN, THAT'S SOME LOYALTY.
YOU REALIZE HE'S THE ONE THAT'S SHOOTING AT YOU, RIGHT?

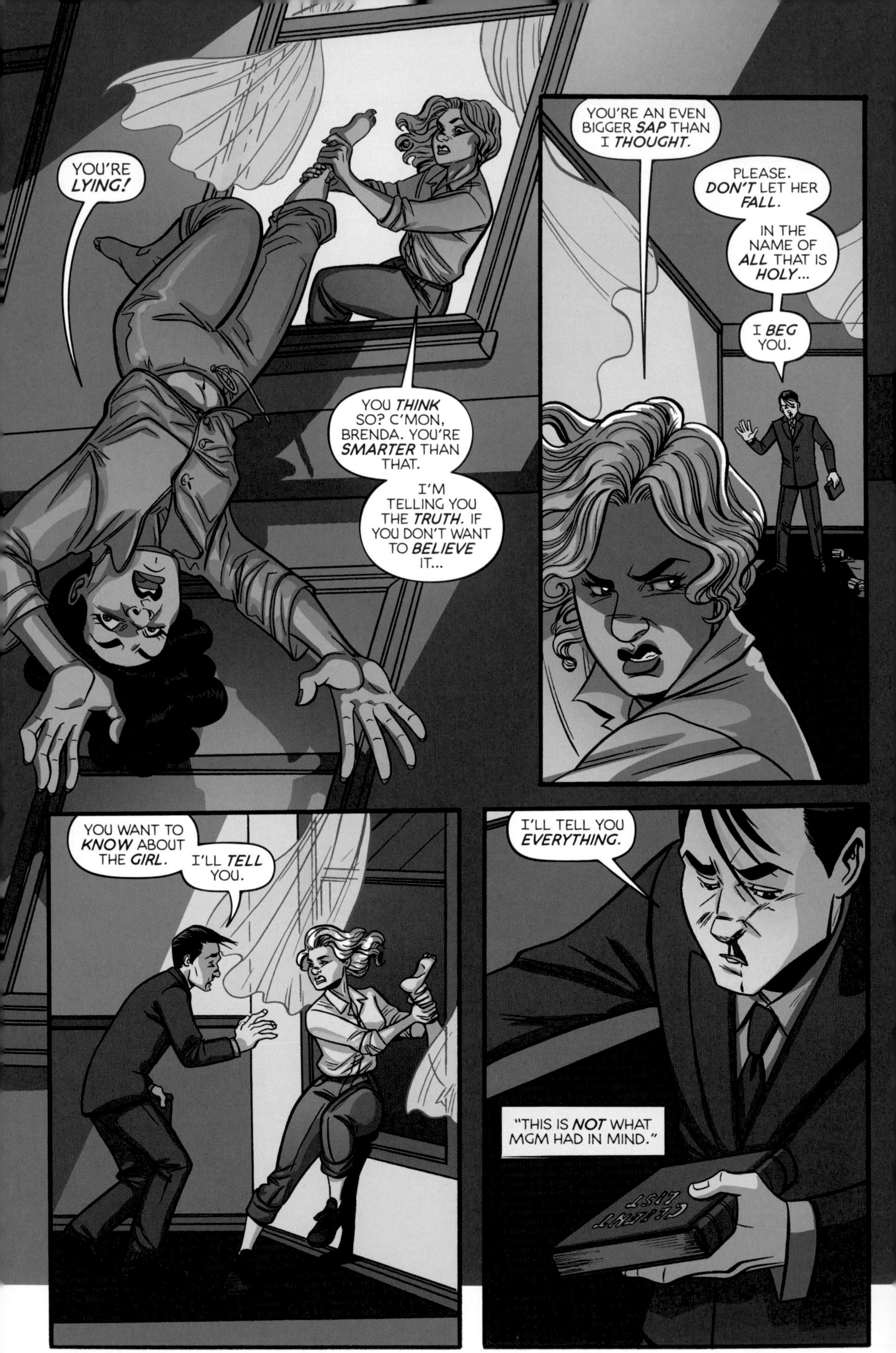
YOU'RE *LYING!*
YOU *THINK* SO? C'MON, BRENDA. YOU'RE *SMARTER* THAN THAT.
I'M TELLING YOU THE *TRUTH.* IF YOU DON'T WANT TO *BELIEVE* IT...
YOU'RE AN EVEN BIGGER *SAP* THAN I *THOUGHT.*
PLEASE. *DON'T* LET HER *FALL.*
IN THE NAME OF *ALL* THAT IS *HOLY*...
I *BEG* YOU.
YOU WANT TO *KNOW* ABOUT THE *GIRL.*
I'LL *TELL* YOU.
I'LL TELL YOU *EVERYTHING.*
"THIS IS *NOT* WHAT MGM HAD IN MIND."

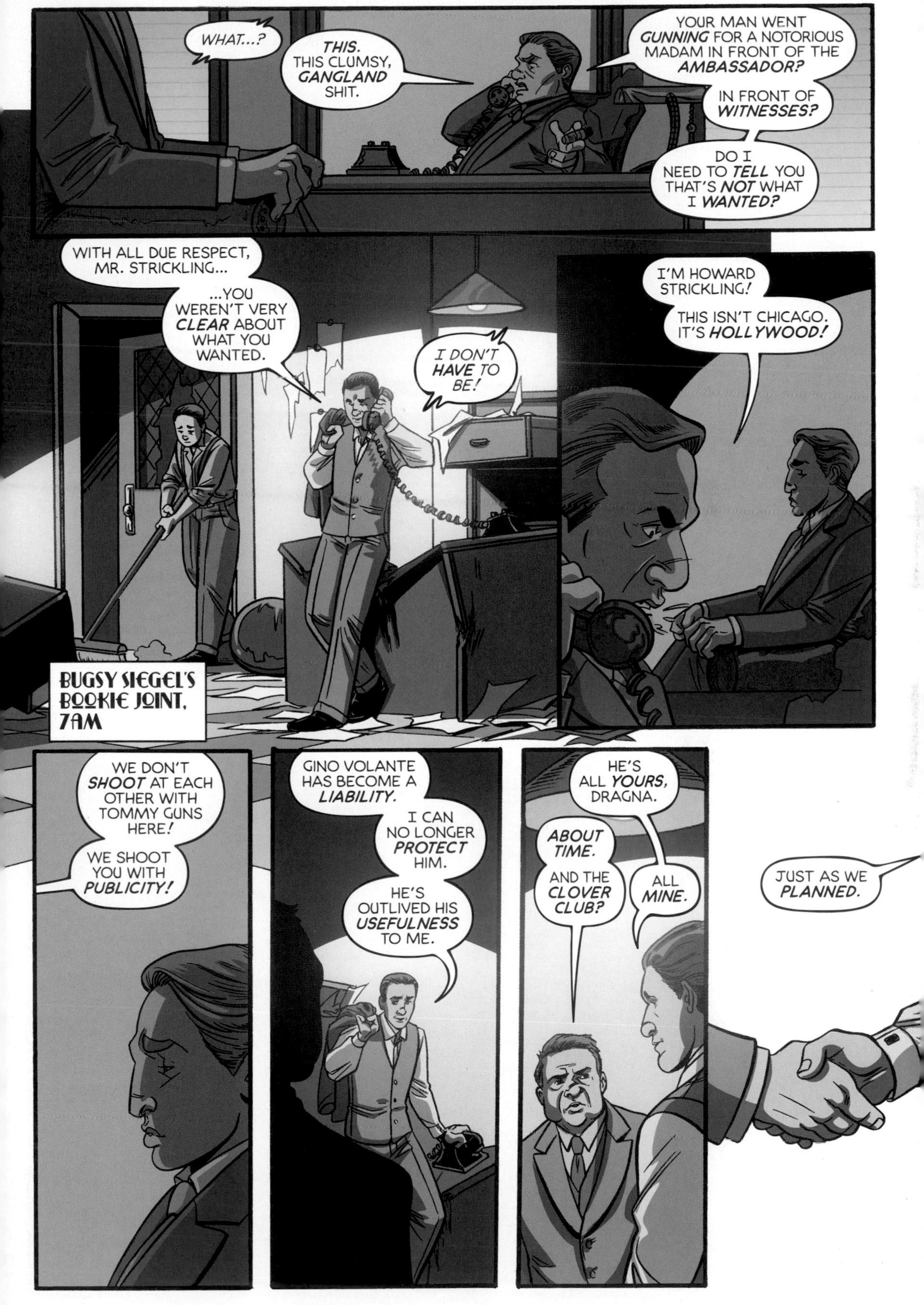
WHAT...?
THIS. THIS CLUMSY, GANGLAND SHIT.
YOUR MAN WENT GUNNING FOR A NOTORIOUS MADAM IN FRONT OF THE AMBASSADOR?
IN FRONT OF WITNESSES?
DO I NEED TO TELL YOU THAT'S NOT WHAT I WANTED?
WITH ALL DUE RESPECT, MR. STRICKLING...
...YOU WEREN'T VERY CLEAR ABOUT WHAT YOU WANTED.
I DON'T HAVE TO BE!
BUGSY SIEGEL'S BOOKIE JOINT, 7AM
I'M HOWARD STRICKLING!
THIS ISN'T CHICAGO. IT'S HOLLYWOOD!
WE DON'T SHOOT AT EACH OTHER WITH TOMMY GUNS HERE!
WE SHOOT YOU WITH PUBLICITY!
GINO VOLANTE HAS BECOME A LIABILITY.
I CAN NO LONGER PROTECT HIM.
HE'S OUTLIVED HIS USEFULNESS TO ME.
HE'S ALL YOURS, DRAGNA.
ABOUT TIME.
AND THE CLOVER CLUB?
ALL MINE.
JUST AS WE PLANNED.

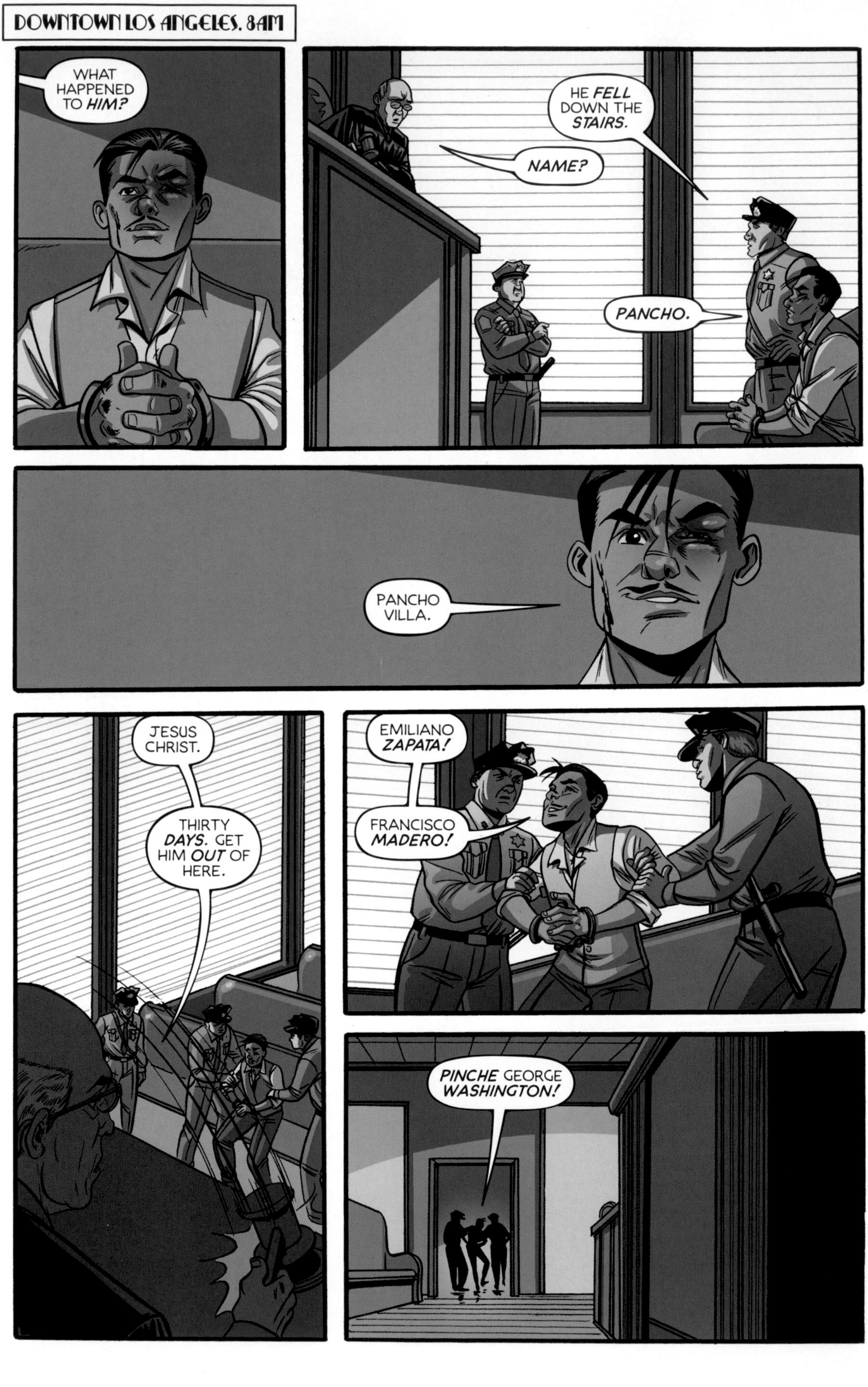
DOWNTOWN LOS ANGELES, 8AM
WHAT HAPPENED TO *HIM?*
HE *FELL* DOWN THE *STAIRS.*
NAME?
PANCHO.
PANCHO VILLA.
JESUS CHRIST.
THIRTY *DAYS.* GET HIM *OUT* OF HERE.
EMILIANO *ZAPATA!*
FRANCISCO *MADERO!*
PINCHE GEORGE *WASHINGTON!*

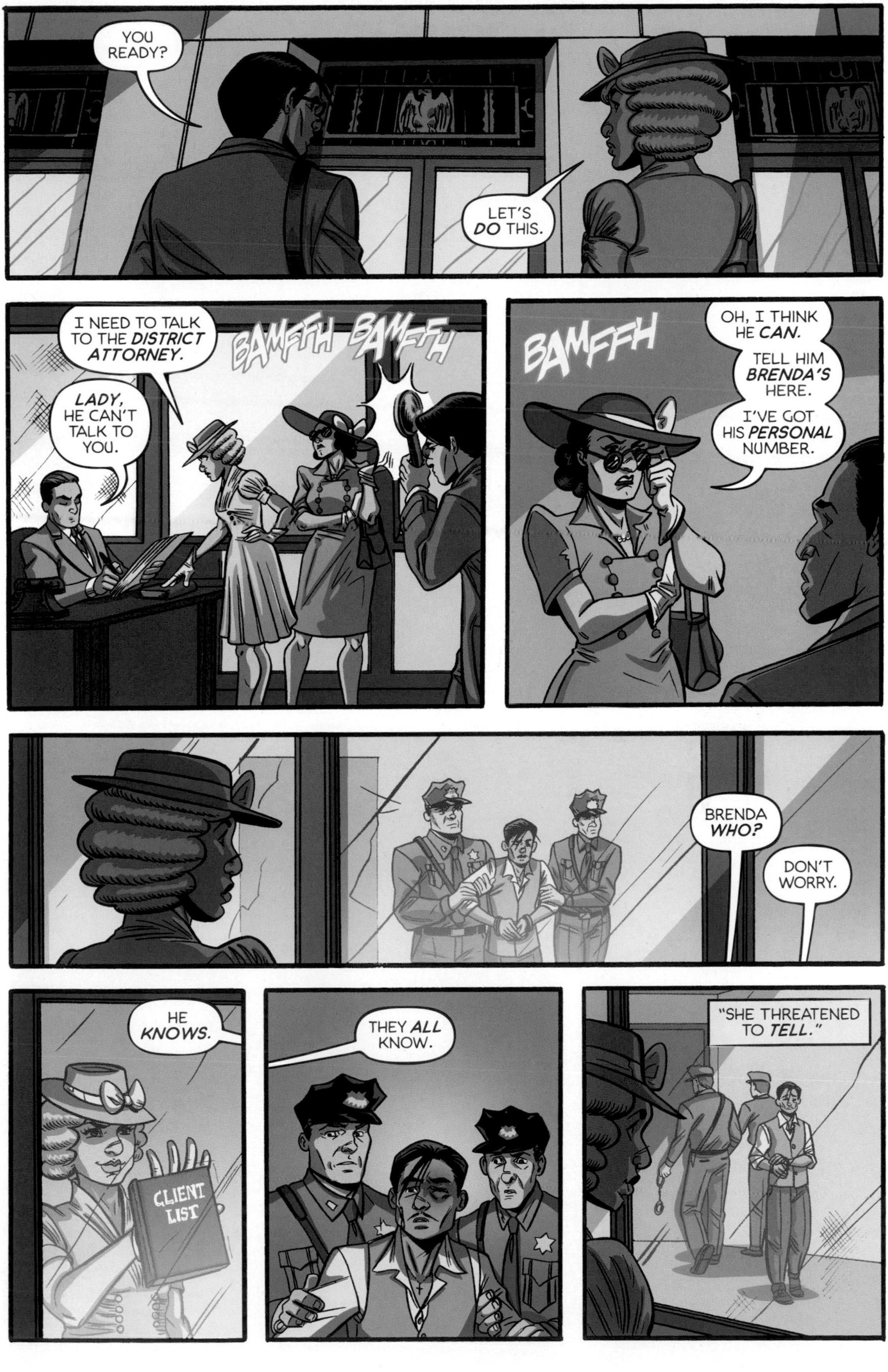
YOU READY?
LET'S DO THIS.
I NEED TO TALK TO THE DISTRICT ATTORNEY.
BAMFFH
BAMFFH
LADY, HE CAN'T TALK TO YOU.
BAMFFH
OH, I THINK HE CAN.
TELL HIM BRENDA'S HERE.
I'VE GOT HIS PERSONAL NUMBER.
BRENDA WHO?
DON'T WORRY.
HE KNOWS.
CLIENT LIST
THEY ALL KNOW.
"SHE THREATENED TO TELL."

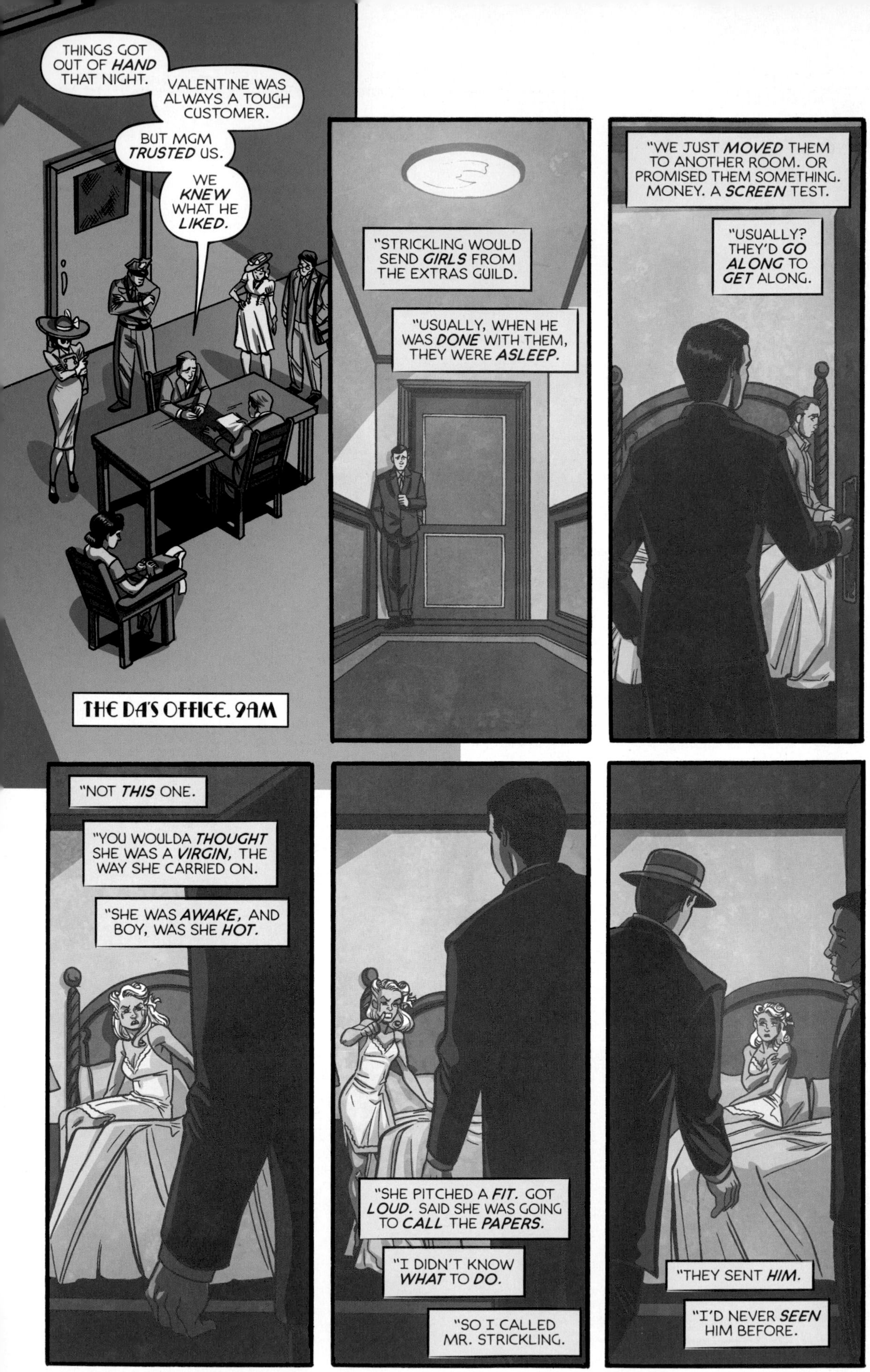
THINGS GOT OUT OF HAND THAT NIGHT.
VALENTINE WAS ALWAYS A TOUGH CUSTOMER.
BUT MGM TRUSTED US.
WE KNEW WHAT HE LIKED.
THE DA'S OFFICE. 9AM
"STRICKLING WOULD SEND GIRLS FROM THE EXTRAS GUILD.
"USUALLY, WHEN HE WAS DONE WITH THEM, THEY WERE ASLEEP.
"WE JUST MOVED THEM TO ANOTHER ROOM. OR PROMISED THEM SOMETHING. MONEY. A SCREEN TEST.
"USUALLY? THEY'D GO ALONG TO GET ALONG.
"NOT THIS ONE.
"YOU WOULDA THOUGHT SHE WAS A VIRGIN, THE WAY SHE CARRIED ON.
"SHE WAS AWAKE, AND BOY, WAS SHE HOT.
"SHE PITCHED A FIT. GOT LOUD. SAID SHE WAS GOING TO CALL THE PAPERS.
"I DIDN'T KNOW WHAT TO DO.
"SO I CALLED MR. STRICKLING.
"THEY SENT HIM.
"I'D NEVER SEEN HIM BEFORE.

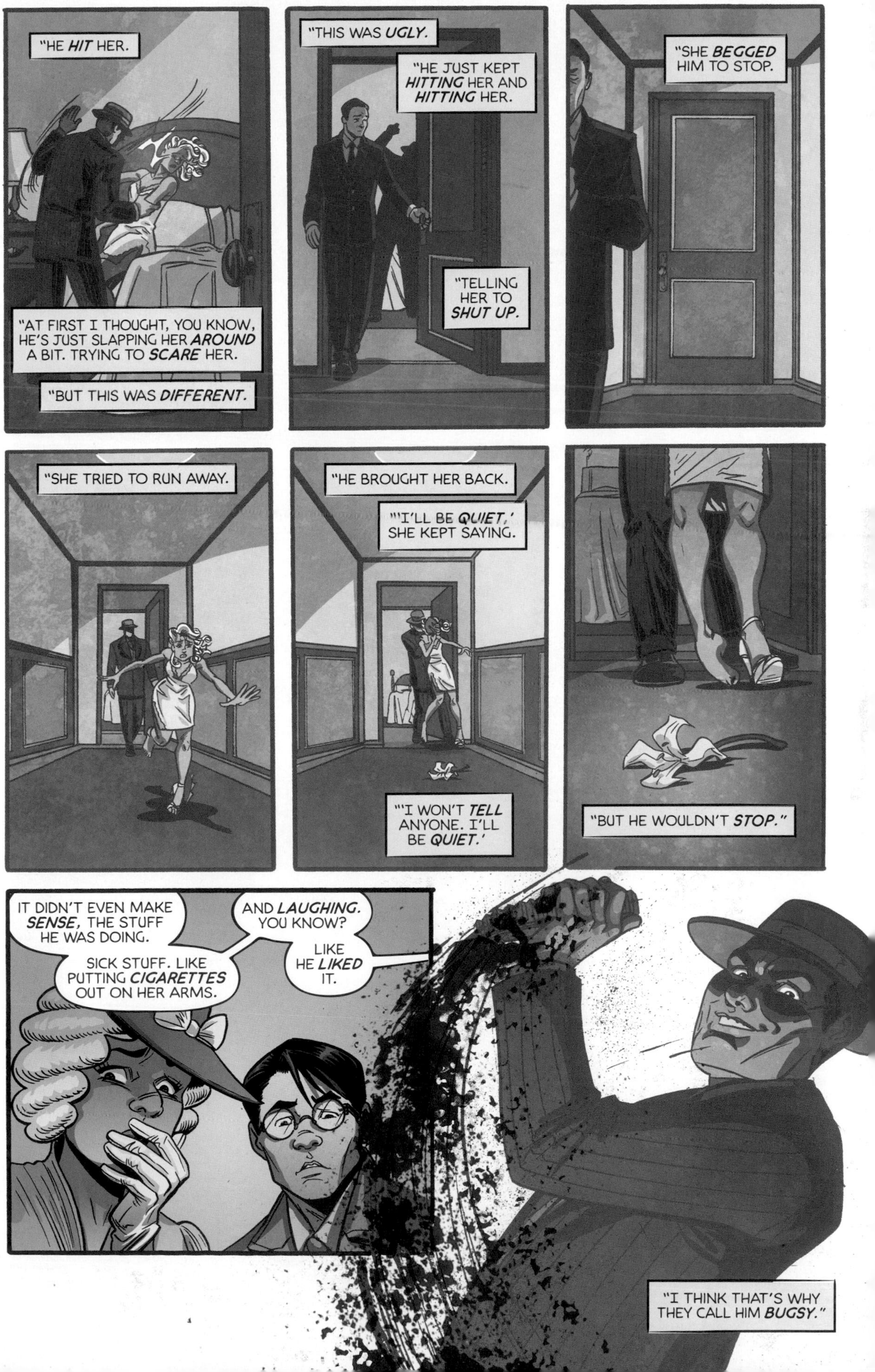
"HE *HIT* HER.
"AT FIRST I THOUGHT, YOU KNOW, HE'S JUST SLAPPING HER *AROUND* A BIT. TRYING TO *SCARE* HER.
"BUT THIS WAS *DIFFERENT.*
"THIS WAS *UGLY.*
"HE JUST KEPT *HITTING* HER AND *HITTING* HER.
"TELLING HER TO *SHUT UP.*
"SHE *BEGGED* HIM TO STOP.
"SHE TRIED TO RUN AWAY.
"HE BROUGHT HER BACK.
"'I'LL BE *QUIET,*' SHE KEPT SAYING.
"'I WON'T *TELL* ANYONE. I'LL BE *QUIET.*'
"BUT HE WOULDN'T *STOP.*"
IT DIDN'T EVEN MAKE *SENSE,* THE STUFF HE WAS DOING.
SICK STUFF. LIKE PUTTING *CIGARETTES* OUT ON HER ARMS.
AND *LAUGHING.* YOU KNOW?
LIKE HE *LIKED* IT.
"I THINK THAT'S WHY THEY CALL HIM *BUGSY.*"

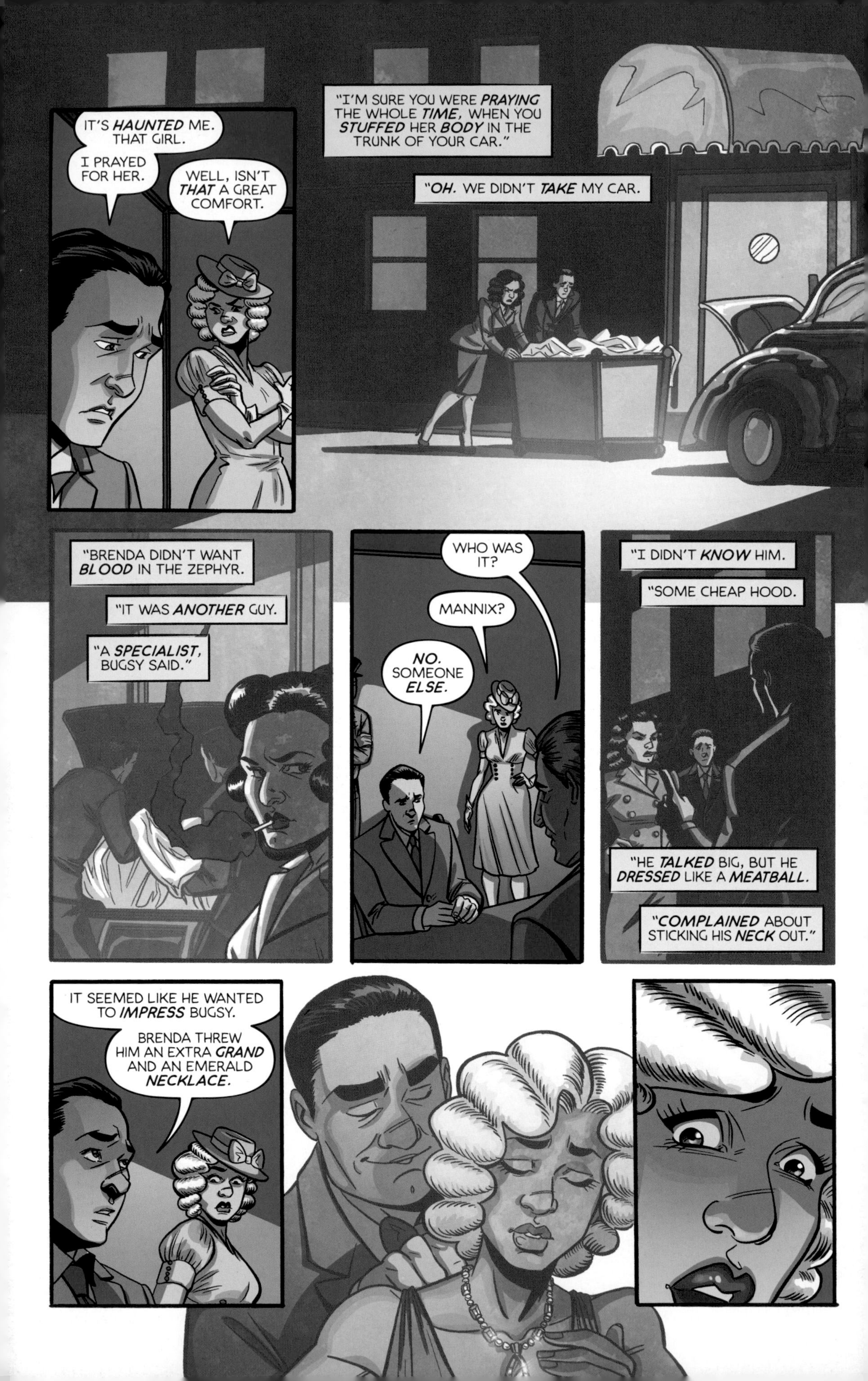
IT'S HAUNTED ME. THAT GIRL.
I PRAYED FOR HER.
WELL, ISN'T THAT A GREAT COMFORT.
"I'M SURE YOU WERE PRAYING THE WHOLE TIME, WHEN YOU STUFFED HER BODY IN THE TRUNK OF YOUR CAR."
"OH. WE DIDN'T TAKE MY CAR.
"BRENDA DIDN'T WANT BLOOD IN THE ZEPHYR.
"IT WAS ANOTHER GUY.
"A SPECIALIST, BUGSY SAID."
WHO WAS IT?
MANNIX?
NO. SOMEONE ELSE.
"I DIDN'T KNOW HIM.
"SOME CHEAP HOOD.
"HE TALKED BIG, BUT HE DRESSED LIKE A MEATBALL.
"COMPLAINED ABOUT STICKING HIS NECK OUT."
IT SEEMED LIKE HE WANTED TO IMPRESS BUGSY.
BRENDA THREW HIM AN EXTRA GRAND AND AN EMERALD NECKLACE.

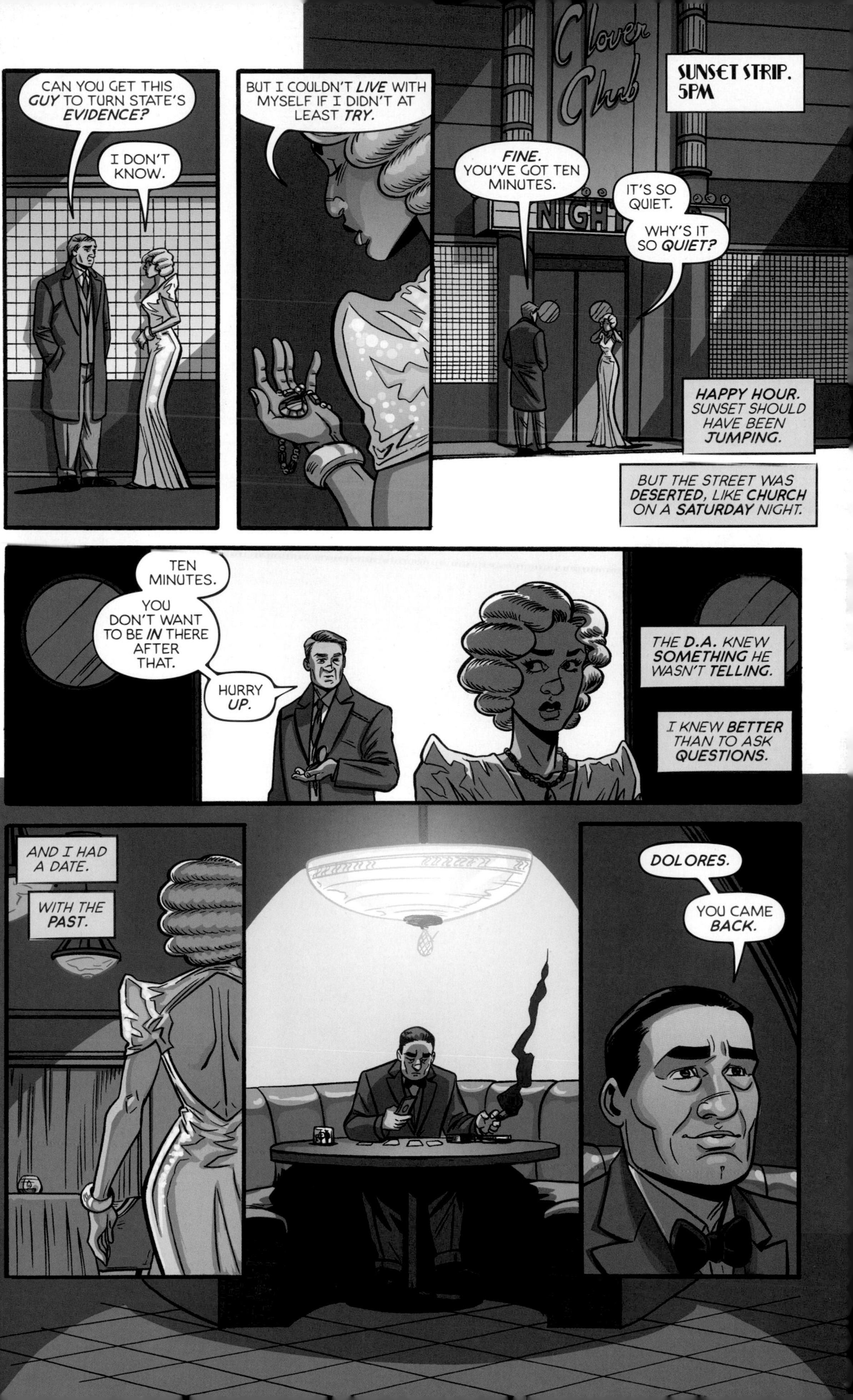
CAN YOU GET THIS GUY TO TURN STATE'S EVIDENCE?
I DON'T KNOW.
BUT I COULDN'T LIVE WITH MYSELF IF I DIDN'T AT LEAST TRY.
Clover Club
NIGHT
SUNSET STRIP. 5PM
FINE. YOU'VE GOT TEN MINUTES.
IT'S SO QUIET.
WHY'S IT SO QUIET?
HAPPY HOUR. SUNSET SHOULD HAVE BEEN JUMPING.
BUT THE STREET WAS DESERTED, LIKE CHURCH ON A SATURDAY NIGHT.
TEN MINUTES.
YOU DON'T WANT TO BE IN THERE AFTER THAT.
HURRY UP.
THE D.A. KNEW SOMETHING HE WASN'T TELLING.
I KNEW BETTER THAN TO ASK QUESTIONS.
AND I HAD A DATE.
WITH THE PAST.
DOLORES.
YOU CAME BACK.

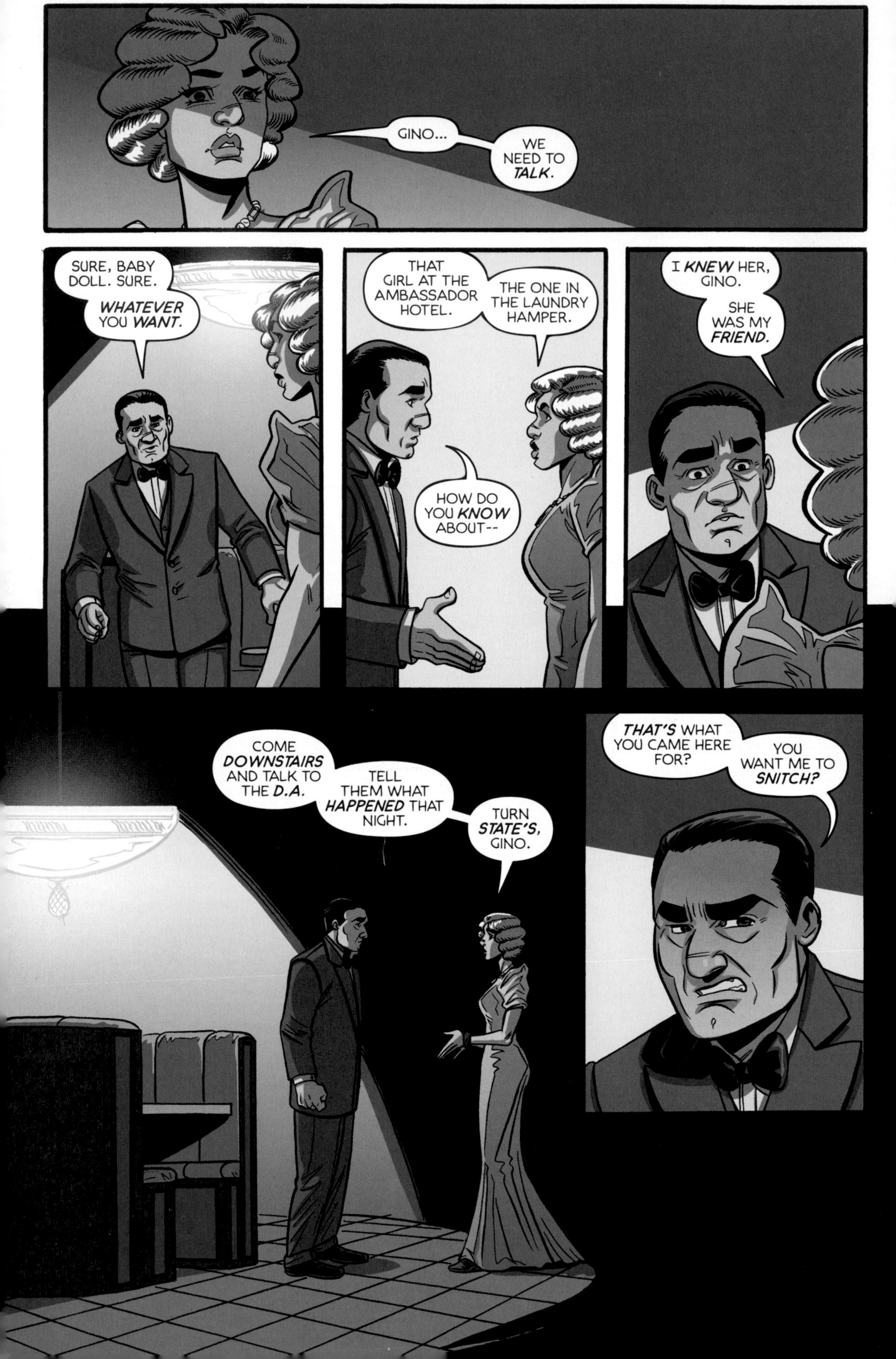
GINO...
WE NEED TO TALK.
SURE, BABY DOLL. SURE. WHATEVER YOU WANT.
THAT GIRL AT THE AMBASSADOR HOTEL.
THE ONE IN THE LAUNDRY HAMPER.
HOW DO YOU KNOW ABOUT--
I KNEW HER, GINO.
SHE WAS MY FRIEND.
COME DOWNSTAIRS AND TALK TO THE D.A.
TELL THEM WHAT HAPPENED THAT NIGHT.
TURN STATE'S, GINO.
THAT'S WHAT YOU CAME HERE FOR?
YOU WANT ME TO SNITCH?

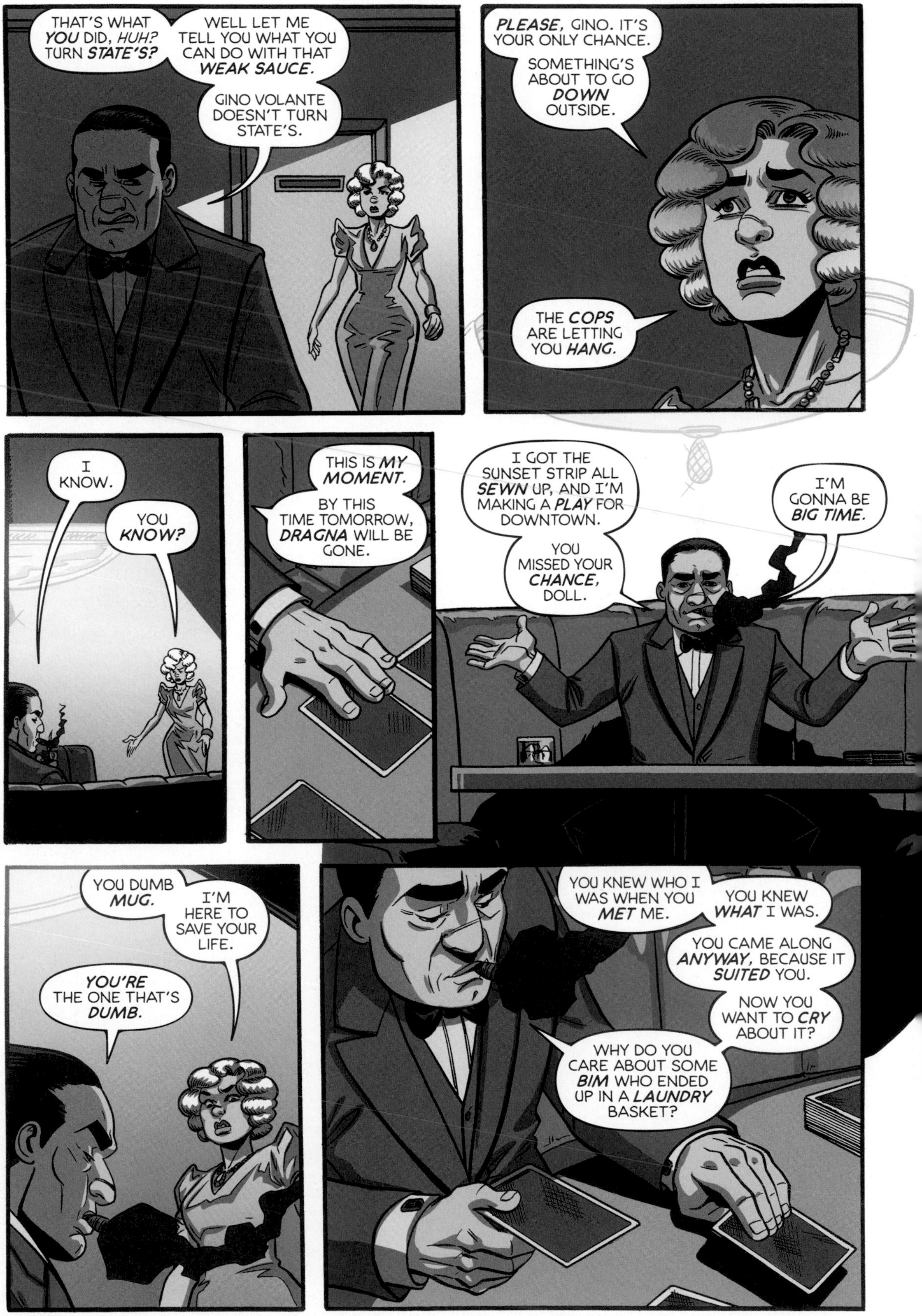
THAT'S WHAT YOU DID, HUH? TURN STATE'S?
WELL LET ME TELL YOU WHAT YOU CAN DO WITH THAT WEAK SAUCE.
GINO VOLANTE DOESN'T TURN STATE'S.
PLEASE, GINO. IT'S YOUR ONLY CHANCE.
SOMETHING'S ABOUT TO GO DOWN OUTSIDE.
THE COPS ARE LETTING YOU HANG.
I KNOW.
YOU KNOW?
THIS IS MY MOMENT.
BY THIS TIME TOMORROW, DRAGNA WILL BE GONE.
I GOT THE SUNSET STRIP ALL SEWN UP, AND I'M MAKING A PLAY FOR DOWNTOWN.
YOU MISSED YOUR CHANCE, DOLL.
I'M GONNA BE BIG TIME.
YOU DUMB MUG.
I'M HERE TO SAVE YOUR LIFE.
YOU'RE THE ONE THAT'S DUMB.
YOU KNEW WHO I WAS WHEN YOU MET ME.
YOU KNEW WHAT I WAS.
YOU CAME ALONG ANYWAY, BECAUSE IT SUITED YOU.
NOW YOU WANT TO CRY ABOUT IT?
WHY DO YOU CARE ABOUT SOME BIM WHO ENDED UP IN A LAUNDRY BASKET?

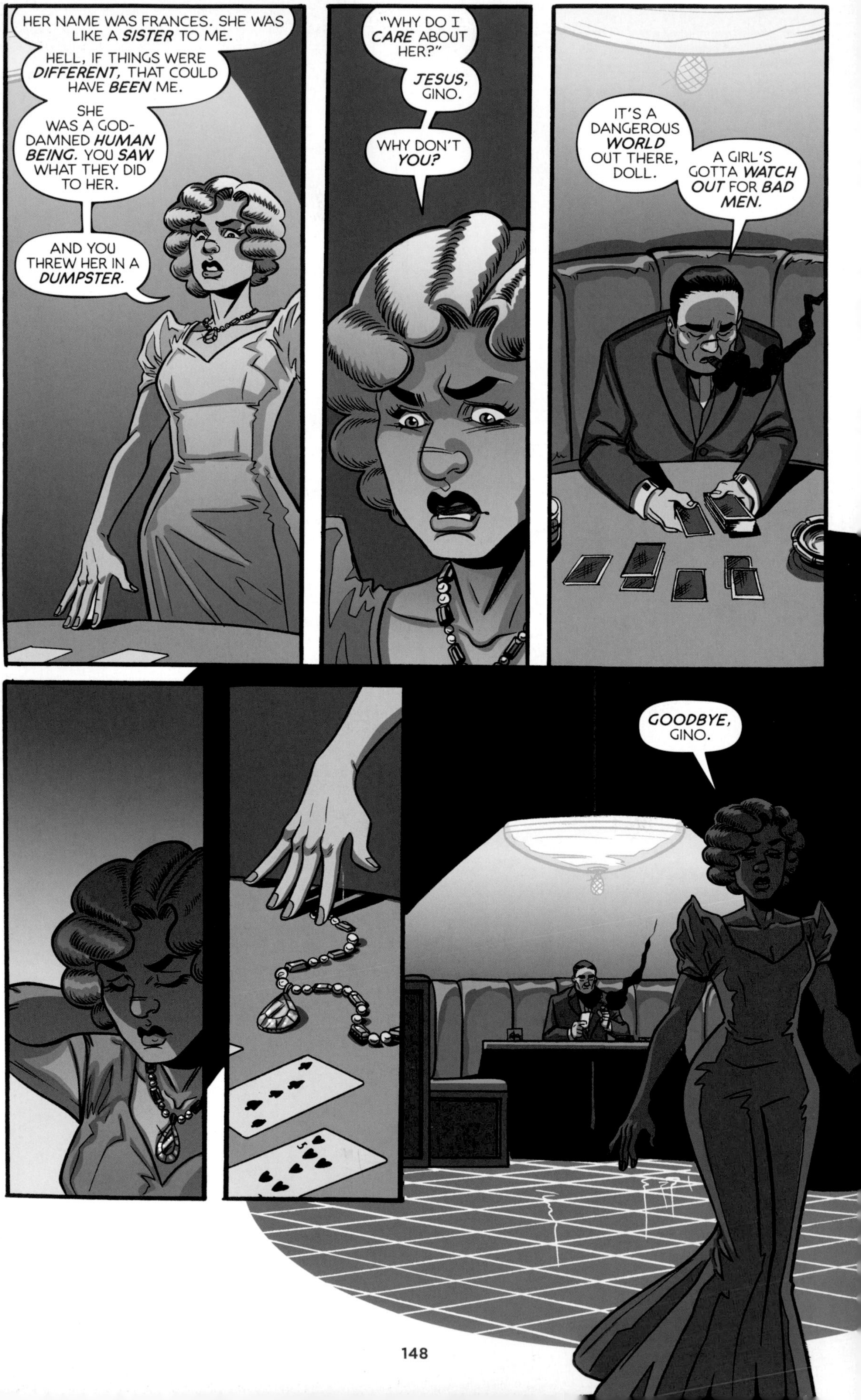

HER NAME WAS FRANCES. SHE WAS LIKE A *SISTER* TO ME.
HELL, IF THINGS WERE *DIFFERENT,* THAT COULD HAVE *BEEN* ME.
SHE WAS A GOD-DAMNED *HUMAN BEING.* YOU *SAW* WHAT THEY DID TO HER.
AND YOU THREW HER IN A *DUMPSTER.*
"WHY DO I *CARE* ABOUT HER?"
JESUS, GINO.
WHY DON'T *YOU?*
IT'S A DANGEROUS *WORLD* OUT THERE, DOLL.
A GIRL'S GOTTA *WATCH OUT* FOR *BAD MEN.*
GOODBYE, GINO.

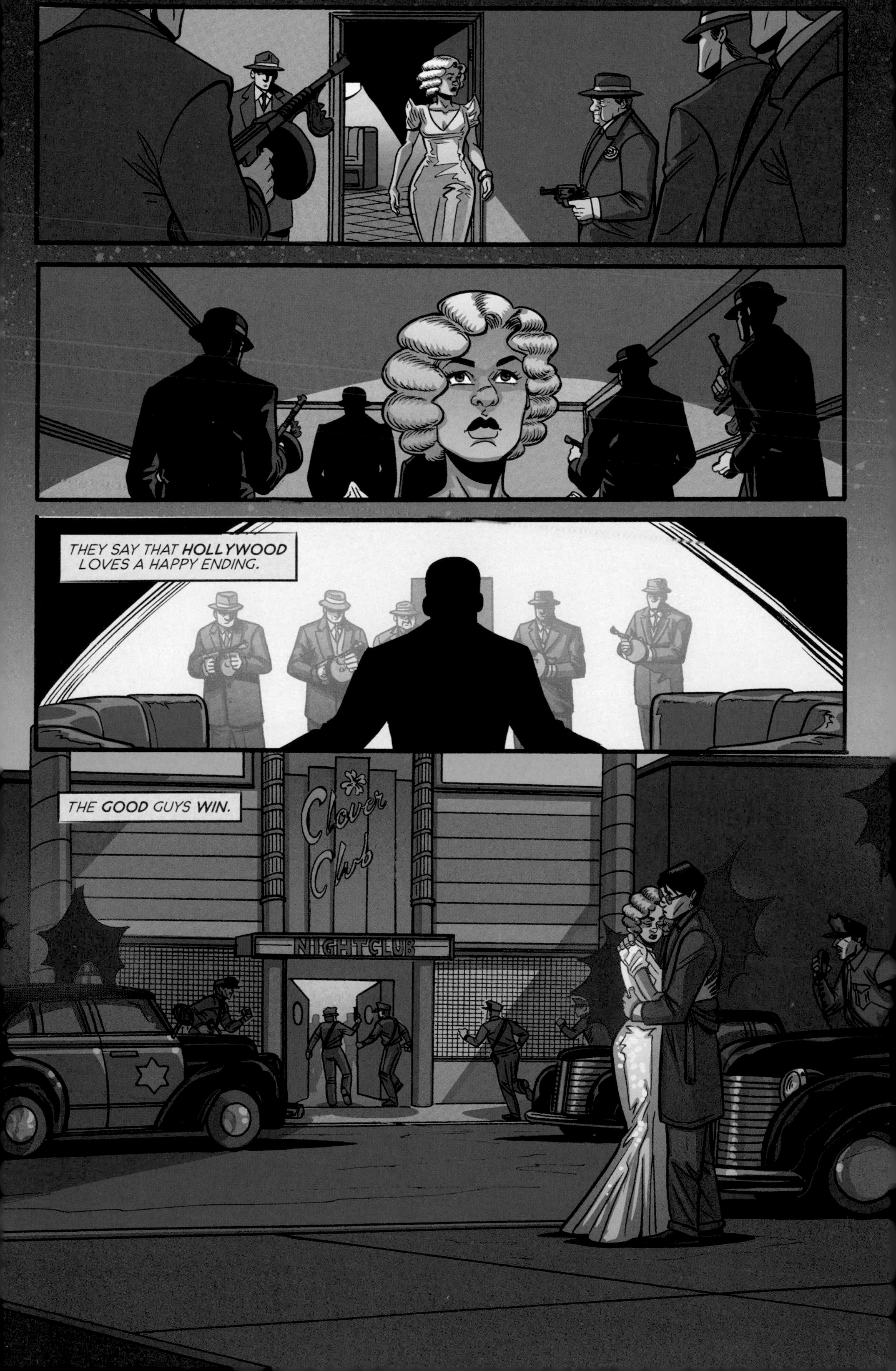
THEY SAY THAT HOLLYWOOD LOVES A HAPPY ENDING.
THE GOOD GUYS WIN.
Clover Club
NIGHTCLUB

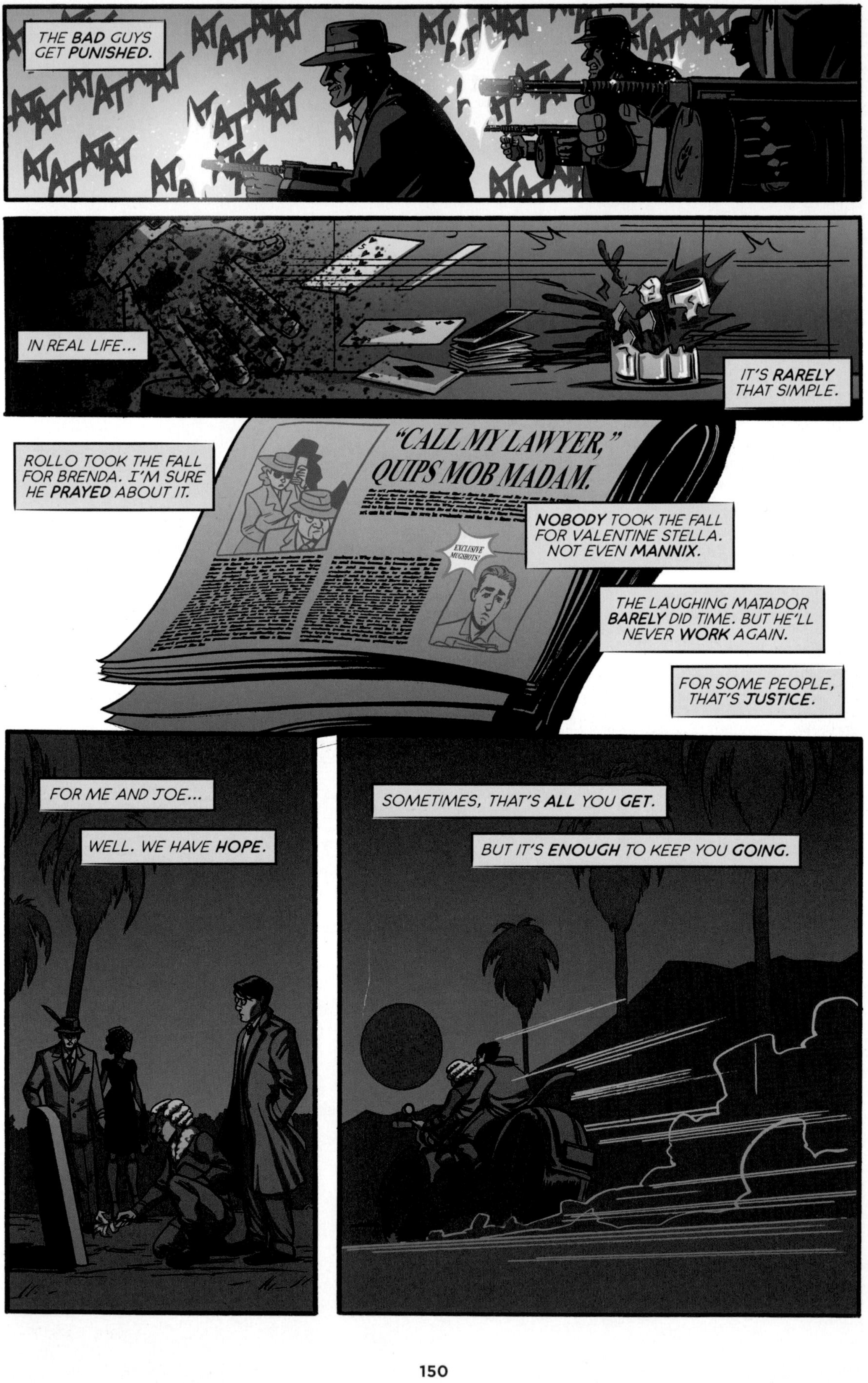

THE BAD GUYS GET PUNISHED.
IN REAL LIFE...
IT'S RARELY THAT SIMPLE.
ROLLO TOOK THE FALL FOR BRENDA. I'M SURE HE PRAYED ABOUT IT.
"CALL MY LAWYER," QUIPS MOB MADAM.
EXCLUSIVE MUGSHOTS!
NOBODY TOOK THE FALL FOR VALENTINE STELLA. NOT EVEN MANNIX.
THE LAUGHING MATADOR BARELY DID TIME. BUT HE'LL NEVER WORK AGAIN.
FOR SOME PEOPLE, THAT'S JUSTICE.
FOR ME AND JOE...
WELL. WE HAVE HOPE.
SOMETIMES, THAT'S ALL YOU GET.
BUT IT'S ENOUGH TO KEEP YOU GOING.

EPILOGUE

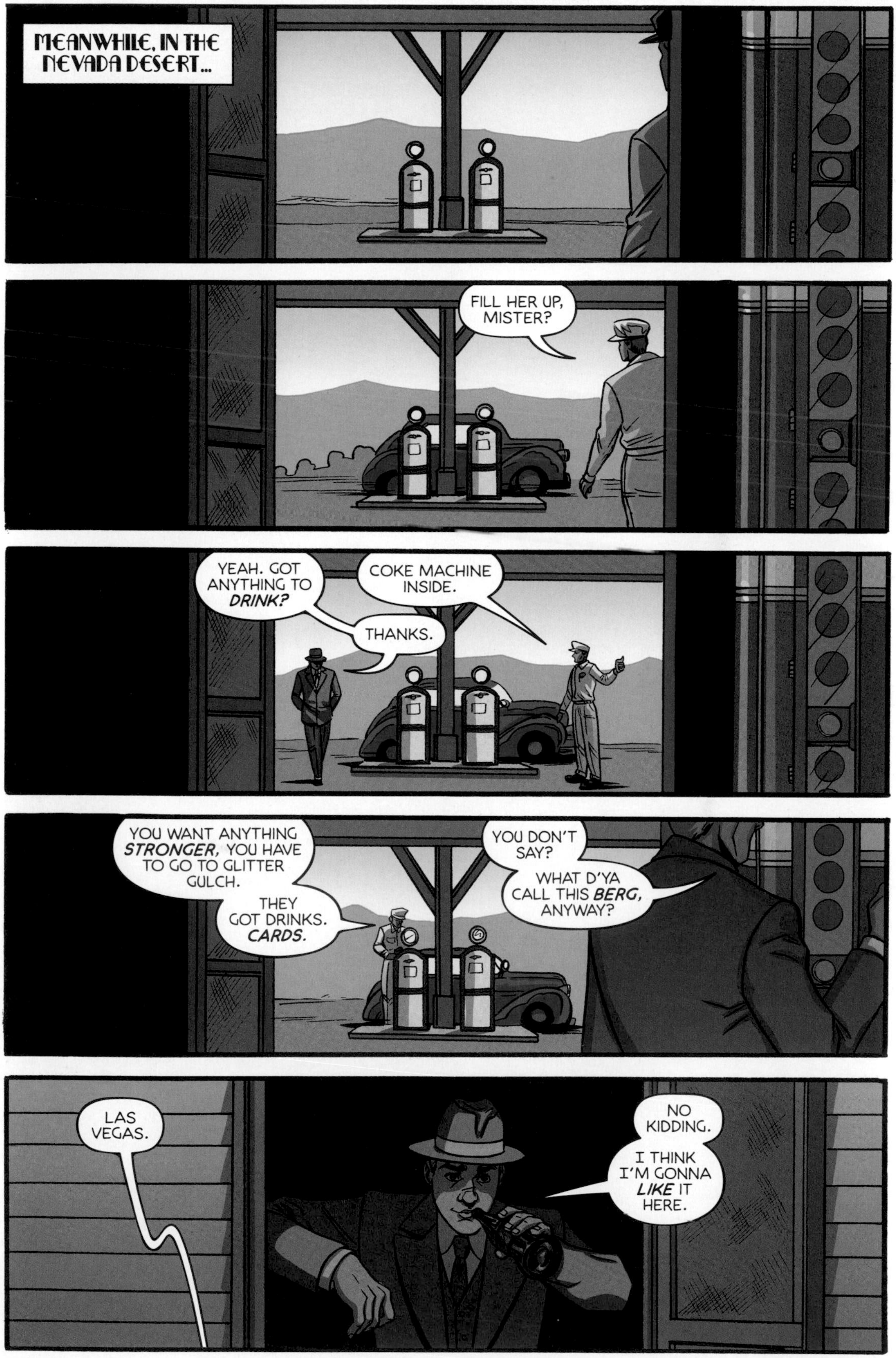

MEANWHILE, IN THE NEVADA DESERT...
FILL HER UP, MISTER?
YEAH. GOT ANYTHING TO *DRINK?*
COKE MACHINE INSIDE.
THANKS.
YOU WANT ANYTHING *STRONGER,* YOU HAVE TO GO TO GLITTER GULCH.
THEY GOT DRINKS. *CARDS.*
YOU DON'T SAY?
WHAT D'YA CALL THIS *BERG,* ANYWAY?
LAS VEGAS.
NO KIDDING.
I THINK I'M GONNA *LIKE* IT HERE.

THE END...?

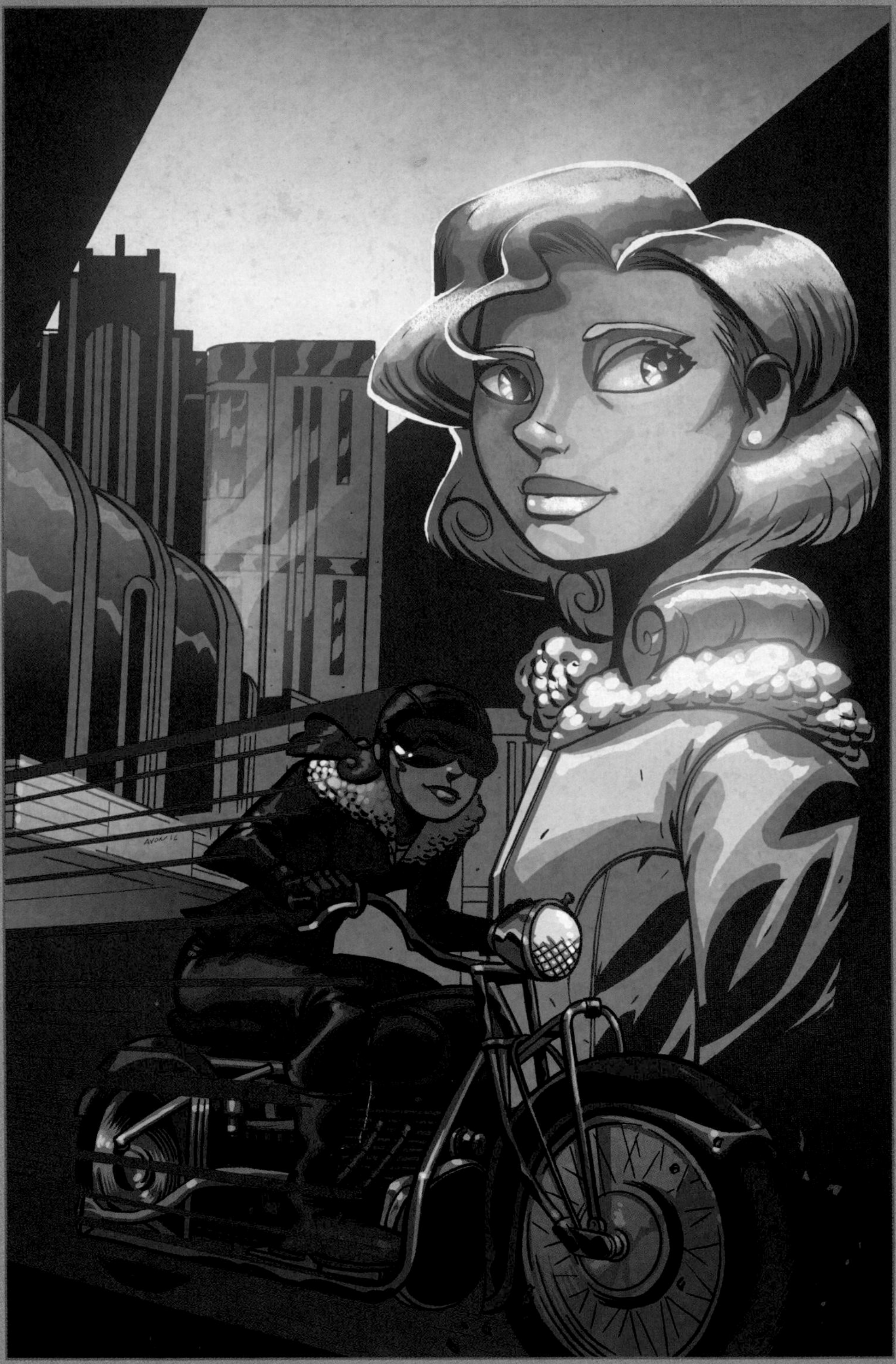

ILLUSTRATION BY

Michael Avon Oeming
& Nick Filardi

"Men are afraid that women will laugh at them. Women are afraid that men will kill them." —MARGARET ATWOOD

My favorite aisle in the bookstore has always been "True Crime." It's a guilty pleasure. Once, when I was visiting my dad's house as an adult, my stepmother caught me with a trashy airport paperback from the "nonfiction" section. "Is that Ann Rule?" She asked, raising an eyebrow.

I was a bit ashamed. In a family of educators, film theorists and English majors, I felt like I'd been caught with a porn mag hidden in my copy of *Anna Karenina*. "Yes...?" I admitted.

"Have you read *The I-5 Killer*? *The Want Ad Killer*? *Lust Killer*? *The Green River Killer*? *The Killer Beside Me*?" Pretty soon she was introducing me to the Ann Rule section on her own bookshelf, and we were exchanging dog-eared paperbacks and recommendations. I was not alone. The fascination with real life killers was shared by both of us. And, judging by the sheer number of cases on *Investigation Discovery* with the word "Killer" in the title, it's shared by a lot of us.

And by "us," I mean, primarily, women. Because for us, the threat that any man in our life—a date, a neighbor, a coworker, a beloved husband, a total stranger—could snap and kill us at any moment, is a very present fear. It's so familiar that we don't even really think about it most of the time. We just adjust our lives to accommodate it, and hope that, if "The Killer Next Door" or "The Killer in the Next Cubicle" or "Sleeping With a Killer" turns out to be a book with our face on it, at least someone like Ann Rule will come along and do the story justice.

Which brings us to the Black Dahlia.

On January 15, 1947, a young woman was out walking with her three-year-old daughter on the 3800 block of South Norton Avenue in Los Angeles. In the tall grass of a vacant lot, she saw what she thought was a broken department store mannequin. But as she got closer, she realized that the bisected body in the grass—carefully posed, and with a smile literally cut into her face—was a human being.

Before her death, Elizabeth Short had led a pretty unremarkable existence as a young, single working class girl in California. Her killer was never found. Her death was never explained. There was no trail of evidence, no sequence of murders, no clever moniker to hang on the killer. So they gave a name to the victim. The Black Dahlia. She was no longer a person. She was a photograph of a vamp with a flower in her hair. She became a True Hollywood Story.

And her killer was never found.

Angel City is not a true Hollywood story. And it's not the story of the Black Dahlia. But it's a story that's informed by a lot of true Hollywood history. It's haunted by Hollywood's ghosts, and scandals. And it's definitely inspired by some of the speculation and history that surrounded the Black Dahlia murder. So in the next pages, we share some of that history with you.

Welcome to Hollywood's True Crimes.
We hope we do the story justice.

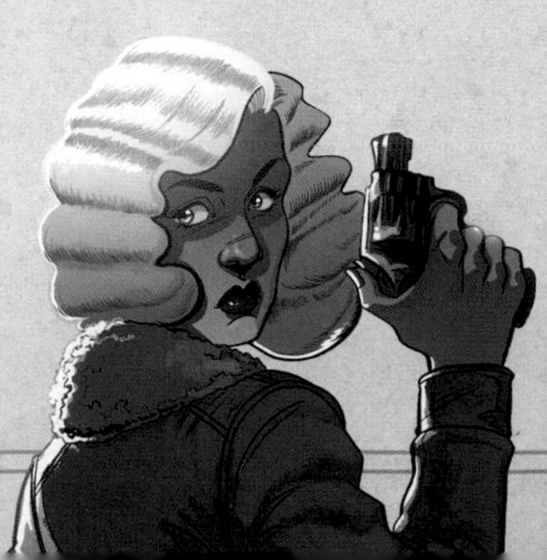

Bugsy Siegel and the "Ice Cream Blonde"

If there was a prize for "America's Favorite Gangster," Benjamin "Bugsy" Siegel would probably win it. From his humble beginnings strong-arming pushcart vendors in Brooklyn with his best friend, Meyer Lansky, to his rise through the Luciano crime organization, to becoming the founder of modern-day Las Vegas, Bugsy Siegel's "rags to riches" story is pretty familiar to anyone who has ever seen a movie. He is perhaps best known as the visionary who created the first luxury gambling hotel in Las Vegas, the Flamingo.

But before he created the Vegas Strip, in a lesser-known chapter of mob legend, Bugsy Siegel took his vision of upscale gambling to another strip: The Sunset Strip.

When Prohibition ended in 1933, Luciano and his fellow bootleggers turned their sights to a new source of revenue: gambling. The racing wires of the time were mostly held by the Syndicate, a nationwide organization that joined the forces of Capone's Chicago mob and Luciano's organization in New York. To consolidate the Syndicate's hold on the West Coast, Ben Siegel arrived in Los Angeles around 1935, when a Los Angeles telephone directory confirms that he kept an address at the Piazza Del Sol apartments on Sunset Boulevard, steps away from the real-life Clover Club. The secret upstairs casino he established there—frequented by a select Hollywood clientele—became a fashionable nightspot.

Bugsy was the strong arm of the Luciano organization, and he got his nickname from his legendary temper. When he lost it, he tended to go right for the face, either pistol-whipping his victim with the butt of a gun, or slashing them across the face and throat with a knife. Bugsy and Meyer called themselves "Murder, Inc," so it isn't hard to imagine what he was sent to Los Angeles to do. But Ben Siegel himself may have had other ideas about starting over on the West Coast, like many dreamers before him.

As a friend of actor George Raft (who knew Lansky and Siegel from their early days as Brooklyn hoods), the handsome, well-dressed Siegel found new celebrity as a Hollywood socialite. Gossip columnists referred to him as a "sportsman" and a "bon vivant." He rubbed shoulders with Hollywood royalty and actual royalty: William Randolph Hearst, Mary Pickford, Douglas Fairbanks, the Duke and Duchess of Windsor. He had money, and he was good-looking: that was good enough for Hollywood. If anyone knew he was one of the founders of Murder, Inc, they weren't telling.

Or perhaps they just weren't telling the right people.

One of the Hollywood celebrities who ran in the same circle as Siegel was Thelma Todd, aka "The Ice Cream Blonde." A popular movie actress in the 20s and 30s, Todd was one of the Hal Roach players, and appeared in 120 films alongside stars like Laurel & Hardy and the Marx Brothers. A vivacious vamp onscreen, Todd was a smart cookie who had wanted to be a teacher, but was pushed into acting by her ambitious mother after she won second prize in a beauty contest.

In 1935, Todd was divorcing her husband, self-styled "agent" and manager, Pat DeCicco, and looking for a way to retire gracefully from acting. She opened "Thelma Todd's Sidewalk Café" in Malibu, trading on her famous name to segue into the restaurant business. The Spanish style building had a seaside café on the first floor, a private dining room and nightclub for Hollywood elites on the second floor, and Todd's private apartment on the third floor.

Accounts differ as to how much Todd's deadbeat ex-husband Pat DeCicco had to do with the operation of the café itself, but one thing seems clear from all accounts: DeCicco had ties to the Syndicate, and his mob friends were either using Thelma's café as a front for their gambling operations, or forcing her into using their restaurant suppliers, or both. The spacious 15,000 square foot building was convenient to the West Side, more exclusive than the Sunset Strip, and had a view of the Pacific Ocean. If the Syndicate wanted an upscale casino that catered to the Beverly Hills crowd, this was a perfect target for expansion.

The only problem was Todd herself. It wasn't long before Thelma got wise to what was going on, and she wasn't happy about it. But when she tried to evict DeCicco and his mob friends from the premises, she was told she'd better play ball. Letters to her family at the time indicate that she was receiving threats from an unknown source, and worried about having fallen in with a "bad crowd." But the Ice Cream Blonde was no pushover. On Dec 11th, 1935, Thelma went to the office of District Attorney, Buron Fitts, to file a complaint against the mobsters who were trying to muscle in on her café. She made an appointment to come back in five days.

Five days later, Todd was dead. Her body was found slumped over the wheel of her Phaeton in the garage of the Seaside Café, the engine running, the door shut. The cause of death was officially "death due to carbon monoxide poisoning." Her broken nose, two broken ribs, and bruises around her throat were never explained.

Turns out, Buron Fitts was being paid off by the mob. The public uproar and inquiry surrounding Todd's death forced a grand jury investigation, but there were no convictions. Witnesses were "not as cooperative" as they could have been. The case was closed before Christmas; the final verdict was that Thelma Todd had either fallen asleep in the garage, or committed suicide. Eventually the rumors surrounding her death died down, and nobody remembered the Ice Cream Blonde.

The Café's business never rebounded from the scandal, but the building that housed the Seaside Café is still there. It sold for 6 million in 2014. Curiously, it was listed as having "no onsite parking."

In her will, Thelma Todd left Pat DeCicco one dollar.

In 1973, Buron Fitts reportedly took his own life with a .38 caliber pistol at the age of 78.

Further reading:

THE BLACK DAHLIA FILES: THE MOB, THE MOGUL AND THE MURDER THAT TRANSFIXED LOS ANGELES by Donald H. Wolfe

THE ICE CREAM BLONDE: THE WHIRLWIND LIFE AND MYSTERIOUS DEATH OF SCREWBALL COMEDIENNE THELMA TODD by Michelle Morgan

THE LIFE AND DEATH OF THELMA TODD by William Donati

BOARDWALK GANGSTER: THE REAL LUCKY LUCIANO by Tim Newark

"Girl 27"

In the late 30s, MGM Studios, home of such squeaky-clean family hits as *The Wizard of Oz*, was the highest grossing studio in Tinseltown. If they called, you answered. If they screwed you over, you stayed quiet. And if you couldn't stay quiet, studio "fixers" like Eddie Mannix made sure you did. But there was one girl who refused to back down—even if it took another 50 years for anyone to believe her story.

In 1937, MGM threw a party for its regional salespeople to show its appreciation for a banner year. The week-long sales convention culminated in a dinner at the Ambassador Hotel and a "Wild West" party at a remote studio location.

"Yippee! Get Set for Wild West Show at Roach's," announced the Wednesday schedule. "It will be a stag affair, out in the wild and woolly West where 'men are men.'"

An agent put out a call: chorus girls wanted by MGM. Pay was $7.50 and a hot meal. 120 young dancers reported for wardrobe and makeup at Hal Roach Studios in Culver City. Fitted for "cowgirl" costumes—cowboy hats, bolero jackets, short suede skirts and boots—they boarded a bus for "Rancho Roachero," a remote converted barn that was used by producer Hal Roach as a filming location.

One of the chorines—listed in the manifest as "Girl 27"—was 20-year-old Patricia Douglas. She thought she was answering a casting notice, but after a couple of hours waiting around a banquet hall with no camera crew, miles from anywhere, she must have wised up that this was no movie call.

Finally, at 7pm, 300 boozed-up conventioneers descended on the ranch—and on the girls that they assumed came along with the "stag affair." There were 300 cases of scotch and champagne at the open bar. The female performers who'd been hired for the event—including a 13-year-old Dorothy Dandridge, who'd been contracted to perform with the Dandridge Sisters—were left to fend for themselves until the "party" was over.

As the night went on, things got ugly. Patricia tried to hide out in the ladies room, complaining to an attendant that a man she had danced with was an "annoying creep" who was trying to "cop a feel." The "annoying creep" was David Ross, a 36-year-old salesman from Chicago. When Douglas told Ross she didn't drink, he and another salesman held her down and poured booze down her throat. Later that night, Ross sexually assaulted Douglas in the parking lot. A parking attendant found Douglas staggering out of the lot with two black eyes.

No police report was filed. When Patricia returned to pick up her check two days later, she tried to tell the cashier what had happened to her, "so it doesn't happen to anyone else." Unmoved, the cashier handed her $7.50.

A sad story, and if Patricia had been after hush money, that might have been the end of it. But she wanted something else. "I just wanted someone to believe me," she said. She wanted MGM to "stop having those parties." Patricia Douglas filed a complaint against Ross with the LA District Attorney.

When the D.A. did nothing, the 20-year-old went to the press. Amidst tales of studio orgies, ruined virtue, a grieving mother and a wild stag party, MGM went into a panic. The story threatened not only the studio's family-friendly image, but their standing with stockholders.

Enter Eddie Mannix. The studio fixer went after Douglas with everything at his disposal—Pinkerton agents digging up dirt, the other girls at the party who could be bribed with money and jobs—anything to discredit Douglas and her story. It was a tough case. If ever there was a perfect witness, Patricia Douglas was it. The Pinkertons reported that Douglas didn't drink, and lived with her mother.

A parade of witnesses perjured themselves for MGM money and jobs. When Douglas lost the case, MGM hoped they had shamed and frightened Girl 27 into giving up.

They hadn't. Instead, Douglas slapped a civil suit, not only on David Ross, but Eddie Mannix, Hal Roach, and "John Doe One through Fifty" for "unlawful conspiracy to defile, debauch, and seduce (women)... for the immoral and sensual gratification of male guests." When that suit was dismissed, she filed an identical suit in federal court.

It may have been the first time a female plaintiff made a federal case—a civil rights case—out of a sexual assault. She'd named the people and institutions responsible for harming her, and called the "party" what it was: a conspiracy. Incredibly, she'd pushed through three different courts, and the wall of silence that a powerful institution like MGM can build with money and influence. But in the end, the case was dismissed when MGM's lawyers didn't even show up.

It wasn't until the 2000s, when filmmaker David Stenn stumbled upon Douglas' case, that the story of "Girl 27" was exhumed from the deep, deep hole that MGM tried to bury it in. Stenn found and interviewed the 87-year-old Patricia Douglas in her home in Las Vegas. At first, she wasn't sure why anyone would be interested in her story, and felt she hadn't "accomplished" anything. But as Stenn showed her the movie he was putting together, the truth dawned on her.

"Pretty gutsy, wasn't I?" she reportedly said. "I guess they just got my Irish up."

Patricia Douglas never received any personal consideration from the studio, but the documentary *Girl 27* tells her story.

MGM quietly discontinued its practice of holding conventions for its regional salesmen.

Further reading / viewing / listening:

IT HAPPENED ONE NIGHT... AT MGM by David Stenn (*Vanity Fair*, April 2003)

GIRL 27 a documentary by David Stenn (2007)

YOU MUST REMEMBER THIS: MGM'S EDDIE MANNIX AND THE LIVES HE RUINED
a podcast by Karina Longworth (*Slate*, November 2015)

"Aggie Underwood and the City of Forgotten Women"

The real Aggie Underwood is an amazing character. A pioneer of crime reporting on the LA beat, she not only may have solved the Black Dahlia murder, but through her efforts, pioneered the "battered woman" defense.

As a young wife and mother with two small children in Los Angeles in 1926, Aggie asked her husband for money to buy some stockings. When he told her no, she went out and got a job as a switchboard operator at a local newspaper, the *Los Angeles Record*. According to Aggie's autobiography, *Newspaperwoman*, she was instantly hooked by the chaos of the newsroom. By 1930, Aggie was a working reporter with a growing reputation. William Randolph Hearst, who owned the *Herald-Express*, tried to woo her away from the *LA Record* many times before she finally accepted in 1935.

It was at the *Herald-Express* that Aggie's career as a crime reporter really took off. Over the years she covered the city's most gruesome and shocking crimes, and developed a reputation for having a hard head and an even stronger stomach. It was noted that she attended the 1936 autopsy of actress Thelma Todd "without fainting." Once, when trying to lock down an exclusive, she hid a wanted murderess in her home—while her daughter's Girl Scout troop held a meeting in the next room.

One of her most famous assignments at the time was a series of profiles on the "Forgotten Women" of Tehachapi Prison, an all-women's prison opened in 1933. It was there that she met Nellie Mae Madison, the first woman in California to receive the death sentence.

The child of Irish immigrants, Nellie Mae Madison had eloped at 13, been married five times, smoked, and drank whiskey. She put five bullets in the back of husband #5. At her trial, she was so emotionless on the stand, the press called her "the Sphinx Lady." She didn't cry. She didn't beg for her life. She told the jury she wasn't even in the room at the time of the murder, although neighbors had heard them fighting for six days. Cold, childless, disaffected, she was roundly considered to be a monster. When she was sentenced to death, nobody complained.

Nobody, that is, except husband #4, who was still friends with Nellie Mae. He begged her to appeal the case and go public about the spousal abuse she'd suffered at the hands of her recently deceased spouse. So, Nellie Mae told Aggie Underwood the story that her defense team had deemed too "sordid" for the ears of the court. And Aggie told it to the world.

Mr. Madison was an abusive cheater and a drunk. After Nellie Mae caught him in bed with a sixteen-year-old girl, her husband beat her for six days. During that time, he bragged about only marrying her for her money, and forced her to sign a note that said they weren't married. She was so afraid for her life, she said, that she bought a gun. When Madison reached under the bed to grab a butcher knife and threatened to "cut her heart out," she panicked and fired repeatedly before he had the chance to turn around.

Aggie's story turned the tide of public opinion. Letters of support for the battered wife—most of them from other women—came pouring in from all around California. Even the jurors who had originally convicted Nellie Mae Madison petitioned the governor to commute her sentence and get her off death row. Aggie's story not only saved Nellie Mae Madison's life, but helped to legitimize the idea that prior abuse, and the psychological trauma it causes, could mitigate a sentence.

Nellie Mae Madison was probably Aggie's most celebrated story until January of 1945, when the body of Elizabeth Short turned up in a vacant lot. Aggie was reportedly the first reporter on the scene of Short's murder, and some say she even coined the name "Black Dahlia." It was also her last story as a reporter at the *Herald-Express*.

After scooping every other paper in town by interviewing Red Manley, the last person to see the "Dahlia" alive, Aggie was pulled off the Black Dahlia case by higher-ups at the paper. Everyone at the *Herald-Express*, including Aggie, thought it was strange that the highest-ranking crime reporter at the paper had been taken off the highest profile case in the city. Aggie had nothing to do, so to drive home the point, she spent the day sitting at her desk, in the middle of the newsroom, knitting.

Day two and day three went by with no change, and the most celebrated crime reporter in LA continued to sit in the middle of the newsroom, knitting. After three days, publisher William Randolph Hearst—perhaps tired of being the laughingstock of his own paper, promoted her to City Editor. This made Aggie the first female city editor on a major paper in America. It also took her off the crime beat.

Was Aggie getting close to the Black Dahlia killer? Decades later, when questioned by her grandsons to name the killer, Aggie reportedly said, "he's dead, and it doesn't matter anymore."

Aggie remained the City Editor of the *Herald-Express* until she retired in 1968. She kept a baseball bat and a starter pistol in her desk, and supposedly fired the starter pistol in the air whenever the newsroom got too quiet.

Nellie Mae Madison was released from prison on March 24, 1943—exactly nine years after the murder of Eric Madison. She married her sixth husband shortly after her release, and the two of them remained married until she died of a stroke in 1953.

Further Reading:

NEWSPAPERWOMAN by Agness Underwood (1949)

DID L.A.'S TOP CRIME REPORTER OF THE 1930S AND '40S CRACK THE BLACK DAHLIA CASE? by Joan Renner (*LA Magazine*, July 2013)

UNWITTING PIONEER OF THE BATTERED WOMAN DEFENSE by Cecilia Rasmussen (*Los Angeles Times*, February 2007)

THE ENIGMA WOMAN: THE DEATH SENTENCE OF NELLIE MAY MADISON by Kathleen Cairnes

THE *PACHUCO* WAS THE ORIGINAL " REBEL WITHOUT A CAUSE."

In the 1930s and 40s, Los Angeles had the highest concentration of Mexican nationals outside of Mexico. The younger generation were torn between two worlds: alienated from the Mexican culture of their parents, they still didn't feel accepted as "American" by their anglo peers. So the teens made their own culture, with its own style and its own slang. Like the "Teddy Boys" in London, this generation of Chicanos created their own defiant subculture: *Pachuco*. Sporting high pompadour hairstyles and distinctive "zoot suits," which included long tailored coats, high-waisted pants, padded shoulders and wide-brimmed hats, *pachucos* exuded a cool swagger that didn't come from fitting in with anglo ideals. *Pachucas*—the female counterparts of the *pachucos*—also defied gender conventions in ways that were shocking at the time: either by dressing in tailored slacks and men's suits themselves, or with above-the-knee skirts, often with bobby socks and saddle shoes. You can still see traces of *pachuco* style in LA car culture today.

Things began to heat up for the *pachucos* at the beginning of World War II, when the Wartime Productions Board started rationing the amount of fabric that tailors could use for suits. Some say the new austerity measures deliberately targeted the zoot suiters, and in a defiant act of cultural pride, zoot suiters started ordering their suits from bootleg tailors, becoming literal fashion outlaws. The extravagant suits, with their "fingertip length" jackets and generous, baggy pants, were seen as unpatriotic during wartime. Add to that the general racial tensions that were brewing in the city, and the thousands of US military servicemen that were descending on Los Angeles from nearby bases, looking for booze, girls and entertainment—by some counts, 50,000 GI's every weekend—and you had a powder keg ready to go off.

On May 30th, 1943, a group of anglo sailors walking in downtown LA spotted a group of Mexican girls going in the other direction, and started following them. Between them stood a group of young men in zoot suits. Accounts differ about what happened, but a fight broke out between the GI's and the zoot suiters. One sailor, Joe Coleman, was struck on the head from behind, and had to be carried back to the Armory by his mates. There, the story of the fight grew and became more distorted with each re-telling.

By June 3rd, a gang of about 50 sailors with makeshift weapons were assembled, and headed toward East LA, looking for anybody in a zoot suit. Their first victims were a couple of 13-year-old boys who happened to be wearing a zoot suit in the wrong place at the wrong time. The servicemen pulled the young men from a movie theater, tore their zoot suits from their bodies, beat them, and set the suits on fire.

What followed was a violent conflagration between servicemen and the *pachucos* that lasted for 5 straight days. The LAPD, who looked on the zoot suiters as Mexican American gangs, did nothing to stop the GI's; in fact, by some accounts they accompanied the GI's with orders not to arrest them. Over a period of several days, hundreds of people were injured and over 500 Mexican-Americans were arrested.

The violence escalated and spread; by Tuesday night, an angry mob of 5,000 had gathered downtown, including civilians. They headed south to Watts, and to East LA, targeting not only zoot suited youth, but Mexican-Americans and African-Americans of all ages. Even the press seemed to get in on the mob mentality. One paper published a gleeful guide on how to "de-zoot" a zoot suiter: *"Grab a zooter. Take off his pants and frock coat and tear them up or burn them."*

Finally, on June 7th, hostilities ceased when the Navy and Marines confined all servicemen to barracks, and declared LA to be off-limits to military personnel. The LA

City Council passed a resolution that made it a crime to wear a zoot suit within city limits, punishable by 30 days in jail. Blame for the violence was officially laid at the feet of the "Mexican American gangs," and the military declared that the servicemen were acting in self-defense.

On June 18, Eleanor Roosevelt, first lady and wife of President Franklin Roosevelt, was quoted in the *LA Times* as saying:

"The question goes deeper than just [zoot] suits. It is a racial protest. I have been worried for a long time about the Mexican racial situation. It is a problem with roots going a long way back, and we do not always face these problems as we should."

The headline in the *Los Angeles Times* read: "Mrs. Roosevelt Blindly Stirs Race Discord." An editorial in the same paper speculated that she might be a communist.

———

In 1978, playwright Luis Valdez immortalized *pachuco* culture in his play, "Zoot Suit," and incidentally launched the career of Edward James Olmos, who portrayed the archetypal character, "El Pachuco" in both the play and movie. The film, which Valdez also directed, was nominated for a Golden Globe.

Further Reading:

LUIS VALDEZ, "ZOOT SUIT" (play), 1992, Arte Público Press

THE AMERICAN EXPERIENCE: THE ZOOT SUIT RIOTS OF 1943 (PBS)

HISTORY 101: THE ZOOT SUIT RIOTS by Ojibwa (*Daily Kos,* January 2014)

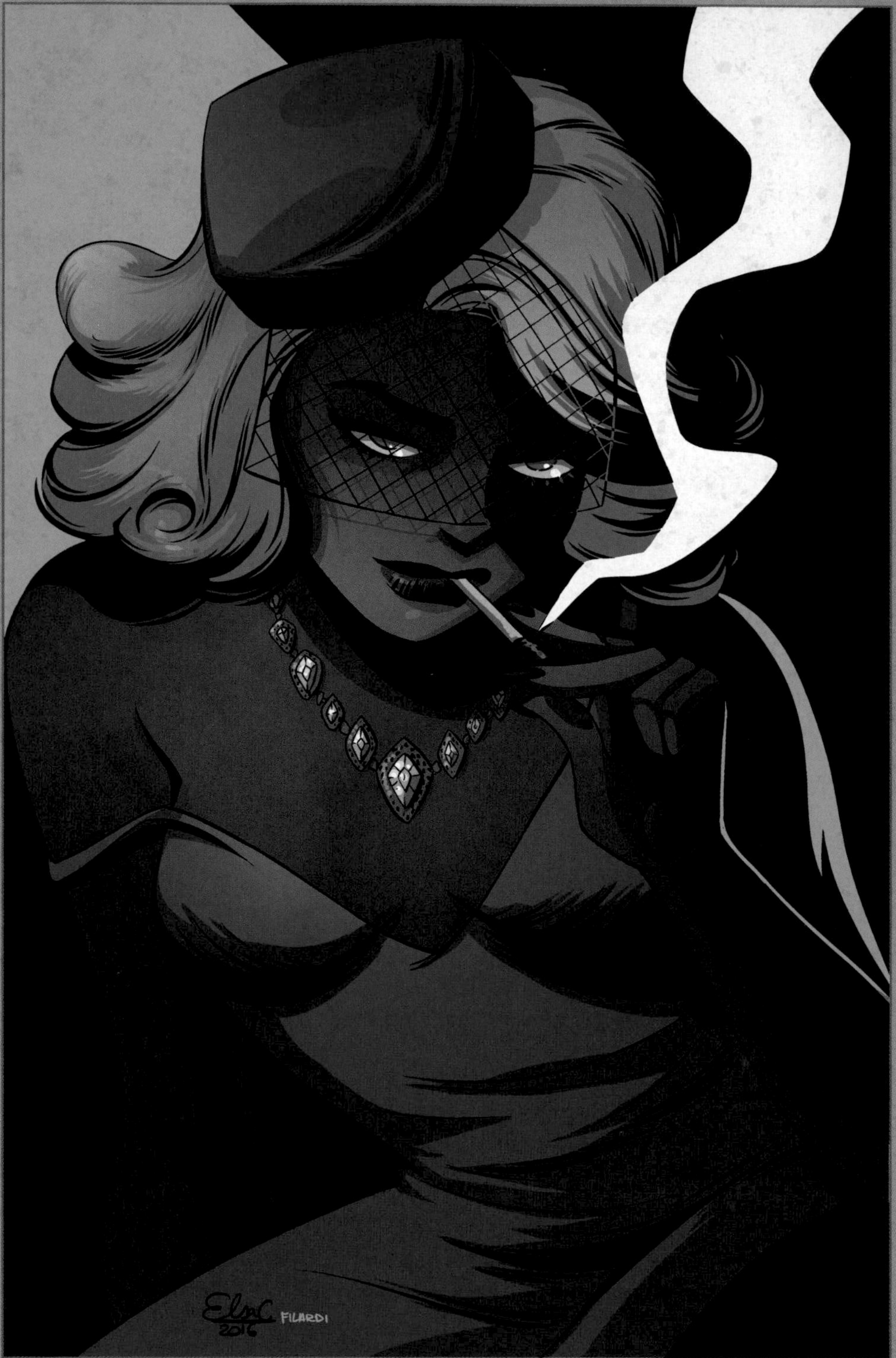
2016 FILARDI

ILLUSTRATION BY

Elsa Charretier
& Nick Filardi

ANGEL CITY #1

Cover Process

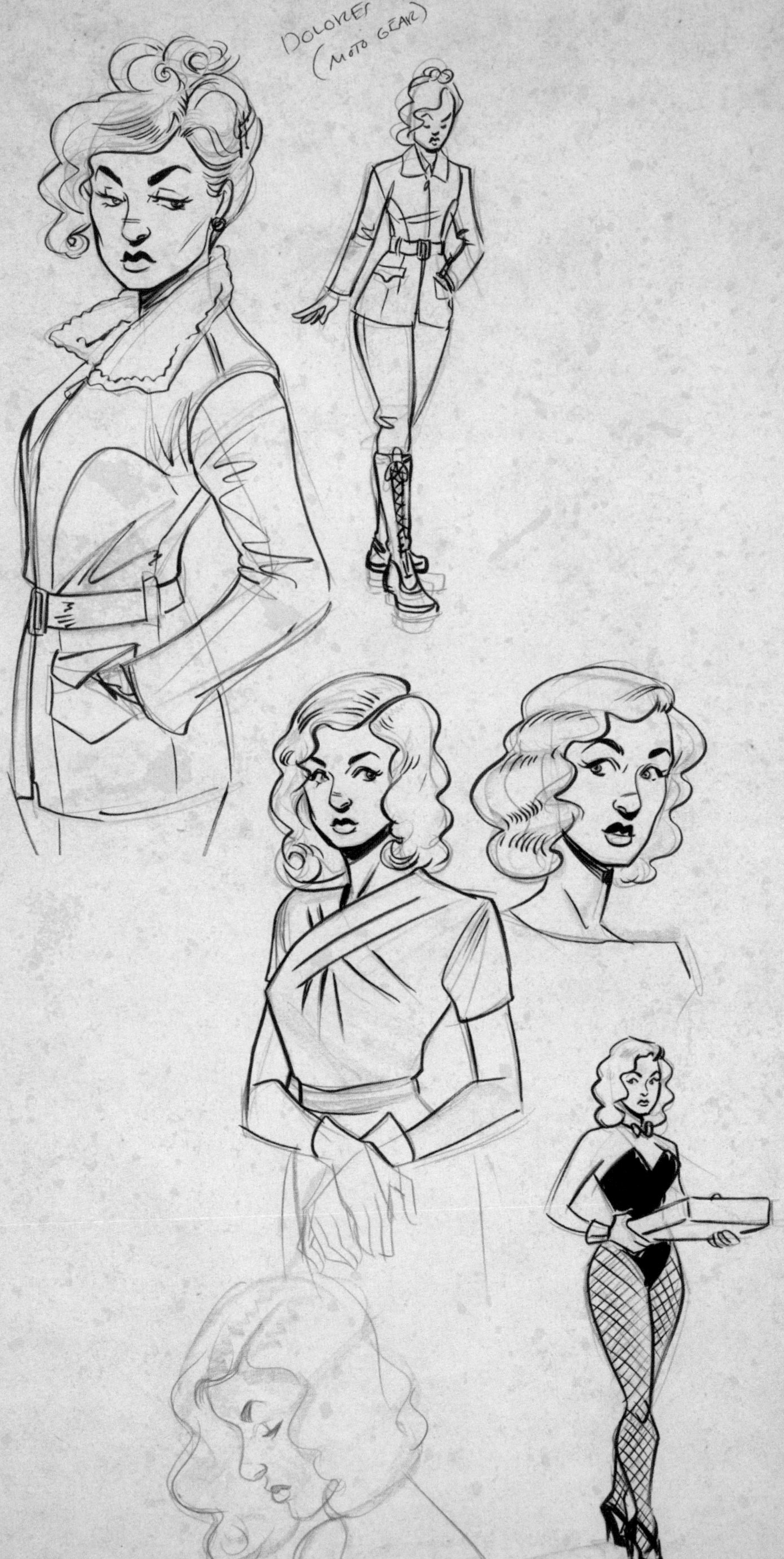
DOLORES
(MOTO GEAR)

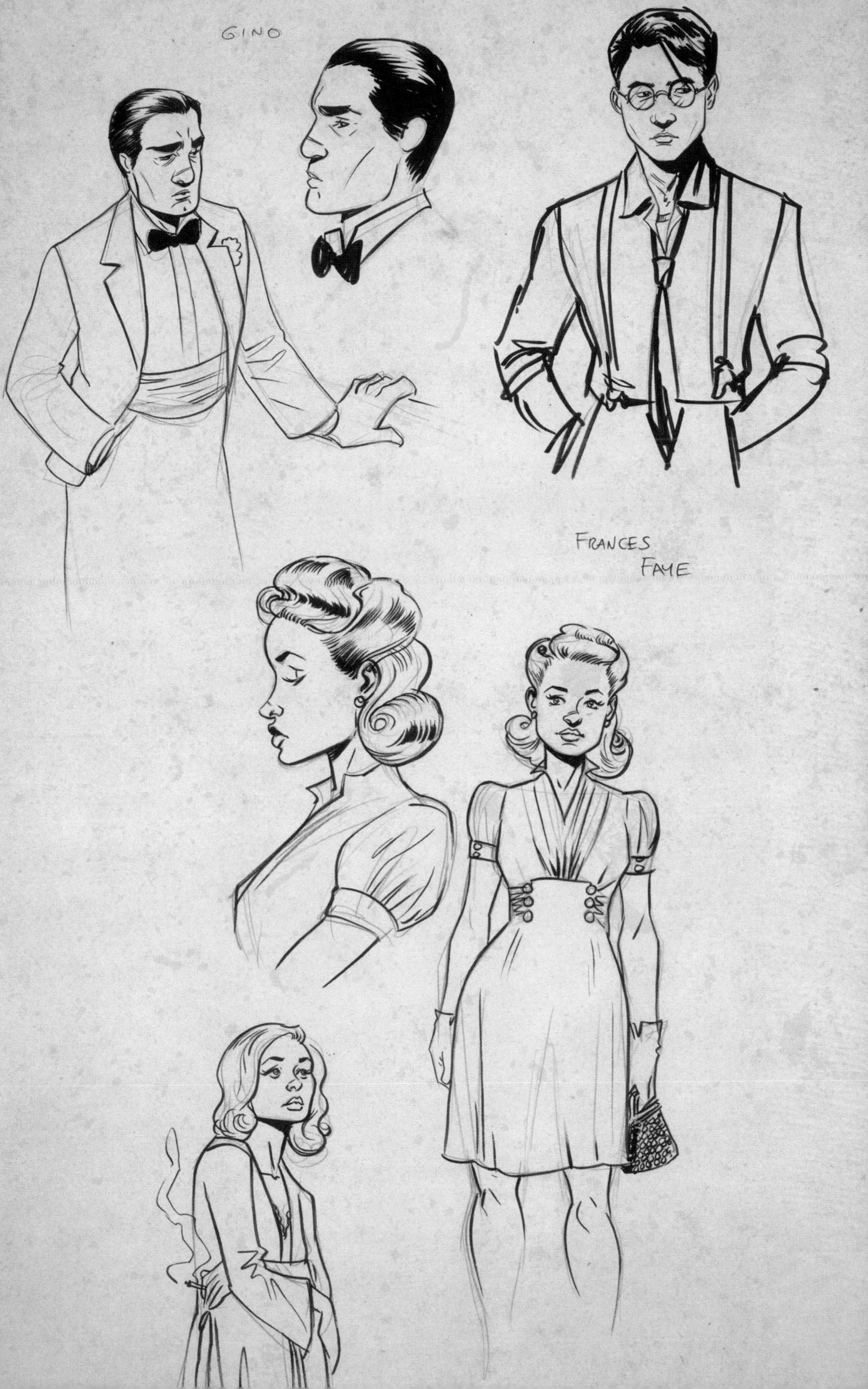
GINO
FRANCES
FAYE

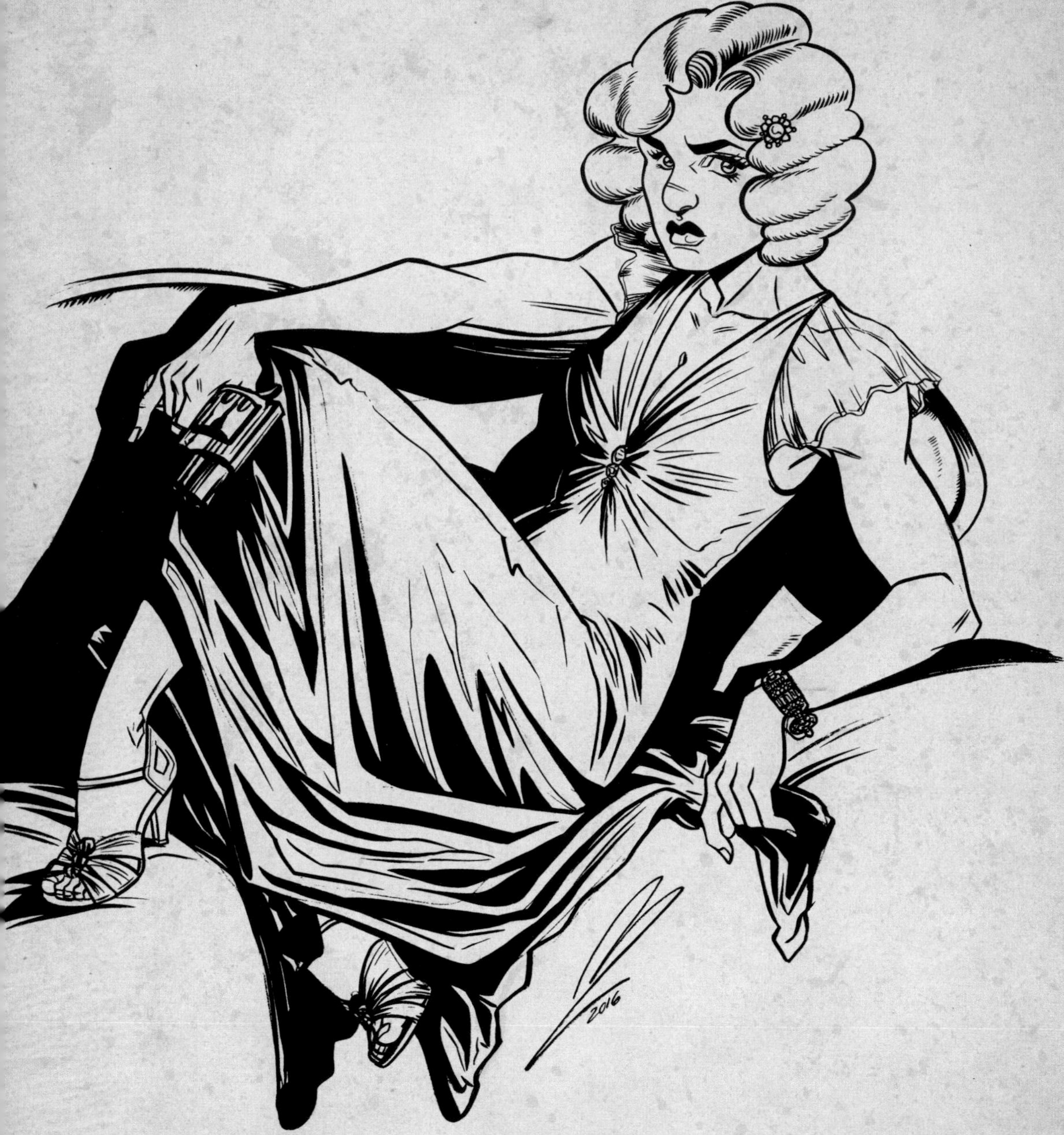
2016

Janet Harvey is an award-winning writer of comic books, movies and games. She has written for Image Comics, Tokyopop and DC Comics, including the first full length adventure of Cassandra Cain in the "No Man's Land" storyline. She recently wrote and directed her first feature film. She lives in Texas, where it's legal to shoot trespassers.

Megan Levens is a comic book artist best known for her work on *Buffy the Vampire Slayer* Season 10 for Dark Horse Comics, and her collaborations with writer Jamie S. Rich on Image Comics's *Madame Frankenstein* and Oni Press's *Ares & Aphrodite*. She has also contributed to several Vertigo anthologies, including the finale of *Fables*, and illustrated the creator-owned *Spell on Wheels* with Kate Leth and Marissa Louise (also for Dark Horse). Currently she is boldly going and drawing various *Star Trek* projects for IDW. Megan is owned by a Boston Terrier and a grumpy old cat, who live with her in Kansas City.

Nick Filardi grew up going to Sarge's Comics in New London, Connecticut. He studied comics at Savannah College of Art and Design. He now resides in Florida with his fiancée and 3-legged dog. You can find his work in *Cave Carson has a Cybernetic Eye*, *Powers*, *Heartthrob*, and the odd *Deadpool* issue. Find his terrible jokes, convention appearances, and typos at his Twitter account *@nickfil* and his color work at *instagram.com/nick_filardi*.

Crank! letters a bunch of books put out by Image, Dark Horse and Oni Press. He also has a podcast with Mike Norton (*crankcast.net*) and makes music (*sonomorti.bandcamp.com*). Catch him on Twitter: *@ccrank*.

READ MORE FROM *Oni Press!*

ARES & APHRODITE
love wars
JAMIE S. RICH & MEGAN LEVENS

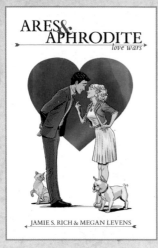

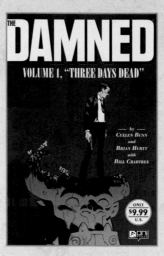

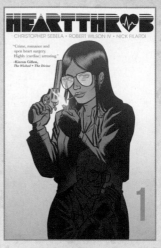

ARES & APHRODITE
By Jamie S. Rich and
Megan Levens
168 pages, softcover, color
ISBN 978-1-62010-208-4

THE
DAMNED
VOLUME 1, "THREE DAYS DEAD"
by
Cullen Bunn
and
Brian Hurtt
with
Bill Crabtree
ONLY
$9.99
U.S.

THE DAMNED, VOL 1:
THREE DAYS DEAD
By Cullen Bunn, Brian Hurtt,
and Bill Crabtree
152 pages, softcover, color
ISBN 978-1-62010-385-2

HEARTTHROB
CHRISTOPHER SEBELA • ROBERT WILSON IV • NICK FILARDI
"Crime, romance and open heart surgery. Highly (cardiac) arresting."
–Kieron Gillen,
The Wicked + The Divine
1

HEARTTHROB, VOL 1:
NEVER GOING BACK AGAIN
By Christopher Sebela,
Robert Wilson IV, and Nick Filardi
136 pages, softcover, color
ISBN 978-1-62010-338-8

"STUMPTOWN IS, FOR MY MONEY, THE PERFECT RUCKA BOOK."
STUMPTOWN
GREG RUCKA • MATTHEW SOUTHWORTH

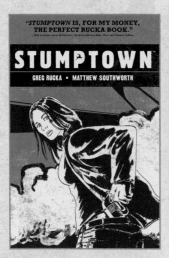

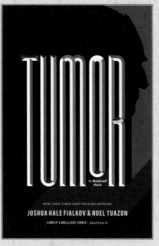

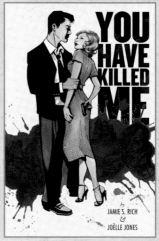

STUMPTOWN, VOLUME ONE
By Greg Rucka and
Matthew Southworth
160 pages, hardcover, color
ISBN 978-1-934964-37-8

TUMOR
A Medical Noir
NEW YORK TIMES BEST-SELLING AUTHORS
JOSHUA HALE FIALKOV & NOEL TUAZON
"SIMPLY A BRILLIANT COMIC" SEATTLE PI

TUMOR
By Joshua Hale Fialkov
and Noel Tuazon
248 pages, hardcover, b&w
ISBN 978-1-62010-326-5

YOU HAVE KILLED ME
by
JAMIE S. RICH
&
JOËLLE JONES

YOU HAVE KILLED ME
By Jamie S. Rich and
Joëlle Jones
192 pages, softcover, b&w
ISBN 978-1-62010-436-1

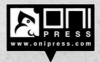

ONI PRESS
www.onipress.com

For more information on these and other fine Oni Press comic books and graphic novels visit www.onipress.com.
To find a comic specialty store in your area visit www.comicshops.us.